W9-AQJ-322

2-

CLASSICAL
BEARINGS

NEW HANOVER COUNTY
PUBLIC LIBRARY
201 CHESTNUT STREET
WILMINGTON, N C 28401

CLASSICAL BEARINGS

INTERPRETING
ANCIENT HISTORY AND CULTURE

PETER GREEN

THAMES AND HUDSON

For Gene Borza and Kathleen Pavelko
who have been there and understand the landscape

Any copy of this book issued by the publisher as a paperback is sold subject to the condition that it shall not by way of trade or otherwise be lent, resold, hired out or otherwise circulated without the publisher's prior consent in any form of binding or cover other than that in which it is published and without a similar condition including these words being imposed on a subsequent purchaser.

© 1989 Peter Green

First published in the USA in 1989 by Thames and Hudson Inc.,
500 Fifth Avenue, New York, New York 10110

Library of Congress Catalog Card Number 89-50628

All Rights Reserved. No part of this publication may be reproduced or transmitted in any form or by any means, electronic or mechanical, including photocopy, recording or any other information storage and retrieval system, without prior permission in writing from the publisher.

Typeset by Jahweh Associates in Linotype Bembo 10/12pt

Printed in the German Democratic Republic

CONTENTS

After the fifth century BC the historian's outlook underwent an enlargement in time. When Greek thought, having attained a consciousness of itself and its own worth, set out to conquer the world, it embarked on an adventure whose development was too vast to fall within the view of a single generation, and yet its consciousness of its own mission gave it a conviction of the essential unity of that development. This helped the Greeks to overcome the particularism which had coloured all their historiography before the time of Alexander the Great.

R.G. COLLINGWOOD, *The Idea of History*

Each venture
Is a new beginning, a raid on the inarticulate
With shabby equipment always deteriorating
In the general mess of imprecision of feeling,
Undisciplined squads of emotion. And what there is to conquer,
By strength and submission, has already been discovered
Once or twice, or several times, by men whom one cannot hope
To emulate – but there is no competition –
There is only the fight to recover what has been lost
And found and lost again and again; and now, under conditions
That seem unpropitious.

T.S. ELIOT, *East Coker*

The data furnished by the classical philosophers and the historians are incontrovertibly precious. The classical legends which present the prelogical experience of a people who had just risen out of the Neolithic mist are perhaps more precious still. But in the last analysis these overtly expressed conceptions are of less importance than the information we derive incidentally from the manner in which they are presented. The obvious content of literature is less significant than the mechanism of thought and language employed by its authors. Attic Greek is our surest guide to Athens, classical Latin our surest guide to Rome. Nothing mirrors the nature of a civilisation so clearly as its habitual medium of expression.

R.R. BOLGAR, *The Classical Heritage*

PREFACE AND
ACKNOWLEDGMENTS

I T IS OVER A QUARTER OF A CENTURY since I published my first volume
of classical essays, mainly remembered today for its opening salvo
against the academic establishment. The appearance of the second
collection (1972) coincided with my own translation to a permanent
academic position in the USA, an ironic twist of fate lost neither on me nor on
my friends. I have now worked as a full-time professional classicist and
ancient historian for eighteen years. Can it be (as Kenneth Grahame's
narrator wondered at the conclusion of *The Golden Age*) that I too have
become an Olympian? In *The Shadow of the Parthenon* I reflected that my
views might just 'have become a little less rebarbative (but not, I hope,
boringly so) with the onset of middle age'. I need not have worried. In my
seventh decade they are as rebarbative as ever, but now for rather different
reasons. The stuffy and sclerotic conservatism I was complaining about in
1960 has almost entirely vanished: the trouble is that in England at least, if not
in the States, it seems (as a last vindictive gesture) to have taken the whole
tradition of classical education with it. Thus where, as a young maverick, I
was blasting away at the aridities of grammar and textual criticism and loudly
extolling the virtues of translation, I now find myself highly suspicious of
translation as anything but a second-best crutch, a substitute for the paramount
necessity of learning Latin and Greek, and learning them well, as the prime
desiderandum for even beginning to appreciate ancient culture.

In my end is my beginning: this new volume, like my first, opens with an
essay on the state of the classics today, and ends by discussing the problems of
translation. But there the resemblance ends. The problems have changed,
and so, I hope, have I. Though I have always had a visceral and instinctive
distaste for theoretical fads and fashions, I have never consciously occupied
the position of odd-man-out for the mere pleasure of being different. Yet
once again I find myself at odds with a whole array of new orthodoxies. At
least, I comfort myself, they are different from the devils I belaboured in my
youth: they also, amusingly, put me in the unusual role of *laudator temporis*

acti. When I was young I was always being advised to modify my brash anti-establishment views. Now the wheel has come full circle, and I run the risk of being dismissed as hopelessly old-fashioned. Still, there is a clear distinction (though not everyone draws it) between being blind to progress and holding out against ephemeral trends. I am, and take pride in being, that least trendy of creatures today, a passionate liberal humanist. I actually believe that truth exists – *magna est veritas et praevalebit* – and that it is the scholar's sacred duty, in his human and fallible way, to recover as much of it as he can. Those who argue from the relativism of knowledge to the worthlessness of such historical endeavours are, almost invariably, ideologists with an axe to grind. Sub-Stalinist sneers about 'bourgeois objectivism' merely serve to confirm me in my conviction that the end does *not* justify the means, that agitprop is the ultimate betrayal of all scholarship, and that Ranke's ideal, history written *wie es eigentlich gewesen,* was, at the deepest level, right after all.

Nor, I fear, have I much more time for the basic concepts, much less the jargon, of post-structuralist criticism, which has always struck me as, at best, an elaborate intellectual game, and, worst of all, one that makes up its own rules as it goes along, a nice example of a category described, on my British driving-licence, as a 'track-laying vehicle steered by its tracks'. This trivialisation of research into mere arbitrary modes of discourse strikes at the very heart of the humanist tradition. It also represents a fundamental fallacy. I am inclined to agree with Stein Haugom Olsen's verdict, in *The End of Literary Theory* (1987), that

given its metaphysical premise, literary theory is necessarily reductive and positivistic. Though literary theorists have normally denied it, literary theory, because it is reductive and positivistic, poses a threat to humanist values. 'Literature' is a value concept, and the literary work is defined through the value which it is expected to yield. Literary theory has never been able to come to terms with this. If, with deconstruction, literary theory has entered a crisis from which it does not recover, this may be no bad thing (p.211).

The study of European and American literature, poetry in particular, has always been one of my deepest and most abiding joys. That fact may not be immediately apparent from the present volume, which (partly as a direct result of the critical climate in which I have existed for the last eighteen years or so) has concentrated more on other, less elusive, aspects of civilisation. But it is worth emphasising, in any case, that I believe, firmly, in the validity of authorial intention: in the indissoluble relationship between the writer's life and personality, on the one hand, and the work written, on the other: and in the symbiotic link between that work as expressed and the 'real world' from which its substance is drawn.

Finally, then, *Classical Bearings* can be described in the words that Bernard Knox used to characterise R.P. Winnington-Ingram's recent (1980) study of Sophocles: it is a 'defiantly old-fashioned book', which 'makes no reference to the raw or the cooked, no mention of codes, mythemes or *bricolage*', and functions 'in apparent unconsciousness of the dilemmas posed by the signifier, the signified, *parole* and *"la différence"* ', while 'its critical vocabulary lacks basic adjectives – liminal, binary, diachronic – and key nouns – intertextuality, deconstruction, metatragedy' [*CR* 32 (1982) 8]. Like the systems of Freud or Marx, those of the structuralists and their successors can be raided for useful insights; but to adopt any such ideological stance *in toto* puts the free critical intelligence into blinkers, and leaves its owner a mere exponent of whatever creeping theological monadism he may have chosen to embrace. If that puts me into the today much-despised category of English empiricist, so be it. The badge is an honourable one, and I wear it with some pride.

Of the essays in this volume, I and XVI were originally composed as lectures to be delivered in Tulane University during my tenure there, in Fall 1986, of the Mellon Chair in Humanities. III is, in substance, the Dougherty Lecture given in the University of Texas at Austin (1984), with additional material from my article 'Longus, Antiphon, and the Topography of Lesbos', first published (1982) in the *Journal of Hellenic Studies*. IV, V, VI and X are revised and augmented versions of pieces that first appeared in the *New York Review of Books*. II, VIII, and XI had a very similar genesis, being developed from review-articles and notices in the *Times Literary Supplement*. VII was originally published in *Greek Roman and Byzantine Studies* (1979); XII in the *American Journal of Ancient History* (1978); XIII in *Classical Antiquity* (1982), and XIV in *Echos du Monde Classique/Classical News and Views* (1981). XV was originally written and delivered as the first Mario and Antoinette Romano Lecture at the State University of New York at Binghamton (1988). IX formed the opening chapter in *The Sexual Dimension in Literature* (1983), edited by Alan Bold. I am grateful to Mr Bold, to the Graduate Schools of Tulane University and the University of Texas at Austin, and to the editors of the various periodicals listed above, for permission to reprint material that first appeared under their aegis. Translations from Ovid in Chapter XIII are my own, and taken from my forthcoming Penguin Classic, *Ovid: The Poems of Exile*. I would also like to thank the staff of Thames and Hudson for their encouragement and support: in particular for the degree to which they were willing to accommodate the whims of a more than usually obstinate author. To be published by such a house is a rare privilege.

Austin, Texas   PETER GREEN
August 1988

ABBREVIATIONS

AC	*L'Antiquité Classique*
AIA	*American Institute of Archaeology*
AJA	*American Journal of Archaeology*
AJPh	*American Journal of Philology*
Amer.Hist.Rev.	*American Historical Review*
Amm. Marc.	Ammianus Marcellinus
Anc.World	*The Ancient World*
Ann.Brit.Sch.Ath.	*Annual of the British School at Athens*
Anth. Pal.[AP]	*Anthologia Palatina*
Apollod.	Apollodorus Mythographus, *Bibliotheca*
Epit.	*Epitome*
Appian	Appianus Historicus
BC	*Bellum Civile*
Iber.	*Iberica*
Mithr.	*Mithradateus*
Syr.	*Syriaca*
Ap. Rhod.	Apollonius Rhodius
Arch.Miss.Scient. et	
Litt.	*Archives de missions scientifiques et littéraires*
Arch. News	*Archaeological News*
Architect.Rev.	*Architectural Review*
Arist.	Aristotle (Aristoteles Philosophus)
Gen.Anim	*De Generatione Animalium*
Hist. Anim.	*Historia Animalium*
Nic.Eth.	*Ethica Nicomachea* [*Nichomachean Ethics*]
Metaph.	*Metaphysica*
Pol.	*Politica* [*Politics*]
Probl.	*Problemata*
Aristoph.	Aristophanes Comicus
Acharn.	*Acharnenses* [*Acharnians*]
Eccles.	*Ecclesiazusae*
Thesm.	*Thesmophoriazusae*
Arrian	Lucius (Aulus) Flavius Arrianus
Succ.	*Successores*
Artemidorus	Artemidorus Daldianus Oneirocriticus
Athen.	Athenaeus, *Deipnosophistae*
Athen.Arch.Annal.	*Athenian Archaeological Annals* = 'Αρχαιολογικὰ 'Ανάλεκτα τῶν 'Αθηνῶν
[Aul.] Gell.	Aulus Gellius, *Noctes Atticae*
Bengtson, *Griech. Gesch.*[4]	Hermann Bengtson, *Griechische Geschichte von den Anfängen bis in die Römische Kaiserzeit,* 4th ed., Munich 1969
Bull. Assoc.G.Budé	*Bulletin de l'Association G. Budé*
Bull.Met.Mus.Art	*Bulletin of the Metropolitan Museum of Art*
Caes.	C. Julius Caesar
Bell.Afr.	*Bellum Africanum*
BG	*Bellum Gallicum*
CAH	*Cambridge Ancient History*
Canad.Rev.Comp.Lit	*Canadian Review of Comparative Literature*

Cat.	C. Valerius Catullus
Cic.	M. Tullius Cicero
Acad.	*Academicae Quaestiones*
Ad Attic.	*Epistulae ad Atticum*
Ad Fam.	*Epistulae ad Familiares*
Brut.	*Brutus [De Claris Oratoribus]*
De Div.	*De Divinatione ad M. Brutum*
De Invent.	*De Inventione Rhetorica*
De Leg. Agrar.	*De Lege Agraria Orationes*
De Nat.Deor.	
[ND]	*De Natura Deorum*
De Offic.	*De Officiis*
De Orat.	*De Oratore*
De Opt.Gen.	
Orat.	*De Optimo Genere Oratorum*
De Republ.	*De Re Publica*
Phil.	*Orationes Philippicae in M. Antonium*
Pro Arch.	*Oratio pro A. Licinio Archia*
Pro Mur.	*Oratio pro L. Murena*
Pro Rab. Post.	*Oratio pro Rabirio Postumo*
Rhet.Her.	*Ad Herennium*
Tusc.Disp.	*Tusculanae Disputationes*
Verr.	*Actio in Verrem* [Verrine Orations]
Class.Bull.	*Classical Bulletin*
Class. and Mod.Lit.	*Classical and Modern Literature*
Class.Journ.[CJ]	*Classical Journal*
CP[h]	*Classical Philology*
CQ	*Classical Quarterly*
CR	*Classical Review*
Class.Weekly/World	
[CW]	*Classical Weekly* or *World*
Daremberg-Saglio	C. Daremberg and E. Saglio, *Dictionnaire des Antiquités grecques et romaines d'après les textes et les monuments*, 1877-1919
Demetrius *De Eloc.*	Demetrius *De Elocutione* [*On Style*]
Demosth.	Demosthenes Orator
Diels-Kranz *[DK]*	H. Diels, *Die Fragmente der Vorsokratiker*, 6th ed. rev. W. Kranz, Berlin 1952
Dio Cass.	Dio Cassius Historicus
Diod.[Sic.] *[DS]*	Diodorus Siculus Historicus
Diog. Laert.	Diogenes Laertius, *De clarorum philosophorum vitis* [*Lives of the Philosophers*]
Dion.Hal.	Dionysius Halicarnassensis
AR	*Antiquitates Romanae*
Ditt.*Syll.*[3]	W. Dittenberg, *Sylloge Inscriptionum Graecarum*, 3rd ed., 1915-24
Durham Univ. Journ.	*Durham University Journal*
Edin. Rev.	*Edinburgh Review*
Enc.Brit.[11]	*Encyclopedia Britannica*, 11th ed., 1910-11
Eur.	Euripides Tragicus
Orest.	*Orestes*
Eustath.	Eustathius, Bishop of Thessalonike
FGrH	F. Jacoby, *Fragmente der griechischen Historiker*, 1923-
G.and R.	*Greece and Rome*

Hdt.	Herodotus Historicus
Hesiod	Hesiodus Epicus
WD	*Works and Days*
Th.	*Theogony*
HH [*Pyth.*] *Apoll.*	Homeric Hymn to [Pythian] Apollo
Hieron. *Chron.*	Hieronymus [= St Jerome] *Chronica*
Hippocr.	Hippocrates Medicus
Morb.	*De Morbis*
Nat.Puer.	*De Natura Pueri*
Hist.	*Historia*
Hom.	Homerus Epicus [Homer]
Il.	*Iliad*
Od.	*Odyssey*
Hor[ace]	Q. Horatius Flaccus [Horace]
AP	*Ars Poetica*
Epist.	*Epistulae*
HSCPh	*Harvard Studies in Classical Philology*
HThR	*Harvard Theological Review*
IG	*Inscriptiones Graecae*
ILS	H. Dessau, *Inscriptiones Latinae Selectae*, 1892–1916
Isidor. *Orig.*	Isidorus, *Origines*
JHS	*Journal of Hellenic Studies*
JŒAI	*Jahresheft des Österreichischen Archäologischen Instituts*
JRS	*Journal of Roman Studies*
Juv.	D. Junius Juvenalis
Sat.	*Saturae* [*Satires*]
Kirk-Raven-Schofield	G.S. Kirk, J.E. Raven, M. Schofield, *The Presocratic Philosophers*, 2nd ed., 1983
Livy	T. Livius Patavinus
per.	*periochae* [epitomes]
Lobel-Page [L-P]	E. Lobel, D. Page, *Poetarum Lesbiorum Fragmenta*, 1955
Lucian	Lucianus [Lucian of Samosata]
Bis Accus.	*Bis Accusatus*
Luct.	*De Luctu*
Lucr.	T. Lucretius Carus
Lycophr.	Lycophron Tragicus
Alex.	*Alexandra*
Macrob. *Sat.*	Macrobius, *Saturnalia*
Marm.Par.	*Marmor Parium*
MDAI(A)	*Mitteilungen des Deutschen Archäologischen Instituts (Athen. Abt.)*
MH	*Museum Helveticum*
Nat.Geogr.	*National Geographic*
Nepos	Cornelius Nepos
Eum.	*Eumenes*
De Reg.	*De Regibus*
Neues Jahrb. f.klass. Altert.	*Neues Jahrbuch für klassisches Altertum*
New Cath. Enc.	*New Catholic Encyclopedia*
Nic. Damasc.	Nicolaus Damascenus Historicus
Ovid	P. Ovidius Naso
AA	*Ars Amatoria*
Am.	*Amores*

EP	*Epistulae ex Ponto*
Her.	*Heroides*
RA	*Remedia Amoris*
Tr [*ist.*]	*Tristia*
Paus.	Pausanias Periegetica
PCPhS	*Proceedings of the Cambridge Philological Society*
*PIR*²	*Prosopographia Imperii Romani Saeculi I,II,III*, ed. E. Groag and A. Stein, 2nd ed., 1933
Plato	Plato Philosophus
Gorg.	*Gorgias*
Phaed.	*Phaedo*
Phaedr.	*Phaedrus*
Symp.	*Symposium*
Plaut.	T. Maccius Plautus
Mil.Glor.	*Miles Gloriosus*
Most.	*Mostellaria*
Plin. *Epist.*	C. Plinius Caecilius Secundus, *Epistulae*
Plin. *HN*	C. Plinius Secundus, *Historia Naturalis* [*Natural History*]
Plut.	Plutarchus Biographus et Philosophus [Plutarch of Chaeronea]
Mor.	*Moralia*
Vit.	*Vita* [Life of]
Aem.Paull.	*Aemilius Paullus*
Alex.	*Alexander*
Ant.	*Antonius* [Mark Antony]
Caes.	*Caesar*
Crass.	*Crassus*
Dem.	*Demosthenes*
Demetr.	*Demetrius* [Poliorcetes]
Marcell.	*Marcellus*
Nic.	*Nicias*
Phoc.	*Phocion*
Pomp.	*Pompeius* [Pompey]
Pyrrh.	*Pyrrhus*
Sull.	*Sulla*
P.Oxy.	*Oxyrhynchus Papyri*, ed. B.P. Grenfell and A.S. Hunt, 1898–
Proc. Class. Assoc.	*Proceedings of the Classical Association*
PWK	A. Pauly, G. Wissowa, W. Kroll, K. Ziegler, *Real-Encyclopädie d. klassischen Altertumswissenschaft*
Quad.Urb.Cult.Class	*Quaderni Urbinati di Cultura Classica*
Quint.*Inst.Orat.*	M.T. Quintilianus, *Institutiones Oratoriae*
Quint.Curt.[QC]	Q. Curtius Rufus, *Historiae Alexandri Magni Macedonis*
RBPhil	*Revue Belge de Philologie et d'Histoire*
RE	See *PWK*
Rev.Arch.	*Revue Archéologique*
REA	*Revue des Etudes Anciennes*
RhM	*Rheinisches Museum*
Sallust	C. Sallustius Crispus
Hist.	*Historia*
Schanz–Hosius	M. Schanz, C. Hosius, *Geschichte d. Römischen Literatur*, vols. I and II (1927, 1935)
Sen.	L. Annaeus Seneca
Consol. ad Marc.	*Ad Marciam de Consolatione*

De Ben.	*Be Beneficiis*
De Brev. Vit.	*De Brevitate Vitae*
Ep.Mor.	*Epistulae Morales*
SHAW	*Sitzungsberichte der HeidelbergerAkademie der Wissenschaften, Philos.-Hist.Klasse*
Sidon.Apollin.	Sidonius Apollinaris
Statius	P. Papinius Statius
Silv.	*Silvae*
Steph.Byz.	Stephanus Byzantius
Suet.	C. Suetonius Tranquillus
Cal.	*Caligula* [Gaius]
De Vir.Illustr.	*De Viris Illustribus*
Div.Aug.	*Divus Augustus*
Div.Claud.	*Divus Claudius*
Div.Jul.	*Divus Julius*
Tib.	*Tiberius*
Tac.	C. Cornelius Tacitus
Ann.	*Annales*
Dial.	*Dialogus de Oratoribus*
TAPhA	*Transactions and Proceedings of the American Philological Association*
Theogn.	Theognis and the *Theognidea*
Theophr.	Theophrastus Philosophus
Caus. Plant.	*De Causis Plantarum*
Hist. Plant.	*Historia Plantarum*
Vert.	*De Vertigine*
Thuc.	Thucydides Historicus
Val.Max.	Valerius Maximus
Vell.Pat.	P. Velleius Paterculus
Vitruv.	Vitruvius Pollio, *De Architectura*
Xen.	Xenophon Historicus
Anab.	*Anabasis*
Cyrop.	*Cyropaedia* [*Institutio Cyri*]
Hell.	*Hellenica*
Mem.	*Memorabilia*
Symp.	*Symposium*

I

PRECEDENT, SURVIVAL, METAMORPHOSIS: CLASSICAL INFLUENCES IN THE MODERN WORLD

(✿)

WHAT WE HOPEFULLY LABEL the 'classical heritage' is, ultimately, a phenomenon as elusive as Lewis Carroll's Snark – liable to turn into a Boojum when cornered – and as mutable as Proteus, the original Old Man of the Sea. About the one general point of agreement is that by 'the classics' we mean the Graeco-Roman tradition: and even that has been challenged, on occasion, by hopeful Sinologists or students of the Upanishads whose cultural allegiances outstrip their historical common sense. Anyone who pursues this subject for long will soon begin to sympathise with Aristotle's revealing remark – 'The more time I spend by myself, the more attached I have become to myths.'[1] The myths, of course, are modern no less than ancient; and even the ancient ones have been put, as we shall see, to some modern uses that would have baffled, and sometimes shocked, their Greek or Roman exponents. *Mimesis*, for instance, it has recently been argued,[2] is really not in the pattern, but in the mind of the observer, and offers not so much a technique of conservation as strategies for improvement.

Such trends have not stopped those old enough to hanker, wistfully, after a belief in metaphysics from promoting classical culture and art – products of *mimesis* in a very different sense – as 'a prophylactic against unacceptable aspects of the modern world'.[3] Aristotle, of course, is invoked as authority for both views. No serious artist today, critics argue, can work through the canons of classical art; yet that art has never been more widely or intensely admired. Hence the oddly impassioned ongoing debate over Andrew Wyeth: not so much is he a good artist, but is he an artist at all? Classical education, based on a deep knowledge of the Latin and Greek languages, is, at best, a flourishing minority cult for enthusiasts; yet today classical scholarship has scaled fresh heights of methodological precision and technical sophistication, while Greek and Roman authors are reaching a wider audience – even if only through the distorting glass of translation – than ever before. The situation,

15

in short, is redolent of paradox, something that properly invites closer scrutiny.

In some ways, of course, we are shaped by the legacy without being consciously aware of it. This is most strikingly true as regards the language we speak. English is an immensely complex repository of assimilated loan-words. By far the largest proportion of these – indeed, it has been estimated, over three-quarters of our entire vocabulary, and 50 per cent or more even of the 10,000 most common words we use – are of Latin or Greek derivation.[4] In short, like it or not, we *are* our history: a history shaped irrevocably by Greek concepts and Roman law and administration: by the common Greek speech of the *koine* and the Latin of imperial bureaucracy, transmitted through the Eastern and Western churches respectively; by Ciceronian rhetoric and Aristotelian logic: by that all-pervasive Platonic philosophy to which – as Whitehead claimed,[5] with only minimal hyperbole – the work of every subsequent thinker formed no more than a series of extended footnotes.

The same is true, *a fortiori*, of former provinces such as Spain or France, where, as in Italy itself, culture was largely continuous, and the language remained a mutation of Latin. To an even more striking extent Greece forms an historical and linguistic continuum. In Germany, by contrast, where the Roman legions and administrators never settled, classical loan-words are notable by their absence, while Teutonic myth (as Wagnerian addicts are uncomfortably aware) remained lumpish, violent, and primitive, shot through with most unclassical infusions of improbable Brobdingnagian lusts and forest *Schwärmerei*.[6] Most significant of all for our present purposes, Latin and Greek were, and have remained, unashamedly elitist in function: the languages of scholarship, of the Church, of the Imperial civil service, of the great humanists, of upper-class, often aristocratic, thinkers and writers who believed in that hieratic cosmos of fixed class-distinctions popularised by the Stoics. Language preserves the dichotomy of Us and Them. Anglo-Saxon terms are simple and basic: indeed, Old English betrays its linguistic, one had almost said tribal, primitivism by repeatedly borrowing words for general concepts, though it already possessed numerous terms denoting aspects of those concepts – something calculated to put any social anthropologist on the alert. Thus, it had no noun to express colour, though enough individual colour-identifications to fill the spectrum; no verb 'to move', though verbs in plenty for specific types of movement, from running to swimming: no generic terms for family relationships, but labels for just about every member of the family. For all but the very simplest concepts or abstractions, above all for scientific neologisms, Latin and Greek 'provide virtually every derivation'.[7]

In Greece (see n.19 *ad fin.*) this linguistic dichotomy has been fixed, apparently for ever, as a political confrontation between conservative right (*katharévousa*) and populist left (*dhemotikí*). Such ingrained elitism, however variously our own prejudices may choose to describe it – the pursuit of excellence (or *arete*, or *virtù*), nostalgic conservatism, a class-bound and reactionary attachment to outmoded privilege – lies at the very heart of the classical tradition, and, ever since the early nineteenth century, has proved an increasingly divisive factor in determining our conscious attitude to the legacy as we perceive it. The great paradox of the Graeco-Roman world for us today is the way in which its unparallelled intellectual and artistic fecundity of invention in the arts and sciences was dedicated throughout (with brief exceptions only) to the maintenance of a privileged *status quo*. The ancient economic ideal was not – you may be surprised to learn – our own goal of increased productivity, but stability of revenue.[8] Stoic cosmology envisioned a changeless uniformity of order, in heaven as on earth, a 'natural law' that justified the prescriptive rule of imperial Rome or Byzantium, and was eagerly borrowed, not only by medieval thinkers (who revamped it as the Ladder of Being), but also by men of the Renaissance as distinguished as Hooker or Sir Thomas Elyot.[9] Shakespeare gives vivid expression to this concept in *Troilus and Cressida* (? 1603):

> The heavens themselves, the planets and this centre
> Observe degree, priority and place . . .
> Take but degree away, untune that string,
> And hark, what discord follows!

It is no accident that the Greek and Roman verbs (*neoterizein, res nouare*) habitually translated as 'to rebel' or 'to make a revolution' in fact simply mean 'to produce change (or novelty)': all change was, by definition, disruptive of the social order. The number of classics professors who are ferocious reactionaries should not really surprise us. *C'est leur métier*: conservation is, on every count, their proper business.

Here, of course, we run into yet another paradox, since one of the greatest Greek gifts to the world is commonly held to have been democracy. No one would argue with that; and yet we should never forget the severe limitations, of both extent and duration, that applied to the original experiment. It had no other parallels in neighbouring Near Eastern countries; while within Greece itself it was far from universal, and certainly not (as is sometimes supposed) coterminous with the rule of the city-state (*polis*). The example, of course, that we know best is that of post-Cleisthenic Athens from the late sixth to the mid-fourth century BC; and even here political equality, *isonomia*,[10] neither took in slaves and women, let alone foreign residents (*metoikoi*, metics), nor did anything to disturb a social class-system still firmly rooted in blood-lines, privilege, capital, and unabashed snobbery. The best and the brightest (a fair equivalent of the Athenian *kaloi k'agathoi*) might give the many-headed garlic-breathing landless rabble the vote: but they were not required to invite its members to dinner, much less introduce them to their daughters. Some of Aristophanes' bitterest jokes – Euripides' mother as greengrocer, Strepsiades marrying above his station[11] – are solidly class-

based. The *banausos*, originally simply an artisan, acquires pejorative associations.[12] Manual labour of any sort, especially at the behest of others, is looked
down on. The modern reader who studies Aristotle's *Politics* (*c.* 325 BC)
finds, to his astonishment, that learning to play a musical instrument is
rejected as a banausic manual occupation, unsuitable for gentlemen, and that
a clear distinction is made, not only between the educated (*pepaideuménos*) and
the vulgar (*phortikós*), but also, despite the franchise, between the banausic
and the free (eleutheros). [13]

This attitude foreshadows the *de facto* collapse of *polis* democracy, and the
reversion to authoritarian (or, at best, oligarchic) rule during the Hellenistic
period: and it was the Hellenistic rather than the classical legacy, politically
speaking, that was transmitted, via Rome, to the medieval and modern
world. The snobbery, the elitism, the contempt not merely for trade but for
all applied science (this being in the hands of technicians and artisans),[14] the
obsession with stability and the fixed world-order – these remained constant
throughout, and form one of the most significant elements (though seldom
recognised as such) in the whole classical tradition. Variations on this attitude
confront us in virtually every classical author, since, for Greeks and Romans
alike, writing, like the study of history or mathematics, was the prerogative
of educated rentiers supported by a private income. For fifteen hundred years
and more this expression of a socially fixed order – fixed, indeed, by divine
dispensation – met with no serious objections. Indeed, until the late eighteenth
century, and in some areas much longer than that, it was accepted as virtually
axiomatic, a moral postulate no less praiseworthy than Alexander's conquests
(which themselves began to acquire some strange cultural justifications after
aggressive imperialism went out of fashion). It was not until the egalitarian
1940s that liturgical editors were shamed into excising, from that peculiarly
insipid hymn 'All things bright and beautiful', the tell-tale stanza proclaiming:
'The rich man in his castle,/The poor man at his gate,/God made them high
or lowly/And ordered their estate.'

The scholars, politicians and divines of the Renaissance would have
dismissed as subversive drivel Lewis Mumford's speech at the 1943 Stanford
Conference, on the theme of 'The humanities look ahead', when he castigated
the Greeks for 'their failure to embrace humanity . . . to address the soldier,
the sailor, the craftsman, the farmer, and to give hope and faith to the
common man . . .'[15] Their respect for the common man stood on a par with
Plato's in the *Republic*, and lower than that it is hard to go. They looked to the
past for practical advice on good government, even for moral uplift, while
never doubting that it was they who had the prerogative to govern, that their
moral rectitude was a class, almost a private family, issue between themselves
and God.

Nothing else has so laid the classical tradition open to attack in our own
time as this sanctified perpetuation of class privilege, and the prescriptive
dogmatising on anything from literature to the natural order – look at

Aristotle's *Poetics* no less than his cosmological pronouncements – that forms its natural concomitant. Thomas Gaisford, Professor of Greek at Oxford in the early nineteenth century, is reported [16] to have declared – during a Good Friday sermon! – that 'the advantages of a classical education are twofold – it enables us to look down with contempt on those who have not shared its advantages, and also fits us for places of emolument not only in this world but also in that which is to come'. We may laugh at Gaisford's eschatological pretensions – the notion of professors forming a *corps d'elite* in heaven has its own weird charm – but the class prejudice was all too palpable, and, worse, as we have seen, directly derived from Graeco-Roman social mores.

From the American War of Independence until the aftermath of World War II this elitism provided one of the stock charges against a classical education, though there were plenty of others. Perhaps most deleterious, certainly in the USA, was that disdain for history, that wholesale rejection of the past – above all the European past – which has always formed so prominent a strain in American anti-intellectualism (itself a central feature of the egalitarian process). Look to the future: the past is irrelevant – or, even if relevant (in the fashionable sense of containing one's roots), obscured and corrupted by the elitist garbage of centuries. Up with hot-gospellers and down with the Apostolic Succession. Above all, down with humanism (often equated by the semi-literate faithful with Satanism), and with any prescriptive dogma except that trumpeted from the pulpit. Refugees from the past have, of course, a special incentive 'to excise history from their lives'. [17] No monuments, no ruins, no bunk. The foreshortened perspective thus produced (something from which in the fifth century BC both Herodotus and Thucydides had to struggle free: trends tend to be cyclic) leads, of course, to foreshortened judgments. Those who cannot recall the past are indeed condemned to fulfil it [18] – a more cogent reason than many, as Polybius saw no less clearly than Santayana, for the study of Graeco-Roman culture.

The sheer number of points at which the classical tradition has come under attack during the past two centuries testifies eloquently to its influence – and, indeed, to its staying-power. The Romantic Revival, in both literature and the visual arts, fought to break away from precedent and *mimesis*, in any form, and, as a result, put a premium on self-generated originality, pure inspiration. Scientific progress, while loosening the stranglehold of Protestantism, also contrived to render by far the larger part of ancient science and medicine (if not pure mathematics) wholly obsolete, thus undermining the prescriptive authority of Greek and Roman texts as a whole. The French Revolution, the American and Greek Wars of Independence, inevitably disseminated a political egalitarianism squarely at odds with the Hellenistic and Roman systems inherited by the Renaissance. The fixed world-view became a scientific and a political anachronism: Aristarchus and Galileo, lone wolves both, had not lived in vain. Economics moved from static to dynamic objectives. The rhythms of written prose approximated, with unconscious populist zest, ever closer to the vernacular.[19] Heroic *gestes* went out of fashion. The revolt against prescriptive patterns led not only to impressionism in art, but in mathematics to the development of non-Euclidean geometry,[20] and in linguistics to post-Chomskyan systems of grammar.

A new, more functional approach to education as, primarily, vocational training – attacked, without noticeable success, by countless humanists[21] – had the effect, while paying lip-service to classical studies, of relegating them to the status of cultural 'top-dressing'. There was no longer any need, it was argued, to turn to the classical past for anything practical: certainly not to learn how to express oneself or to solve problems of conduct, two reasons regularly advanced by Renaissance humanists.[22] The way to the stars – and, *a fortiori*, to Star Wars – was to be achieved by increasingly complex high technology, not through familiarity with Homer: the past was expendable, its function over, to be jettisoned like the first stage of a rocket. All the more regrettable, then, that those with the largest investment in the classical legacy, the scholars dedicated to its preservation, should in so many ways have failed to meet the challenge. The faults by no means lie all on one side.

Nor, in the case of the humanities, has it been only the professionals who are to blame. Perhaps the most insidious danger to which our Graeco-Roman roots have been exposed since the Industrial Revolution has been the temptation to use antiquity not so much to view modern problems (whether political, ethical, psychological, social or artistic) in true perspective, but rather as an idealised, and increasingly unreal, refuge from the harsh stresses and demands of contemporary life. (Visually, the dislocated marble statues and timeless sunlit colonnades of De Chirico embody this mood to perfection: his long lancing shadows suggest a world like that of Tennyson's Lotus Eaters, in which it was always afternoon, the apotheosis of *ataraxia*.) The Greeks looked back to a lost Golden Age: they would have been surprised to hear that they themselves were living in it.

Meanwhile this kind of escapist passivity bred its own, equally unreal, equally escapist reaction. Nietzsche and Schliemann, Gladstone and Arnold, Carlyle and Froude between them set several generations of classically educated Englishmen, weary of industrial squalor, Victorian pieties, and the emergent bourgeois state, to emulate that 'action, nobility, and moral and physical strength'[23] which they professed to find in early Greek epic. When war came in 1914 men like Rupert Brooke or Julian Grenfell saw themselves, with mythic insouciance, as Homeric heroes. Gallipoli was, after all, in the Thracian Chersonese, well on the way to Troy, so that Patrick Shaw-Stewart could write:

> I will go back this morning
> From Imbros over the sea:
> Stand in the trench, Achilles,
> Flame-capped, and shout for me.

The botched strategy and mudbound mass slaughter that followed quickly put paid to such romantic fancies: Shaw-Stewart might have done better with Thucydides, or even Archilochus, in his pocket rather than the *Iliad*.

The ancient world, though never (for complex reasons) effectively tech-nologised, went through just about every modern reaction to the great fundamentals of life, most often in a disconcertingly sophisticated manner. As a result we have a constant, and constantly varied, sense of *déjà vu* in studying its history: it is we moderns who are so selective in our approach to it. Perhaps this is why the past obstinately refused, and still refuses, to die. I find it symbolically appropriate that the end of World War I should also have marked the completion of Marcel Proust's obsessional exploration of *temps perdu*. '1918 was the end of a myth', Robert Ogilvie wrote of this period.[24] Not so much the end, surely, as the *beginning* of a profound mythic revolution, a subterranean bombshell as powerful as any other upheaval that marked the years between the wars (what Auden so aptly labelled the Age of Anxiety), and, incidentally, revealing the archetypal durability of charters and patterns that had their genesis among warring Mycenaean baronies in the Peloponnese, 1500 years and more before the birth of Christ.

The much-publicised ransacking of myth, for their own ends, by Freud and Jung gave fresh force and significance to familiar literary landmarks: the toybox of the conscious mind stood revealed as a dangerous repository of unconscious dynamite. Paradoxically, again – since the Oedipus complex, however firmly acclimatised as a Bronx joke, has won few serious adherents, while the evidence for Jungian archetypes tends to go soft on close investiga-tion[25] – the shaky scholarly underpinnings of such theories made no difference to their epidemic appeal, a fact of life which Robert Graves and Arnold Toynbee (to take only the two most obvious examples) were to cash in on with some gusto. Diagrammed by Lévi-Strauss as a problem in man's autochthonous origins,[26] Oedipus remained (what indeed he had always been) a powerful property for poets – though Sophocles might have blinked a little at the version Ted Hughes presents in his ballad entitled (inevitably) 'Song for a Phallus':[27]

> The Dickybird came to Oedipus
>   You murderous little sod
> The sphynx [*sic*] will bite your bollocks off
>   This order comes from God.

Yet Sophocles himself had invented, it seems, Oedipus' agonising process of self-discovery, self-blinding, exile, and miraculous assumption at Colonus: having a well-developed fifth-century sense of guilt and retribution to keep his unruly erotic urges in check, he could not stomach the archaic tradition, according to which Oedipus, that incestuous parricide, remained ruler in Thebes till the day he died, eyes intact, leaving rich flocks to be fought over by the sons he had cursed.[28] The dominant characteristic of living myth is its infinite adaptability to fresh needs.

Homer himself provides a remarkable instance of this. As countless new translations, not to mention a remarkable recent TV documentary,[29] make very clear, many of us are still in search of the Trojan War. Schliemann's veracity, and psychological balance, may have taken a beating lately,[30] but Achilles, Agamemnon and Odysseus still fascinate. That kind of attraction, of course, always arouses academic distaste: hence the passion (camouflaged as scholarly honesty) for proving everything of the sort, from Troy to the Troezen Decree, a fantasy or a fake. The anti-romantic reaction had, in fact, begun long before 1914: as early as 1842 the cartoonist Honoré Daumier produced an acid series of lithographs in *Charivari*,[31] depicting, *inter alia*, Odysseus and Penelope reunited in bed – a stout, elderly, decidedly plain matron rather wistfully contemplating her nightcapped, toothless, open-mouthed, snoring and clearly senile husband. Such an attitude looked forward to similar Gallic *jeux d'esprit* of the 1930s: Jean Giraudoux's *The Trojan War Will Not Take Place* (1935), with Hector and Odysseus working to sidetrack battle via negotiation, or Jean Giono's *Birth of the Odyssey* (1938), in which Odysseus figures as an aging, neurotic fantasist, spinning ever taller stories to excuse his erotic escapades.

Yet the *Iliad*, even in an age that had no time for heroics, retained all its pristine emotional power. In the late summer of 1940, after the fall of France, Simone Weil saw it as a 'poem of force', a marvellous evocation of that cold and stony cruelty, backed by divine caprice, which forms a fundamental (and often disregarded) aspect of antiquity, and to which the expansionist activities of the Third Reich had given a new and fearful validation.[32] Auden's haunting variation on this theme, 'The Shield of Achilles', binds together modern statistical propaganda, marching legions and weed-choked fields, all the horrors of totalitarianism and, centrally, the Crucifixion, thus not only synchronising history, but turning Homer's counterpointed picture of civilisation and war inside out, so that what Hephaestus offers Thetis is no longer peace amid conflict, or even the conflict itself, but a blight obliterating both:[33]

> She looked over his shoulder
>   For vines and olive trees,
> Marble well-governed cities
>   And ships upon untamed seas,
> But there on the shining metal
>   His hands had put instead
> An artificial wilderness
>   And a sky like lead.

The reworking of Graeco-Roman myth by modern poets and playwrights is an enormous theme on which I can do no more than touch here. But its very size and universality are worth stressing. The need for roots, however cynically exploited, is not a mere temporary fad: and some roots run very deep. To jettison the past not only foreshortens our perspective; it also impoverishes the psyche. Too many ahistorical critics have emphasised that 'the dead writers are remote from us because we *know* so much more than they did'; we still need Eliot's famous rejoinder:[34] 'Precisely, and they are that which we know.' There is a nightmarish poem by the Irish classicist Louis MacNeice, belonging to his last phase (1962), when, like Webster, he was much possessed by death. In a surreal scene of London at night, fogbound and with all the bridges down, Charon appears as a Thames ferryman:[35]

> He looked at us coldly
> And his eyes were dead and his hands on the oar
> Were black with obols and varicose veins
> Marbled his calves and he said to us coldly:
> If you want to die you will have to pay for it.

The density and interpenetration of past and present achieved here is only possible on a basis of tradition known, assimilated, and present as a potent, all-pervasive element in the inherited bloodstream of a culture. Here jazzy modernity need be no impediment: can, indeed, enhance the effect. Consider, for example, Kit Wright's 'Fortunes of War', a hilariously funny ballad in which the narrator, a renegade Trojan loaded with stolen loot, finds Cassandra living in 'a grey block of flats' off the Fulham Road in London, and uses her prophetic powers to make a fortune betting on the horses.[36]

The technique bears a certain affinity to that of the modern Greek poet Yannis Ritsos, in his great dramatic Mycenaean soliloquies.[37] Here, with a kind of unselfconscious synchronicity, Chrysothemis will talk to a reporter from a newspaper chain; automobiles coexist with chariots, and telephones with messengers; Phaedra chain-smokes; Persephone, on vacation from Hades, complains about the blinding Greek sunlight; and the aged Helen, warts and whiskers sprouting from her withered face, sits in squalor amid dirty coffee-cups while church bells sound outside. Here, of course, history and culture form, more than elsewhere, a single unbroken continuum. Greece is Greece *is* Greece, so that even Ritsos, a communist poet imbued with the populist post-Byzantine tradition of *Romaiosyne* (that anti-classical obsession with nationalism and the Christianised culture of the New Rome in Constantinople), also thinks naturally and by instinct in the archaic mode. 'That grey ghost Helen,' exclaims Wright's narrator, 'was she what they all died for?': it might have been Ritsos' Helen that he had in mind.

Sometimes the use of the myth is esoteric, and knowledge of it inessential: no one, let's face it, is the worse off for not realising that Eliot's *The Cocktail Party* is an adaptation of Euripides' *Alcestis*,[38] while in Cocteau's *Orphée* the 'themes and symbols are part of the mythology of Cocteau, not of Orpheus'.[39]

But few would argue that Prometheus – to take an obvious example – does not stand at the very heart of society's perennial balancing-act between authority and freedom, or that a knowledge of the metamorphoses undergone by that Protean figure down the ages [40] does not immeasurably enhance our understanding of the human condition. From such a viewpoint myth and history serve a common purpose. Anyone who supposes that the totalitarian ills of this century are something new and unprecedented should turn back to Thucydides' analysis of civil war (3.82-83), parts of which, with their description of double-think, calculated atrocities, and what today might be labelled 'bourgeois objectivism', read as though written by George Orwell. *Those who cannot recall the past are condemned to fulfil it.*

Perhaps the most useful thing to be done at this point in a state-of-the-art report is not so much to pursue any specific aspect of the classical legacy – that will come later – but rather to attempt a provisional balance-sheet in historical terms. We have to admit, from the outset, that a good number of the criticisms levelled at classical learning, and the humanities generally, have been, and in some cases still are, well-founded. I have, in the past, formulated such charges myself,[41] and have already suggested others here. As regards the actual literature of antiquity, and the cultural values to be extrapolated from it, the most common complaint, of course, is that it is irrelevant to our own age. Historically fallacious, as we have already seen, this charge remains a perennial favourite with the instant-culture brigade. To make it stick, we must assume that the only knowledge worth having is practical and functional: that all education should be career-oriented, primarily towards industry, commerce, administration, and the applied sciences; and that the liberal arts can only be tolerated, if at all, as a recreational or decorative luxury.

For the past forty years or so, ever since World War II in fact, this attitude has been far more dominant than all but the most honest humanists care to admit. Here is that embattled liberal Norman Foerster, writing in 1946:[42] 'It is believed, if not always asserted, that the good life of man consists mainly in the pursuit and possession of material advantages . . .' The ideal is seen as 'a living world of experience, not a dead world of records and books'. There are, of course, good, if not sufficient, reasons for this. We often forget the extent to which Renaissance humanists utilised the newly recovered texts of antiquity *as sources of knowledge*, as 'authorities on matters of fact in such spheres as astronomy, geography, zoology, medicine'.[43] As has been well said,[44] 'the past fortunes of the classical heritage are there to show us how social aspirations and interests can affect the course of education'; the rise of modern science and technology, to look no further, has largely robbed these ancient texts of any factually prescriptive value they might once have had. This is the main reason why the classical legacy as a whole (viewed by functionaries solely in functional terms) has been sidelined in such quarters like the Epicurean gods, a cultural anachronism worth no more than the occasional polite genuflection for the sake of past glories.

Here the humanists have not, unfortunately, always served their own cause to advantage. Too many of them, seeing modernism as the Great Enemy, have in response adopted, with unseemly relish, that fundamental Graeco-Roman elitism which professed to despise all aspects of commerce, industry, and technical knowledge as 'banausic': a view which, though it had the backing of writers as diverse as Xenophon, Aristotle, and Seneca,[45] still played straight into the Great Enemy's hands. When modernists dismissed this attitude as anti-egalitarian (which it was), and fundamentally unrealistic, traditional humanists – accepting the challenge, but too often somewhat hazy about the realities of life – clung to the classics as the embodiment of good taste, the proper intellectual training for a corps of post-Platonic Guardians whose business was government, and whose leisure, what the Romans termed *otium*, embraced such interesting minor skills as pastiching English poetry into Greek or Latin verse.[46] They made the classic mistake of despising both science and industry without a proper understanding of either. Small wonder that their opponents, just as mistakenly, dismissed ancient literature as a mere florilegium for the privileged. Worse, the traditionalists' sclerotic conservatism was, notoriously, symbolised by the fact that professional classical scholars still clung, with fierce exclusiveness, to the editing and textual criticism which had constituted a necessary rescue operation in the Hellenistic Age and, to a lesser degree, during the Renaissance, but which now should have served, at best, as means to a greater end – full cultural understanding.

This end, unfortunately, scholars all too seldom pursued. They were not comfortable with literary value-judgments or aesthetics, which they tended to dismiss, defensively, as emotionalism or non-quantifiable hot air. This, combined with innate snobbishness, made some of them take a kind of inverted pride in accepting the modernists' criticisms. In 1938 one commentator observed, ruefully, that the humanities 'build no bridges and raise no crops; they cure no fevers and point no guns'.[47] Are such things, it might be asked, their business? In a sense, yes. This pessimist might have done well to reflect that in fact the humanities can, and should, build bridges between nations, raise plentiful crops of ideas, cure the fevers of irrationalism, and, if pushed, point the gun of irrefutable argument and consensus. There have, it is true, been attempts, more often than not inept, to justify the classics in practical terms (see p.26 below); but in retreat humanists have more often tended, like so many Hellenistic intellectuals before them, to contract out, to avoid involvement, to live – as Epicurus advised[48] – unnoticed, their ideal, similarly, the negative *ataraxia*, or mere absence of upset.

Too many advocates of classics since the war have tended to speak with the unattractive voice of privilege in retreat, frothing on vaguely about law and order, faith in God (the relation of Athens and Jerusalem is, of course, an enormous problem in itself), the expression of values, or the spirit of man, while at the same time sneering (like Plato, like Seneca) at 'soulless technicians' and new-style layabouts,[49] for whom culture has 'somewhat sinister aristo-cratic connections' and work, especially if they happened to be students, is 'figuratively as well as literally a four-letter Anglo-Saxon word'. The ideal, as for Archimedes, was a situation in which 'no utilitarian purpose or aim contaminated the purity of an unsullied intellectual life'.[50]

Like all ideals, this one has been much abused for sectarian purposes, and by scientists at least as much as by humanists. The claims of pure scholarship are too often advanced as a cover for ivory tower *ataraxia*. Snow's two cultures (content today, in all likelihood, to regard themselves as being in binary opposition, another fashionable state) will never value each other at their true worth until the cumulative, and ingrained, misapprehensions of over two millennia have been scraped away. Modernists must learn that they cannot jettison the past like so much trash: the result is liable to be a mindless orgy of trend-catching and anti-literacy, best typified by the appalling popularity, a decade or two ago, of the jargon-laden, hyped-up, and pro-foundly ahistorical works of Marshall McLuhan, designed to flatter just about all the prejudices of a TV generation in which functional illiteracy was already well advanced.[51] Egalitarianism should level up, not down.

On the other hand, scientists have every reason to resent cheap, ill-informed, and superior sneers at their approach to the life of the intellect: minds that can conceive the DNA double helix are not to be brushed aside so easily. Things have changed a good deal since Archimedes' day. At the same time this vast increase in the substance and complexity of our scientific knowledge does not alter the fact that a scientist's mode of perception tends to lack the historical perspective, the broadly human element, fundamental to a balanced view of civilisation. It would be ironic if a new prescriptive dogma, that of the scientific planner, were to replace the old discarded certainties of the Renaissance humanists. The stereotypes certainly do not make things easier. If modernists regard classicists as innocents clinging to an obsolete past and meaningless privileges, they themselves figure in the demonology of their opponents as robot technocrats, all brain and no heart, with a regrettable weakness for left-wing planned economies, and virtually deaf to the true voices of humanity. Still, I think Robert Ogilvie was probably right when he said that 'there can never be any prospect of a civilisation being centred on science',[52] on the grounds that 'however valuable a scientific education may be for the enrichment of the intellect and the comprehension of the material universe, it does not supply the substance in which men can find themselves and move themselves'. The consistent *de haut en bas* sniping at scientific attitudes by nervous or prejudiced humanists – totally unjustified in itself – makes it extremely hard to achieve consensus on so vital a concern. But consensus there must be: we are all in this together.

What, then, is the sum of the whole matter? The classical heritage is with us whether we like it or not. It is there in the language we use: it permeates our literature and art: its legacy remains operative in scientific areas as disparate as

26

pure mathematics, orthopaedic surgery, or the analysis of conic sections; it still, to an extraordinary degree, dominates our philosophical thinking. A fair proportion of tribal nonsense has been handed down, inevitably, along with the rare gifts: a geocentric, up-and-down, heaven-earth-and-hell cosmology; a theory of 'humours' that still encourages us to talk about people as sanguine, phlegmatic, or bilious; a complex astrological determinism which continues to surface, in a debased form, in the popular press, and has, equally, left its mark on the language: 'Men are still jovial, mercurial, or saturnine, talk of fortunate conjunctions of events, believe in unlucky numbers, and thank their stars.'[53]

Still, the educational monopoly enjoyed by the Renaissance humanists and their successors, which in the long run may be seen as the worst thing ever to befall the classical heritage, is, at last, broken. As Sir James Mountford stressed twenty years ago, in a Presidential address to the British Classical Association:[54] 'Gone are the days when all men who had claim to education and who in their various spheres moulded the current of events had a common background and training in the classics.' The discipline is back in the open marketplace where it belongs, to stand or fall on its own merits. Gone, too, one would like to believe, are those spacious justifications of elitism on pseudo-practical grounds: the classics as an unmatchable training for the mind, with Latin as the supremely logical language, the kind of thing that elicited (as early as 1938) a derisive comment from Louis MacNeice, himself an excellent (and professional) classical scholar: [55]

We learned that a gentleman never misplaces his accents,
    That nobody knows how to speak, much less how to write
English who has not hob-nobbed with the great-grandparents of English,
    That the boy on the Modern Side is merely a parasite
But the classical student is bred to the purple, his training in syntax
    Is also a training in thought
And even in morals; if called to the bar or the barracks
    He always will do what he ought.

Nor will it suffice today to retreat into pedantry for its own sake, to emulate Didymos Chalcenteros, the Elder Pliny, Browning's Grammarian, George Eliot's Mr Casaubon, or even the legendary English headmaster who is said to have told his class:[56] 'Boys, this term you are to have the privilege of reading the *Oedipus Coloneus* of Sophocles, a veritable treasure-house of grammatical peculiarities.'

This quintessentially Hellenistic attitude tempts me to conclude on something of a personal note. For some years now I have been occupied with the writing of a full-scale political, social, and cultural history of the Hellenistic Age, between Alexander's death in 323 and the abolition of the last Successor kingdom by Octavian in 31. As my research proceeded I found (to quote from my introduction) that 'I could not help being struck, again and again, by an overpowering sense of *déjà vu*', and being fascinated by 'the ornate, indeed rococo, glass in which Alexandria, Antioch and Pergamon reflect contemporary fads, failings, and aspirations, from the urban malaise to religious fundamentalism, from Veblenism to *haute cuisine*, from funded scholarship and mandarin literature to a flourishing drop-out counter-culture, from political impotence in the individual to authoritarianism in government, from science perverted for military ends to illusionism for the masses, from spiritual solipsism on a private income to systematic extortion in pursuit of the materialistic and hence plutocratic dream'.

Quite apart from some jolting lessons to be learnt here about the constant elements in human nature (a very different thing from mankind's evolutionary acquisition of knowledge) – *déjà vu* on a truly cosmic scale – it is this depressingly familiar scenario, rather than the currently more popular Periclean myth, which remains, in essence, the legacy of the Graeco-Roman world. As such it was accepted until new winds of freedom blowing through Europe and America – somewhere between the Age of Enlightenment and the Romantic Revival – created a boom in the fifth-century Athenian democratic ideal, together with its great literature, art, and architecture. (No one in later antiquity, we may note, had ever thought of including the Parthenon among the canonical Seven Wonders.) Yet that ideal was, as we have seen, highly uncharacteristic of Greece, and soon lost in any effective sense; in Rome it never caught on at all. If we are to do better than Auden's hypothetical academics who 'read the *New Yorker*, trust in God, and take short views',[57] we need to know not only how the metamorphosis took place, and why, but what our own organic relationship to this past may be within the seamless evolution of historical time. We cannot escape reality by living wholly in the past: but equally we cannot afford to stunt our humanity and destroy our understanding by ignoring that past as irrelevant.

The rise of Western civilisation has been a slow, hard-won, and infinitely precarious process that took at least seven millennia to bring to its present less-than-perfect state, and which (since in all things it must fight, and hopefully tame, nature, the perpetual struggle of *nomos* against *physis*) can be more easily lost than is often supposed. A major symptom of intellectual malaise today, and one directly attributable to neglect of, even contempt for, the past, is a failure of critical and moral standards. As E.R. Dodds – a classical scholar with a highly tuned moral sense – reminded us in 1964, this is an age 'when educated men find it increasingly hard to distinguish good literature from bad, sense from nonsense, the difficult insights of the creative innovator from the sham insights of the charlatan on the make'.[58] Hence, perhaps, the iconoclastic urge to deconstruct the lot. We can all think of names to fit the categories.

A few years earlier, in 1953, Kathleen Nott published a devastating, though isolated, humanistic attack on new-style critical and philosophical trends, reminding us, *inter alia* (p. 323), that a good deal of Greek science had been as much on the mark as modern cultural theories were off it, and that Aristarchus of Samos, whose heliocentric theory had been formulated long before Galileo or Copernicus, suffered, just as they did, from religious bigotry. Miss Nott's book was called, significantly, *The Emperor's Clothes*: its targets were just the kind of thing that Dodds had in mind, even if Dodds himself was less fiercely Lucretian in his attitude to religion. Not that the Graeco-Roman intellectual tradition (as should by now be very clear) offered any guarantees to a free world, either politically or socially: that authoritarian streak was far too pervasive. The Nazis had a field-day with Plato's prescriptive legislation in the *Republic* and the *Laws*[59], while Marxist dialectic found its roots not only in Hegel, but far further back, among pre-Socratic thinkers such as the enigmatic – and ultra-aristocratic – Herakleitos.[60]

On the other hand, the perspective and discipline offered by thinkers of unsurpassed subtlety and no technological interests, over two millennia ago, at least gave modern intellectuals a critical edge, inoculating them against mere mindless agitprop and sloganeering: against the visceral claptrap of killers with guns in their hands and stocking masks on their heads. Far from being a mere cultural luxury or intellectual game, the maintenance of our classical-humanist legacy, at the highest level, is a vital and, yes, entirely practical element in the never-ending struggle to hold off barbarous recidivism and the gut-law of the jungle. Neither ancient nor modern democracy has been so successful that we can afford to be complacent about their ultimate survival.

That is why over-emphasis on the purely literary or artistic worth of the legacy bequeathed to us, of immense importance though that is, can, I think, lead us unconsciously to undervalue its crucial role in what Eliot called, in *East Coker*, 'the fight to recover what has been lost/ and found and lost again and again: and now, under conditions/ that seem unpropitious'. Not all of us would subscribe to Eliot's uncompromising claim that the only serious reason to retain the classics is the promotion of Christianity (or even, indeed, that the two are ultimately compatible): the historical irony of that assertion should be appreciated today in Athens, Jerusalem, and (if it comes to that) Alexandria. But Dodds' reasons for keeping classics as a university subject are clear and cogent: 'Cut off the classics, and you cut off all scholarly understanding of medieval history, of Roman law, and of the development of Christianity: you sever the Romance languages from their source; you exclude all serious study of the major influences that have moulded English and French literature.'[61]

Every word in that bill of particulars rings true; but Dodds might have paused longer to ask himself just *why*, except on purely academic or aesthetic grounds, this loss of historical perspective was so undesirable. I have a horrific memory, from my days as an ex-service undergraduate at Cambridge, of reading an article [62] by that apostle of wet but privileged liberalism, Sir Harold Nicolson, arguing that 'the charm of the Greek and Latin language is that they offer us a lovely irrelevance; that they provide an escape from the material values of the modern world'. It is true, as we have seen (and as Nicolson noted with relish), that some attempts at the time to claim practical relevance for classical studies were ill-grounded, indeed downright embarrassing. But I hope to have demonstrated in general – what the more detailed studies here assembled will confirm – that the active preservation of our ancestral heritage, and of the languages that enshrine it, is no mere cultural diversion, but a matter of the most vital and immediate concern to us all.

II

VICTORIAN HELLAS

L ORD ACTON, that bottomless well of aphorism on the moral condition of his age, remarked, about 1859, that 'two great principles divide the world and contend for the mastery, antiquity and the Middle Ages' – the world, of course, being restricted to Europe in general, England in particular, and America by courtesy. The dualism that these conflicting principles generated – Athens and Jerusalem, Christ against Socrates, even (or perhaps particularly) Doric versus Gothic – obsessed Victorian intellectuals to a quite extraordinary degree. Yet for some impenetrable reason (all the odder when one considers the peculiar dominance of classical as opposed to medieval studies at most major English schools till well after the Second World War) it is only the Gothic side of the Victorian age that has, till very recently, received regular scholarly attention. Our library shelves are loaded with monographs on Carlyle and Ruskin, on the Pre-Raphaelites or the Tractarian movement: yet the scholars who have nervously tackled any aspect of the impact of Hellenism on Victorian culture and society – surely a topic of fundamental importance – could, till very recently, be counted on the fingers of one hand. Now, to join the ranks of Bush, Clarke, Anderson, and DeLaura, we have Richard Jenkyns and Frank M. Turner, who between them have filled the larger part of this regrettable gap.

Perhaps the absence of systematic investigation is why, hitherto, our attitude to Victorian *Klassizismus* has so often been defined by a series of anecdotal snapshots, lacking the overall view: we have had our Plutarchs, but failed to produce a Thucydides. Dean Gaisford (cf. p. 19) reminding his congregation that the study of Greek literature not only lifts one above the common herd, but often leads to well-paid appointments; the headmaster for whom Sophocles' main attraction was as a repository of idiosyncratic grammatical usages (cf. p. 27); Thomas Arnold's nervously censorious dictum that no man could properly read Aristophanes till he had turned forty; Walter

Pater proclaiming to generations of Oxford undergraduates, through that rather soupy cavalry moustache, the credo of burning with a hard, gem-like flame; the same undergraduates, a few years later, marching down the High, arms linked, chanting choruses from Swinburne's *Atalanta in Calydon*; Gladstone announcing that Homer's world 'stands between Paradise and the vices of later heathendom'; Browning's Grammarian settling *hoti*'s business and giving us the doctrine of the enclitic *de*, dead from the waist down; and endless sub-classical pederastic maundering, of the sort that Wilde put into the mouth of Lord Henry Wotton ('Grace was his, and the white purity of boyhood, and beauty such as old Greek marbles kept for us', etc., etc.). The cumulative impression, perhaps not entirely false, and certainly loaded with an overplus of paradox, suggests not so much a serious historical or sociological appraisal as a Max Beerbohm cartoon – perhaps his famous sketch of the Victorian elder statesman making, without thought of emolument, a flat but faithful translation of Virgil's *Georgics* into English hexameters.

A *vue d'ensemble* was badly needed; and now, by a piece of serendipitous good timing, we have two of them at once: Richard Jenkyns' *The Victorians and Ancient Greece* and Frank M. Turner's *The Greek Heritage in Victorian Britain*, both published in 1981. Between them these two volumes go a long way towards filling what had been a surprising lacuna in both English cultural history and classical *Rezeptionsgeschichte*. Even more felicitously, they complement each other very well, and, further, suggest with some eloquence, through their contrasts and omissions, just how vastly complex and in many ways elusive a subject they are dealing with: controversial, too. Jenkyns' forte is for social history, pure literature, and the visual arts; Turner primarily concerns himself with the history of ideas, as manifested in the interpretation, and application, of Greek political, religious, or mythological phenomena. He is using the Victorians' attitude to classical antiquity as an instrument for probing Victorian intellectual life. He is not concerned, and tells us so, with 'Greek mythology or allusions to Greek culture as displayed in Victorian poetry and literary prose'. Here he stands in sharp contrast to Jenkyns, whose investigation of George Eliot's use of classical symbolism in her novels constitutes a critical *tour de force*. Nor does Turner deal with the role of the classics in Victorian education, or – wisely, I would judge – with the technical side, linguistic or philological, of classical scholarship.

Thus both Turner and Jenkyns have areas where they overlap little or not at all: Jenkyns on tragedy, poetry in general, painting, and the whole matter of *fin-de-siècle* decadence (which he treats as a huge and mildly risqué joke, whereas Turner restricts himself to some asides on the contortions performed by Jowett and other liberal Anglicans over Platonic homosexuality); Turner on the Athenian constitution, Aristotle's *Ethics*, and the seemingly all-pervasive phenomenon of ancient intellectual and moral concepts being used, consciously or unconsciously, as grist for modern religious or political propaganda mills. Where they *do* overlap – on Homer, say, or Plato – they thus tend to take very different views of the material they are studying. Seldom can two books with a common theme have produced less otiose duplication: a pity their authors could not have collaborated. Turner would be all the better for a measure of Jenkyns' style, broad cultural background and (on internal evidence) sharp eye for misprints; Jenkyns, in turn, could do with Turner's structural tidiness, clarity of exposition, and ability to extract cogent intellectual generalisations from the most complex and disparate material.

Though in its own way an overview, Jenkyns' *The Victorians and Ancient Greece* is also the apotheosis of the anecdotal method, as chock-full of good stuff as a Christmas pudding, and at the same time the living embodiment of Blake's apothegm, scrawled in the margin of Reynolds' *Discourses*: 'To Generalise is to be an Idiot. To Particularise is the Alone Distinction of Merit.' A scholar of formidable erudition, enviably wide reading, and impeccable (i.e. middle-of-the-road, professionally unexceptionable) taste, Jenkyns also writes nice prose, and has a pretty wit. This he exercises, as did Juvenal, with tart concision, against safe, or safely dead, targets – as when he describes Swinburne 'sticking out his tongue at Christianity like a naughty child', or remarks of the late Sir Richard Livingstone that he 'provides a fair test of the taste of his time, since he never had an idea of his own in his life'.

Structurally, *The Victorians and Ancient Greece* is an enjoyable mess. Jenkyns divides it into a baker's dozen of chapters, with titles such as 'The Origins of Hellenism', 'The Consequences of Sculpture', 'Homer and the Homeric Ideal', 'Change and Decay', and so on, with sub-headings on 'Christianity and the Greeks' (why not a separate chapter?) and 'Sophocles and Public Order' or 'Boswellism' or 'Plato's Decline'. This, however, is about the extent of his ability to sort the thread of an articulate argument. Each of these divisions functions as a kind of great baggy Jamesian holdall into which he shovels, thick and fast, endless discrete facts, quotations, siftings of novels, plays, poems, tracts, pamphlets: a racy *catalogue raisonné* where the reader struggles from anecdote to aside to aphorism trying, for the greater part in vain, to distinguish the wood from the trees, bogged down by relentless detail, yet always persisting, drawn on in part by the sheer fascination of the material, in part by the frequent crisp and illuminating judgments flung off between one recherché story and the next. Discussing Hardy, he remarks: 'There is no terrible inevitability about the fates of Tess or Jude: they are merely accident-prone.' He neatly deflates the Victorian poet's unfortunate habit of pastiching Greek drama: 'All these men assumed that to be Greek was to succeed: it had become an end in itself.' Nor has he any time for Victorian sentimentality: the reunion, in *Daniel Deronda*, of the dying Mordecai with his sister is knocked off as 'the sort of scene that makes an old-fashioned Hollywood weepie seem caustic', a verdict recalling Wilde's claim that one would have to have a heart of stone not to laugh at the death of Little Nell.

With this kind of temperament Jenkyns is at his most effective when anatomising the complex morbidities and hypocrisies of Victorian attitudes to sex, and *a fortiori* to the presumptive sexual licence, both straight and gay, that so bothered them about classical antiquity. He is particularly good on the coy and ambivalent awkwardness about trendy Greek nudity (as opposed to mere nakedness) that emerges from a study of Ruskin or Pater: Ruskin could enthuse happily over the Venus de Milo's proportions, but the discovery, on his wedding-night, that his bride actually possessed pubic hair and was, as they say, hot to trot, seems to have left him impotent for life.

In this connection Jenkyns notes, correctly, the rather nasty obsession with the Pygmalion legend shown by both poets and artists throughout the Victorian period. Shaw had endless predecessors here, most of them less intellectually sadistic and more emotionally prurient. In 1868 Burne-Jones painted a sequence of four pictures about an artist whose statue came to life. At the time he himself was caught up in a somewhat tepid and cerebral entanglement with his Greek model, whose idea of sex, it is safe to say, was a good deal more direct than his. The second picture, with the statue still safely marble, was entitled 'The Hand Refrains'. In the fourth, the artist is kneeling before a now living, but still marmoreal and bloodless, lady whose breasts he eyes with a lubricious yet somehow apprehensive devotion. This picture is captioned 'The Soul Attains'. And what, as Jenkyns rightly asks, about the hand now? There is something at once chauvinistic and anaemic here. An animated statue is the ultimate in personal playthings, to be moulded by male fantasy, but it lacks the sexual aggressiveness and unpredictability of a real woman. No wonder (Jenkyns seems to imply) that so many Victorian males turned instead to the high-minded, and officially sublimated, pederasty that could be extracted from Plato, or, blended with hearty Christian athleticism and cold baths, was read, by Pater and others, into the savage military regime of classical Sparta. There may be some truth in this, but the roots of Victorian homosexuality lay deeper, and reached far further, than one would ever guess from reading Jenkyns' obiter dicta on the subject.

In particular, the obsession with adolescent boys, unlike its supposed Athenian prototype, was neither vigorous nor unabashed: instead it tended towards a Baudelairean pedestal-and-gutter dualism, heavy with moral earnestness, symbolised at one end of the scale by the marshmallow encomia of aesthetes like John Addington Symonds, and at the other by the pederastic male brothels that proliferated in central London towards the end of the century. Such crude realities remained very much *sub rosa* at the time: as Jenkyns says – another of those peppy aphorisms that too often in this book substitute for serious analysis – 'the love that dared not speak its name has now become so insistently communicative that we easily forget how little was known about it a century ago'. I think he probably underestimates Victorian sophistication in the process of appraising Victorian public reticence; it remains true, however, that in those pre-Freudian days passionate but sexless attachments between members of the same sex certainly existed, and were described in language of an uninhibited sort that would certainly raise eyebrows today. Jenkyns prints a couple of choice specimens from, of all people, Disraeli.

But if there was naivety, there was also hypocrisy. Not all the high-minded admirers of the *Phaedrus* could keep their hands to themselves behind closed doors, and too often the invocation of Greek precedent was used to justify anything-but-cerebral activities. The 'Fleshly School' of poets did not get its name by accident. There was also a good deal of Pecksniffian propaganda from self-styled Uranians about 'ladslove' 'passing the love of women' (the Biblical allusion, too, was absolutely in character). The notion that Plato, like some special spiritual detergent, washed all such activities whiter was, in every sense, peculiarly seductive. Jenkyns invites us to laugh – and we do laugh – at all the dim and sentimental poetasters who hymned white boyish limbs in slim limp-bound volumes of bad verse; who more often than not ended up in Italy, where the local youths knew a profitable game when they saw one; and who astonished their innocent relatives by the size of the bequests they left to their houseboys. But he never makes any attempt to *explain* this odd phenomenon: his forte is for exposition rather than problem-solving.

The sentimentalism and confused thinking characteristic of Victorians who invoked antiquity in defence of their pederastic inclinations is a by no means isolated phenomenon. It also manifests itself in such diverse areas as climate, social life, and, above all, religion. More mush, more pure drivel, must have been written about ancient Greece in the nineteenth century, and, on the face of it, by those who should have known better, than at any other period. There were few, if any, truly original classical scholars in England during this period, Jenkyns argues, which is debatable. But his claim that 'at the very moment that Nietzsche was revealing to Germany the fierce, Dionysiac side of the Greek soul the English were marching boldly backwards towards Winckelmann and Goethe' is undoubtedly true. From Shelley to Wilde, the classicising obiter dicta astound by their banality, emotionalism, and lack of intellectual honesty. The most energetic myth-making was, to a quite remarkable extent, carried on by those – Englishmen following an outdated German banner – who had never been south of the Alps. 'Kennst Du das Land wo die Zitronen blühn' was a rhetorical question calculated to provoke the reply, from a well-travelled Hellenist: 'Yes, but you don't.'

To such people, as Jenkyns says, 'Hellas became a sort of heavenly city, a shimmering fantasy on the far horizon'. Symonds peddled the most incredible nonsense (which even moderate attention to a few key texts, e.g. Hesiod's *Works and Days*, let alone autopsy, should have sufficed to dispel in Housman's canonical three minutes) about the Greeks living in 'perpetual sunshine and perpetual ease – no work . . . that might degrade the body . . . no dread of hell, no yearning after heaven'. In other words, an educated *rentier's* paradise, magically freed from English weather and English religious puritanism, where the elect (as opposed to manual workers, slaves, women, and other such neglectable *canaille*) could sit around discussing their souls and eyeing pretty boys. Modern Greeks, too, were included in this rose-tinted scene: happy Mediterranean peasants with less work and more food than would be their lot in the dank north. 'Summer leaves them not', Symonds pontificated (the endemic illusion of the tourist who assumes that everything goes on exactly the same when he isn't there). His further comment is even more revealing: 'There is surely some difference between hoeing turnips and trimming olive boughs; between tending turkeys on a Norfolk common and leading goats to browse on cytisus beside the shore.'

The South, in short, was by definition more romantic than the North, the past than the present. Hence W.S. Gilbert's gibe at 'the idiot who praises, in enthusiastic tone/ all centuries but this and every country but his own'. If cytisus sounded better than turnips, a peplos was more poetic than trousers. Yet the past was still refracted inexorably through the present: as the classicising pictures of artists like Leighton or Alma-Tadema make all too clear, the Victorian concept of antiquity was, in the last resort, a stylised never-neverland done up in fancy dress.

This depressing conclusion is reinforced, with massive, detailed, meticulous, and (in the end) relentless documentation, by Turner, who gives equally short shrift in this area to the Victorians' much-vaunted intellectual pretensions. He demonstrates conclusively that 'disinterested or dispassionate criticism was simply not the order of the day': that the Victorians, almost without exception, used the ancient world as back-up material for their own social, moral, religious or political prejudices, while at the same time allowing those prejudices totally to dictate the interpretations they formulated of classical authors and institutions: that even (or perhaps especially) the most high-minded of them were ready to ignore, suppress, distort or domesticate any feature of Greek society that appeared patently at odds with their chosen vision. It is a bleakly pessimistic view of human intellectual endeavour; and there is, alas, a horrible degree of truth to it. From *stasis* on Corcyra to the latest round of ideological agitprop, the message remains the same: *tantum religio potuit suadere malorum*. A pity, I always feel, that *religio* has come to be so exclusively associated with 'religion' in the narrower sense: its binding moral force can, and does, embrace any prescriptive dogma or taboo, from Marxism to voodoo (not to mention voodoo economics). The one quality it *always* lacks, almost by definition, is reasoned objectivity, a respect for truth-telling due process. This latter habit, so awkward for chiliasts and rain-makers of every stamp, has therefore been dismissed as 'bourgeois', a label by now about as meaningless as 'fascist', but through these new associations perhaps due for an honourable revival.

Turner is well aware that the distorting vision of belief is a phenomenon not by any means restricted to the Victorians. He shows us, in scarifying detail, just how William Mitford, the eighteenth-century pioneer of Greek historiography in England, the friend of Jeremy Bentham, used classical Athens in particular as a didactic model (and awful warning) to support and promote Country party doctrine on the virtues of the balanced English constitution and the radical perils of democratic government. Hobbes, who translated Thucydides, took a very similar line. Nor was the practice exclusively English. J.G. Droysen's advocacy of Macedonian dominance for the fractious Greek states, under Philip II and Alexander III, was directly conditioned by his activities as a rabid monarchist and Prussian nationalist: having, like Grote, ineffectually pursued a parliamentary career, he ended by projecting his frustrated ambitions on to the ancient world, just as he had earlier used that world to justify his own political ideology.

If men like Arnold, Grote, Gladstone, Jowett and Burnet were – as Turner amply demonstrates – shaped in their attitudes to Hellenism by the position they took on contemporary political, social, or religious issues, can we claim that the scholars of this century are any more immune from such influences? In particular, the onset of totalitarianism (infecting Left and Right with fine impartiality) has intruded a refracting lens that subtly – or not so subtly – modifies our assumptions about antiquity in ways few could have foreseen a century ago. Sir Karl Popper's famous assault on Plato is a good case in point: would *The Open Society and its Enemies* have been written with quite such virulent fervour (or even perhaps written at all, at least until Gulag-time) had Hitler not invaded Popper's native Austria? Do we not in large measure owe our pervasive concept of Plato-as-totalitarian to the *Anschluss*, and to the Nazis' embarrassing habit of pilfering educational ideas from the *Republic*? What did Rostovtzeff's ideas on the Roman middle classes owe to his traumatic brush with the Russian revolution? How far were Syme's views on Augustan *Realpolitik* crystallised by first-hand observation of Italian fascism, with Mussolini's bully-boys cracking liberal skulls down the road from the American Academy? A similar scrutiny of some fashionable contemporary trends might prove instructive: what, for instance, could be more attractive than deconstruction in an era of bankrupt morality, collapsing social values, creeping illiteracy, self-doubt, smart slogans, media glitz, and the triumph of relativism?

Till the latter part of the eighteenth century what we may term the Romano-Christian view of the ancient world held the field. Despite such isolated phenomena as the Cambridge Platonists, despite the efforts of pioneers like Colet, Cheke, and Erasmus, Greek culture never really took a firm hold in England at the Renaissance: it is symptomatic that the first translation of Aeschylus only appeared in 1777 (cf. below, pp.267 ff.). Greek interests developed, as Turner reminds us, only when 'the values, ideas and institutions inherited from the Roman and Christian past became problem-atical'. A new wind, too, was blowing from Germany, where the *Neue Humanismus* of the University of Göttingen, not content with revolutionising classical historiography and philology, had expanded into the area of Biblical studies, with incalculable consequences: the sharp critical tools thus put into the hands of liberal theologians produced a conservative reaction much akin to that angry panic generated by the teaching of the Sophists in fifth-century Athens. Nor was this new groundswell exclusively religious. Political radicalism had come of age; the American and French revolutions were to demonstrate, graphically, just what practical results ideological theory could achieve. Conservatives, searching for counter-propaganda, turned to Greece, which, having been so little studied, 'could represent almost any value or outlook that a writer wished to ascribe to it'. It is a nice paradox, not least in an age that parrots the slogans of Greek democratic freedom *ad nauseam* – one more Hellenistic habit to add to the rest – that the polemical writing of Greek history should have begun in the 1780s as a vehicle for Tory propaganda.

Yet conservatives and radicals, freethinkers and Christian apologists, all alike assumed the classical heritage as common property for the purpose of their great debate. As Turner rightly insists, 'that now dissipated general familiarity with the classics was one of the distinguishing and self-defining marks of the social and intellectual elite of Europe'. No longer, alas: one more casualty of a dying aristocratic tradition, bayed about by anti-elitist levellers (see above, pp. 20 ff.). The predominance, throughout the nineteenth century, of the Oxford school of Literae Humaniores – Mods and Greats – also ensured that generations of statesmen, divines and academics took it for granted that the ancient world and their own enjoyed a symbiotic relationship, moral no less than cultural, that what they thought and wrote about Greece would profoundly affect contemporary political, religious, philosophical and moral discourse. (R. G. Collingwood in his *Autobiography*, written during the dark days of World War II, reflected grimly on how much logical positivism had shaped the attitudes of Oxford-educated politicians in the Thirties.) The converse corollary of this assumption – that contemporary beliefs and prejudices must, inevitably, colour their own attitudes to antiquity – seems not to have been grasped with anything like the same degree of certainty.

Yet as the century progressed, the changing interpretations of Greek history, mythology, philosophy and religion must surely have given the more thoughtful some moments of acute self-doubt. Bishop Butler and Bishop Hampden, Hegel and Vico, Max Müller's Aryanism, Utilitarianism, Comte, Nietzsche, Ruskin, Pater, Freud, Marx, Bergson, Jung – the gods of the copybook headings succeeded each other with dizzying speed. New dogmas contradicted old shibboleths, scholarship was public, *engagé* (with many scholars doubling as politicians, and vice versa) in a manner reminiscent of the Byzantine theological riots. Those who pride themselves, today, on having achieved a greater degree of objectivism might do well to reflect that this represents not so much the triumphant surmounting of academic bias as an evaporation of interest in what were once burning issues. Where the issues are still alive the distorting sense of committal remains as strong as ever.

Hugh Lloyd-Jones has pointed out (*Times Lit. Supp.* 24 June 1981) that Nietzsche's *The Birth of Tragedy* was meant as 'an attempt to utilise the understanding of antiquity in order to construct a philosophy for the author's own contemporaries'. By now it should be clear that this was no mere aberrant exception. Apart from those works of 'pure' scholarship that Turner excludes from his survey (and not even they were always immune: even to edit Plato or Aeschylus meant getting involved in their ideas), it would be hard to find a Victorian essay in ancient literature, history, or philosophy that was not, at the same time, in some sense a work of propaganda. The presumed *likeness* of fifth-century Greeks to the Victorians was a notion, Turner argues, 'fundamental to Victorian intellectual life', and he offers a brilliant analysis of the various devices employed by nineteenth-century thinkers to let them see Greece in their own image, and utilise its culture for their own ends (while, at the same time, refuting each other's theories with dogmatic vigour: Jowett's unorthodoxies actually got him prosecuted). The reinvention of the past has always been a flourishing intellectual industry.

To providentialists, the Greeks were precursors of Christianity. Those who, like Thomas Arnold, believed in Vico's cyclic theory of world history could argue that Periclean Athens and Victorian England both represented the apogee of the cycle, and thus should be treated *in pari materia*. Comtean positivists adapted Greek religious and philosophical phenomena to the three-stage model of intellectual development (religious, metaphysical, positivist). Hegelians, similarly, saw in the passage from the archaic to the classical world the triumph of *Moralität* over mere *Sittlichkeit*. As Turner says, 'these several philosophies of history did not function in hermetically sealed compartments', nor were those who argued for analogies between Greece and Britain always fully aware of them. For a nation of pragmatists the result was conceptual muddle and steaming but unacknowledged emotionalism. Yet however eclectic their treatment, these notions supplied, one way and another, the framework for a century of polemic and speculation.

It is thus a great virtue of Turner's method that he approaches his subject not generically, but in linear, evolutionary, historical terms – diachronic rather than synchronic, as the new jargon has it – tracing patterns of influence as they develop. Thus both constants and variables get their proper emphasis. If Victorian thinkers shared one characteristic throughout, it was that of political and intellectual elitism solidly rooted in the English class-system; if they had a constant common enemy, it was the bugbear of commercialism, materialism, and selfish bourgeois Philistinism (very often with romantic or iconoclastic modernism thrown in as an antisocial makeweight). For both attitudes they could invoke a wealth of precedent from the ancient world. To that extent Matthew Arnold had a point. They tended, further, to believe in the uniformity of human nature (if not in the common nature of that uniformity), and to stress moral or ethical issues (though seldom from the same standpoint). But this was about the limit of their common ground, as becomes very clear – to take one of Turner's more striking examples – from their treatment of Plato.

Till after 1840 the Platonic corpus, untaught and largely untranslated, lay in a kind of intellectual limbo: Plato's thought was held to be impractical, and thus (as Macaulay informed readers of the *Edinburgh Review*) irrelevant to an age of progress. (In 1816, during the debate over the Elgin Marbles, the experts consulted came down squarely in favour of realism and naturalism in art: trendy idealism was still waiting in the wings.) A character in Thomas Love Peacock's *Crotchet Castle* (1831) observes that contemporary universities also regarded Plato as 'little better than a misleader of youth'. In due course, however, liberal Anglicans such as Sewell and Blackie and A.E. Taylor got hold of Plato and used his doctrines to uphold traditional Christian ethics against utilitarianism – whereupon his university status at once rose appreciably. The utilitarians, in turn, employed Plato's moral and political philosophy as a surrogate to *replace* Christian values: where Taylor had 'transformed the *Republic* into a Hellenic *Pilgrim's Progress*', Grote saw Plato as a kind of radical Benthamite, a questioner of all established values. In this tug-of-war the figure of Socrates perhaps suffered most: his irony forgotten, he was presented successively as a liberal deist, a radical gadfly, a substitute Christ-figure and mystic, or a no-nonsense early Victorian Methodist.

To Christian scholars, of whatever denomination, the fact that it was Grote – of all people – who wrote the standard nineteenth-century work on Plato (its conclusions still a starting-point for much argument today) came as a supremely unpalatable irony. Blackie, for instance, held it to be 'no less inappropriate than Voltaire's composing a commentary on the fourth Gospel'. Jowett, for his part, created a Hegelian Plato; his disciples employed this odd figure to encourage, in Turner's words, 'a collective civic life in which the individualism of the mid-Victorian period would come under the benevolent direction of the state and of a civic elite that resembled Mill's vision of bureaucracy'. Through the agency of Oxford and the Civil Service examinations, the Empire struck back: it is not hard to see how Rhodes or Kipling would look at the *Republic*. Pater, on the other hand, could treat the doctrine of Forms as a vindication of the senses; Nettleship and others related the *Republic* to the medieval, and thus anti-commercial, monastic ideal: while Ernest Barker put the same dialogue to work as a handbook inculcating service to the state. After beginning the century in neglect, Plato ended it with a revival that out-dazzled the Renaissance. Though Grote had been worried by the philosopher's political, as Martineau was by his moral, illiberalism, it was left for our own age to tar and feather Plato as an out-and-out totalitarian. The symbiotic exploitation of past and present continues.

Equally startling, though in political rather than religious terms, is the metamorphosis of the Athenian constitution, as seen by English historians, from a late eighteenth-century hobgoblin embodying all the worst features of lawless anarchy, political chaos, and disregard for personal security, to an

Edwardian model of idealised social-cum-political aspirations for classically educated servants of empire to imitate. Turner's chapter on this remarkable transformation is at once an object-lesson in disinterested research and an historiographical horror story. No man can be wholly impartial, and we catch a glimpse of where Turner stands from his uncharacteristic encomium of Zimmern's *Greek Commonwealth*, which he describes as 'one of the most sensitive, eloquent, evocative and humane works ever written about Athens in this language'. Such judgments, pro or con, are rare in Turner's study, and all the more effective as a result. More often he is casually, and savagely, dismissive. Frazer gets short shrift for transforming Demeter and Persephone into mere wheatsheaf dolls, while Andrew Lang is sunk without trace: 'At his best he was only a gifted amateur and at his worst a polemical bore.'

On the nineteenth-century historians Turner's objectivity is withering, his wit caustic. Skilfully he relates their treatment of evidence to their own political and moral predilections, noting Arnold's obsession with 'the ideal unity of the Greek polis as the means of overcoming modern democratic pluralism', Grote's disconcerting habit of equating the Athenian Assembly with Parliament, Pericles with the Prime Minister of the day, Cleon with some radical Opposition spokesman. We can see why Sparta was so highly regarded at the opening of the century but condemned at its close, why Mitford rehabilitated the *tyrannoi*, why Grote trod so gingerly in his treatment of Solon and Peisistratus ('this scenario too closely resembled the confiscation of property during the French Revolution and Napoleon's later tyranny to suit Grote's polemical purposes'), how Gladstone's Peelite view of Homeric politics brought him into conflict with the utilitarians, how and why the hot potato of slavery was handled more boldly from 1867 onwards (not only the end of the American Civil War but the passing of the Second Reform Bill), how views of Macedonia in the fourth century BC were conditioned by Anglo-German relations before 1914, just as earlier, for Droysen, they had been conditioned by the unificatory ambitions of Prussia. Finally, we are left with an unforgettable image of London buses, early in World War I, carrying extracts from Pericles' Funeral Oration on official war-propaganda posters. 'The debate over the Athenian constitution,' Turner concludes, 'was primarily a debate over the conservative image of democracy and not over democracy itself.' It would be hard, in the face of the evidence he musters, to argue with that verdict.

The same mastery of material and independence of judgment inform every topic on which he turns that shrewdly penetrating eye of his. Max Müller's Aryanism, for instance, like his theories of solar myth, offers a tempting target to the modern cynic (of Heracles' death in the pyre on Mt Oeta Müller wrote: 'Another magnificent sunset . . .'): but Turner puts his finger unerringly on the quality that endeared this pompous Teutonic eccentric to Victorian England, the notion that the original nobility of the Aryan race would save mankind from Darwinism (has this theory ever been adduced as an explanation for anti-Semitic activities?), that the embarrassing habits of theft, murder, lying, incest, adultery, homosexuality, promiscuity, sodomy and castration attributed to the Greek gods or heroes by our sources were all late accretions, that, as Müller assured his readers, 'in all these tales there is nothing of which, *in its old shape*, we ought to be ashamed'. No wonder he was offered a knighthood and made a Privy Councillor! Turner also gets to the heart of Gladstone's odd obsessions about Homer, sees precisely why Jebb and Arnold were far from pleased by Schliemann's archaeological discoveries (Tiryns in particular so offended Jebb's preconceived notions of high Homeric culture that he argued strongly for the ruins being Byzantine), and pinpoints the advantages enjoyed by Aristotle's *Nicomachean Ethics* as an instrument of education: it was sensible, it upheld social elitism (thus appealing equally to Anglicanism and the aristocracy), it did not evoke mystical or radical yearnings in the young, much less challenge traditional beliefs regarding the sanctity of property or the family, and (as Mark Pattison in an unguarded moment admitted) it was an ideal text from which to set examination questions.

Is there any kind of central causality lurking behind these diverse phenomena? One obvious factor, scarcely touched on by either Jenkyns or Turner, has to be the all-pervasive impact of the Industrial Revolution. Few men had the vision of a painter such as J.M.W. Turner, who boldly absorbed the new monsters of iron and steel, steam and coal, into his romantic palette and traditional iconography (see, e.g., *Rain, Steam and Speed*, 1844). Far more characteristic is that strain of social and literary Luddism that runs through English criticism from Arnold to Leavis, that universal lament for the loss of rural innocence, that non-stop jeremiad against Blake's 'dark Satanic mills' and the horrors of industrialism. In the course of a slamming attack on Arnold's *Culture and Anarchy* Jenkyns remarks, without following up the implications of his *aperçu*, that in Arnold's vocabulary 'coal, railroads and machinery are words as automatically pejorative as incense or chalice in the literature of the Protestant Truth Society'.

This is hardly to be wondered at. The Industrial Revolution undermined (often in a most literal sense) the very foundations of English rural, and still predominantly aristocratic, landownership; by providing new avenues to great wealth it opened up the closed circle of traditional political power; it destroyed old values as well as the landscape, and brought a dangerous air of egalitarianism into society along with the poisonous smoke from its factory chimneys. The English upper classes, taught – by Plato and Aristotle among others – to despise banausic occupations, saw in Greek culture the perfect rearguard action against these rising forces of mercantilism. Jenkyns remarks at one point that 'the extent to which [the Victorians] underestimated Plato's hatred of democracy is remarkable'. It is not remarkable at all. Those who were classically educated, who regarded their knowledge of Greek as a badge of ascension in the class structure, detested and feared egalitarianism: they were elitist through and through (see above, p.18). Arnold's quarrel with John Bright is symptomatic. No accident that so many classicists have been quite ferocious right-wingers. Greek culture was not only pre-industrial and supposedly tolerant of gentlemanly vices; it also (if selectively studied) could be held to support private incomes and government by a self-perpetuating elite.

Another by-product of this anti-industrial obsession with antiquity was an increasing interest in what might be termed urban pastoralism: the romantic (not to say oxymoronic) cultivation of country matters by those who preferred to view their sheep through the study window. Nostalgic escapism was the key here: if the Pre-Raphaelites and others medievalised Homer, Theocritus – in fact an earthy and predominantly heterosexual bucolic poet – could be, and was, taken up as the advocate of languorous and genteel rural inversion. Jenkyns notes, in authors as diverse as Flecker, Kenneth Grahame, and T.S. Eliot, 'a concern with landscape and its supernatural associations'. The numinous, it was felt, did not take well to the (industrialised) English countryside: even Kipling's *Puck of Pook's Hill* indirectly chronicles its passing. Anti-clericalists, chafing against what they regarded as soul-killing religious and moral constraints, were not slow to use the classics as a weapon against the stuffier manifestations of Victorian Christianity, especially as regards sexual freedom. 'Thou hast conquered, O pale Galilaean', Swinburne announced, 'the world has grown grey at thy breath'; but nevertheless he and many others continued to fight a vigorous campaign in favour of a resurgent neo-paganism linked especially with Pan. As a symbol of what today we would call the Id, Pan enjoyed a certain brief popularity, cropping up everywhere in *fin-de-siècle* art and literature, but otherwise, as far as one can tell, having no effect at all. The trouble with the new paganism, as Chesterton shrewdly pointed out, was that it was neither new nor pagan; worse, neither it nor the culture from which it sprang had any really organic connection with English society. Arnold's laborious Greek dramas, the Doric façade of a London bank, the notion of Pan piping at Mapledurham – all, in the last resort, were artificial growths.

The really serious problems inherent in Victorian dealings with Greek culture are, as we have seen, religious and political, with a strong social undercurrent of unacknowledged class-conflict. The classics could be used to defend aristocratic government (while at the same time talking about the glories of democracy), anti-commercialism, and the inevitability of a fixed world-order. But at the same time it had to be admitted that Greek beliefs were in many ways – some embarrassing to a degree – incompatible with Christianity. The fact that many Greeks, from Xenophanes onward, had been equally bothered by the moral aspects of Olympianism did not in any way alleviate this problem. Gladstone's Homeric theories, as both Jenkyns and Turner make clear, were crazy; but they were crazy in a desperate cause, to make Homer in some vital sense a precursor of the Christian revelation.

The fact that an otherwise sane figure, of considerable intellectual stature and several times Prime Minister, should be hagridden by such an obsession is in itself an historical fact of enormous significance.

'That Homer had been the Bible of the Greeks,' Jenkyns writes, 'was a Victorian cliché. Where Gladstone was unusual was in his desire that the poet should become the Bible of the English too.' This is neat but impercipient. One can see, only too well, the dilemma facing the *bien-pensants* of the Victorian era: their two great props against social and political destruction, the Greek classics and the Christianity of the Protestant Establishment, were in apparent fundamental conflict with one another, and all efforts to reconcile Athens with Jerusalem, ever since the days of the Early Fathers, had involved an element of more or less dishonest circle-squaring. Attempts to present even Plato, and *a fortiori* Socrates, as an *anima naturaliter Christiana* have always had something a trifle specious about them. In the Victorian age – the age of scientific revolution and anguished religious doubt, of strident dogma and social flux – that dilemma provoked more heart-searching, and spiritual agony, than at any other period since that of Tertullian. But (as both Turner and Jenkyns in their different ways remind us) our own age has no cause for complacency, either: heart and head still tell conflicting stories, and evidence ranging from Auden's 'Shield of Achilles' to the latest televangelist scandal testifies eloquently to the perennial, and seemingly insoluble, nature of the problem. The great merit of these two books is to counter the current distorting fad for synchronicity by establishing an historical context and perspective in which the ongoing debate can be placed and, with luck, illuminated if not resolved.

III

LESBOS AND THE
GENIUS LOCI

THE REMOTE AND BEAUTIFUL Greek island of Lesbos carries
unfortunate connotations for a modern visitor. Most people
know that it was the place where, in Byron's words, 'burning
Sappho loved and sung'. They may have no very clear notion of
the songs in question, and the over–imaginative reconstructions foisted on
them by some of Sappho's modern translators will not help. But they do have
a vague notion of a great lyric poet, known in antiquity as the Tenth Muse.
This, however, is generally eclipsed by what they know, or surmise, about
the particular nature of Sappho's burning and loving. The name of her island
and, even more, the name of its inhabitants offer a constant nudging
reminder of her supposed predilections. When we talk about a Lesbian today
it is not, in all likelihood, a citizen of Mytilene or Eresos that we have in mind.
The Greek Tourist Office, by a kind of modest synecdoche, prefers whenever
possible to refer to Mytilene, the capital, when discussing the island as a
whole. Worse, the legend of Sappho has effectively outgrown all other
knowledge of Lesbos except among specialists: this ignorance is compounded
by the fact that no serious history of the island exists in any language. What
follows here is part of an ongoing attempt, conducted over many years and
sometimes in highly unacademic circumstances, to fill the gap.

For me Sappho has always, therefore, been a witness, valuable if enigmatic,
not only to her troubled age but also to the island where she was born and spent
the greater part of her life. The landscape, weather, vegetation and seasonal
changes of Lesbos deeply affected her attitudes and imagery: the *genius loci* is
very strong in Sappho's work – as I came to discover during several years'
continuous residence on the island during the 1960s. Here, at Molyvos,
ancient Methymna, where Orpheus' singing head fetched up after being
carried 'down the swift Hebrus to the Lesbian shore', I wrote a novel about
Sappho, *The Laughter of Aphrodite*. It obstinately cast itself in the first person,

45

so I suppose it could be said that the island, or at least its most famous ghost, took possession of me. Here, in a relatively untroubled enclave (even with Turkey less than three miles away across the strait) I contrived, with few regrets, to bypass the American and British upheavals of the Sixties. But two recent research trips to the island, in 1980 and 1983, suggest strongly that the isolation and remoteness of Lesbos may soon be a thing of the past. Serious crises in Greco-Turkish relations brought in the army, and gun-emplacements sprang up everywhere. One excellent stretch of early Aeolic wall was demolished by over-enthusiastic military pioneers while the then Ephor (Superintendant) of Antiquities was, as so often happened, somewhere else.

Restrictions have come along with the military. Over large stretches of the island the use of cameras is now forbidden. (To my astonishment, I was stopped from photographing the small monument to Sappho on the bluff overlooking Mytilene harbour: I'm still trying to figure out the rationale of that particular prohibition.) Also, Greek tourists have discovered the place. They swarm in from Thessalonike, patronise the locals with lower-middle-class urban brio, and have even worse beach manners than the Germans, which is saying something. Back in the Sixties one DC3 flew in each afternoon, half full. Now, Mytilene is serviced by four Boeing 737s daily: every seat is taken. Already non-stop package tours are being routed direct to Mytilene airport from Scandinavia and the UK. There are plans to extend the runway yet further, bring in 747s, and make Lesbos a staging-post for the Near and Middle East. When that happens, the island I know and love will cease to exist: many islanders regret this prospect as much as I do. Others, unfortunately among them some of the richest and most influential, do not. As I pursued my researches, in the historical archives of Mytilene, or doing topographical surveys, underwater as well as on land (cf. below, p.50), or taping folk-music and interviews, I was acutely conscious that time, for this as for so many other enclave cultures, was inexorably running out: what I was writing – these pages included – might end up as an epitaph.

'NO MAN,' WROTE JOHN DONNE, 'is an island, entire of itself; every man is a piece of the *Continent*, a part of the *main*.'[1] In a very real sense it can be said that no island is entire of itself either, that it too forms part of the main. Yet at the same time that sundering stretch of sea, however narrow – and in the case of Lesbos it is very narrow indeed – insulates in a way that no man-made political frontiers could ever do. Thus in studying island history one is always conscious of a strong contrapuntal tension between the small world and the larger world scene beyond it, the centripetal and centrifugal instincts. On the one hand there is an existence defined by geophysical accident, yet more often than not pursued with extraordinary and idiosyncratic passion. An enclave untroubled by the intrusive levelling of mass-communications is a marvellous culture-dish, in which dialects, myths, folklore, music, poetry, even political relationships, can develop within narrow yet sustaining limits. On the other hand, this isolation is never total. The islanders themselves will always have one eye across the straits: to expand their frontiers, to trade for the key imports that every island needs, to defend themselves against aggression. They are on the inside looking out: but there is always, too, someone out there looking in, sizing up their small kingdom as a potential outpost of empire, source of wealth, or staging-post on some crucial trade-route.

The island of Lesbos has, for much of its history, been exposed to conflicting claims and ambitions in precisely this way. It lies in the north-east Aegean, handily close to Troy, and, more important, to the Hellespont [Dardanelles]. Through those narrows the grainships on which Athens and other Aegean cities depended made passage from the Black Sea, loaded with south Russian wheat. At least from the archaic period, indeed from the beginning of the Dark Age, say about 1100 BC, Lesbos had a Greek-speaking population, and formed part of that Hellenic world which embraced the entire circle of the Aegean, its inhabitants, as Plato said,[2] resembling ants or frogs clustered round a pond. They shared a common religion, the great international festivals, a similar way of life, Hellenic ancestry, and, above all, the Greek language.[3] Within all these elements there was great scope for variety and individualism: local deities and local dialects could be equally *sui generis*.

One notorious absentee from the list, however, was political unity, or even federation in any serious sense. As late as Metternich's day it was still thought impossible, and with good reason, to define Greece as a whole in political terms.[4] Throughout classical antiquity stubborn local particularism – euphemistically described as the city-state (*polis*) mentality – ensured that the Aegean formed a permanent cockpit for small but intensely ambitious local powers, whose main occupation was fighting each other. As a change from this activity the rival political groups within each city – oligarchs or democrats, conservatives or radicals – would frequently escalate their non-stop bickering, the basic stuff of Greek political life, into open civil war. This process they described as *stasis* (the modern Greek word, appropriately enough in Athens, for a bus-stop), and just how ruthless it could be we know from Thucydides' famous description [5] of a peculiarly virulent outbreak on Corcyra, the modern Corfu – again, like Lesbos, an offshore island.

This tendency to internal fission, sometimes of almost nuclear intensity, is a constant in Greek history. Only under long-term and authoritarian foreign occupation – successively by Macedonia, Rome, Byzantium, the Franks, and, most recently, the Ottoman empire of Turkey – do we find it dormant. Even then it is merely held down by force: since the Greek War of Independence (1821-30) it has once more erupted with undiminished vigour. In antiquity more Greek cities were betrayed by the power-hungry opposition party within the walls than ever fell to a besieger. Alliances were brief, uncertain, and only dubiously ethnic: the old Dorian-Ionian split has been overdone.

Immediate advantage was all. External aggression might remind Greeks, transiently, of their common heritage; but even the great Persian invasion of 480 BC produced a far from united front. Many states preferred collaboration with Xerxes, in the hope of rich pickings under some accommodating satrap. It is well to remember such things at the outset, since the history of Lesbos reflects them all in microcosm. Yet it is also ironic, since, as we shall see, the island's Greekness was an early historical accident, and its perennial ties have always been in substantial part to the Anatolian coastal cities, and to the great land-mass of Asia that forms their interminable hinterland.

WHEN WE EXAMINE THE CONSTANT FACTORS in Lesbos' physical and social ecology, those that remain as applicable today as they were three thousand and more years ago, one symbolically arresting fact strikes us before anything else. In a very literal sense Lesbos *is* part of the continent. At some point, as the Augustan geographer Strabo was well aware,[6] it had broken away from the Ida range and the Troad, a small contribution to continental drift and earth movements in the Quaternary period, perhaps a million years ago. The andesite of north Lesbos matches that of the Troad, and the serpentine in the south-east part of the island recurs on Mt Ida: most rock types and structures, in fact, find close parallels.[7] Geologically, the island falls into two halves, volcanic and crystalline, divided by a long band of serpentine east of the Gulf of Kalloni. To the north and immediate west of the Gulf we find andesite lava and basalt. Beyond these is a wide region of tuffs, the consolidated ash from lava, which gives the western part of the island its wild and desolate appearance, accentuated by deforestation.

It is here, too, in the upland plateaux and valleys between Sigri, Eresos and Gavathà in the north, that we find what is quite certainly the oldest natural phenomenon on the island apart from the rocks of which it is formed: the petrified forest. Over four million years ago, probably when Lesbos still formed part of the mainland, the climate was very different, much resembling that of northern California today, complete with summer fogs, and the area was thickly forested swampland. Trees included not only oaks (*quercus aegileps*, still flourishing here and there) but also giant sequoias, akin to the Californian redwoods. A period of intense volcanic activity buried these forests deep in ash, but at the same time formed a basin that could be percolated not only by rainfall, but also by heavily silicated water from the surrounding hills. This formed the petrifying agent. 'As a result of molecular substitution the cells and other spaces were filled without any damage to the original tissue.'[8] At the same time various minerals coloured this petrified wood in the most arresting manner: iron produced red, yellow and brown formations, copper a bluish-green tint, manganese and carbon streaks of black. Sappho, whose birthplace was nearby Eresos, must have been familiar with these strange stone tree trunks from childhood. Was she, one wonders, as indifferent to them as the modern herdsman (at least until modern archaeological publicity suggested a brisk, profitable, and now, fortunately, illegal trade in tourist souvenirs)? It is hard to believe that her keen eye for natural phenomena would have missed something so exotic.

Were she to return now, she would find the western part of the island far more barren than in her day, when the hills were covered with thick oak forests, thrashed by the fearful gales that Vitruvius knew,[9] and which provided Sappho herself with some vivid emotional imagery. 'Love shook my wits,' she declared, 'like the wind falling on mountain oaks.[10] Elsewhere she describes such a wind, accurately, as 'down-rushing'.[11] The heavy shutters of even the most strongly built modern house testify to its force. Central and eastern Lesbos, in contrast to the west, remain almost as thickly forested as in antiquity. The great pine stands stretching from Lambou Mylai northward past the Gulf of Kalloni towards the Lepétymnos range, and still known today by their Turkish name, Tsamlíki, were familiar to Theophrastus – a native of the island – in the fourth century BC: then as today, they suffered from forest fires.[12] The area embracing the Gulf of Yera (ancient Hiera), the south-eastern hills and the capital, Mytilene, is a vast mass of crystalline limestone, rising in its centre to a sugar-loaf peak about 3000ft above sea-level, and known, with a certain lack of imagination, as Olympos. Above the tree line there still grows a wild profusion of oak, beech and, around Aghiassos, chestnut: planes and poplars are common at sea level. The hills above Mytilene are covered with near-virgin forest: soil erosion and deforestation, the twin scourge of the Cycladic islands in the central Aegean, have made no inroads here. The olive tree, which provides Lesbos with its chief export, fine oil, is ubiquitous: at the last census fifteen million were listed.

The two great inland gulfs also remain unchanged, though the towns after which they were named in antiquity, Hiera and Pyrrha, no longer exist: Pyrrha was destroyed in the third century BC by one of the frequent earthquakes, some of them catastrophic, that still shake the island.[13] The worst in recent memory was that of March 1867, which affected the whole northern and eastern part of Lesbos, and resulted in no less than 684 deaths, together with widespread damage and injury.[14] Seismic action must have been an equally constant hazard throughout the archaic and classical periods. One reminder of Lesbos' volcanic past is the extraordinary number of hot thermal springs, many with reputedly curative properties, in which the island abounds. The best-known is that at Thermi, where a spa has existed since Roman times, dedicated to Artemis Thermia, while the hottest (87.6° Celsius) is near Polichnitos: one nineteenth-century traveller[15] wrote of it: 'The heat of the water is so great, even after its exposure to the air as it flows down the mountainside, that the neighbouring villagers use it as a natural kitchen: they simply plunge their pans and kettles into the stream, and everything is cooked to perfection.'

Not all the sources are thermal: the north of the island in particular has fine perennial cold springs, especially on and near the Lepétymnos range. The Olympos massif also provides abundant spring water, such as we find bubbling up at the delightful plane-shaded oasis of Karinai,[16] on the road to Aghiassos. On the other hand Mytilene, the capital, has never possessed an adequate local source to supply its disproportionately large population, and thus has always been obliged to bring in water from outside. As early as the fourth century BC we find an inscription[17] praising the benefactor who organised additional water supplies, apparently by the diversion of a river. It took the Romans, probably in Hadrian's day,[18] to construct a highly effective aqueduct from Olympos to the city. Substantial remains[19] of this can still be seen at Morià, a mile or two north-west of Mytilene, and at Paspalà, near Lambou Mylai, below the Olympos massif. It entered the city from the north, near the ancient theatre.[20] The aqueduct's carrying capacity has been estimated at 127,000 cubic metres a day,[21] which compares well with modern standards.

At some point in the Middle Ages this aqueduct was among many useful survivals from antiquity, such as good harbours and fine public buildings, that were left either to fall down or to silt up. One of its main sources was the Great Lake (Megali Limni) on the upland plateau immediately north of Olympos, and close to Karinai. The lake has now been drained: but in the late nineteenth century it still survived, a shallow, marshy, reed-choked, stinking wilderness,[22] another case of far-from-benign neglect. In Mytilene itself – the only town on the island that has been in continual occupation, on exactly the same site, since at least the second millennium BC – we find similar indifference at work. The famous canal that throughout antiquity linked the city's northern and southern harbours, and was spanned with arching bridges of fine polished marble (one of which has recently been excavated),[23] silted up so thoroughly in the medieval period that it vanished altogether. Its course is now marked by the long main shopping street. There is a tradition, unconfirmed by any archaeological report, that in about 1900 engineers digging a trench to install water pipes found the remains of an ancient wooden ship buried deep in the subsoil.[24] Other monuments have fared better. Sea traffic has shifted today from the north harbour, the Epano Skala, to the deeper southern basin, but the ancient mole is still *in situ* and clearly visible, its western flank emerging as part of the city walls that can be traced from east to west immediately north of the town. Continuous habitation for nearly three millennia also means that whenever foundations are dug for houses or high-rise apartments (an increasingly popular sport these days), extensive remains appear two or three metres below the surface. At least two such sites were uncovered during my residence in the summer of 1980, one of which included a complex Roman drainage system. On Lesbos the past is very much alive in the present.

EXCAVATION ON LESBOS has always, unfortunately, tended to be *ad hoc* and haphazard, despite the efforts of scholars such as Koldewey, Lamb, Charitonidis, Buchholz, Kondis and, now, the Canadian School. This fact should be borne in mind when we consider the early historical evolution of Lesbos, always struggling to control her own destiny against the strong rival claims of east and west, of Anatolia and the Greek Aegean.[25] It is true that what changes there have been – apart from such obvious innovations, some very recent, as metalled roads, telecommunications, efficient refrigeration and air travel – are for the most part superficial, and that the island's ancient inhabitants saw a landscape identical, in all essentials, to that absorbed by their modern descendants. Yet the man-made record, as we know from better-documented areas, must have differed profoundly from that visible today: and our archaeological evidence, some of it excellent, remains sporadic. Much work still remains to be done. Even so, our knowledge of Lesbian prehistory has improved a good deal since Winifred Lamb, half a century ago, dug the Bronze Age coastal site of Thermi – still the only large-scale excavation carried out anywhere on Lesbos – and also identified late Bronze Age sherds at Antissa.[26] We now know that Antissa was in fact occupied as early as Troy II, in the third millennium BC: other Early Bronze sites (*c.* 2900–*c.* 1900) have been found at Palaia-Methymna, on the north coast; in the Bartholomaios cave, south of Mytilene; at Klopedi (Napé) in the central uplands; and in a cluster of sites on the east coast of the gulf of Kalloni, the ancient 'Euripos of the Pyrrhaeans';[27] Lesvorion (Kourtir) and Chalakies, which may even go back to the late Neolithic period, Perivola, and, possibly, Pyrrha itself. A Middle Bronze site is confirmed at Methymna as well as at Thermi. Late Bronze or Mycenaean remains have been found in a strategic ring all round the coast: at Methymna and Antissa; on the coast north of Sigri; at Makarà and Pyrrha; in the Gulf of Yera; at Mytilene and Thermi.[28] At the same time there has been no serious attempt to relate such material to the literary tradition, which is more often than not dismissed, unexamined, as fictional fantasy.[29] This seems to me unduly pessimistic, and I would like – while, I hope, retaining a proper degree of scepticism – to see what can be extracted from it.

No Greek mythographer, for reasons we will look at in a moment, had access to a tradition that went back much beyond 1500 BC. Thus for the earliest period we are dependent on archaeology alone. At Thermi, the only site for which we possess a continuous record, we find a series of five settlements between about 2900 and 2350 BC. The original inhabitants came, probably, from the mainland. They were a peaceful community, living in an unwalled village by the sea, keeping flocks and herds, hunting, fishing.[30] It is not until the fourth settlement (? 2700) that we find spears, and only the fifth found it necessary to build a fortified city wall for purposes of defence.[31] The site was abandoned, without any signs of conflict, about 2350. Speculation suggests the approach of an enemy from the Thraceward regions, by sea:

Thermi had close links with the north-west Anatolian culture that was centred on Troy.[32] Perhaps the inhabitants withdrew to the mountainous interior of the island. Thermi was not reoccupied till the beginning of the Middle Bronze period, *c.* 1900,[33] and Mycenaean pottery first appears about 1400. Almost exactly two centuries later (*c.*1200) Thermi was finally destroyed in a 'gigantic conflagration' which discoloured the soil all round the site and left an ash-layer in places over half a metre deep.[34]

How far does this evidence agree with the literary tradition? Almost the only account of Lesbos during what we would call the Bronze Age is that preserved by Diodorus Siculus.[35] In antiquity, he says, a number of people colonised the island, and there were many changes of population. Lesbos was originally known as Issa, with Antissa as an offshore island: both are good pre-Hellenic names. The island was occupied, at some point before Deucalion's flood, by a Pelasgian, Xanthos, who made his way there from Lycia and found it uninhabited. Seven generations later, amid the disease and destruction that followed the flood, Macareus, or Macar, a fugitive fratricide from Achaea, migrated to Lesbos with a mixed group of settlers.[36] (It may be no more than coincidence that Cyclopean remains have been found at Makarà, near the entrance to the Gulf of Kalloni; but the similarity of name is at least worth noting.) A firm date would help here. There is a very strong possibility that Deucalion's flood represents memories of the great *tsunami* or tidal wave that swept the Aegean after the gigantic eruption of Thera, in the Cyclades. Thirty-six square miles of the island, an area four times that of Krakatoa, blew out in a rain of ash and basalt boulders, leaving the deep-sunk caldera we see today. Now apart from flooding, Diodorus also speaks of 'epidemic disease . . . due to the corruption of the atmosphere', and we know that an eruption of this size disseminates not only a very heavy ash-layer, but also poisonous gases.[37] The eruption of Thera is now firmly dated to about 1500 by archaeologists and seismologists; it is worth noting that the chronographer Eusebius places Deucalion's flood in 1519.[38] Seven generations represent a period of about 200-250 years, depending on the length assumed for a generation. If we take 1500 as our median point, and treat the eruption of Thera as the main cause for the break in mythographic tradition, then we can, without trouble, date Xanthos the Pelasgian somewhere between 1700 and 1650 in the antediluvian Middle Bronze Age, and Macareus (or Macar) the Achaean *c.* 1450-1400. This latter date coincides with an Achaean-Mycenaean takeover at Cnossos in Crete, and may indicate a period of general mainland expansion. So far, then, archaeology and tradition agree very well.[39]

At the outbreak of the Trojan War (*c.* 1270-60[40]) Lesbos, like Hellespontine Phrygia and the Troad, was allied with Priam's Troy. Lesbos was still known as 'the seat of Macar', but the Lesbians who fought on the Trojan side served under Pylaios, a Pelasgian from Larissa.[41] All we really know about the Pelasgians is that their name was a handy generic mythographer's label for an early, non-Greek-speaking people in Greece or western Asia Minor.[42] Had there been yet another change of population? At this stage it seems unlikely. What in fact we see here, I believe, is the incipient division of the island into those independent, fiercely competitive city-states that ruled it throughout the archaic and classical periods. Macar is the last ruler who is ever described, specifically, as 'king of Lesbos',[43] establishing a common law for all. From now on we are concerned with Mytilene, Methymna, Antissa, Pyrrha, Eresos, and, briefly, Arisbe, rather than with Lesbos as a whole. The myth that represents these towns as being named after Macareus' daughters[44] may well reflect a period of further settlement, intermarriage, and division. The 'Lesbos' (or 'Lepétymnos'), a Pelasgian from Thessaly, who married 'Methymna',[45] was at least powerful enough to name the island after himself: no accident that throughout history Methymna was Mytilene's chief rival.

The founding of Mytilene[46], which rose to preeminence at the expense of the older nearby site of Thermi, was accomplished, according to one tradition, by the Amazons. Now the Amazons have strong Hittite associations, and the city's very un-Greek name recalls that of the Hittite king Mutallu or Muwatallish (1320-1294).[47] Of all the leading cities on Lesbos only Pyrrha has a clearly Hellenic name, and it is tempting to identify it as Macareus' original foundation. The Homeric Hymn to Delian Apollo [48] describes the 'seat of Macar' as *Aeolian*, an interesting claim, since this not only (on linguistic grounds) locates Macareus' origin in Thessaly, but links him with the subsequent great Aeolian migration from Greece that established Lesbos, for ever, as wholly Hellenic. In addition to Pelasgians and Achaeans (i.e. mainland Mycenaeans) it is possible that Lesbos also had a stratum of Minoan immigrants from Crete. This would go a long way towards explaining the remarkable culture that we find flourishing on the island in the time of Sappho and Alcaeus, with its striking emphasis on the arts and, above all, on feminine values. Could these have been brought from Cnossos, and preserved in the enclave society of Lesbos? It is by no means impossible. Literary tradition, confirmed now by archaeology,[49] suggests intense Minoan expansion, not only throughout the islands of the Aegean, but also up the coast of Asia Minor, indeed as far afield as Athens and Megara. If Minos' grandson could reign as lord of Chios, some infiltration of neighbouring Lesbos cannot be ruled out. Further, the collapse of the great palace civilization of Crete *c.* 1380 must, like the comparable fall of the Mycenaean kingdoms in the twelfth century, have produced a major diaspora of well-connected refugees. The natural route for them to follow was the island bridge from east Crete to south-west Caria, and then northward. It was, I would suggest, their culture that provided the key element in crystallising the society of archaic Lesbos. Sappho may have been, as Strabo claims,[50] a 'marvellous phenomenon'; but assuredly she – not to mention Atthis, Anactoria, Gongyla, Telesippa, and the rest of her circle – did not happen in a void.

During the early years of the Trojan War Achilles is said to have led a highly successful series of raids against Troy's allies and strategic outposts.[51]

He overran not only the offshore islands of Tenedos and Lesbos – the latter crucial as a supply base[52] – but also a whole string of cities down the Anatolian coast: Antandros and Adramyttion, where he rustled the cattle of Aeneas from the Ida range; Cyme and Phocaea, Smyrna, Clazomenae and Colophon, even Miletus. Nothing could better demonstrate the symbiotic relationship of Ionia and the Troad with the eastern Aegean islands. Achilles is particularly associated with the conquest of Lesbos[53] – where he acquired as booty a number of beautiful Lesbian women – and, on Lesbos, with the stronghold of Methymna, which he found exceptionally difficult to capture.[54] Why was this? Homer describes the island as *eüktiménē*, 'well built' or 'well-fortified'[55], and the remains of Cyclopean masonry at various key coastal sites – Mytilene, Pyrrha, Makarà, Antissa – confirm this. It is also known at Methymna. Yet the epithet associated with Methymna by Parthenius, *hypsipylos*, 'high-gated', is inappropriate for the early low-lying site.[56] We need to look elsewhere, a little further inland, nearer to the protective flank of the Lepétymnos massif. Here, well off the modern beaten track, but with a commanding view out over the Methymnaean plain and the sea beyond it, lie the remains of what looks remarkably like a hitherto unremarked Cyclopean complex. From a strongly defended advance site on a rise in the plain, walls, and an ancient road, can be traced up into the hills almost as far as the modern village of Vaphiò. There was little that escaped Robert Koldewey's sharp eye, and he makes no comment on this material. Perhaps he never saw it. In any case, until it has had a full archaeological survey judgment must be held in abeyance. But I would like to make the tentative suggestion that this may have been the high-gated fortress that gave Achilles so much trouble.

Winifred Lamb long ago suggested[57] that the great conflagration which destroyed Thermi for ever, about 1200, was also the work of Achilles. But if Blegen's dating for Troy holds good, and I think it does, then Achilles overran Lesbos at least half a century earlier. I would prefer to associate the burning of Thermi with the *second* capture of Troy, by European invaders from Thrace and (?) Hungary, makers of what is known as Knobbed Ware (*Buckelkeramik*), who crossed the straits into Asia Minor just about 1200. They formed part of a vast wave of attackers from the north and east, a movement which brought Dorians into the Peloponnese (led by the 'returning Heracleidae' familiar from myth[58]), witnessed the advance of the marauding Sea Peoples to the very gates of Egypt, and, most interestingly for us, enabled the Thracians and 'Phrygians' who had swarmed in from Europe virtually to destroy the Hittite empire in Anatolia. (It has recently been argued, with some plausibility, that the Troy which the Greeks sacked was not VIIa but VI, hitherto believed to have fallen prey to a vast earthquake, and in itself a far more plausible target, with its wealth of gold and its great batter walls. Since the date of its destruction would be shifted, according to this thesis, from c.1300 to a point nearer 1270/60, my basic conclusions would not be affected.)[59]

The burning of Thermi *c.* 1200 fits precisely into this pattern of events, and the subsequent Aeolian migration from central Greece to the island must be seen in the context of an old world in collapse: not only the Hittites, but also the great Mycenaean baronies, first Pylos, finally Mycenae itself, fell to invaders.[60] The eastward migrations which followed were led, for the most part, by aristocratic Mycenaean refugees: that to Lesbos and the Aeolid is firmly associated with Orestes and his descendants, Penthilos and Gras, who established the dynasty of the Penthilids. Our most reliable chronological scheme from antiquity[61] places this Aeolian migration in 1140, probably a median point; we know that it was a slow and difficult process, which met with strong opposition.[62] However, all the evidence suggests that by 1130-20 the Aeolian settlements were well-established,[63] and the Pelasgian element driven out.[64] The migration was also described as Boeotian,[65] and this agrees well with the Boeotian and Thessalian affinities of the Aeolic dialect in which, later, Sappho and Alcaeus were to write.[66] The literary tradition, as we have seen, regularly ascribes Thessalian origins to settlers on Lesbos.

I HAVE SPENT TIME on this early, formative period in part because scholars claim, pessimistically as I believe, that it is impossible to reconstruct.[67] Yet to understand it is crucial, since it is followed by a gap of almost five centuries. From the time of the Aeolian migrations until that of Sappho and Pittacus and their contemporaries – a period equivalent to that separating Chaucer from our own world today – we know virtually nothing about Lesbos. Apart from two entirely unremarkable apsidal buildings, possible shrines, excavated at Antissa, the earlier of which may date back to the ninth century,[68] the Greek Dark Ages on Lesbos remain impenetrable. Yet when light dawns again it becomes clear that remarkable things have been going on during the night. A sophisticated society is flourishing: aristocratic, highly politicised yet intensely individualistic, with a brilliant poetic and musical tradition predicated on pleasure and the passions, the latter including sex as well as *stasis*. The cities are now fully, and vigorously, independent.

Mytilene and Methymna in particular, at least from the eighth century, were very busy conquering and colonising numerous valuable mainland sites in the Troad and round the Gulf of Adramyttion, notably Sigeion, Antandros, and, later, the great stronghold of Assos. These possessions were known in antiquity as 'the Mytilenaean shore' and 'the coastal cities' (*aktaiai poleis*).[69] Cyme had already been founded independently by collateral descendants of Agamemnon, and we hear of conflict between this group and settlers from Lesbos.[70] Sigeion was said to have been built by Archaeanax of Mytilene – a splendidly aristocratic name: it means 'ancient king' – with stones taken from the ruins of Troy. Methymna, which founded Assos, also absorbed, at some point in the seventh century, the hitherto independent *polis* of Arisbe.[71] In

Mytilene, the royal house of the Penthilids, following the usual Dark Age pattern, was modified into an aristocratic oligarchy. This did not curb the family's arrogance. They went about clubbing their opponents in the streets; one citizen, Smerdis (an Anatolian name, like so many on Lesbos) they beat up in his wife's presence. A successful coup followed, and the Penthilids were eliminated as a ruling clan, though they continued in politics. Smerdis killed a Penthilos (who may have been Pittacus' father-in-law) with his own hands.[72] The pattern of internal politics on Lesbos – violent feuding between cities, and, in cities, between aristocratic-oligarchic and democratic, or, earlier, 'tyrannical' (i.e. anti-oligarchic) factions – was established early, and proved to be perennial.

The only symbol of unity was, as so often, religious rather than political. This was the common shrine of the Lesbians, already established by Alcaeus' day,[73] and dedicated jointly to Zeus, Hera, and Dionysus (the latter, appropriately enough, as 'eater of raw flesh'). This shrine or precinct was almost certainly, with its lush grove and perennial spring, located at Mesa, in the central Kalloni plain, where there is a still-surviving fourth-century temple.[74] Mesa is roughly equidistant from Methymna, Mytilene, and Eresos, the three main cities. Here, chafing in exile, and impatient for the day of revolution (or in his case counter-revolution) Alcaeus wrote, shortly before 600:[75]

> But still I can come to the blessed gods' precinct
> setting foot on the black soil . . .
> where the girls of Lesbos in their trailing robes
> parade to be judged for beauty, and all round
> echoes the holy chant of women every year.

There is an odd blend of violence and innocence, politics and lyricism, about archaic Lesbian history, such as we do not encounter again until another great creative period, that of Elizabethan England. An annual religious beauty competition held in the middle of civil *stasis* is absolutely characteristic. There are also the idiosyncratic touches bred of isolation. Consider the extraordinary Aeolic capitals still *in situ* at Klopedi, from a large late archaic temple, probably that of Apollo Napaios. They are neither Ionic nor Doric, neither plant-forms nor ram's horns, but, as Vincent Scully says,[76] 'wholly themselves – forces, potencies, and beings: eyed, muscular, octopus-armed' – and different from any other capital known to us. The same is true of the unique Aeolic style in wall-building, where polygonal stones were cut and fitted together by using a flexible lead strip, 'with which they made templates of the sides of each block when it had been set, so as to mark on the adjoining blocks the lines on which they should be cut to fit properly'.[77] The technique was observed (along with much else) by Aristotle, during his stay on Lesbos between 345 and 343.[78] A splendid example of Aeolic work, known, with good reason, as *Ho Kalóchtistos*, 'the well-built', is preserved at Apothikai, close to the mouth of the Gulf of Kalloni.[79] It seems to have been the retaining wall for a defensive outpost.

The uniqueness of Lesbos does not lie in its political history, which follows, all too closely, the pattern of internal *stasis* and external warfare common to every Greek state. In the late seventh century Mytilene was fighting Athens to regain control of Sigeion, which Athens had conquered: during this campaign Pittacus, later canonised as one of the Seven Sages, is said to have defeated the Athenian commander, Phrynon, in single combat by trussing him up in a fishing net. The quarrel over Sigeion sputtered on for decades.[80] The rivalry between Mytilene and Methymna usually meant that when the first joined an alliance the second did not, and vice versa. This is true of the most famous episode involving the island during the classical period. In 428, three years after the outbreak of the Peloponnesian War, Lesbos – a powerful naval ally of Athens for half a century – revolted, and made overtures to Athens' enemy Sparta. The revolt was put down, and the Athenian assembly voted to inflict on Lesbos the punishment known as *andrapodismós* – execution of all adult males, every woman and child to be sold into slavery. A state trireme set out for Mytilene bearing this grim warrant. We all know how the Athenians had second thoughts, called a fresh debate (used by Thucydides to enshrine rival notions of *Machtpolitik*), and rescinded the original order; how a second trireme set out in pursuit of the first, its rowers offered special bonuses, sleeping and eating on the rowing benches; how by a supreme effort – the modern diesel ferryboat takes fourteen hours to do the same trip – they got there just in time to stop the execution,[81] even though 1000 leading citizens were put to death anyway to be on the safe side. What we tend to forget is that the original revolt was an attempt by oligarchic Mytilene, very much in the old Penthilid spirit, to unite the whole island under its now authoritarian leadership,[82] and that only democratic Methymna, out of step as usual, refused to fall in with such a plan. This, of course, did not stop Methymna later (412) from going over to Sparta after the failure of Athens' Sicilian Expedition.[83]

Examples of this sort could be multiplied. In 389/8 Thrasybulus of Athens found all the Lesbian cities except Mytilene supporting Sparta.[84] By 378 Athens was making a treaty with Methymna.[85] Oligarchs and democrats succeeded one another on the island with bewildering rapidity. Tyrants who joined the right side at the right time were honoured; others, not. During Alexander's early campaigns this process assumed almost farcical proportions: in 336 the Macedonian generals Attalos and Parmenio banished all the tyrants and brought Lesbos into the Hellenic League; in 335 the pro-Persian mercenary commander Memnon of Rhodes seized Lesbos and brought all the tyrants back again; in 334 the island was recaptured for Alexander and the tyrants were out once more; in 333 the Persians returned, and a new set of tyrants – the previous lot by now being mostly dead – was duly installed. In 332

Alexander's supporters finally established themselves, brought back the exiles, and stabilised the regime. It had been a *mouvementé* but all too typical period.[86] In essence, nothing had changed since the revolutions and counter-revolutions, the violent in-fighting between Pittacus, Melanchros, Myrsilos and the rest in the lifetime of Sappho and Alcaeus.[87]

Lesbos preserved a precarious independence from Persians, Macedonians, and Romans until the first century BC. But in 88 the island not only joined the anti-Roman revolt of Mithridates, but made the even worse mistake of handing over a sick Roman legate to him for execution.[88] Despite a desperate defence, Mytilene fell to the Roman general Minucius Thermus in 80/79, an engagement during which the young Julius Caesar was decorated for valour.[89] Almost twenty years later, in 62, Caesar's rival Pompey came to Mytilene, and gave the city back its freedom. The reason he did so is interesting. It was, says Plutarch, for the sake of Theophanes, a local scholar and historian who had chronicled his campaigns. Pompey also watched the 'traditional contest of poets' (who took his exploits as their theme), bestowed Roman citizenship on Theophanes, and was so taken with the theatre of Mytilene that he later copied it in Rome, though, characteristically, on a far grander scale.[90] We see here a late but typical instance of the way in which on Lesbos a flourishing artistic tradition tended to entwine itself inextricably with politics. The early verse-propaganda (*stasiotikà, stasis*-poems) of Alcaeus set a fashion; and it is worth remembering that even Sappho, whose surviving poetry contains more passion than politics, was nevertheless involved enough to be twice exiled from Mytilene, once (*c.* 600) as far afield as Sicily.[91]

Beginning with Sappho's predecessor Terpander of Antissa, who gave Greece the Phrygian musical scale and the seven-stringed lyre,[92] Lesbos produced a quite extraordinary series of poets, musicians, philosophers and scholars: 'preeminent as the Lesbian singer over foreigners', Sappho wrote,[93] with fierce, and justified, insular pride. The passions that raged against that hauntingly beautiful landscape found their unique flashpoint in art – though, paradoxically, not in the visual arts: Lesbos produced only one indifferent sculptor, and (till Theophilos in this century) no serious painters at all. At the same time one rich house-owner in the third century AD was so enamoured of poetry in general, and Menander in particular, that he commissioned mosaics – not, alas, very good ones – portraying, *inter alia*, Orpheus charming the animals with his music, Thalia the Muse of Comedy, and various scenes from Menander's plays, together with a portrait of the Master himself.[94] It was a small world, yet all-absorbing, all-sufficient. The roll-call includes Arion, famous for his rescue from pirates by an obliging dolphin; Theophrastus, the philosopher and botanist, Aristotle's successor at the Lyceum; Hellanicus the historian; Longus the novelist, author of *Daphnis and Chloe*; and countless minor epic and lyric poets, epigrammatists, iambographers, rhetoricians. The list is rounded off with an art-historian, a champion chessplayer, and a famous illusionist. In our own day both the novelist Stratis Myrivilis and the Nobel prizewinner Odysseus Elytis are from Lesbos. The island remains a creative crucible.

Its ties to the mainland, despite political vicissitudes, have always been close, even though few of those early possessions in the Troad and round the Gulf of Adramyttion remained for long under Mytilene's control. Sappho's brother Charaxos traded Lesbian wine as far afield as Naucratis in Egypt[95]; and a whole network of regular shipping lines linked Lesbos with the cities of Asia Minor. The hot springs, too, brought visitors: a Roman, Claudius Lucianus, from distant Alabanda in Caria, dedicated a fine hunting bitch to Artemis Thermia in gratitude for his cure.[96] A glimpse of the regular to-and-fro traffic is given us in, of all places, the Acts[97] of the Apostles. We find St Paul shuttling between the Troad and Thrace, coasting along from city to city in Macedonia, dropping in at Athens and Corinth, crossing the Aegean to the flourishing city of Ephesus, with its famous cult of Artemis ('Great is Diana of the Ephesians'), sailing along the eastern Mediterranean to Caesarea and Antioch, returning to Ephesus (where he provoked a near-riot in the theatre[98]), and so back to Macedonia and the Troad. From Methymna's old foundation of Assos he was brought across to Mytilene. Tradition claims that he was almost wrecked by one of those frequent storms that rage through the eastern channel.[99] There is also a legend that the faithful begged him to rid the island of a fearful snake, which, interestingly, was said to haunt the great pagan temple at Mesa, and that he duly killed it by the force of prayer.[100] From Mytilene he sailed south, as coastal freighters still do, to Chios, Samos, Priene, and the once-powerful Ionian city of Miletus. Inland lay Pergamon; to the south, the strongholds of Caria – Alinda, Labraunda, Euromos, Heracleia-by-Latmos, Halicarnassos. All formed a natural common nexus for Aegean travellers: the only barriers, then as now, were those of politics and war, and in AD 58, under Rome's imperial aegis, travel was easy.

YET WE MUST END, as we began, with Lesbos itself, the microcosm as opposed to the wider horizon. The richness, variety, peace, and stunning loveliness of the island were a constant attraction throughout antiquity. It is sometimes claimed that the Greeks and Romans had no interest in landscape. This is simply not true. Cicero enthused about Mytilene's natural beauty and setting.[101] The island attracted residents from abroad as early as the fourth century BC,[102] drawn, as now, by the climate, the scenery, the thermal springs, the vintage wines, the cheap cost of living. Aristotle spent much time studying the habits of the marine life – starfish, sea-urchins, gobies, above all oysters – in the Gulf of Kalloni.[103] Longus, who set his pastoral romance *Daphnis and Chloe* on the island, rhapsodised[104] over its thick woodlands of pine and cypress, plane and laurel, its orchards of pears, figs, pomegranates, apples, its immense variety of spring flowers – roses, hyacinths, lilies, violets, daffodils and many others: its vines, olives and plentiful springs, its never-failing rivers, swarming with fish, its rich farmland and pastures, its abundant game (hares in particular).

No visitor to the area round Pyrrha, which he is chiefly describing,[105] can fail to be struck by his accuracy. Nothing has really changed. Since *Daphnis and Chloe* is a work of fiction, modern criticism has paid little attention to the numerous topographical details concerning Lesbos which Longus scatters through his work. Yet just as Longus' women reveal a striking blend of fictional romance and social realism,[106] so the background to his narrative, however much adorned with items of baroque fancy, nevertheless remains solidly based on the geography and ecology of Lesbos itself. The cave of the Nymphs, with its grotto, its spring, and its clutter of statues, may derive from the pastoral property-closet;[107] but Longus' description of Mytilene agrees with those given by Strabo and Pausanias,[108] and many other details – the trailing vines, the wine, the flourishing orchards, the prevalence of hares for hunting[109] – suggest familiarity with the terrain. The description in the proem of the grove of the Nymphs, thick with flowers and trees and watered by a single spring, at once calls to mind the site of the great temple at Mesa, in the Kalloni plain.[110] Most striking of all, since often used as evidence for Longus' *ignorance* of Lesbos, is his vivid description of a heavy snowfall, much at odds with later travellers' accounts of the climate's perennial mildness.[111] But in the winter of 1964, when I was living on the island, snow lay three feet deep in the chestnut forest above Aghiassos, while Methymna (Molyvos) was icebound, with frozen taps and sub-zero temperatures, for ten days, so that all the eucalyptus trees outside the schoolhouse died. The worst winter in living memory was that of 1953/54: the mountains are frequently snowbound. Longus, like Alcaeus, who also describes such conditions,[112] knew what he was talking about.

A very similar picture is presented in the poems of Sappho and Alcaeus, composed about eight centuries earlier. Alcaeus talks of the 'bloom of soft autumn' (on Lesbos October is the loveliest of all months), claims – no exaggeration – to have 'heard the flowery spring coming', notes the chirring of summer cicadas, the long-winged widgeon flying overhead, harlequin necks outstretched.[113] Sappho heard 'the spring's messenger, the sweet-voiced nightingale', that still sings in April from the Aghiassos forest: loved apples and roses, knew that the moon, too, was 'rosy-fingered' on Lesbos after sunset, revelled in the riot of spring flowers, the embroidering of the many-garlanded earth.[114] Now, as then, the island blossoms with cyclamen, anemone, iris, poppy. Sappho writes of an orchard where 'cool water babbles through apple-branches, and the whole place is shadowed by roses, and from the shimmering leaves the sleep of enchantment comes down: therein too a meadow, where horses graze, blossoms with spring flowers, and the winds blow gently'. These are the changeless things: isolation still works its magic.

There are some sixty unique species of flower on Lesbos,[115] and some very rare animals, including the giant salamander and the star shrew.

There are also some odd and very ancient cult survivals, often imperfectly assimilated by the Greek Orthodox Church from clearly pre-Christian sources. In the north especially, among the wild mountains of the Lepétymnos range, such ceremonies are strong and persistent. At the Church of the Archangels in Mandamádhos there is a miracle-working black-faced icon of St Michael (Aghios Taxiarchos). Local cabdrivers, with that passion for cockeyed etymologies characteristic of Greeks from antiquity to the present day, always hang his image above their steering wheel: what else *could* Aghios Taxiarchos be but the patron saint of cabdrivers? This black-faced St Michael (whom I suspect of having undergone a sex change, from Aphrodite or Demeter, with the advent of Christianity) has his shrine heaped with fresh-cut flowers in springtime, and in some mysterious fashion has absorbed the odours of spring into his icon. Bulls, too, are sacrificed and eaten communally in his honour soon after Easter.

But the most remarkable festival of this sort, known throughout the island simply as *O Tavros* ('The Bull'), takes place a little further south, on the spur of the Lepétymnos range known as Saitarion. It blends bull sacrifice with horse racing, and is therefore almost certainly descended from an old Poseidon festival. On the evening of the second Sunday after Easter, horsemen from all the villages in the central part of the island gather at the remote hilltop shrine of St Charálambos to have their mounts blessed by the priest. Later, as the sun sets behind the mountains, a bull and a heifer – garlanded, often with gilded horns, looking exactly like a sacrifice from the Parthenon frieze or the Roman Ara Pacis – are slaughtered for the festival. The onlookers, including the horsemen, dip their fingers in the blood, cross themselves with it on the forehead. The bull's hide goes to the priest, and the flesh is cooked with wheat in great cauldrons near the chapel, to be eaten next day by all comers at the *panegýri*, the festival held in the village of Aghia Paraskeví, down in the plain. By then another celebration has supervened: that of the Aghia Paraskeví horse races, in which both sexes compete (most unusually for Greece) on equal terms. (The first year I witnessed these races, a woman in fact won.) The women of Lesbos are still famed, as in Sappho's day, not only for their beauty but also for their independence; and the horses they ride still roam in wild herds through the hills above the central salt flats.

This heritage survived everything: the long Byzantine centuries: those medieval Genoese adventurers the Gattelusi, who built new and better castles at Mytilene and Methymna; the dilatory Turkish pashas of the Ottoman empire, who ruled the island from 1462 until as late as 1912. To a quite extraordinary degree – as I hope to have demonstrated – it remains intact to this day, complete with the old snarling, revolutionary, radical streak exemplified (though from the other end of the political spectrum) by

Alcaeus. Not for nothing was Lesbos known, after 1944, as 'to kókkino nesí' the Red island. But the ideology, as always, is idiosyncratic. Here, as an appropriate summing-up, is a marvellous graffito observed in Mytilene in the summer of 1983. It reads, slightly ungrammatically, 'kato ta synthemata, zeto ta poiemata' – 'down with slogans and long live poetry'. The spirit of Sappho on Lesbos is, clearly, still alive and well, despite the encroachments of mass-communications and nuclear-based power-politics. Long, against all the odds, may it so continue.

IV

ON THE THANATOS
TRAIL

DEATH, THE ONE IMMUTABLE ELEMENT in every life, is at the same time the one transition that no one can claim as a conscious experience. We do not live through it – a paradox all ages have been disinclined to accept – and putative exceptions to the rule, from Lazarus to mediums' contacts or Ouija-board monologuists, all require a suspension (whether miraculous or not) of the normal laws of nature. Anxiety about death dictates many of our fundamental beliefs and behaviour patterns, and all death imagery, in any age, is manifestly borrowed from the world men inhabit, since it is the only one they know. The disposal of corpses, furthermore, is a universal problem with strictly limited solutions. An archaic Greek and a modern urban European or American share a wide range of assumptions about death, funerals, burial, and the hereafter: where they differ sharply is in the spiritual luggage they carry with them. To study any group's attitudes to death becomes, in a very real sense, a refraction of their ideas about life, their social conventions and priorities, their more persistent sustaining myths. If Freud stressed, in his essay 'Das Unheimliche' (1919), the perennial changelessness of human relations to death, recent thanatology has rather concentrated on the rich cultural diversity which they reveal.

In her remarkable Sather Lectures, *Aspects of Death in Early Greek Art and Poetry* (published in 1979), Professor Emily Vermeule shows an acute sensibility both to the universal and to the unique features of archaic Greek dealings with death, as manifested variously in literature, vase paintings, myth, and the heterogeneous clutter of artifacts dug up from graves (decreasing, more often than not, in direct proportion to the growing wealth and materialism of the group involved). She ranges in time from the Mycenaean Bronze Age to the mid-fifth century BC, a period which she sees (justifiably, I think) as maintaining a more or less consistent system of values and beliefs, though the interpretation of the evidence – literary no less than archaeological

63

– presents endless problems. How far do the Homeric poems, to take an obvious example, reflect actual ritual? Homer's language is a literary amalgam: could the funerary practices he describes be similarly synthetic, culled from a variety of eras and areas? Professor Vermeule reminds me at times of Mrs Moore in *A Passage to India*, who enjoyed mystery but disliked muddle; there is plenty of both in the testimony she accumulates, and if the mystery stimulates her imaginative insight, the muddle too often drives her tidy archaeological mind to distraction. For her the great watershed of change comes about 450 BC, with the development of Protagorean classicism, and this is historically persuasive. The propositions spread by the Sophists – scientific agnostics if not crypto-atheists almost to a man – modified the archaic world-view as nothing had ever done before.

Vermeule's approach is peripatetic rather than chronological: each of her six chapters takes a central theme or peg – the relation of soul (*psyche*) to body, the implications of burial customs, death in battle, the nature of immortality, Eros and Thanatos, the poetic magic inherent in sea monsters – and on this thread strings a brilliant digressive essay, full of asides and illustrations, somewhat in the manner of Sir Thomas Browne, and often with the same poetic concision, paradoxical insights, and glinting elegance of phrase. This makes her work a delight to read, but at the same time puts a severe strain on any reader who prefers his arguments to start at the beginning and then proceed in an orderly manner to their conclusion. Such old-fashioned historicists (for whom I have more than a sneaking sympathy) should probably prepare themselves for entry into Vermeule's labyrinth by first studying Robert Garland's *The Greek Way of Death* (1985), a brisk, well-documented trot through cemetery and underworld which completely eschews Vermeule's hauntingly evocative digressions (Garland refers at one point to her 'engaging belles-lettres style', a damning piece of academic shorthand) and analyses, in unnuanced prose, 'a system of categorisation . . . designed to keep the world of the living rigidly apart from that of the dead' (p. 121). Even so, during the fifth century BC, these psychological barriers begin to come down: grave-reliefs show libation-pourers on the same scale as the departed, the dead and the living actually shaking hands. In Athens, where our evidence is best, democratisation is having its effect. Public funerals, civic tombs, and popular festivals of the dead are offset by a cavalier indifference to old aristocratic grave monuments from the Archaic period, unceremoniously used to fill Themistocles' defence wall in an emergency.

Since Professor Vermeule's earlier work, that brilliant synthesis *Greece in the Bronze Age* (1964), was as tightly argued and organised as a legal brief, her discursive-symbolic approach here is clearly a matter of policy rather than ineptness. The counterpoint of text and illustration, the cumulative pointillist use of images to circle a central concept or object – these suggest poetic rather than scholarly techniques. To understand death, she implies, requires creative insight, plus an analysis which, while using the tools of philological and archaeological expertise, abandons the constricting tramlines of conventional academic judgment. Garland describes laying-out and funeral rites in detail, reminds us that ancient Greeks had no real sense of sin and were thus spared the vulgarity of death-bed conversions, observes that corpses (despite pollution, *miasma*) inspired little of the wormy horror that so engrosses some Christian theologians, stresses the weakness and ineffectuality of the dead, their lack of *menos* (strength) as well as blood, their pathetic efforts, expressed in countless epitaphs, to catch the attention of living by-passers. But Vermeule opens up the whole emotional matrix of death-related beliefs and taboos, sidesteps our innate reluctance, involves us willy-nilly in the psychologically potent material that she uncovers.

Such a programme calls for rare skills: but then Professor Vermeule is altogether a rare scholar, a poet herself, an exotic cemetery-fancier whose pages are enlivened by snapshots of *outré* tombstones, the author of a Homeric-style paean to the Red Sox in the *Boston Globe*, and, on this showing, a splendidly omnivorous reader, not only of ancient Greek poets and their modern commentators but also of authors less often favoured by classicists: Ernest Bramah (the creator of Kai Lung and Max Carrados), Jane Goodall on carnivorous chimpanzees, even E. Howard Hunt. Of her earlier *magnum opus* on the Bronze Age it was remarked that such a work normally formed the climax to a scholar's career before retirement: Emily Vermeule published it in her thirties, filling her spare time (as is clear from *Aspects of Death*) with *New Yorker* cartoons, Ann Landers' advice column, and Snoopy, not to mention Macaulay's essays, Tennyson's *Maud*, *Ruddigore*, Woody Allen, *Measure for Measure*. Sarah Orne Jewett's 'The Gloucester Mother', and all the other variegated literary bric-à-brac one might expect to find in the mental attic of a well-brought-up and incurably bookish American East Coast intellectual. (I'm prepared to bet, on no evidence whatsoever, that she knows *Winnie-the-Pooh* almost by heart.) She also turns out to be on familiar terms with the contents of Boston Irish coffins and the souls of California seals. She has run down a doctor in Düsseldorf who put expiring patients on the scales and proved to his own satisfaction that the soul weighs 21 grams precisely. It has been shown with finality, she says, straight-faced, that the Sirens were not oysters. In short, the lady's centre is not quite in the middle, which strikes me as a decided advantage when it comes to writing a book of this sort.

So is her refreshing lack of dogmatism about a topic which is, at best, both subjective and emotionally fraught, not to say elusive. 'After four years of reading,' she admits, disarmingly, 'I still do not know what the Greeks thought about death, or what Americans think either, or what I think myself.' Seldom can any assertion of ignorance have been so consistently enlightening, so illustrative of the old dictum that what matters is not so much finding the answers as asking the right questions. Her quarry does not really suit the normal methods of academic pursuit. Researchers on death, like translators (see below, p. 268), have invariably reflected, as Sally Humphreys recently pointed out [*JHS* 100 (1980) 97], 'the practices, practical concerns and fantasies of the period in which they were written'. It would be idle to hope that the Greeks themselves were immune from this kind of amiable self-delusion, much less that over the space of half a dozen centuries and the whole Aegean basin they should show any tidy consistency of belief or practice. One of Professor Vermeule's most acute insights is the awareness that 'poets, critics, historians, archaeologists, artists spend their working lives as necromancers, raising the dead in order to enter into their imagination and experience', and her rarest achievement in these Sather Lectures is the ability to move at ease between the modes of vision which the five categories listed represent.

This, I think, is why she shows herself so sensible on those endless apparent inconsistencies and self-contradictions about death to which the early Greeks were no more immune than any other group. They are, as she says, necessary ambiguities, in an area where both reason and experience are at a discount: 'It is the artist who reintegrates the elements of the dead when he has need to.' Pedants who worry about dead Tityos having a liver for the vulture to nibble at (or about the remarkable regenerative powers displayed by that of Prometheus in similar circumstances) will get cold comfort from this book. One cannot somehow imagine Professor Vermeule coming out with Dr Garland's blunt assertion 'There is no evidence that the prospect of dying filled the Greeks with much apprehension'. But then what *can* one say about the Greek afterlife? Less actively punitive, it is true, than Puritan hellfire or the sadistic intricacies of Dante's Inferno, but still a depressing if ill-topographised region, peopled with insubstantial wraiths whose one regret is that they are not still quick with blood and *menos*, alive, on earth. But then what about all those dismal archaic poets who on the face of it embraced the modern life-as-a-vale-of-tears philosophy, who argued (as Louis MacNeice summed it up) that 'never to have been born was best, call no man happy this side death'? *Do I contradict myself? Very well, I contradict myself.* Ancient Greeks did not conduct their lives, let alone envisage their deaths, for the benefit of tidy-minded latter-day professors.

The early Greeks, as Vermeule says, took death extremely seriously: but their efforts, nevertheless, were for the most part aimed at circumventing it. Nor was it thought of as final. Thanatos seems to have been strictly a negative concept. The Greeks 'had no word for irreversible death: one does not die, one darkens'. What darkened could, with luck and intelligence (*nous*, that much prized and much abused Greek trait), be relit. Thus immortality tended to wear human, and at times disconcertingly physical, lineaments. However much lip-service might be paid by Homeric hero or Hesiodic peasant, by pre-Socratic thinker or black-figure vase-painter, to the separation of immortal spirit and perishable corpse, the two in practice preserved an obstinate, wholly understandable alliance. This is something that goes far beyond the liminality or marginal between-state, after burial but before decomposition, which Dr Garland notes (pp. 38 ff.) as keeping the soul of the deceased in a temporary and taboo-ridden limbo: the relationship, as we shall see, was far more complex and symbiotic. Ghosts (*eidola*) were – and indeed remain – hard to visualise except in human form: and as Vermeule reminds us, 'the grave has always been the easiest place to try speaking with the dead', who from Homer's day to that of Aeschylus were viewed as quite horrendously active, and, if the situation called for it, could be endowed, not with substance perhaps, but at least with unequivocally anthropomorphic features.

What becomes abundantly clear from the evidence assembled in *Aspects of Death* is that the instinct for immortality, the denial of death, the striving for survival in essentially human form are traits that have been present ever since the dawn of mankind, long before the Greeks gave the concept their own idiosyncratic stamp. A corpse would be left beside the fire, given a tool, a weapon, a piece of meat. Its face or head would be clumsily daubed with the colours of life. Despite the *psyche* (always an ambivalent factor anyway), Greek emphasis was always on proper treatment of the physical cadaver and its formal separation from the still-living community: the elaborate ritual of mourning and burial – as much a comfort for the survivors as a service to the dead, and virtually unchanged, apart from minor Christian modifications, from the Bronze Age to the present day: as Dr Garland says, 'a three-act drama with precise regulations governing the most minute details of procedure'. First came the laying-out of the body (*prothesis*); then the procession to the place of burial (*ekphora*); lastly the disposal of the inhumed or cremated remains, followed by a ceremonial feast over which the deceased was held to preside in spirit. The women's ritual dirge, the libation to the dead, the formalised gestures of mourning – all formed part of an ageless procedure over which, with minor variations only, our literary and visual sources all concur.

The soul, by contrast, was never clearly visualised. This is all too understandable. Sometimes it seems to have been thought of as minuscule, at best bird-sized, a notion Homer had perforce to jettison when circumstances demanded it: as Professor Vermeule demurely concedes, it would be 'poetically awkward for Odysseus, when speaking with the *psychai* of his dead friends, to go down on all fours outside the mouth of Hades with a magnifying glass'. Its exit from the body, via mouth or wound, 'bewailing its fate', may denote the moment of Homeric death, but still remains puzzling, since it is only associated with the body when leaving it, and is certainly not synonymous with consciousness or the life-force (Garland p. 18). It is likened to a 'puff of smoke'. It is represented in art as a winged manikin, perching sadly on the head of the deceased. The truth of the matter is, as Vermeule so clearly sees, that 'the *psyche* cannot be truly separated from its body, because the Greeks are not really good with ghosts, nor are they able to describe the dead consistently in language other than that which they use for the living'. Paradox is all. Similarly with Hades, official home of Stygian gloom and darkness, which acquires mysterious and unexplained stage-lighting simply to serve Homer's dramatic needs.

Such problems abounded: the somatic, like cheerfulness, would keep breaking in. Where were the dead united? In Hades? In the grave? Both? Could they eat? Defecate? Have sex? One reason for Oedipus blinding himself was to avoid the shame of meeting his parents in Hades. Did that mean that the body's condition could affect that of the *psyche*? And what about the social etiquette of first and second wives or husbands running into one another in the hereafter, a surprisingly persistent worry? (Or perhaps not so surprising: the eschatological projections of daily life were strikingly crystallised for me by the anxious query, to a religious advice column, of an American lady who wanted to know whether she should be buried with her dentures, only to be reassured that in Heaven everyone would have a perfect set of teeth.) Again, rational exegesis is, clearly, not only inappropriate but irrelevant in such a context. Professor Vermeule stresses, rather, the emotional needs that generate poetic paradox of this sort, so that in scrutinising archaic Greek eschatology we wind up (as doubtless she intended that we should) also examining ourselves.

The topography of the early Greek underworld was as elusive and inconsistent as the true appearance of its denizens. No one, as Odysseus complained to Circe, ever went to Hades in a black ship, and a cartographer would have considerable trouble if required to map Persephone's domain or the route thither. (Christians had comparable problems in the Age of Reason: witness the ingenious Tobias Swinden's monograph, *An Enquiry into the Nature and Place of Hell*, first published in 1714. This must have found a ready market, since it appeared in a second edition, revised and augmented, in 1727.) Was it subterranean, or far in the West by the shores of Ocean? Below, rather than Beyond, in most versions, with access by way of woods, lakes, and, particularly, caves. Even within the *Odyssey* the topography varies. Circe directs Odysseus to a rock marking the confluence of three (? subterranean) rivers. Hermes leads the slaughtered suitors along 'dark, mouldy ways' to a white rock by the region of dreams. Aristophanes in *The Frogs* talks of a lake or swamp of dung, various unpleasant beasts and serpents, the mired floundering of wrongdoers, the bliss of Eleusinian initiates. Instructions buried with Orphic (or perhaps Pythagorean) adepts mention landmarks such as a white cypress and spring to the right of the house of Hades. Charon the ferryman enters the scene comparatively late, an import perhaps from Magna Graecia. Retributive punishment (as Aristophanes and other sources make clear) certainly existed, but lacked the vivid relish and intensity which early Christianity brought to its compensation-fantasies about the Roman ruling classes roasting in hell-fire for all eternity. Hades was drab, colourless, bloodless, in every sense non-vital.

Ex nihilo nihil fit: this blurred picture of mouldy paths, underground rivers, mephitic swamps, guard-dogs, ferrymen, dark windy plains, rocks, myrtle-groves, dank caverns and drooping poplars has to come from somewhere, and those with personal knowledge of the Greek landscape will probably jump at Professor Vermeule's tempting suggestion that literary descriptions of Hades bear an odd resemblance, monsters and all, to the subterranean caves and streams of Greece's limestone ranges, with their stalactites and exotic prehistoric fauna. The Dirou Caves in the Peloponnese – at least until they were floodlit for tourism – yawned dripping and grim at the visitor, a serrated and more than metaphysical gullet (*stomion*) to the nether regions. Could Cerberus have originated in dim memories of cave-hyenas, or that grossly female monster Lamia as a pigmy cave-hippo? Professor Vermeule tosses out the suggestion only to reject it, but the idea remains attractive. (On the other hand the Empusa, with one brass leg and the other of cow-dung, presents, in these terms, a somewhat more intractable problem.) In any case, we once again have an aspect of the afterlife, its terrain this time, rendered in familiar terms. In the midst of death, the Greek might have said, we are in life. The landmarks remain comfortingly familiar. That, of course, is true for all of us: what, if anything, made the Greek approach unique?

Perhaps its most characteristic feature (though one that often recurs elsewhere) was the thirst for posthumous fame, from Achilles' obsession with '*undying* renown' (*kleos aphthiton*) to Horace's literary monument, *aere perennius*, outlasting bronze, the basis for his proud claim *non omnis moriar*, 'not all of me will die', a phrase which, with its built-in ambiguity (which bit lives?) could serve as Professor Vermeule's epigraph. An early Greek was certainly more concerned with his *kleos* among future generations than with that 'intact survival of both body and mind', complete with food, sex and work, which drove the Egyptians, those obsessional industrialists of the hereafter (cf. below, pp. 83-4, 88-9), not only to mummify their corpses but to credit them, hopefully, in their future existence with the grossest of physical functions. 'I eat with my mouth,' one such is made to proclaim, 'I have motion in my behind.' *Caco, ergo sum.* Homer's dead do not eat, much less shit; rather, says Professor Vermeule, with characteristic wry amusement, 'they wander loose in an ill-defined countryside . . . and . . . discuss . . . the brilliance of their funerals . . . like patients in a hospital solarium telling each other about details of [their] operations . . . '. Or, as Dr Garland puts it, 'the principal activities of the Homeric dead appear to be gossip, sententious moralising, and self-indulgent regret'.

A later age, more concerned with rewards, punishments, and good intentions (the last-named being something wholly alien to archaic morality), seems to have believed that the afterlife for the virtuous would consist of one long drinking-party, interspersed with quiet sessions of draughts (miniature gaming-boards have been found in many graves): Socrates in Plato's *Republic* (2.363D) accuses the Orphics of claiming that the reward for the just in Hades is 'eternal inebriation'. The *carpe diem* principle normally involved sex as well as good food and drink, the eternal hedonistic trinity: were the dead, then, also thought of as fucking? By the Etruscans, undoubtedly: occasionally by the Greeks too, as one grave-relief from Cos graphically demonstrates. At the same time such unions do not seem to have produced issue, fertility in the hereafter being something of an oxymoron. Further, though intellectuals from Euripides to Plutarch and Juvenal derided the whole idea of Hades as a fairy-tale fit only for children, Lucian in the second century AD [*Luct.* 2, cited by Garland p.76] asserted that the common populace still took the myths of Homer, Hesiod, and the rest as gospel, in particular convinced 'that there is a deep place under the earth called Hades, and that it is large and commodious and dark and sunless'. A horrific papyrus fragment of about the same date [see Page, *Select Papyri III: Literary Papyri, Poetry* (1941) 416-421] not only confirms this, but shows that by now Roman imperialism had added some grisly touches to people's conception of the afterlife. The visitor to Hades (a husband or lover determined to hunt down and reprimand his profligate mistress even in the afterlife) picks his way, quaking with fear, to the Shores of Ugliness, where dogs are tearing at the entrails of corpses, beheaded or crucified, while others are impaled or hanging with their throats cut. The air is thick with the stench of spilt blood, and the Furies, wearing wreaths, are laughing in mockery at these modes of execution.

Such fantasies are a long way indeed from the Mycenaean and immediately post-Mycenaean Greeks who are Professor Vermeule's prime concern. Seagoing by necessity, disputatious by nature (whether with sword or, much later, syllogism) the early Greeks, she claims, evolved a mythology of death that stressed – as we might expect – the splendours and miseries of warfare, the cognate joys of hunting, the cruel sea's chill vicissitudes and ingurgitant monsters. Her acute, wide-ranging, and eruditely witty analysis of these phenomena is the most welcome contribution I have seen in years to a subject that has hitherto (for whatever murky reasons) remained largely the monopoly of dull or tendentious Germans, prosing on at inordinate length about *Totenkultus* and *Unsterblichkeitsglauben*. (One exception, as fresh and stimulating now as when it was first written, is Erwin Rohde's *Psyche* [4th ed. 1907: English translation 1920], to which both Vermeule and Garland owe, and enthusiastically acknowledge, a major debt.) Bronze Age heroes in particular ate meat, drank wine, split skulls and skewered livers with abandon, glorying in life like those circling lions to whose presence Gilgamesh awoke from a clouded dream of death. Hades for them was no more than a grey shadow-house, peopled by dim *eidola* rather short on *phrenes* (wits): the self, the man himself (*autos*) remained, however illogically, a physical manifestation. One thing most people remember about Achilles from Homer is his ghostly admission that he would rather be a day labourer in this world than a king in the next. Vermeule sums up this complex attitude with a Herakleitan paradox that forms one of her chapter titles: 'Immortals are mortal, mortals immortal.' Immortality as such the heroic mind found tedious, ill-defined, lacking (another paradox) in essential humanity. Polly Garter in *Under Milk*

Wood sums up the Greek attitude: 'Isn't life a terrible thing, thank God?'

Professor Vermeule sees this relish for the here-and-now, I think rightly, as 'part of the Greek legacy to the West, and almost a definition of humanism' (many ideological humanists would, to their own loss, disagree). As is the generation of leaves, mused Glaucus in the *Iliad*, so is that of mankind: the transience (as the Elizabethans knew so well) sharpens wit, heightens pleasure, casts a sundial's shadow. *Sunt lacrimae rerum*: brightness falls from the air, after the first death there is no other. It is the monument of words that survives, made all the more precious by the frailty of the wordmaker: *ephemeroi*, the Greeks called humans, 'creatures of a day'.

Thus it is with justice that violent rather than natural death dominates these lectures, not least when we reflect on the precarious social conditions of Homeric or archaic Greece, the endless hazards of battle and disease. In such a society, Vermeule emphasises, 'war is a habit, the natural way of life for an adult, a pastime and the only path to honour', and she goes on to remind us how much this attitude conditioned Greek literature: 'Is there another epic tradition so well informed about the human anatomy, or so eager to break it apart for our amusement and edification?' (Like all wars, this one had unexpected by-products, including medical experience that showed to good effect in the Hippocratic treatises on fractures and head wounds.) Battle is symbolically predicated on the archetypal patterns of hunting: lion and boar merge, respectively, into the triumphant and the defeated warrior. Patroclus, the lion in victory, becomes a boar as he dies. Metaphor confers status. Leonine predators thirst for blood, feed on raw flesh, a Dionysian banquet minus the palliating religious ecstasy.

Professor Vermeule links this aspect of battle with the uneasy memories of head-hunting and cannibalism that surface here and there in Homer. Such practices, she notes, are still reported today – stark fact, not fantasy – most recently from the combat areas of Vietnam and Cambodia. She even refers, breezily, to 'the kind of snack or pacifier heroes so longed for at Troy, an enemy liver to eat or a head to play with'. The influence of W.S. Gilbert is detectable here and inappropriate. This is battle-axe grinding, pursuant to the author's vision of the Happy Warrior, and strikes me as overdone. To accept war's inevitability, as Homer and the early lyric poets do, is not to treat it (something *Aspects of Death* strongly suggests) as unalloyed fun. Vermeule's prize example of a battle-glutton is, of all people, Odysseus, who in fact made vigorous attempts to dodge the draft by feigning insanity, and distinguished himself throughout a ten-year campaign by unheroic pragmatism. That gift of war from Zeus to which he alludes (*Iliad* 14.83 ff.), and which Vermeule takes at face value, in fact carries overtones of savage irony.

Both Hesiod and Archilochus similarly allude to a god's gifts – poverty and drowning respectively – in terms that leave no doubt whatsoever about the bleak emotions they arouse in the recipient. Even as early as the *Iliad* the old heroic battle ideal is beginning to come under fire: openly from Thersites, indirectly through Achilles' own introspective doubts. Archilochus, the seventh-century hard-case colonist, will fight because fight he must to survive: but he sees no shame, and much common sense, in throwing away his shield, taking to his heels, and living to fight another day. Hesiod is about as antiwar as an archaic poet could get, which does not stop him, in his grimly pragmatic fable of the Hawk and the Nightingale, from recognising the compulsion of superior force:

Now I will tell you a fable for the princes: they themselves well understand it.

> Thus did the Hawk address the dapplenecked Nightingale
> as he bore her aloft through the clouds, caught in his claws.
> Pitifully, skewered on those curving talons, did she lament,
> but he, in his arrogant power, made this speech to her:
> Why scream, silly creature? A far stronger one has got you:
> you shall go wherever I take you, singer though you be.
> Just as I choose, I can let you go or make you my dinner.
> Witless are they who try to take on the more powerful:
> they're done out of victory, suffer hurt as well as shame.
> So spoke the swift-flying Hawk, that long-winged bird.
>
> *Works and Days* 202-212

From this passage a thematic trail leads unbroken to the authoritarian Sophists invoking Natural Law, the might-is-right ethic propounded (with truly Hawk-like insouciance) by the Athenian envoy in Thucydides' Melian Dialogue.

If Professor Vermeule's approach has a weakness it derives, I think, from her bright, and perhaps apotropaic, unwillingness to take death seriously. Here her fondness for *New Yorker* cartoons, especially of the comic-grisly sort, is symptomatic. There is more than a touch of the Victorian nursery, of Harry Graham's *Ruthless Rhymes*, about her bouncy attitude to dismemberment: when a Homeric head flies off one almost expects her to cry '*Touché*!', like Thurber's famous cartoon duellist. This, combined with her gift for witty aphorisms, doubtless enlivened her lectures no end: but to the extent that it leaves us feeling that death in antiquity must have been a gas for everyone concerned, it presents a false picture. What one misses is the agony and the terror, the formulaic violence of lamentation, the desperate battle against that awful sense of total eclipse. The tearing of hair and clothes, the laceration of breasts, the dreadful graveside keening – these are not among the aspects of death on which Professor Vermeule chooses to dwell. She prefers her obsequies unmessy, and is, I would guess, relieved when a Homeric victim is dispatched painlessly by Apollo's 'gentle arrows', or has death spread round his head like a soft mist, as though he were a hospital patient being put out with intravenous sodium pentathol. Greek death poetry, she claims, 'often deceives us with its ornamental black wit, a kind of formal black humour', which of course is true: but this side of it can very easily be overstressed by the unwary. By way of contrast she might try Andromache's lament over Hector, or – since Greece, as readers of Ritsos' great Mycenaean soliloquies know, is seamless and timeless – a modern Maniot *moirologhion* (dirge), perhaps that for a shot-down English airman transcribed by Patrick Leigh-Fermor in *Mani*, which I still cannot read without a prickling of the scalp and an onset of tears.

Similarly, Professor Vermeule is irritated by classicists who blame the Bronze Age for the savagery, actual or latent, in Homer, and treat the *Iliad* as a mere traditional backdrop for the evolution of the 'new spiritual Greek'. The trouble is, they happen to be right, and Professor Vermeule's reminder that the Periclean Age was no less brutal (to the examples she cites we might add the habit of genocide and that disgusting form of execution known as *apotympanismós*) cannot alter the fact. Homer *does*, demonstrably, control and civilise such raw urges, a process further developed by succeeding generations, despite occasional temporary setbacks like those inflicted by the Sophists or the bitter prolongation of the Peloponnesian War, both of which led to outbursts of barbarous recidivism. We have another paradox here, one arising from Professor Vermeule's own work, since elsewhere she herself demonstrates the civilising element in Homer with considerable subtlety and perception. But then logic, as she remarks at one point, is not fruitful in the sphere of death: a valid point, as we have seen, and one with which her audience at Berkeley doubtless sympathised. If the Greeks could legitimately contradict themselves on a topic that lay beyond both thought and experience, then why not a Sather Lecturer?

Contradiction, as she tells it, was built into the evidence she investigated from the (below-)ground up. She found baffling discrepancies between her three main sources of material: the contents of graves, visual representations of death-related topics by artists, and what poets wrote - mythologically or otherwise – about the hereafter. This is not altogether surprising. Each step in that sequence represents a further retreat from the brutal realities of coffin and corruption, a comforting slide into the hopeful fantasies of eschatological wish-fulfilment. The smell of death (as Hemingway knew so well) is the first thing to go when the artists take over. The dropped jaw, the blank staring eyes, the voided bowels all soon follow. Today even the professionally sanitised final truth of an open coffin is the exception rather than the rule. One unnoticed twentieth-century revolution is the virtual removal of corpses from the public domain. People talk about the censorship of sex: that of death has been far more efficient and complete.

Other difficulties that Professor Vermeule encountered have long been familiar to historians. She admits, for example, that 'it is not easy, professionally or temperamentally, for an archaeologist to make confident connections between tombs and thoughts'. Amen to that: artifacts are no substitute for the

Logos. Who could have extrapolated *Gilgamesh* from Sumerian mud bricks, or the *Iliad* from a Dipylon funerary vase? What Ariadne's thread can lead us safely from the symbolic iconography of a Minoan seal-ring to the cults and beliefs that inspired it? The grave is indeed, as Marvell wrote, a fine and private place; whether its occupants embrace may remain an open question (see above, pp.69-70), but what Malraux termed the voices of silence are singularly uncommunicative, not only about the afterlife, but even, after the collective death of a culture, with respect to the human motives of those who went through the formal ritual of burial and separation. For Professor Vermeule this difficulty became a kind of ongoing battle between herself and her material, which at times seems to have acquired disconcertingly human characteristics. It proved recalcitrant, she tells us, it resisted attempts to impose order on it: evidence of that long struggle is still apparent. Some of her problems have a mildly spooky quality about them. Photographs of tombstones refused to come out, references were inexplicably lost, arrangements went mysteriously wrong. After a while one begins to wonder whether Professor Vermeule may not have been hexed, somewhere along the way, by an angry Greek ghost who resented her reminder that the dead in antiquity were thought of as being somewhat weak in the head.

Greek poets, she notes, with perhaps excessive pessimism, were not much interested in bones or funerals, preferring instead to coin snappy aphorisms about the brevity of life. This is interesting and significant, not least through its striking contrast with the more physical, not to say skeletal or maggoty, sense of *memento mori* that we find in Roman and Christian literature. Sophocles may allude tangentially in the *Antigone* (411-12) to the desirability of remaining upwind of a decomposing corpse, and Polygnotus may paint a death-demon that eats the flesh off corpses, and is blue-black in colour, 'like the flies that cluster on meat' (Paus. 10.28.7): but these are exceptions. Similarly, serious archaic artists – with the exception of certain late black-figure vase painters – took more interest in mythological themes involving death than in the actualities of bereavement. One is reminded of the long-standing belief, recorded by Plutarch (*Vit. Sol.* 15), that the Athenians had a marked taste, and talent, for euphemism. By contrast, the practical tradition of burial in the archaic period primarily concerned itself with personal factual details – family and background, virtues, achievements – of the deceased, and thus generated a type of painting (especially on *lekythoi*, unguent jars, placed in the grave) with little of the mythological or fantastic about it, together with funereal epigrams largely lacking in supernatural imagery. All this changed in the fifth century, which sees a remarkable elaboration of general concepts regarding the afterlife, and the sophisticated spread of mythological themes, both literary and visual, into every area of human awareness, from the theological to the erotic. Though Professor Vermeule does not say so, it seems clear that this evolutionary process must have been directly linked to the rapid spread and increase of literacy that took place during this period, the growing habit of using mythological paradigms as a yardstick or touchstone for diurnal conduct and, in the widest sense, for human comfort.

During the earlier archaic period, however, as she rightly observes, the evidence lacks both uniformity and cohesion. This bothers her more than is necessary. There was no real need to underplay the post-Homeric evidence to the extent that she does: in the process we lose a lot of Hesiod and Archilochus and Mimnermus (to name only three of the most important witnesses) that could have been highly enlightening. Professor Vermeule concentrates more, first, on mythological iconography (legendary heroes, figures of the under-world, winged demons, marginal allegories, all aptly and idiosyncratically illustrated), and, secondly, on the physical detritus surviving from burials. The latter in particular poses endless questions. What was the purpose or function of the gifts people put in graves? Did these weapons, jewellery and vases complete the dead person's identity underground, or give him a start in his new life beyond? Dr Garland takes the commonplace example of a strigil (body-scraper) so often buried with young men. Would the deceased use it in some *outre-tombe* wrestling-school? Was it a token of his athletic prowess on earth, or simply a personal item that could not be left behind? Answers here tend to be arbitrary, and are never clear-cut or decisive. Professor Vermeule more often than not goes for the identity-completion theory, while frequently implying that of the new career after death. Neither preference would be easy to prove.

Just as man, according to cynics from Xenophanes onward, inevitably creates God in his own image, so he displays an ineradicable tendency to furnish the afterlife with properties reminiscent of his existence here on earth. Similarly, the dead had to be supplied with food and, *a fortiori*, with drink. Such pleasures, most often in the form of a banquet, were regarded as the highest reward for a virtuous life. The universality and frequency of libations suggests that, whatever the dead may have done about intercourse, toping seems to have been endemic. Funerary urns had pierced bottoms, sometimes connected to clay tubes, to facilitate the passage of liquor to these thirsty if insubstantial recipients. Honey, milk, water, wine and oil in combination offered as rich a liquid sustenance as antiquity could conceive. The vessels from which this mixture was poured were broken afterwards, much as glasses will still be broken today on occasion in a Greek taverna. Correspon-dence was paramount. Indeed, the grave itself seems to have been viewed in much the same way, as in some sense a desirable residence, or at the very least a way-station. Much evidence – roofs, doors, painted façades – suggests a house, or at any rate a bedroom: a new home, a comfortable setting for the Big Sleep. Yet did bodily functions call for support once the flesh had failed? Vermeule is inclined, against the evidence, to think not – but still, despite herself, slips into treating the grave as a home at times. She claims, to be sure, that 'in the Bronze Age the most ambitious tombs, the *tholoi*, were not replicas of normal houses': the ambivalent word there is 'normal'. In fact, the inner space defined by a *tholos* bears a most striking inverted resemblance to those circular huts known as *tourlotá*, built to this day by the nomadic pastoral herdsmen of Epirus, the Saracatsani [see J.K. Campbell, *Honour, Family and Patronage* (1964) pl. 4 opp. p.208: P. Leigh-Fermor, *Roumeli* (1966) pl. opp. p.24]. Leigh-Fermor notes [ibid. 27-32] the immutable conservatism of Saracatsani patterns in building and dress: some of the designs on Saracatsani wedding dresses show unmistakable Geometric influence, dating back to at least the eighth century BC.

The lectures on which *Aspects of Death* is based have become legendary in Berkeley, and it is not hard to see why. Besides being an immensely distinguished archaeologist and prehistorian, Professor Vermeule is the kind of widely read humanist who, to our infinite loss, has become virtually extinct in overspecialised academic life (a special bouquet, therefore, to the American Philological Association, which surprised everyone by making *Aspects of Death* its choice for the prestigious Goodwin Award of Merit). To students fed for too long on windy jargon, bureaucratic trash, or emotive but inarticulate slang, her resilient and sparkling prose must have come as a revelation. Nor has elegance of style been achieved at the expense of intellectual strength. Her extensive (and often very funny) notes show her equally at home in an extraordinarily wide range of topics; the wit and poetic insight have a solid underpinning of scholarship. Even where she cannot find answers, where she admits, as she often does, to bafflement or muddle, she illuminates by the keenness of her vision and the unlooked-for parallels she so often adduces. Her sense of the interplay between Eros and Thanatos results, *inter alia*, in some deadpan sexual one-liners, e.g. on Ixion and Tityos 'trying to rape the great goddesses, unaware that immortality cannot be achieved by friction'. The biggest compliment I can pay her is that, having read and reread her book with ever-increasing fascination, I am now in the process of rethinking the entire subject for myself. She gives a fresh angle to everything she touches: Hades will never look quite the same again.

V

THE TREASURES
OF EGYPT

B Y THE TIME THAT the Tutankhamun exhibition closed in San Francisco, it had been seen by more than eight million people, almost all of whom had to apply for reserved tickets: the potential audience was probably twice as large again. Museum directors and their PR men have, in the past decade or two, become experts at what one critic nicely terms 'the techniques of hype and hoopla', the hard sell of cultural packages, from the Chinese show of 1973 to 1978's 'Pompeii AD 79': not surprisingly, since the windfalls that such happenings generate can be immense. The 'Tut craze' proved the biggest money-spinner of the lot. The New Orleans Museum of Art, for instance, let it be known that a 'minimum of $69.4 million was pumped into the New Orleans economy' in no more than four months, as a direct result of the Tutankhamun exhibition being on view there.[1]

In the *New Yorker*'s 'Talk of the Town' column for 25 December 1978 there was an interview with Tutankhamun himself ('We found the boy king in the pale pink sitting room of his suite, wearing a Turnbull and Asser djellabah and sipping Perrier'), in which he was asked if his spectacle had a theme, and replied, with commendable bluntness: 'Yes, it's about gold, man. Heavy metal.' So it was, and in more ways than one. When Robert Hughes characterised the art world as 'the last refuge for nineteenth-century laissez-faire capitalism' he was not indulging in mere idle hyperbole. The Egyptian government alone made about $7 million out of Tut's peregrinations around the USA and Canada, all altruistically earmarked (despite rumours to the contrary) for revamping the somewhat tacky display facilities of the Cairo Museum.

Yet this, clearly, was not an exorbitant slice of the cake. Ahmed Abushadi, press counsellor to the Egyptian Embassy, described it as 'peanuts', and is on record[2] as saying: 'We didn't bring the show here for the money, or we'd have demanded a fair share of the millions made by cities around the country on it.' Heavy metal, indeed. It is interesting, too, that a large amount of the cash-flow came from what was labelled 'Tutsploitation' or the 'Tut glut': Tut beer mugs, T-shirts, tote-bags, stationery, posters, paper dolls, whiskey decanters, and, at a slightly more pretentious level, the replicas of Egyptian artifacts marketed, as an exclusive monopoly, by the Metropolitan Museum of Art. These ranged from simple ankh pendants or crook-and-flail pins to a slap-up gold-surfaced copy of the exquisite statuette of the goddess Selket, going for a mere $1,850, and unkindly described by Frank Schulze (n. I above) as 'neo-sleazo'. Museum boutiquefication in itself strikes me as a comparatively harmless trend, which has the advantage of bringing attractive historical designs within reach of almost anyone who can appreciate them. No one is forced to buy the grungier items, much less go broke in pursuit of limited-edition exotica. *Caveat emptor*. But a large market exists, and as long as it does, laissez-faire commercialisers will continue, quite legitimately, to milk it for their own benefit.

This, of course, raises the far more intriguing question of just *why* a collection of grave-goods from the tomb of a minor, and in his own day little esteemed, New Kingdom pharaoh (*c*.1343-1325 BC: dates disputed) should have 'managed to agitate almost the entire surface of American culture'.[3] Not all the hoopla, obviously, can be put down to clever hype and promotion. You need an intrinsically magnetic commodity to market in the first place. The stunning artistic quality of the Tutankhamun material has to be one major factor in the exhibition's success: but another, perhaps even more potent, is the prodigal use of what has always been the rare, royal, and ornamental metal *par excellence*, lustrous, indestructible, untarnishing, infinitely malleable and ductile, its smooth, soft, almost liquid yellow sheen a never-failing visual and tactile delight.[4] *It's about gold, man*.

No accident, then, that the exhibition catalogue, *Treasures of Tutankhamun* (1976), the Met's more elaborate survey *Tutankhamun: His Tomb and his Treasures* (1976), and two publications sponsored by *Newsweek*, *Treasures of the Egyptian Museum* (1969) and *The Gold of Tutankhamun* (1978) – the latter the most sumptuous, scholarly, and exquisitely produced art-book to have come my way in years: lucky the coffee-table that gets it – all blazon the young king's famous gold-and-lapis mask across their dust-jackets, and give pride of place, in full seductive colour, to the other golden artifacts that cluttered his burial-chamber in more-than-royal abundance: statuettes, shrine-panels, daggers, sandals, and, above all, coffin-cases, of which one – the innermost of Tutankhamun's three – weighs no less than 2,448 lbs of pure beaten 22-carat gold. Two of these volumes even have golden end-papers. Their cumulative impact is undeniable. The contents of the Shaft Graves at Mycenae – gold masks and daggers there, too – look like mere provincial *Edelkitsch* by comparison. An art-book such as *Egyptian Treasures from the Collections of the Brooklyn Museum* (1978), which has only one gold piece to offer – an admittedly exquisite fly necklace – and a limited range of other material, is, in a sense, subsidised by the Tutankhamun treasure-trove. This kind of cultural surf-boarding has also, inevitably, spilt over into popular fiction, complete with antiquities-smuggling, sexy female Egyptologists, and variations on the obligatory Mummy's Curse. Among more sensational finds, the Valley of the Kings has also given the world a barrelful of romantic clichés.

The effect is all the more arresting, in historical terms, when we reflect that Tutankhamun died young, and that by royal Egyptian standards his burial was (it seems safe to say) a cut-price and makeshift affair: he had had little time to accumulate heavenly treasure. If *his* tomb yielded such wealth, what must have gone into those, say, of Chefren, or Amenhotep III, or Rameses II, the self-styled victor of Kadesh (1300 BC), the grandiose builder of Karnak and Abu Simbel?[5] The depredations of tomb-robbers, mostly ancient, who made an almost clean sweep of the royal burials at Thebes, ensure that such a question must remain for ever rhetorical (though from tomb-paintings and documents we can glimpse something of that lost splendour): there is a nice eschatological paradox here, since the more visibly magnificent preparations an Egyptian made to ensure his own ultimate survival, the more liable he was to have his mummy destroyed – and with it, his chance of life hereafter – by ruthless thieves in pursuit of fabulously rich pickings.

A convicted tomb-robber was impaled through the anus; but the long catalogue of rifled burial-chambers makes it clear that many felt the enormous rewards more than justified the risk (which was, in any case, much reduced by the systematic bribery and collusion of court officials). Indeed, it is by pure luck that Tutankhamun's own burial survived intact. At least two near-successful attempts were made to rifle it soon after the boy-king's death: the thieves penetrated the antechamber but missed the inner sanctum. Then Rameses VI (d. 1134 BC), excavating his own tomb slightly above and to one side of Tutankhamun's, blocked the entrance to the latter with rubble, leaving it hidden – and forgotten – for three millennia. The sheer antiquity of this funeral treasure-trove, the dazzling glimpse that its priceless wealth and artistry offered into a lost world of wholly alien power and privilege, and – by no means least – the archaeological drama associated with its recovery from the silent earth: all these factors combined to ensure a powerful, and continuing, public fascination, not only with Tutankhamun (who, his relation to the 'heretic pharaoh' Akhenaten apart, was historically negligible), but with the whole enigmatic, yet extraordinarily well-documented, civilisation to which he belonged.

EVEN A CURSORY ACQUAINTANCE with the diffuse modern literature on ancient Egypt makes it clear that the so-called 'Tut craze' forms part of a far wider, and older, phenomenon than mere gold-mania or archaeological romanticism, let alone the hype generated by a well-publicised travelling exhibition. Such things, of course, have their place in the overall picture: they are symptomatic of that persistent, acquisitive process of exploitation that began with the tomb-robbers of the Twentieth Dynasty and has continued almost to our own day, a colourful saga of amateur eccentrics, quirky obsessional scholars, con-men, and rip-off artists. Sometimes, indeed, we find all these qualities united in the same person: Giovanni Battista Belzoni (1778-1822) is a nice case in point.[6] It was Napoleon's savants who not only opened the way for the first scientific Egyptologists, men such as Champollion and Mariette, but also, at the same time, made ancient Egypt fashionable, with quite horrendous results. What has been well described by Brian Fagan (n.6; p.361) as a 'surge of nationalistic lust for the precious and exotic' led to an orgy of looting, a series of treasure-hunts thinly disguised as 'scientific investigation' and carried out under the aegis of gunboat diplomacy. Private purchase became a well-organised and corrupt racket; surreptitious excavations and smuggling abroad of finds were a commonplace. Museums, too, carried on a brisk under-the-counter traffic in stolen antiquities, justifying themselves with the familiar argument that at least they were rescuing priceless material from oblivion.

The excavation of Tutankhamun's burial in 1922 by Howard Carter becomes a good deal more comprehensible when viewed against this louche background: it is entirely appropriate that the latest, and liveliest, account of it – stressing the shady private manoeuvres as well as the public success story – should be by none other than Thomas Hoving, ex-director of the Met, main begetter of the Tut exhibition, master publicist, and (as several reviewers have pointed out, with heavy-handed implications) an entrepreneur whose own personality strikingly resembles that of his hero Carter (if hero is the right word in this context). Hoving reveals, *inter alia*, that Carter and his patron Lord Carnarvon privately, and illegally, 'cased' the inner chamber before bringing in any official representatives of the Egyptian Antiquities Service; that they were, to say the least, high-handed in their disposal of artifacts (what may be described as 'The Affair of the Lotus Head in the Fortnum and Mason Wine Case' is instructive here); and that they had, for some time, been involved in the clandestine sale of Egyptian antiquities to American museums. The minor inaccuracies scattered through Hoving's text are irksome, but do not invalidate his main point: that such behaviour was commonplace rather than anomalous. In obeying, all too literally, the Biblical injunction to spoil the Egyptians, Carter and Carnarvon were simply doing what all their predecessors had taken for granted; indeed, they were far more scrupulous than most. It is sad, but perhaps not surprising, that Carter, a prickly maverick who never learnt the art of compromise, was denied in his lifetime the academic recognition he so richly deserved; another minor scandal to add to the rest.[7]

Archaeological curiosity, then, laced with a dash of romance and scandal, and floated on the Tut revival, may partly – but by no means entirely – have accounted for this recent Egyptological craze, and consequent publishing boom. *Publishers Weekly* at the time estimated a total of almost fifty Tut-related titles in print. To judge from a personal sampling, I would guess the overall tally to have been, in fact, far larger, much of it, significantly, in paperback. You could find titles galore (often reprints of works fifty and more years old) on Egyptian temples, archaeology, medicine, civilisation, daily life, art, chronology, hieroglyphics (and language generally), literature, religion, and magic: a lot of this material was both arcane and technical, including facsimile reproductions that looked marvellous and cost the earth. Who bought such books, and why?

At one level the attraction is obvious enough. Both the culture itself and those who rediscovered it constitute a powerful natural draw for the large audience of amateurs who insist on having their past perspectives dramatic, vivid, and larger than life. The process of rediscovery contains its own special lure. Not all Victorian Egyptologists were mere rapacious treasure-hunters, and the development of scientific archaeology on the Nile, in the hands of great pioneers such as Flinders Petrie of University College London, and J.H. Breasted of the Oriental Institute at Chicago, is in itself as fascinating and romantic a saga as one could hope to find. Today, moreover, refinements of technique are available that would have been way beyond even Petrie's wildest dreams, of which he had not a few.

Scholars today are even ready to bombard the pyramids with cosmic ray muons in search of hidden chambers and galleries: and there can be few more brilliant examples of scientific skills implementing archaeological retrieval than the use of the computer to reconstitute Akhenaten's totally demolished and dispersed temple to Amun-Re at Karnak by matching up almost 40,000 recycled building blocks (and, incidentally, the reliefs carved on them). In a less spectacular, but no less effective, use of multidisciplinary scientific techniques, contemporary Egyptologists are expanding our hitherto sketchy knowledge of predynastic Egypt into the palaeolithic period, far beyond the Badarian and Merimden cultures of 5-4000 BC.[8] Hence the attraction of books such as T.G.H. James's *The Archaeology of Ancient Egypt* (1972), an excellent piece of *haute vulgarisation* done by a first-class scholar for the general public, and primarily concerned, again, with the physical recovery of Egypt's past.

For anyone like myself, brought up in the classical tradition, where before 750 BC the literary pickings are nil, and even the archaeological evidence (despite show-pieces such as Mycenae, Pylos, Cnossos and Troy) tends to be sporadic, the sheer mass and variety of Egyptian material available from the third and second millennia almost defy belief: it reaches right back to the dynasties of the Archaic or Thinite Period (*c.*3100-2778 BC). Scholars may debate whether Narmer and Menes (the traditional uniter of Upper and Lower Egypt, the first pharaoh of the First Dynasty) were one and the same man: but we have Narmer's personal cosmetic palette, and much besides, including ivory gaming sets, inlaid ebony boxes, alabaster vases, copper tools, and some surprisingly realistic portraiture, too soon thereafter to be fixed and stylised.[9]

Perhaps more important, from the Fifth Dynasty onwards, c.2400 BC, we have a considerable literary record for the Old Kingdom: funerary prayers, autobiographical testaments, royal decrees, the famous 'pyramid texts', other theological and didactic poems.[10] When we move on into the Middle and New Kingdoms, the evidence multiplies to a staggering degree. Frescoes, bas-reliefs, statues, furniture, exquisite *objets d'art*, elaborate games and toys are reinforced by a wealth of military records, hymns, harpers' songs, school texts, love lyrics, and prose tales somewhat akin to those in the *Arabian Nights*.[11] Nothing, it's true, even approaches the creative or intellectual achievements of Greek literature, and the prevailing tone – bureaucratic where not theological – in fact suggests a Near Eastern tradition much closer to the world of the Old Testament or the Hittite and Eblaite archives. But the age of this material alone makes it noteworthy: almost all of it predates the collapse of the Mycenaean kingdoms in Greece (c.1150 BC).

THUS ONE MOST SEDUCTIVE ASPECT of Egyptian civilisation is the vivid, rich, and uniquely bountiful manner in which it opens up for our bemused inspection a world as far removed in time from, say, the Rome of Augustus as Augustus' Rome is from contemporary New York. The sheer hoary antiquity of Egypt was already impressing tourists in Herodotus' day, when Pharaonic culture was virtually a spent force. The initial appeal, of course, is that incredulous sense of kinship one feels across the centuries with these cheerful, humorous, energetic, and erotically inclined people, whose religion never got in the way of their pleasure, and indeed seems in many ways designed to enhance it. The beer-swilling artisans, the pernickety letter-writers, the elegant, svelte, fashionable ladies, the ambitious bureaucrats and dedicated hunters, all come across (we delude ourselves) as the sort of people we know, and have met.

There is something a little factitious about such an attitude, as Diderot saw during the brouhaha over the first discoveries at Herculaneum. He commented, ironically, on the astonishment generated in an antiquarian, M. Fougeroux, by the fact that these first-century Italians actually used cooking-pots and table-utensils, just like modern men. ('Que ne s'étonnait-il aussi qu'ils eussent une bouche et un derrière?' he enquired waspishly.) In any case, it very soon becomes apparent that with Egypt the differences far outweigh the similarities: that this was an exotic (not to say freakish) culture, which demands a real effort of the imagination on our part to comprehend: totally conditioned by its surroundings, rooted in concrete particularities, indifferent to abstractions or theories as to the outside world, deeply suspicious of change, an early Shangri-La dedicated, with unswerving hedonism, to the preservation of the status quo up to, and above all beyond, the grave, at whatever cost.

To begin with, the country's geography and ecology were, and remain, unique.[12] From Aswan to the Delta, Egypt's existence is wholly predicated on the Nile and its annual inundation. South of Memphis the country is simply one long narrow oasis, never more than twelve miles wide, between burning desert wastes: an enclave in every sense. Rain is rare, and in Upper Egypt almost unheard-of. The sun beats down daily out of a cloudless sky: Akhenaten's attempt to create a kind of solar monotheism was logical enough. Control of the Nile – essential for human survival – demanded, and got, centralised, efficient, conservative government. A natural symbiosis grew up between Upper and Lower Egypt, between the red land of the desert and the rich black soil of the Delta. The predictability of the Nile flood produced a stable agricultural pattern, together with a relatively advanced, but non-theoretical technology. The existence of the desert meant that Egypt evolved, at least to begin with, in virtual isolation.

The ever-visible, sharply drawn contrast between that narrow, luxuriant, unbelievably fertile strip and the barren sun-scorched landscape encroaching on it must have given these Nile-dwellers a proto-Manichaean cast of mind. Their ideal life was, surely, seen as an oasis – all brightness and shade, music, coolness, good food and drink, love-making, the teeming bird-life of the marshes, colour, sensation. Death, by contrast, will have been envisaged as the negation of all this (cf. above, p.69): the parching waterless desert, bare burnt rock, the mirage at noon. We might have expected such a dichotomy to produce something more akin to the Horatian *carpe diem* philosophy of hedonism rather than the complex and *outré* Egyptian attempt to beat death at its own game: and indeed the trend existed. The famous harper's song from the Middle Kingdom tomb of King Intef advised men to eat and drink their fill, to make love, to 'follow your heart and your happiness', since death is the irreversible end for all men: you can't take your good things with you, so make the most of them while you're still here.[13] This scepticism regarding both the reality of the afterlife and the effectiveness (for those who hoped to achieve it) of tomb-building – a scepticism shared, we may assume, by generations of tomb-robbers if by no one else – came in for some sharp criticism from more orthodox later poets: not surprisingly, since it ran flat counter to the whole observable pattern of Egyptian belief.

There are two options available to the dedicated hedonist. He can accept this life as a one-shot, and squeeze it for all it's worth on the grounds that he won't get a second chance; or, alternatively, he can predicate an afterlife that continues, indeed possibly improves on, this world's pleasures, and do all he can to ensure that he makes the transition with as little change to his enjoyable mundane existence as possible. The ancient Egyptians went, with quite extraordinary thoroughness, for the second approach. As has often been pointed out, they were not so much possessed by death as obsessed with life, and determined to prolong it, or a semblance of it, in any way open to them.

Hence, *inter alia*, the mummification of corpses: the body must be preserved as nearly as possible as it was before death.

The contrast between the pathetic physical remains of Tutankhamun (the embalmers botched their job) and that magnificent funeral mask, one of the very finest surviving portraits from antiquity, or indeed from any period, is instructive: the true immortality, as some writers were aware even at the time, is that conferred by art. Yet from the age of the pyramid-builders on, a seemingly illimitable amount of time, money and skill was expended on the business of projecting this world's investments into the next: mummification became more elaborate, coffin-texts multiplied, complex ritual was reinforced by posthumous offerings. To an outsider all this must have looked very odd. The afterworld itself was endowed with all the functions of this life, work and sex included. Most of the gods seemed to be animals or birds: Ptolemaic Greeks had a derisive saying, 'Like an Egyptian temple, magnificent to look at, and inside a priest singing a hymn to a cat or a crocodile'. Egyptian myths contradicted each other at every turn, and no one cared to rationalise or reconcile them: it was all enough to drive a logical Greek mind to drink.

The Greeks in fact reveal two standard reactions to Egypt: derision and awe. These have more in common than is generally supposed, being both based upon profound ignorance. There was the potent mystery of the unknown, an awareness of dim and alien antiquity that suggested superhuman wisdom, the sheer colossal scale of Karnak or Memphis or the pyramids. There was also that astonishing theocratic conservatism which so appealed to moral authoritarians like Plato, and is most apparent in the visual arts: not only were painting and sculpture (and music, it would appear) wholly subsumed to a didactic-religious function, but for centuries their formal conventions remained fixed and immutable, with a firm ban on innovation of any sort.[14] Such absolutism has by no means lost its appeal in some quarters even today: one more element of attraction to add to the rest.

Early Greek mercenaries, on the other hand, made a conscious effort not to be impressed. (No accident, I feel, that those Greeks who succumbed to the lure of Mysterious Egypt always had some pretensions to intellect, whereas the common man remained immune, if not actively contemptuous.) They cut graffiti on the legs of Rameses II's giant statues at Abu Simbel ('written by Archon son of Amoibichos, and Hatchet son of Nobody'). To the strange outsize creatures and gigantic monuments they saw they gave names designed to scale such conceits down to size. The very word 'pyramid' is Greek for a small bun of that shape. An 'obelisk' was a kitchen skewer or spit, a 'crocodile' a garden lizard. Ostriches they called *strouthoi*, i.e. 'sparrows'. The theriomorphic cults of cat, ibis or baboon were still attracting derisive comment in Juvenal's day.

But in earlier times a great deal of this reductionist nomenclature was, I suspect, mere whistling in the dark to keep up one's courage. For Herodotus, as for many later Greek writers, Egypt remained a place of marvels and magic, and a fertile source of fictional anecdote (e.g. visits supposedly made there, in search of arcane wisdom, by such figures as Solon, Thales, or Pythagoras). Behind the great temples, the sphinxes and pylons and elaborate religious ritual, lay (they were convinced) the immemorial wisdom, and more than human powers, of the mysterious East, expressed in hieroglyphs as potently symbolic, to a Greek eye, as they were incomprehensible. The quasi-occult myth thus generated has proved singularly resistant to progress or knowledge. Since Champollion's day, after all, scholars have been deciphering the hieroglyphic, hieratic and demotic scripts with increasing assurance and accuracy.

Today we have a very fair notion, based on extensive literary and iconographic evidence, of what these people knew as well as what they believed: and about the former, at least, there is nothing mysterious or arcane at all. Their medical records show the same mixture of common sense and sympathetic magic as we find in the Greek tradition a thousand years later. Their mathematical knowledge, far from being ahead of its time, was both primitive and pragmatic – though, as such, quite adequate to construct a pyramid with accurate mensuration. They were indifferent astronomers, far inferior in this respect to the Babylonians. They reveal themselves as masters of no lost transcendental philosophy: since they were unacquainted with the zodiacal system even their reputation as astrologers has been overblown. The mystical-sounding *Book of the Dead* reads in places more like a Baedeker to the underworld than anything else, and its eschatological symbolism, though complex, is amenable to patient analysis.[15] No great hidden truths there – and some remarkably silly spells.

YET OVER A CENTURY OF increasing scholarly light in dark places has completely failed to destroy the myth of Egyptian hermetic wisdom. A remarkable succession of occultists, numerologists, Pythagoreans and the like (satirised memorably by Samuel Butler in *Hudibras*, and known to Egyptologists, unkindly, as 'Pyramidiots') continues to promote any number of arcane theories, most prominent among them being the notion that the Great Pyramid of Giza was a kind of 'gigantic prophecy in stone, built by a group of ancient adepts in magic'.[16] What is more, these fantasies command a large and apparently insatiable market. Another profitable element in the current Egyptological boom at once falls into place.

Whatever scientific critics may say – and most of it is pretty scathing – about such professional bagmen of fantasy as Immanuel Velikovsky or Erich von Däniken,[17] there can be no doubt that these popular purveyors of pseudo-science – 'paradoxers', as Carl Sagan calls them – have touched a most responsive nerve in the public psyche, and can therefore (like anyone else in that rewarding position) ignore their detractors while laughing all the way to the bank. The putatively transcendental qualities of the Great Pyramid are equally big business: one reason, perhaps, why paperbacks on Egyptology tend to wind up in bookstores among titles dealing with such topics as I Ching numerology, Zen, Vedanta, UFOs, the Bermuda Triangle, or works like Ouspensky's *Tertium Organum*. A half-educated age that questions all established beliefs will inevitably create its own crop of synthetic absolutes and instant folk-dogma. These are then sold to the unwary, packaged in a pseudo-scientific format that apes the external trappings of scholarship.

It's an ill wind that blows no one any good, and genuine Egyptologists probably have this trend to thank for the republication of many classic works that would otherwise be unobtainable – or, at best, prohibitively expensive. Who would have thought to find Budge's exemplary interlinear edition and translation of *The Book of the Dead* – or, even less probably, his invaluable, but highly technical, *Egyptian Hieroglyphic Dictionary* – available in paperback?[18] It would be over-optimistic to deduce from such phenomena a renaissance in formal Egyptological studies. The real give-away is the absence from the paperback lists of Sir Alan Gardiner's monumental *Egyptian Grammar*: indispensable for all serious students, it offers nothing to the pseudoscientific fringe. A trickle of linguists doesn't float glossy reprints. The real market for these publications, it seems clear, lies with the would-be adepts who hope to tap ancient Egypt for anything from hyperkinetic energy to prophetic wisdom and, for all I know, the music of the spheres: for anything, in fact, rather than the fascinating culture that the scholars have actually unravelled. But then, for such devotees of the arcane, what kind of fun is public, non-hermetic knowledge?

The entertaining notion of the Great Pyramid as a predictive code-matrix in stone, to be cracked by enterprising numerologists, got a great boost in the nineteenth century from Piazzi Smyth, the then Astronomer Royal for Scotland, whose work on the subject – a masterpiece of misconceived mathematical ingenuity – was, ironically enough, responsible for Petrie's first youthful investigations at Giza. Brilliant scientists, like other men, can have their dotty obsessions: Sir Isaac Newton's astrological notebooks are quite an eye-opener. The trouble is that their reputations sometimes induce unwary readers to take the nonsense on trust. Mystical mathematics, as Pythagoras and Sir Thomas Browne knew, can be horribly attractive: in such cases reason is no deprogrammer. It took Petrie very little time to check, and refute, Smyth's theories: but as he said afterwards, 'it is useless to state the real truth of the matter, as it has no effect on those who are subject to this sort of hallucination'. I suspect that there are more of the latter around than one thinks (it would be interesting to inspect the sales figures of those publishers who specially cater to them), and that their perennial hunger for such esoterica constitutes a major factor in the recurrent 'Tut craze'.

Certainly the trade for the converted remains as brisk as ever. The Great Pyramid is still being touted as a 'blueprint for human destiny' (the Egyptians, of all people, cared not a jot for human destiny apart from their own, but no matter), while Egyptian culture emerges as (what else?) the heir to Atlantis, another splendid catch-all for dotty speculation; and the vulgar notion, so unaccountably popular with serious Egyptologists, that the pyramids were simply what their builders claimed them to be, i.e. monumental sepulchres for great pharaohs, is stigmatised as 'crankier than all the fantasising of the pyramidologists and the UFO freaks'.[19] (Here we detect a characteristically modern obtuseness: it's assumed without question that to channel infinite energy, capital and ingenuity into such superstitious flummery as tomb-building is the mark of a 'primitive' or 'barbarian' mentality irreconcilable with the Egyptians' supposed superior wisdom.) The collateral notion of the pyramids, or pyramidal objects generally, as a source of mysterious energy is also flourishing. Special pyramidally-shaped tents are very popular: their inherent forces can be harnessed, one gathers from the literature, to do anything from dehydrate meat to sharpen razor-blades (provided the latter are laid along a north–south axis). One adept even claims that half an hour or so in a pyramid converted his cat to vegetarianism. Tom Hoving had to fend off a character who wanted to embrace Chefren's statue outside its glass case, his object being to test the power of the life-giving rays that 'most assuredly emanated from the ancient divinity-being and would beyond doubt cure most, if not all, maladies of mankind's oppressed and feeble bodies'.[20]

So it goes: every generation gets the nonsense it needs and deserves. One merit this material certainly possesses is that of drawing attention to the persistence, irrational optimism, and almost infinite elasticity of human belief. The otherwise sensible authors of *Egypt Observed* (n. 12 above) still cherish the old chimera of a 'mummy's curse' operating out of Tutankhamun's tomb, even though its prime disturber, Howard Carter, lived on till 1939: and the apotropaic furore over Skylab – with hundreds of apparently sane people making a concerted effort to raise its orbit by willpower – showed that the market for instant magic has scarcely been touched by the progress of science.

THIS IS ALL A GREAT PITY, since the culture of Egypt was quite extraordinary enough in sober fact; to credit the Egyptians, in addition, with being the guardians, if not the inventors, of every sort of hermetic wisdom, arcane science, prophetic skill, and perennial philosophy merely detracts from what they *did* do. (The collected works of Bacon are an impressive achievement in their own right: why over-egg the pudding by throwing in those of Shakespeare too?) It is also seriously misleading, since it implies a gift for conceptualisation which was the one thing, notoriously, that the Egyptians lacked, and which constitutes their most fundamental distinction from natural generalisers like the Greeks, who couldn't rub two facts together without coming up with a hot universal theory. Jon Manchip White[21] puts the case with admirable concision:

The Egyptians were devotees of the concrete object: they did not traffic in speculations or abstractions. They were not metaphysicians but practical men. Just as they failed to appreciate the fundamental principles underlying their building, engineering, mathematics, astronomy or medicine, so they failed to interest themselves in the principles and possibilities of hieroglyphic writing. It would hardly be going too far to say that the ancient Egyptian dreaded theorizing and abstract thinking. He felt at home only with what he could experience with his five senses. Even his attitude to so nebulous an experience as death or survival after death was practical and positive. It is therefore not surprising that the Egyptian language contains no words of a truly abstract nature.

It is easy to forget that Egypt's omnipresent bureaucracy got on very well without a coinage; that surviving Egyptian literature contains nothing identifiable, in our terms, as philosophy, hermetic or otherwise; that the proliferation of irreconcilable Egyptian myths (which bothered no one in Egypt) strongly suggests the pre-Hesiodic localism of Greece before rationalising intellectuals got at it; and that the quarrelling of the Egyptian gods (e.g. over the struggle between Horus and Set) makes Homer's Olympus look a model of genteel decorum by comparison. Horus at one point decapitates his mother Isis in a fit of pique, a fact eventually noticed by Ra: 'Who *is* this headless woman?' he enquires. Even Ares and Aphrodite manage a little better than that. No accident that Akhenaten's aberrant excursion (as his successors saw it) into monotheism and realistic art provoked so violent a reaction: both are symptoms of a nascent capacity, and inclination, for independent intellectual thought.

The natural focus of Egyptian civilisation (as the Akhenaten case forcibly reminds us) was not intellectual but theological, indeed theocentric. The power inherent in the god-king achieved its peak of faith during the Old Kingdom (2778-2300 BC), a faith that built pyramids not only as a memorial of great rulers, but as a 'palace of eternity' for the occupant. A spell on the wall of one Fifth Dynasty pyramid declares: 'A staircase to heaven is laid for Pharaoh, that he may ascend to heaven thereby' – an interesting gloss on Zoser's early Step Pyramid. The diorite statue of Chefren (Fourth Dynasty, c.2580 BC) from Giza reveals this consciousness of absolute divine power in all its unquestioning majesty.

Originally, it was believed, only Pharaoh made the crucial transition to a life hereafter. However, as time went on, and the aristocracy multiplied, and something resembling a middle class of craftsmen and scribes and other officials developed, eligibility for eternal life soon became general, while Pharaoh's own role, though as autocratic and theophanic as ever, grew increasingly politicised by a series of historical conflicts, including periods of anarchy and foreign rule, such as that of the 'shepherd kings', the Hyksos (c.1730-c.1580 BC). Yet despite such inroads of temporal interest, throughout Egyptian history almost all the surviving monuments and writings – the pyramids, the huge temples, the tomb paintings, the jewellery, the literature, whether imaginative or didactic – were designed for one single, dominant, all-obsessional purpose: to ensure that the dead continued to enjoy, in a paradise as like their previous existence as possible, all the amenities and pleasures of this world.

It is entirely typical of the Egyptians that, having once opened up a potential afterlife to anyone who could afford the necessary preparations – mummification, elaborate ritual, coffin-texts[22] and so on – they seem to have applied only the most perfunctory moral sanctions over the actual business of admission. True, there was what the Greeks called a *psychostasia*, at which the dead man's soul or heart was weighed against the feather of truth, *maat*, with a hybrid monster known as the Devourer ready to put away anyone who failed the test: but there is no evidence to suggest that in fact anyone did fail it. Hell-fire had no takers in the Nile Valley. A written profession of innocence was an adequate substitute for the thing itself: bureaucracy triumphed even in death. No other culture – except perhaps our own[23] – has ever manifested so intense, persistent, and physically sensuous an addiction to the simple fact of being alive. The most common prayer for the departed is 'bread, beer, and prosperity'.

How many people got the pleasure? If we visualise ancient Egyptian society (appropriately enough) as a pyramid, how far down did the privileges extend? Further, certainly, as time went on: after the revolutionary upheavals of the First Intermediate Period (2300-2065 BC) the peasantry got at least an embryonic bill of rights, while the easygoing Egyptian temperament shielded workers from the grosser forms of exploitation. The myth of pyramid workers driven on under the lash is a myth only, reinforced in recent times by Goldwyn and De Mille: during the months of inundation peasants were only too glad of public employment. It remains true, nevertheless, that then, as in later ages, Egypt was essentially a monolithic two-class society, with the aristocracy, the priesthood, the court bureaucracy and some skilled function-aries forming a *de facto* elite, and the fellahin a toiling invisible majority, about whose lives and feelings we know very little.

The afterlife was a privilege that came expensive, a club with an enormous entrance fee. No elaborate burial awaited the peasant, but a shallow pit in the hot sand – and, thus, natural mummification at no cost. Perhaps this was how the practice originated. The little *ushabti* figures in the graves of the rich, 'answerers' who substituted for the dead man when he was called upon to do menial work in the hereafter, are socially eloquent: we know the faceless underlings who gave such a notion currency. For the ambitious a certain upward mobility was possible. 'Be a scribe', boys are advised again and again. 'You will not be like a hired ox. You are in front of others.' Ancient Egypt had no monopoly of such attitudes. The *apparatchik*, the *petit fonctionnaire*, are perennial and ubiquitous: any strong bureaucracy offers them rich soil in which to flourish.

Perhaps what fascinates most today about Egyptian civilisation is, para-doxically, its static self-assurance. To an age of transient governments and crumbling creeds it presents the spectacle of massive energy, absolute faith, and virtually limitless resources harnessed, for almost three millennia, to a unique, unswerving vision of immortality and the good life. Further, what Eliot called the 'strong brown god' remains perennial, outlasting creeds and dynasties. Nothing can change the rhythms of the life-giving Nile, though ingenuity continues, as always, to exploit and conserve its gifts: the great pharaohs of the Old and Middle Kingdoms, who believed that bigger was better, and embodied that belief in memorable achievements, would surely have approved the building of the Aswan High Dam. Islamic Egypt is Egypt still: Nasser's funeral has a place beside Tutankhamun's, and we sense the continuum between them. When the last cache of pharaohs' mummies was shipped downriver to Cairo by the archaeologists, the banks of the Nile were lined with wailing women, and men fired off their rifles in salute.

By emphasising this sense of continuity, finely illustrated general surveys of Egypt[24] serve a really useful purpose. Photographs of mosques, minarets, potters' kilns, *souks*, feluccas, desert tanks, and the crowded polyglot streets of Cairo and Alexandria are interleaved in a diachronic simultaneity with those of grave-goods, temples and hieroglyphs. Sometimes a modern picture, e.g. threshing spice crops, will gloss an ancient one – it is Egyptian tomb-paintings, characteristically, that give us our fullest record of ancient daily life – stressing the changeless quality of Nilotic culture. 'To subsist in bones,' sniffed Sir Thomas Browne, 'and to be but Pyramidally extant, is a fallacy in duration', thus brushing aside the monolithic faith that could – and did – move mountains, and boasted a longer run for its money than Christianity has yet notched up. Here, surely, is the key to the current – and perennial – obsession with Egypt of the pharaohs. Nothing, in the last resort, not even gold, is more insidious than unshakeable belief.

DELPHIC RESPONSES

[*Note: This essay is a revised and expanded version of a review I wrote, for the* New York Review of Books, *of the late Professor Joseph Fontenrose's monograph* The Delphic Oracle: Its Responses and Operations, with a Catalogue of Responses *(1978). The review provoked a lively public correspondence between the author and myself, with an additional letter from Professor Ernst Badian. In the interests of fairness, and because the discussion seems to me to raise points of general interest, I have printed this correspondence at the conclusion of my essay. Professor Fontenrose continued the debate in private, and I have tried to take account of his later points (where not merely amplification of the public ones) in the body of my essay. I am thinking particularly of the nature of* pneuma, *and of Plutarch's valuable statements on this, on mantic possession, and on the Delphic Oracle in general. In the interests of space I have not reprinted Professor Fontenrose's long and detailed private letter to me, but any reader who would like a copy of it need only send me a stamped addressed envelope. It is pleasant to report that after this exchange Professor Fontenrose and I met, for the first time, in San Francisco and got on famously: I found myself recalling Orwell's charming admission that his polemics against Stephen Spender (or what he thought Spender stood for) became quite impossible once he and Spender had actually got together and taken each other's measure as human beings. The whole episode reinforced my conviction (which I am sure Professor Fontenrose fully shared) that scholarly honesty and disagreement are perfectly compatible with personal friendship.*]

P SYCHOLOGICALLY, DELPHI STOOD at the centre of the Greek world. Geographically, it lies west and north of Athens: just over a hundred miles distant by road, about eighty as the eagle flies, which it does less often nowadays because of noisy tourist traffic and diesel fumes. Ancient pilgrims, hardly less numerous (if differently motivated) than their modern counterparts, lacked those mixed blessings conferred by the internal combustion engine, though their grumbling at local rapacity has a timeless flavour. So does Delphi itself, which, numinous and awesome (the scenery seems to have been a factor in Apollo's choice of venue[1]), has long outlasted all human attempts to channel or domesticate its power. Perched some fifteen hundred feet above the Pleistos Valley, between the twin peaks of Parnassos and the steelblue waters of the Corinthian Gulf, the site possesses a tremendous beauty that ignores rather than defies exploitation. Godhead seems inherent in the landscape: as Georges Roux remarks,[2] 'comme si le dieu n'avait pu rendre ses oracles qu'en un lieu naturellement chargé de puissance divinatoire'. Shimmering with afternoon sunlight, the towering precipice of the Phaedriades cliffs reaches up in close and easy communion with heaven. Water is best, said Pindar, and the Castalian spring, crystalline, eternal, still quickens inspiration. The Pythia drank from the sacred spring before giving utterance.[3] Drawing water seems to have been a regular feature of oracular shrines. Deep under the limestone, seismic forces turn in uneasy sleep. During the three winter months, Dionysus was thought to take over from Apollo. Byron claimed to be disappointed with Delphi. My guess is he was scared.

For over a thousand years, while its reputation and treasures grew, suffered intermittent setbacks, stagnated, and in the end dwindled away through the psychic attrition generated by intellectual scepticism or the rival prophets of Christianity, Delphi's oracular shrine drew generation after generation of consultants, all eager to tap that mysterious *dynamis*, that supranormal power or vision inherent in the *genius loci*. There the Pythia, the priestess of Apollo, seated on a tripod in the *adyton* (inner sanctuary), and attended by cult officials, as well as a crowd of unofficial seers, exegetes, versifiers, and what Roux nicely terms 'professionels parasitaires',[4] would respond to questions as if Apollo himself were answering them. The Delphic *vox dei* guaranteed and sanctioned, as an ultimate authority, anything from the foundation of cities to legislative reforms or the institution of cults, besides pronouncing on a host of lesser personal affairs. The oracle, in short, to quote Roux once more, 'patronnait les notions morales et juridiques sur lesquelles étaient fondés la condition et le comportement de l'homme grec'.[5] In plain utterance, *not* pentecostal babble, the Pythia expressed the god's decisions, which might then be versified by his Delphic exegetes. It is important, for reasons that will become apparent in a moment, to appreciate *ab initio* the enormous moral and civic prestige that Delphi enjoyed, at all levels, during the archaic and classical periods.

Despite natural religious conservatism (which undoubtedly did play a significant role in its history), the Delphic Oracle was anything but a static phenomenon. Indeed, its evolution, and crises, closely reflect the intellectual no less than the spiritual development of the Greeks who consulted it. We are often told – by Professor Fontenrose among others – that Delphi was not in business as a consultative oracle before about 750 BC. Yet the site was occupied from at least the Late Helladic III period (*c.* 1400), and has yielded in some areas a thick crop of Mycenaean votive figurines.[6] Mythology and cult survivals combine to suggest that in the Bronze Age rocky Pytho much resembled archaic or classical Delphi. Apollo was arguably a Mycenaean deity, a thesis not incompatible with the role he plays in Homer. The oracle's period of greatest prestige is said to have begun early in the sixth century, which looks plausible, and to have reached its absolute zenith *c*. 500, shortly before the onset of the Persian Wars. From about the time of Alexander's death in 323 it entered upon an era of steadily declining influence and wealth that continued, despite occasional brief revivals (e.g. under Hadrian) until, in AD 391, Theodosius shut down all oracles and placed a general ban on divination.

With minor modifications, most scholars would accept this general picture. At the same time what we need to know, but are seldom told, is just *why* the graph of the Oracle's success, decline, and ultimate eclipse should have run the way it did. Professor Fontenrose has made an exhaustive study and catalogue of all known oracular responses in *The Delphic Oracle*: but he is not an historian by trade, and this is not the sort of question that gets much of his attention. While it would be unfair to blame him for not doing what he never set out to do, it remains true that his comparative indifference to the historical and evolutionary dimension of the Oracle's operations does tend to handicap him in understanding why, at different periods, things happened as they did. 'The decline', he says offhandedly, 'runs parallel to the decline of the Greek *polis*.' Well, so in a way it does: but this is merely to substitute one aspect of the conundrum for another. The true key to the puzzle surely lies in the rapid, tension-ridden, and spiritually fraught evolution of the Greek intellect from Hesiod's time to that of Aristotle. The mysteries of the universe bear one aspect in the *Works and Days* and quite another in the *Meteorologica* or the *Nicomachean Ethics*: and one measure of the difference between them will undoubtedly have been the attitude of an intelligent man, at each period, to judgments or prospects derived from the utterances of a possibly entranced peasant-priestess sitting on a tripod, over a by-no-means-certain hole in the ground. To map such distinctions is a prime duty of the modern scholar, for which arbitrary identification with the forces of fashionable enlightenment offers no adequate substitute.

The early stages of any society are marked by the propitiation and, where possible, the exploitation of unknown natural or more-than-natural powers, always in uneasy symbiosis with man's own slowly developing control of his environment. Magic and experimental science advance hand in hand, often indistinguishable, setting up their flimsy ring-wall against chaos. As human control widens and is consolidated, the resultant shrinkage of the unknown will curtail divine prerogatives. All weather-gods, for example, are diminished by meteorology. Rationalism, especially of the Sophistic sort, tends to be an addictive drug, its main side-effect hubris, e.g. the Protagorean notion of man as universal yardstick. No accident that the months immediately prior to the outbreak of the Peloponnesian War saw what was 'perhaps the last occasion [but see below, p.109] on which the Delphic Oracle was to be consulted by a Greek state on a major political issue, unconnected with cult or

93

ritual'.[7] Nor was this merely due to the fact that public consultations came a great deal more expensive than private ones. The slow erosion of *polis* power, even before Philip II's victory at Chaeronea in 338, and the subsequent appearance of all-powerful Hellenistic monarchs themselves hedged about with the trappings of divinity, whose will was executed for the most part by mercenaries, all had its effect on the nature, popularity, and prestige of Delphi, which acted as a kind of barometer for the Hellenic world.[8]

Earlier, things had been different. The eighth-century world of Homer and Hesiod, barely emerged from the Dark Ages that followed the collapse of Mycenaean civilisation, and still cherishing a half-forgotten past, with all its totems and taboos, was nevertheless compelled to look outward, to build anew, to colonise, to explore. In this process Delphi became intimately involved, its approval boosting the morale of pioneering city-founders and establishing long-term links with the colonies they set up.[9] The eighth century hung, in terror and excitement, between old myth and new history. The uncharted West was to yield up its rich secrets; the hoary nightmare terrors of the East – beaked griffins and sphinxes, demons cannibal, castrating, incestuous – would, eventually, be tamed and rationalised. But these early pioneers still went in terror of the unknown: the outer world remained strange, baffling, unpredictable, while the gods – only mildly converted, since Homer's *Odyssey*, to moral principles rather than mere inscrutable self-interest – still required to be placated at every turn. In so numinous and arbitrary an atmosphere, with the margin of terrified ignorance still so wide, the oracles provided an essential psychic lifeline:[10]

Without Delphi, Greek society could scarcely have endured the tensions to which it was subjected in the Archaic Age. The crushing sense of human ignorance and human insecurity, the dread of divine *phthonos* [envy, jealousy], the dread of *miasma* [pollution] – the accumulated burden of these things would have been unendurable without the assurance which such an omniscient divine counsellor could give, the assurance that behind the seeming chaos there was knowledge and purpose.

Further, and surprisingly in a people with so marked a gift for conceptual thought, the ultimate realities remained obstinately physical, something to bear in mind when investigating Delphic oracular procedures. Words were winged, while the soul, however rarified, had a tangible essence. Behind it and similar personal abstractions lurked breath, sperm, phlegm, spinal fluid.[11] Chthonian commerce with the underworld was a ritual commonplace (cf. above, pp.66ff.). Through pierced funeral urns, as we saw earlier, libations flowed down to the thirsty dead: and from Ge (Earth) there was said to reach the Delphic Pythia a *pneuma*, something less than wind and more than spirit, intangible yet physical, something that – for lack of a better term – we have to call inspiration. As Parke says,[12] 'the fact was that the ancient world found it extremely difficult to imagine a spiritual force. Inspiration was pictured as being a material and mechanical operation, however fine and subtle the essential spirit which produced it.'

Rational inroads on this world-outlook began early, but took a long while to achieve any substantial effect. The rediscovery of writing came, ironically, at about the same time as the (presumptive) establishment of the Delphic Oracle in its familiar historical form – that is, about 750 BC. What followed – the development of written law-codes, the investigations of the first Milesian physicists, the swing away from tribal to civic institutions, from symbolic to conceptual thought, what we often call, in shorthand, the 'Greek miracle' – for a long while touched only the more progressive upper echelons of society, and even there found a stubborn, unpredictable backlash of emotionally based traditionalism. The intellectual revolution had come too fast for the average psyche to keep up with it, so that archaic patterns of belief and the New Learning pulled devastatingly one against the other, often in the same person, heart against head.

A century earlier, in the time of Solon or Croesus, even under the Peisistratids, traditional piety still remained virtually intact, and the archaic attitude to divinity well-nigh universal. A few intellectual gibes at anthropo-morphism or the gods' immorality, complaints about the new disruptive powers of money – these scarcely constituted an opposition movement. *Nothing in excess*, said Delphi: or, as Alcman put it, don't try to climb the sky, or marry Aphrodite. In this world earth and heaven are still contiguous, numinous, an all-embracing structure bonded by divinity and the prerogatives of blood. This was the universe that received its last late apotheosis from the epinician (victory) odes of Pindar; and in it Delphi's role remained as central as the shrine's sacred stone, the *omphalos* itself, *yin* to the chasm's *yang*, Housman's 'midland navel-stone beside the singing fountain', which stood in the *adyton*, the holy of holies, where the Pythia gave utterance, and marked (or so they said) Delphi as the meeting-point of eagles circling the world. The *adyton's* physical constitution remains baffling – it seems to have had an earth floor, perhaps under a single layer of paving,[13] and to have been a few feet below the level of the rest of the shrine – but as a symbol it could hardly be bettered. Whether it began life as a sacred pit (*bothros*), or even as a Mycenaean tomb, makes little difference to its evident numinous impact.

In 548 the temple was destroyed by fire: the rebuilding was completed by 514, in marble, sumptuously beyond the terms of their contract, by the Athenian Alcmaeonids. It is during this period that we hear about the 'Delphic maxims' – 'Nothing in excess', 'Know yourself', 'Go bail and ruin is nigh'. Parke's comment is apt: 'The oracle had developed in moral stature. In the seventh century it had stressed blood-guilt and ritual purification: in the sixth it was going further into the question of individual responsibility and the consciousness of one's limitations.'[14] Yet it was in 546 that the Oracle received what is generally held (wrongly, I think, on reflection) to have been a severe psychological setback in the political field. This was in the matter of Croesus, king of Lydia, who ruled from his capital, Sardis, in what is now northwestern Turkey.

However much of Croesus' dealing with Delphi we are prepared to write off as *post eventum* fabrication (a game that has been played to excess), his lavish offerings to the Oracle – and to several other 'prestigious Greek sanctuaries', as Professor Fontenrose says, all, though he omits to mention this, also oracular centres – are an undoubted fact (Herodotus [15] describes them in detail, clearly as an eyewitness) and need to be explained. Though Professor Fontenrose would like to regard them as simply part of a generalised effort to curry favour with the Greek states (which would imply political unity of a kind unknown at the time: why should Athens or Corinth care what a barbarian monarch spent on Pytho?), even he has to concede that Croesus 'may very well have consulted the Oracle'. Nor can there be much doubt about the topics of his consultation, which were anything but mundane. Croesus wanted an alliance with Sparta, and, more important, he had ambitions to conquer the Persian empire: not for nothing did he lay out two gold staters as a present for every Delphian. It seems clear that the Pythia gave him encouragement (whether equivocal or not) on both counts, though the nature of that encouragement has been misunderstood (not least by Croesus himself) and should really be viewed as a nice specific demonstration of the two most famous Delphic maxims. Croesus, having been told that if he crossed the Halys River into Persian-held territory he would destroy a great empire, duly did just that on both counts. He suffered a shattering defeat and capture by Cyrus (546 BC): his Lydian empire collapsed overnight.

Herodotus' demonstration[16] that Croesus himself bore sole responsibility for his fate may have relieved those who found the Oracle's ambiguity unsettling;[17] but I very much doubt whether the Delphic authorities were among them. Croesus' character had been tested, and found wanting. He had certainly acted in excess, proving himself a classic overreacher. He had been found singularly lacking in self-knowledge, since he had committed the elementary error of pushing the evidence in the direction he wanted it to go. Not only did he destroy a great empire, thus fulfilling the oracle, but learned, the hard way, some unwelcome truths about himself. Delphi had seen through him precisely as Solon did: he was the millionaire who both believed wealth to be the *summum bonum*, and used it indiscriminately to bludgeon golden opinions out of the world. The spirit of his offering was scrutinised by the god, and found, correctly, to have been no more than a common bribe. He duly reaped his reward. The oracle was, at one level, a very shrewd summing-up of the odds – in this case, the clear realisation that the forthcoming conflict would be decisive one way or the other, that there would be no stand-off, that one side or the other would be totally destroyed. But it also, as I have suggested, read the flaws in Croesus' psyche all too well. Delphi, in short, had no cause whatsoever for worry: indeed, the Oracle had provided a salutary object-lesson for rich patrons everywhere.

This *démarche* over Croesus has been credited with more influence on the subsequent policy (if we can call it that) of the Delphic priesthood than it in fact ever exerted. If anything, the Pythia's credibility was enhanced: Herodotus for one knew a good moral lesson when he saw it, and we have no reason to suppose that Apollo's priestess was any less percipient. It is true, of course, that as a result of Cyrus' victory Delphi (like the Greek world generally) developed a firm and lasting conviction of Persian military invincibility, and that this was to play no small part in determining the oracles received by the Greeks at the time of Xerxes' invasion in 480. Realistic assessment was the name of the game: an Athenian victory at Marathon in 490 made no difference to the perception of overwhelming Persian superiority a decade later, while between Salamis and Plataea the odds had changed dramatically, so that Delphi's pronouncements now became more optimistic. The interesting thing is that its earlier pessimism in no way diminished Greek faith in its oracular powers, which suggests that modern students may have seriously misunderstood its functional role in Hellenic society. Two other points made about the oracular response to Croesus – that it reinforced the progressive shift of emphasis at Delphi away from political involvement to more purely religious or private topics, and that it called in question Delphi's traditional trump card, i.e. the gift of prophecy – I am now very much inclined to doubt. The falling-off of public consultation was an undoubted fact, but (as we have seen) it had ample historical reasons without invoking as *prophasis* Delphi's sound advice to a hubristic sixth-century Lydian king: and as far as prophecy went, the forecast received by Croesus was as accurate as any. If he chose to misread it, that was his affair.

Far more important was the fact that the fate of Croesus, as Herodotus well knew, dramatised two problems that much concerned the Greeks of his day: the relationship between an individual's actions and his destiny, and the whole question (by 430 a hotly debated issue) of belief in oracles as such, a debate crystallised by the contrasting attitudes of Herodotus and Thucydides.[18] Professor Fontenrose wants to relegate the issue of prophecy and prediction entirely to popular legend, an attempt I find unconvincing: but he has to concede that the chresmologues (expounders of oracles) *did* make guesses about the future, and sometimes their guesses came unstuck. Aristophanes[19] lampoons the breed mercilessly: the Sophists had done their anticlerical work all too well. By the late fifth century diviners *et hoc genus omne* were coming in for a good deal of public ridicule: particularly galling, after all the optimistic ballyhoo of the oracle-mongers, had been the total failure of the Sicilian Expedition.[20] By no means all the criticism now came from intellectuals. It is, though, an index of Delphi's enormous and unique prestige how little the shrine was affected by this movement.

Even so, for believers (who still constituted the majority) problems that had been around ever since Xenophanes' mocking assault on anthropomorphism now became acute. Could Apollo deceive those who trusted him?[21] Were Aeschylus' Cassandra, or the *Ion* of Euripides, to be taken seriously in their bitter accusations against the god? Did not justice, piety and generosity

97

bring, inevitably, their own meritorious reward? To such a question, as we know from Hesiod, the Archaic Age had returned a dusty, and realistic, answer: but post-Sophistic meliorism had bred, as so often happens, a touching faith in the validity of good intentions. Reading the Delphic apologia that Herodotus preserves, with its clear verdict on Croesus as a self-promoting and greedy adventurer solely responsible for his own grim fate, we sense the relief that such a verdict must have brought to the faithful. We may also reflect that whoever else had been bowled over by the trendy excitements of the New Learning, Apollo, cultural figurehead though he was, most certainly had not. Delphi's morality remained refreshingly archaic: to conservatives that was one of its biggest draws. Modern scholars may argue that the Croesus episode was a case of what later Greek mathematicians and astronomers called 'saving the appearances';[22] the faithful knew better.

That there were occasions, not least during the Persian Wars, when Delphi *did*, arguably, try to save the appearances does not necessarily, or even probably (see below, p.106), imply conscious cynicism and fraud. This seems to me an important point, and one which Professor Fontenrose, like many other modern scholars, does not always fully appreciate. Indeed it is striking how seldom, throughout its long and chequered history, we find any suggestion of deliberate charlatanism on the part of the Oracle's representatives. Not even the early Church Fathers bring such a charge.[23] They could, and did, regard the Pythia's utterances as diabolically inspired, even as induced through a vaginal penetration by the *pneuma*, but never as merely fraudulent. This Apollo was no mere straw adversary. When the Spartan king Cleomenes I suborned the Pythia for his own advancement (491 BC) this episode remained a scandalous exception to the rule, and was always treated as such. No one, it is safe to say, was surprised when Cleomenes came to a bad end, committing suicide in a fit of insanity.

As Dodds says,[24] 'the rarity of open scepticism about Delphi before the Roman period is very striking', and this could hardly have been the case, century after century, had the operation of the Oracle depended on mere human manipulation and trickery. Apart from the occasional late Epicurean or Cynic, the proponents of this theory of deliberate fraud have, for the most part, been rationalising academics, whose *parti pris* position too often produces facile misinterpretation of the evidence, those written accounts of allegedly contemporary statements that have come down to us. It is worth remembering (to quote Dodds again, ibid.) that 'anyone familiar with the history of modern spiritualism will realise what an amazing amount of virtual cheating can be done in perfectly good faith by convinced believers'. To picture the Delphic priesthood as a group of sophisticated political propagandists manipulating some hypothetical Mediterranean intelligence network seriously misrepresents the climate in which Delphi operated, and Professor Fontenrose (even though he does it for all the wrong reasons) is surely right to dismiss such a theory out of hand. Nor would anyone argue with his assertion (p.165) that 'there was a good deal of pious fraud in the gathering and keeping of oracle collections: and there was a good deal of credulity and superstition in the popular acceptance of circulating oracles'. This will not do, though, as an argument for dismissing any inconvenient Delphic pronouncement with the assertion that it originated outside, and was then foisted on Apollo – an *ersatz* prophetic cuckoo in the Delphic nest – by some unscrupulous seer.

The persistent ambivalence of even intellectual fifth-century Greeks to supernatural phenomena can be documented from a variety of sources. As late as 413 BC (following a much-publicised war of rival oracles pro and con the expedition as such) Nicias lost an army in Sicily by refusing to retreat for twenty-seven days after a lunar eclipse. Socrates himself was not above giving the young Xenophon – who, eager to enlist under Cyrus the Younger, wanted the stamp of oracular approval for his venture – a quick, and perfectly serious, lesson on the proper way to frame a question for the Pythia.[25] Xenophon, in effect, had forced a card with his enquiry, since he wanted to know to which gods he should pray and sacrifice in order to complete his journey and return home unscathed. Apollo duly told him to which gods he should sacrifice, but promised nothing. Socrates, on learning of this, made the obvious comment that in fact Xenophon should have asked the god whether it was better for him to go or stay, rather than deciding that issue for himself. The exchange must have remained at the back of Xenophon's mind, an ironic comment on human wishful thinking, during his long slog north from Cunaxa to the Black Sea.

The general picture that emerges, then, is one of genuine faith, on the part of consultants and priesthood alike, set against a slow attrition of the overall sphere in which that faith operated. Man-the-measure-of-all-things would (as we can see in the pages of Thucydides) increasingly apply his reason to matters political and strategical without taking any account of divine guidance. Though Delphi appears not to have lost any immediate prestige as a direct consequence of oracular tergiversations during the Persian Wars[26] – as we have seen (above, p.97), there may have been perfectly sound reasons for this – it is hard not to infer that the Pythia's unlucky long-term second-guessing at so famous a crisis in Greek history must have led, inevitably, to a mood of cautious separation from power-politics. Statesmen, for their part, began to develop a more Protagorean streak of self-reliance in their military or diplomatic manoeuvres, thus reinforcing the current intellectual trend. Henceforth public affairs and direct predictions – especially in combination – began to disappear from Delphi's repertoire. There were exceptions. The practice of 'neutralising' a territory by getting the Pythia to recognise it as 'non-plunderable' (*asylon*, hence 'asylum'), i.e. as a demilitarised zone protected by its sanctity, a nice application of cult to political strategy, long remained popular. The real decline of the Oracle began under Roman domination. The Romans had their own divination system,[27] and were not, by and large, interested in Greek oracles. Competition also developed from astrologers (*mathematici*), spiritualists, do-it-yourself mediums who required no tripod, and adepts of Graeco-Egyptian magic.

It is of the greatest possible interest to check all these presumptive trends against the exhaustive analytical statistics of Delphic responses that Professor Fontenrose has amassed in *The Delphic Oracle*, and which – particularly in the subdivision by topics and themes – constitute by far its most valuable feature. A perusal of these tables confirms virtually all the patterns noted above. Professor Fontenrose summarises the situation with characteristically succinct precision:[28]

The Historical responses that survive tend to show not only that the Delphic shrine's pronouncements, *from 450 BC at latest* [my italics], were pretty much confined to sanctions of laws and proposals, particularly on religious subjects, and to prescriptions of cult acts; and that exceptions, if any, were safe statements which anybody could make; but also that the responses often had the same form as the question, which was expressed in one of two or three stereotyped forms. Not one can be considered an extraordinary utterance.

He reinforces his arguments with parallel responses from the oracle at Didyma, to which he might have appended some of the inscriptions on lead found at Dodona, where the oracle spoke for Zeus.[29] The revision and reappraisal of this vast mass of diverse material is a fine achievement (though on the epigraphical side already a trifle outdated): scholars who may or may not agree with Professor Fontenrose's conclusions, or even with his categories, will nevertheless be consulting his quadripartite Catalogue of Responses – Historical, Quasi-Historical, Legendary and Fictional – for many years to come. The second volume of H. W. Parke and D. E. W. Wormell's *The Delphic Oracle*, entitled *Oracular Responses* (1956) covers virtually the same ground, and avoids Fontenrose's rigid classification system; but it includes as genuine much material that even the moderately credulous would reject as spurious, and is even more out-of-date regarding inscriptions.

Many of Professor Fontenrose's tables are historically most suggestive (though one feels this wasn't why they were compiled in the first instance). Take, for instance, Table X (p. 54), sub-headed 'Occasions of Quasi-Historical Consultations'. From this we can deduce that after the mid-fifth century (dates are conspicuous by their absence here) plague and famine have been brought under some kind of control, a wider range of recourses, whether physical or psychosomatic (e.g. the temples of Asclepios), exist for the sick, exile is recognised as being due to political machinations rather than the hand of God, war remains an imponderable, portents and prodigies still have their effect on the superstitious majority; few cities are being founded – the blank spaces on the map have retreated beyond the confines of the Mediterranean – but interstate problems remain insoluble (what wouldn't we give today for oracular responses on Iran or Nicaragua?). In general, it would seem from this evidence, the god and his oracle have suffered a slump as regards the affairs of this world, but retain a bullish reputation over the divine imponderables of cult, worship, and theology. As for private consultation, the improper desire to treat the Pythia as a substitute for Ann Landers appears no greater in historical times than at any previous period. It is all extremely plausible.

Yet, despite everything, I found myself, on first and second reading, entering worried caveats against both the incidental methods and, on occasion, the underlying assumptions of this brilliant and idiosyncratic monograph. Professor Fontenrose is, to begin with, a rationalist of the most convinced sort, and as we know from a distinguished fellow-mythologist,[30] 'it is a property of your rationalist that he is unable to understand any type of mind other than his own', an apothegm which often recurred to my mind while studying the Fontenrose version of Delphic history. Indeed, so hot is the author against anything that might even remotely smack of superstition or the occult (which he dismisses, as a theory, in one casual phrase) that he is sometimes led to administer a brisk flogging to some hapless academic horse long since relegated to the scholarly glue-factory. Too many of his cockshies have been knocked down already, so that he is reduced, in a fine rationalist frenzy, to pelting them on the ground. He even seems anxious to convince us that Apollo was not a sun-god, and I can't think, offhand, of any serious scholar who has believed *that* since the high old days of W.H. Roscher. At times, too, the arguments are disingenuous: an attack on Dodds' theory of mediumship for the Pythia ignores the fact that Dodds, no less than Fontenrose, makes a clear distinction between Apollonian 'mantic' (i.e. prophetic) enthusiasm and irrational Dionysiac frenzy.

It is also noticeable that some of Professor Fontenrose's stylistic and topical categorising (never mind the reductionism) seems a little inconsistent. 'Folkloristic' motifs are a sure sign, for him, of spuriousness, however many oracles embodying such features are firmly credited to Delphi by early, and major, literary sources. The distinction, however, enables him to sequester all early oracles in a separate 'popular' category, which can then be disregarded as not only spurious and ahistorical, but also as *non-Delphic*. He puts, similarly, much reliance on the standard introductory formula for 'historical' oracles as an indication of genuineness, what an ancient author would have termed a *sphragis*: but this formula, unfortunately, also shows up in some 'legendary' or 'quasi-historical' examples. Marcia Dobson pointed out,[31] correctly, that on this showing the oracle reported by Herodotus (5.82) as having been given to the Epidaurians *c.* 625 BC (Fontenrose's Q63) 'either . . . cannot be genuine because it is folkloristic and anachronistic [Fontenrose's choice], or its formulaic coding would prove it authentic'. Noel Robertson declared, even more bluntly:[32] 'The equation of "historical" and authentic is stultifying . . . Fontenrose argues from apples to oranges.'

Since the exemplary French excavation reports on Apollo's temple at Delphi, advocates of mysterious rocky chasms and mephitic vapours have been few and far between (the vapours themselves, amusingly enough, may well have begun their toxic life as the brain-children of ancient rationalisers, anxious to offer a credible explanation of how Delphi *worked*: cf. above, p.98).[33] Yet the foundation legend of the goatherd who became 'inspired' on the site, and is clearly envisaged as having inhaled fumes of some sort, like an unwary vintner among the wine-vats – his goats got stoned too – points to something more physical, less symbolic.[34] The Pythia, Professor Fontenrose assures us, spoke coherently and 'was not seized with a frenzy'; few today would argue that she was. The metaphor of inspiration, however, is still there to remind us of its origins. What it commemorates are all those mysterious substances – opium and hashish among the oldest – that since time immemorial men have drawn into their lungs like smoke to stimulate visions and illuminate the brain. Perhaps the question of the Pythia's condition must remain undecided. But I do not think the possibility of drug-assisted *enthousiasmos* should be discarded altogether. Best, in the circumstances, to see what can be made of the evidence offered by reliable eyewitnesses, which is not much.

Plutarch, in fact, is the only surviving ancient author whom we know to have had first-hand experience of Delphi, and to have written about what he saw. His statements concerning the Oracle and its operation should therefore be studied with some care. The two main essays in which he discusses oracular matters are the *De Pythiae Oraculis* ('On the Oracles of Delphi', *Mor.* 394D-409D) and the *De defectu Oraculorum* ('On the Obsolescence of Oracles', *Mor.* 409E-438E). At the turn of the first and second centuries AD, when he was writing, Apollo had clearly lost a good deal of his prestige; but of this fact Plutarch is very conscious, and often draws sad contrasts between past and present. Oracular utterances, he says, are now marked by poverty of diction, verbal slovenliness, and metrical errors (396C-D). They are also (402B) now given in prose, a fact taken by one of the characters in Plutarch's dialogue as a sign of non-inspiration, of Apollo's absence. Plutarch cites Herakleitos (*c.* 500 BC) for the Sibyl's 'unembellished' (*akallópista*) words enduring, through the god, for a thousand years (a citation nowhere mentioned in Professor Fontenrose's study). The implication cannot be missed: once the Sibyl was literate, or at least endowed with the literacy of Apollo; but today her utterances have lost their ancient staying-power.

It is further emphasised (cf. p.97) that prophecy is indeed the Pythia's proper function, a claim that promptly elicits a barrage of ridicule from Plutarch's interlocutor Boëthus (398F-399A). *Inter alia* Boëthus cites a famous tag from Euripides,[35] to the effect that 'the best prophet is the shrewd guesser'. To Boëthus' scepticism a second participant in the discussion, Sarapion, responds (399B-E) with a list of prophecies allegedly fulfilled: once again prognostication is assumed to be Delphi's main function. Yet another discutant, Theon, cites Herakleitos once more for the pregnant statement that Delphic Apollo neither speaks plain nor conceals, but offers signs (*semainei*), an unexpectedly modern perception.[36] He also comments on the later removal of obscurity and introduction of clear speaking (406E-F), a passage which precisely fits the transition from archaism to classicism. Formerly, Theon argues (407A-B), circumlocution and mystery were revered as manifestations of divine power. Later, however, a more sophisticated public looked for precise information, and came to suspect metaphors and riddles as bolt-holes for prophetic error. Most disrepute was produced (407C, cf. Aristoph. *Birds* 968 ff.) by itinerant oracle-mongers conning 'servants and women' with charlatanry and false predictions. Theon also emphasises, correctly, that in early times 'powerful states and monarchs and tyrants' (407D) consulted the shrine on political matters, and that it was this made *double entendre* necessary, since it was unadvisable to provoke such potentates to hostility with unpalatable truths, and 'there were things that it was as well for tyrants not to know, and enemies not to learn in advance' (407E). This ambiguity of response, firmly linked by Professor Fontenrose to folklore, is in fact associated with Delphic Apollo by almost every major literary figure of the fifth century.

Theon goes on to remark that the more commonplace subjects of consultation tend to take place in times of peace and tranquillity, with the clear implication that more serious public appeals are equated with periods of crisis. This, again, is just what we might expect. The weakness and desolation of oracles in Plutarch's own lifetime is specifically contrasted (412A) with their vigour and high repute during the Persian Wars, a claim to bear in mind when one is tempted (as one so often is) to draw parallels between Delphi's tacking and veering – collaboration, some would call it – during Xerxes' invasion and the pro-Nazi pieties of Radio Vichy after 1940. Now, we learn – that is, about AD 100 – people not only pester the god with enquiries (413B) about 'treasure-trove or legacies or illegal marriages', but put him to the test with 'shameful and ungodly' trick questions. Depopulation (413F-414B) is offered as a rather feeble excuse for the fall-off in oracular maintenance.

But the most important evidence is that concerning the actual process of divination by the Pythia. The voice is that of the priestess, not the god ventriloquising (414E, 404B), much less inserting himself in some mysterious way into the Pythia's body, a vulgar notion to which the vapour theory might well have seemed preferable.[37] Diction and metre are also the property, as it were, of the priestess. After delivering her utterance, and 'leaving the tripod and pneuma'[38] – which again suggests a *localisation* of inspiration – the priestess apparently came off a high, like Corybantic revellers, says Plutarch, when the music changes rhythm, relaxing into a state of peaceful calm. What was her prior state if not possession of some sort? Apollo, however, 'provides her only with the visions, and makes a light in her soul as regards the future',[39] a useful distinction, and not contradicted by talk of 'incorporating the god once a month in a human body' (398A).

Inspiration, as Herakleitos makes clear, popular suppositions to the contrary, no more involves delirium than did the infinitely crafted poetry-making of Pindar or Dylan Thomas. Yet there remains that elusive *pneuma* to consider.

Plutarch refers to it as *anathymiasis*, 'exhalation', while at the same time (433A) claiming that it has some kinship with the soul. This supposition would suggest that he thought of it as inspiration: but it also seems to be physical, a kind of random gas occurring sporadically (433C-E), sometimes strong, sometimes weak, and perhaps subject, like springs after earthquakes, to blockage or change of location (434B-C), an argument probably evoked by its palpable absence in Plutarch's own day. Yet another speaker, Ammonius, pooh-poohs the dependence of prophecy on 'some particular state of the air or its currents' (435B); but students of ritual pollution (*miasma*) will know how indivisible a nexus existed in classical times between the physical and the moral or spiritual, how *miasma* was seen as an infection, an epidemic in the air, that could attack body or soul indifferently, and in precisely the same way. An identical teasing ambiguity clouds every discussion of Delphic *pneuma*. Perhaps in the last resort the exhalation/inspiration dichotomy is meaningless, the retrojection of modern categories onto an archaic outlook which made no real distinction between the two concepts. Plutarch's use of the word *atmos* (steam, vapour) does, even so, have obstinately physical connotations. One does feel a certain sympathy for Professor Fontenrose when he claims that 'the most certain statement about Delphic procedure is that the Pythia sat upon a tripod when under the god's inspiration she spoke his oracles'.

It may, however, be more useful to examine Professor Fontenrose's *vue d'ensemble* than to pile up further criticism on points of detail, which he has already collected from reviewers in the classical journals, a breed prone by nature to concentrate on the trees rather than the wood.[40] The most remarkable conclusion he reaches, so remarkable that he feels constrained to defend it at length in his final summing-up, is that, to quote his own words, 'the results of this study demand a rejection as non-genuine of almost all responses said to have been spoken in the first three centuries of the Delphic Oracle, roughly 750-450'. *Almost all*? The first *three centuries*? In other words, the entire period during which, as we have seen, Delphi operated in conditions of maximum belief – involved, as never afterwards, in the total continuum of Greek awareness and faith – is here relegated at a stroke to the negligible vulgar grab-bag of fantasy and legend. How, one wonders, are we then to explain Delphi's massive moral ascendency in this period as the source of unimpeachable legislative and ethical arbitration?

The arguments and statistics by which this end is achieved range from the brilliant to the circular. Consider this example. Professor Fontenrose first suggests (what is quite possible) that some narratives have had oracles inserted into them by story-tellers in the course of time. Not, I would have thought, a very common practice, but let that pass. He then proceeds (p. 108): 'And some quasi-historical – or pseudo-historical – narratives set within the centuries after 800 may contain oracles called Delphic *when first told* [italics mine]. So in both traditional legends, when told in the historical period, and in later narratives, storytellers and writers *introduced oracles* [italics mine] as pronouncements of the Delphic god.' The occasional insertion has become widespread if not universal practice. By such devices the evidence for the days of Delphi's true glory is discounted. What I find most striking is the sheer passion and ingenuity with which Professor Fontenrose contrives to jettison almost everything except the mundane, the unremarkable, the explicable, the trite, the commonplace. Was it for *this* that Croesus and the Greek cities laid out such wildly munificent offerings, that official delegates thronged each monthly session of the Pythia, that poets and philosophers celebrated Apollo's dark utterances? Is it really conceivable that for three hundred years such dull and quotidian responses not only satisfied the clients but somehow bred a wholly different, *and false*, literary tradition? Even granted that major political consultations were rare, and that the bulk of the business handled dealt with everyday matters, did *no* great crisis ever strike a prophetic spark from the Pythia to match the poets' vision of her? How, for that matter, did Herodotus' Athenian audience so readily believe, on previous experience, in the genuineness of the oracles he retailed?

Professor Fontenrose claims to have followed exclusively objective criteria: but the more one looks at his categories, the clearer it becomes that he has, perhaps unconsciously, set up a working model in which the only responses recognised as historical are, almost by definition, those that avoid any taint of ambiguity, second sight, or supernatural knowledge: as he says, 'simple commands and statements, none requiring uncommon foresight or cleverness', so that the whole archaic history of this extraordinary institution prior to the mid-fifth century can be treated with the same kind of patronising and dismissive contempt that Victorian missionaries reserved for, say, Haitian voodoo. Historically, to look no further, this is misleading in the extreme. It suggests, *inter alia*, that the only response of Greek writers to three centuries of Delphic involvement in city-state affairs was a stream of imaginative and disregardable drivel, bearing no relation to the facts.

Since a large proportion of the *testimonia* that have survived does indeed – like most ancient historical evidence – need correction for retrospective special pleading or incidental propaganda, such wholesale dismissal can be made to look speciously attractive. For some scholars, too, as we have seen (above, p. 22), radical scepticism is the name of the game: they thrive on forgeries, interpolations, and misattributed MSS. It is clear – and Plato (*Rep.* 427B) confirms this – that very many consultations *did* have to do with 'foundations of cults, sacrifices, and other worship of gods, daimones, and heroes'. Spurious colonising oracles *do* need weeding out. Folklore motifs *have* crept into the tradition. So (though far less often than some would like to believe) have forgeries, as Herodotus (7.6) was well aware. Over the Persian War prophecies, however, even Professor Fontenrose is forced to admit the unlikelihood, in such a public case, 'that anyone could successfully circulate these oracles as Delphic if they were not; for elder Athenians would presumably have known that they were false'. Just so. 'If they be rejected as completely unhistorical,' he continues (p. 126), 'then the whole story of Themistokles' interpretation . . . (that the wooden walls were ships) has to be removed from history.' Yet this doesn't stop him making great play with Athens' supposed lack of archives and media – even though elsewhere he shows himself well aware that the Peisistratids and the Spartan kings, to look no further, accumulated collections of oracles, of which the interest was not, one supposes, limited to cult-practices and queries about legacies.

The Persian war oracles, Professor Fontenrose says, if authentic, 'are extraordinary and unusual pronouncements'. So they are, and not surprisingly: it was one of the most extraordinary and unusual crises in all Greek history that called them forth. On such an occasion Apollo could, one might hope, at least offer something better than a merely routine response. It is interesting, too, that in 479 the *Persians* took Delphi's increasingly pro-Hellenic utterances seriously enough to try (without success, it would seem) to sign up a sympathetic counter-oracle of their own. Whether the hexameter texts that Herodotus reproduces represent the Pythia's *ipsissima verba* may be open to doubt, and Professor Fontenrose has some sensible remarks on the prevalence of prose responses; but they surely were Delphic productions. If (to take a personal example) I was capable, at the age of sixteen, of turning passages of Shakespearian blank verse into very passable Greek iambics, it should not have been beyond the powers of the Oracle's secretariat to work prose into a pastiche of Homer. There may well have been officials whose special job this was. To go further and doubt the veracity of these pronouncements altogether, as Professor Fontenrose would clearly like to do, suggests a fundamental lack of historical perspective. That, in the last resort, is what is wrong with his carefully researched, pragmatic, and in so many ways ultra-sensible book: it cannot see beyond the mode of historical perception that it is prepared to accept as real (cf. below, pp. 120ff.). If Professor Fontenrose had been dealing with, say, a Catholic historian of the Renaissance, he would have a ready pejorative label for that sort of thing: dogma. As it is, he comes closer than he realises to those earnest Stoic dummies who figure so prominently in Plutarch's essays on Delphi: who in their highminded way try to explain everything intellectually, and end up making the whole operation sound like a presidential fireside chat. It is useful, and necessary, to have scholars who make it their critical business to scrape off the accretions from site or topic. With Delphi, as with the Acropolis, the process is highly revealing; but in both cases much of value may be jettisoned along with the expendable detritus. The oracles (*pace* Milton) were perhaps not so dumb after all.

Professor Fontenrose wrote:

Peter Green finds much that is valuable in *The Delphic Oracle*, but disagrees on central issues, primarily on what responses reported for the archaic period we can consider authentic. The matter boils down to this: can we accept the responses reported by Herodotos as genuine pronouncements of the Pythia? These responses are mostly very different from the Historical responses (those that have contemporary attestation). No verifiable response of any oracular establishment, past or present, is anything like those that Herodotos reports for Delphi; it is always more like those that I classify as Historical. Therefore Green and others who want to save the appearances must demonstrate that the oracles which Herodotos quotes are authentic, in substance if not in form. Inspirational talk about archaic Delphi won't do; we must have evidence that is cogent, not circular argument. The case for trusting Herodotos' reports cannot be made from those reports alone. That is what Green does. He asserts two crises in response to which the Delphic Oracle changed its modes. First it gave Croesus assurance of victory, and he was defeated. Thereafter the Delphians considered the Persians invincible and so discouraged opposing them when Xerxes invaded in 480. But the Greeks defeated the Persians at Salamis and Plataea. So the Delphians gave up prediction as a bad job and spoke only safe directions and statements. That is, Green deduces the crises of the Oracle from Herodotos' accounts and then uses the crises to verify the accounts. Furthermore we should notice that ten years before Salamis the Athenians and Plataeans routed the Persians at Marathon. Why did the Delphians continue to think them invincible?

To speak of 'three centuries of Delphic involvement in city-state affairs' (the archaic period) is simply to reassert the conventional view. How much 'involvement' is demonstrable? Even in the Quasi-Historical responses Delphi seldom takes the initiative. In reality, men went to Delphi for sanctions and directions, believing in the Pythian Apollo's special authority at his sacred shrine. Zeus' Oracle at Dodona was as highly esteemed as the Delphic throughout Greek history, although consultants received only yes/no answers or the name of a god to sacrifice to, determined by lot or a similar device.

Professor Green says that in respect to the Pythia's frenzy, vapours, and chasm I am flogging dead horses. He has misapplied the metaphor: a flogger of a dead horse is trying to make the horse get up and go, not punishing a horse that he thinks alive. Green asks, 'Who, today, would argue that [the Pythia] was [seized with a frenzy]?' Well, look at Robert Flacelière's *Greek Oracles* (1965), p. 50: 'All our sources confirm that when the Pythia was prophesying she was in a state of frenzy.' None of them does (unless one says that Lucan confirms this), but Flacelière has written on Delphic subjects for forty years, and he mentions 'noxious fumes' on the same page. Not only that, he says in the same book that 'Phoebus Apollo . . . was also the sun-god' (p. 35). Green says that I seem 'anxious to convince [readers] that Apollo was not a sun god' (also a dead horse), although I mention this matter only incidentally in the preface as an example of outdated beliefs that persist even among classical scholars. And it does persist.

Contemporary scholars like Dodds and Parke attribute possession or trance, if not frenzy (and this is a product of possession), to the Pythia, although Plutarch, a Delphic priest, says plainly that Apollo did not speak with the Pythia's vocal chords: she spoke in her own words, reflecting the truth that Apollo revealed to her. Green apparently accepts possession, as well as a physical *pneuma* and a chasm (although he asserts that 'advocates of rocky chasms . . . have been few and far between'): he mentions a chasm (the omphalos was '*yin* to the chasm's *yang*', whatever that means – it sounds fine), and the hole over which the Pythia sat (a figment of fantasy).

I was careless when I set Dodds beside Rohde for the idea that the Dionysiac cult at Delphi inspired the alleged mediumship of the Pythia. There my topic is her supposed possession, and I should not have run it together with Dionysiac influence. I quote Dodds: '. . . Apollo's Delphic utterances are always couched in the first person, never in the third.' I then show that in many responses the Pythia refers to Apollo in the third person: Dodds made an incautious statement. This was my criticism of Dodds, not what Green says it was. Dodds does distinguish between mantic and telestic (Dionysiac) *mania*, but the possession that he posits for the Pythia is Dionysiac; it is not the mantic *manikê* of Plato, which is not so described and is largely a play on words.

In fact, Green often misrepresents what I have to say or credits me with something that I have not said. For example, the reader of his review will suppose that I have imputed fraud and cynicism to the Delphic priesthood. In fact, I make it clear from the outset that I do not; I never mention it and it should be plain that I consider fraud unnecessary for the sort of response actually spoken.

It seems that I am a rationalist, showing 'a fine rationalist frenzy', but after reading the review one may ask, 'Who's in a frenzy now?' Green's is an obscurantist frenzy, an outburst of that Delphic piety of which I speak in my preface. In his remarks on my objective criteria, which he denies are objective, he confuses 'historical', as I define the term, with 'authentic'. An Historical response, in my classification, is simply one spoken within the lifetime of the earliest authority who reports it.

Green ends up granting that Herodotos' oracles may not be the Pythia's *ipsissima verba*, though he starts by accepting them as quoted. When all is said, he does no more than reassert the conventional view of the Delphic Oracle's utterances and operations. He does not come to grips with the evidence that I present for my conclusions; and I am afraid that a reader of the review will not learn much about the book's content. I expect more of the same kind of thing. As I say in my preface, 'I am aware that my argument, however well-founded, will not prevail against the will to believe'.

Professor Badian wrote:

May I add a note in amplification of Peter Green's excellent and much-needed discussion of the background to the disappearance of political prophecy and advice from the repertoire of the Delphic Oracle?

First, his insistence on the fact that what has seemed to rationalist interpreters politically motivated did not seem so to contemporaries and very probably was never consciously so can be confirmed by the observation that the 'victims' of that supposed motivation (the Greeks in 480, the Athenians after 431, to mention only the most obvious) never protested, in fact went on consulting the Oracle as a matter of course. Modern parallels may be illuminating. Historians writing about our own age in a more 'rationalist' future may well conclude that the modern equivalents of the Delphic Oracle – in particular, economists and the queer fish who swim in 'think-tanks' – base their political predictions and advice on personal and political prejudice. Nonetheless, we know that this is not the common perception: however often the predictions and advice turn out to be wrong, the faithful come back for more and pay heavy tribute for it. And it is clear to any unprejudiced observer that, whatever unconscious prejudice may (and often does) enter into the oracular predictions obtained from inspired computers, the men and women concerned in fact see themselves as conscientiously applying their science according to recognized principles –

just as the priests and the Pythia did. The dissociation of the past from present reality here, as elsewhere, has made for very bad history.

There is perhaps a footnote to be added, against the background that Peter Green has sketched for us. (It is not intended as an alternative but as a supplement.) It may be argued that, within that cultural framework, the political activity of the Oracle came to a stop when its politicization became deliberate and patent. It did not stop in 431: far from it. As late as 371 BC, the Thebans consulted the Oracle (and all others they could think of) before risking resistance to Sparta. And in one of the most extraordinary documents surviving from the fourth century BC, we find Philip II of Macedon and the Chalcidic League led by Olynthus consulting the Oracle in 357/6 on whether they should make peace and on what terms. (The Oracle approved. A few years later, Philip was ready to attack and destroy Olynthus. Needless to say, it has often been maintained that the Oracle was trying to aid Philip in 357/6, but this is totally implausible.) It was in 356 that the Thebans controlling a majority of votes on the venerable Amphictyonic Council that governed the Temple, began to use that control to have their enemies condemned of sacrilege. One result was that a Phocian commander, himself among the victims, seized Delphi in 356 and began to use its funds for Phocian military purposes. The Amphictyonic Council, separated from the actual sanctuary, declared a 'Sacred War', which lasted for ten years, and in that 'Great Schism' between Delphi and its governing body religious issues were soon all but irrelevant and the Greek states divided according to political and military interest. In the end, Philip II gained control of Delphi and reunited it with the Council, which he also came to control; and after years of complicated manoeuvring, in 339 BC he used the pretext of leading another 'Sacred War' in order to launch the offensive that led to his victory at Chaeronea and his domination over the Greeks.

Legend connects Philip and Alexander with many favourable oracles from Delphi. But political acceptance of the good faith and 'science' of the interpreters of Apollo is last attested precisely before the events of 356–338: the 'Great Schism' and its consequences, which made it clear that both the Oracle and its Governing Council had become a piece of political machinery.

To these letters I replied as follows:

Professor Fontenrose's categories are a kind of card-forcing. His 'Historical' category, however much he may hedge his bets over authenticity, carries a specious air of trustworthiness: his 'Quasi-Historical' category, despite carefully noted exceptions, does not. His 'Legendary' grab-bag is even vaguer, still more dependent on 'common-sensical' assumptions. Plenty of scope for subjective judgments here. If he were sorting, say, the Alexander-historians, *every single one* of our surviving sources would get the 'Quasi-Historical' label, since 'Historical' for him simply means 'attested by a contemporary witness'. Since few contemporary references to the Pythia's operations survive from the period 750–450, whereas those centuries offer plentiful material that must, in F.'s terms, be described as 'Quasi-Historical' or 'Legendary', it is not hard to see how, using this model, much historical (small h) evidence can be discredited simply by its formal resemblance to these two latter categories. In other words, we have a built-in *presupposition* of spuriousness for the period of Delphi's greatest influence and prestige.

F. takes me to task for not using the word 'historical' (non-capitalised) in his own *outré* sense. But why on earth should I? The only way that F. can assert that 'the Historical are commonplace directions and statements' is by setting up a model that relegates anything else to the 'Quasi-Historical' or 'Legendary' bins: this is where circularity creeps in. For F., to demonstrate that the Herodotean oracles are authentic means conforming to the guidelines *he* has set up. *Of course* Herodotus is our only direct source for the Persian War oracles; what we have to do is to estimate the likelihood of their genuineness against a broad background of historical probability, not argue their invalidity on the basis of categories we ourselves have created. (Incidentally, I defy F. to point out a passage in my review where I actually accept the Herodotean oracles *as quoted*: the gist, in prose or verse, is what matters, a distinction for which the Troezen Decree provides illuminating parallels). F. wants to cut Delphi loose from socio-historical developments altogether because this is the only way his arguments will work. If he wants to know why the Delphians continued to think the Persians invincible after Marathon, it is, clearly, because they could tell the difference (as F. seemingly can't) between a minor campaign and a major invasion.

What I or F. may believe about the validity (as opposed to the *modus operandi*) of Delphi is strictly irrelevant in historical terms; what *does* matter – as I emphasised in my review – is the attitude of *the Greeks themselves* at any given time. Here we have a distinction of prime importance, which F. constantly confuses. What bothers him, seemingly, is the supposed 'will to believe' among modern scholars rather than the degree and nature of belief at various stages in antiquity; and behind that there lies the *simpliste* rational objection that *because* oracles are superstitious nonsense they couldn't possibly have 'worked'. Whether we allow that last inference or not (I'd be inclined to argue it), all this is strictly beside the point. For the record, I believe in mantic possession (as did everyone in the ancient world) but not in gibberish; in the *pneuma*, but not in physical vapours; in a hole, but not in a rocky chasm. The *pneuma* (see below) was a quasi-physical conceptualising of divine possession, while Georges Roux (*Delphes*, pp. 110-117) has shown that some kind of symbolic chthonian hole may well have existed under the tripod in the *adyton*. To what extent Robert Flacelière qualifies as a 'serious scholar' in the field of Greek religion is a matter for debate; certainly he can't be blamed for the laxness of his translator. What he actually wrote (p. 71 French ed.) was: 'Le délire de la Pythie est attesté par toutes nos sources', and goes on to make it quite clear (cf. p. 51) that he is referring to Platonic *mania*, the utterance of *enthousiasmos*, a common meaning for *délire*: no frenzy, no gibberish. 'Frenzy' may indeed be a 'product of possession', but is not (as F. implies) its inevitable consequence. What Plutarch (*Moral.* 397C, 404B, 414E are presumably the passages F. has in mind) is at pains to emphasise, as H. W. Parke (*Greek Oracles* p. 79) clearly saw, is that Apollo did not occupy the Pythia's body in any vulgar *physical* sense: Parke comments, accurately (a point I also made in my review), that 'the ancient world found it extremely difficult to imagine a spiritual force'. F.'s quibbling over Dodds' definition of mantic possession speaks for itself; and the reader of my review must be left to decide whether it gives the impression that F. 'imputed fraud and cynicism to the Delphic priesthood'. On the one occasion where I discuss F.'s arguments in this context I emphasise his total rejection of such a theory.

Delphi was there for consultation: 'involvement' does not of itself imply initiative. That is as true of the Persian War oracles as of any other: the Athenians, for instance, wanted Delphi's opinion, and got it. Like Dodona, like Didyma, the Pythia doubtless did issue a majority of responses that were run-of-the-mill; but this is no reason for treating the minority of significant exceptions as spurious. Here Professor Badian's line of approach strikes me as far more useful. As he says, people who want to believe will, under normal circumstances, believe regardless, and can cheerfully accommodate, or explain away, any number of false responses: but if they are confronted with blatant, and public, political manipulation, then at the least they will stop asking religiously inspired political questions. I would argue, myself, that by the time of Philip's *démarche* with the Chalcidians, politicisation was already well advanced, so that consultation had become conscious propaganda rather than in any sense an act of faith; the same could just be true of the Thebans before Leuctra in 371 (Pausanias 4.32.5), though they did have a long-standing record of reliance on the Pythia in military matters, which persisted even after their annihilation by Alexander. Professor Badian's *terminus ad quem*, then, may be updatable (I suspect the truth to lie somewhere between his date, after 356, and that advanced by Parke, c.431), but methodologically his arguments are of the greatest value. However, we still need an historical analysis of Delphi's changing role in the affairs of the Greek city-states between the eighth and fifth centuries BC. Because of its preconceptions, Professor Fontenrose's monograph not only fails to provide this, but in some respects is liable to prove a stumbling-block for future research.

VII

STREPSIADES, SOCRATES, AND THE ABUSES OF INTELLECTUALISM

I N PLATO'S *Theaetetus,* Socrates at one point (155E) offers to help search
out the truth of some well-known thinkers' hidden opinions. When
Theaetetus responds eagerly to this offer, Socrates cautions him as
follows: 'Take a good look round,' he says, 'make sure no non-initiate
is listening.' Ironical or not, this remark at once reminds us of the student-
gatekeeper in Aristophanes' pseudo-Socratic 'Think-Tank' *(phrontisterion:*
143, cf. 140), who informs Strepsiades that the information he is about to
impart must be regarded as 'secret truths' *(mysteria).*[1] Socrates then goes on to
define 'non-initiates' in this context: 'These are they who think nothing exists
beyond what they can grasp in their two hands and who refuse to admit that
actions and origins and abstraction generally have any real substance.'[2]
Theaetetus, agreeing, describes such persons as 'stubborn and obstinate'.
Socrates corrects him. They are, more precisely, *amousoi,* without the Muses,
gross, crude, lacking in both taste and mental cultivation. There is a similar
attack in the *Sophist* (246A–B), and later in that dialogue (259E) the Eleatic
Stranger links the epithet *amousos* with an equally derogatory one: *aphilosophos,*
of which perhaps the most accurate translation would be 'non-(or anti)-
intellectual'.

Plato's immediate object in both cases was to discredit the materialists and
sensationalists, and adherents of such thinkers as Protagoras or Democritus.
Yet the description of the materialist may have more general application. To
find a significant example we need look no further than Aristophanes' *Clouds.*
Strepsiades is there portrayed as the classic *amousos,* in terms that clearly
foreshadow Plato's definition: and this Aristophanic sketch of Strepsiades as
amousos is balanced by a brief attack on false intellectual values. The main
satirical function of the *Clouds,* I would argue, was to demonstrate the
disruptive impact of progressive ideas, advanced dialectic, upon social and
familial stability: intellectual *Entwicklung* as a lethal solvent of what Gilbert
Murray so memorably termed the 'Inherited Conglomerate'.[3] In the process

Aristophanes found himself faced, simultaneously, with two distinct but related phenomena: (i) the inability or disinclination of the common man to grasp generalisations, abstractions, or intellectual metaphors of any sort: and (ii) the dangerous tendency of some intellectuals to incur ordinary people's suspicion through *abuse* of the rational process, by allowing their abstractions to degenerate into mere cloudy obscurantism and misapplied metaphor, with a concomitant air of the initiates' closed shop, something particularly stressed in the early scenes of the *Clouds*.

The confrontation between Strepsiades and the Aristophanic Socrates dramatises both problems with acute – and very modern – psychological insight. This, at first sight, is surprising. What Plato thought of Aristophanes' intellectual abilities we may deduce from the fact that in the *Symposium* Aristophanes is the only speaker *not* to analyse Love in abstract terms. K.J. Dover has suggested that Plato put such a speech into Aristophanes' mouth precisely because the latter was a comic poet and thus by definition not credited with the intellectual equipment of a philosopher.[4] Neither the flattering Platonic epigram on Aristophanes, nor the story that Plato, in response to the Sicilian tyrant Dionysius' request for a work that would explain the Athenian state, sent him the plays of Aristophanes to read, offers any evidence that the philosopher admired the playwright's *intellect* (as opposed to his imagination, charm, or eccentricity). Indeed, the anecdote about Dionysius suggests that Plato, finding Athens' democratic politics irrational to a degree, regarded Aristophanes' comic fantasies as the most eloquent – and characteristic – embodiment of that craziness in literary form: no wonder he wanted to ban the artists from his ideal *politeia*.

The identification of rational intellectualism with the ability to abstract or generalise is a cliché today: but just how early in the history of Greek thought this concept became generally accepted is a matter for debate.[5] Some abstract terms only entered the Greek language during the fourth century BC: two well-known examples are *poiotēs* ('quality') and *posotēs* ('quantity'). Plato, in whose *Theaetetus* the former first occurs (182A), actually apologises for using what he describes as a 'grotesque term' *(allótokon ónoma)* . The latter is not found earlier than Aristotle (see, e.g. *Metaph.* 1028a 19). Such symptomatic phenomena as parataxis – well described as 'the unsophisticated tendency to state logically subordinate ideas as separate, grammatically co-ordinate propositions'[6] – suggest strongly the fragile base on which fifth-century rationalism rested.[7] Similarly with the intellectual abuse of abstraction through misapplied metaphor: though this topic is familiar enough today [8], to find it treated as a joke for the groundlings in 423 BC throws fresh light on the general dissemination of progressive thought in post-Periclean Athens. For that reason alone it would be worth examination.

Throughout the *Clouds* Aristophanes is at great pains to delineate Strepsiades as a person with a mind not merely pragmatic but anti-conceptual. His dominant aim in life is to get rid of his debts and to make money[9]: his outlook is unblushingly utilitarian.[10] His first question about geometry (202 ff.) aims to discover its practical benefits. His thinking is shaped and governed by traditional anthropomorphism. '*Who* rains, then?' he asks, on being told that Zeus does not exist, and goes on to admit his prior belief that rain was caused by Zeus pissing through a sieve (363, 373). A few lines later (379 ff.) this anthropomorphic functionalism produces a highly significant misunderstanding between him and Socrates. If Zeus is not the prime mover, he asks in effect, then who is? Socrates has a ready answer. 'Vortex', he declares – a notion to be found in Anaximander, Empedocles, Anaxagoras, Anaximenes, and the Atomists, and variously held responsible for such diverse phenomena as the rotation of the heavenly bodies, spontaneous generation, the rise of civilisation, dizziness, and stones in the gall bladder.[11]

Thus Aristophanes' audience, it seems clear, would have had at least some familiarity with the term Vortex (*Dinos*), and have been prepared to laugh at Strepsiades' reaction. The old farmer instantly, and predictably, *personifies* Vortex as a new usurper in the Ouranos-Kronos-Zeus sequence.[12] For him Heaven is still the scene of an unseemly, time-bound, and all-too-human dynastic scramble: attempts by Anaxagoras and others to monotheise and philosophise Zeus into a universal avatar of Pure Mind have made not the slightest impression on him. Abstractions leave him cold, metaphors he treats as puzzling aspects of physical reality. Thus he also, though we do not learn this till later (1473-74), identifies this 'Dinos' with the large pot, also known as a *dinos,* that is set up as a stage-property outside Socrates' door. His terminology is concrete and personalised, with a touch of magic – the begetter of metaphor – about it: verbal coincidence suffices to predicate essential identity. For Strepsiades one god has simply been replaced by another [13], and the *dinos* is naturally his image.

In a series of encounters, mostly in the first half of the play, Aristophanes develops Strepsiades' character as a non-intellectual through two main techniques: (i) by making him misunderstand a whole range of images, metaphors, and concepts: (ii) by demonstrating his thought-processes in action on various clearly defined situations. In both cases his incapacity for intellectual abstraction emerges clearly and most often forms the point of the joke. We must therefore assume that this joke was one which an Athenian audience would appreciate. The misunderstandings are set up in a variety of ways. On his first appearance at the Think-Tank, Strepsiades is told (137) that his knocking has caused an idea to abort: being used to dealing with nervous pregnant goats, he shows instant and literal interest. This point is well emphasised by Dover.[14] I agree with him that we have no strong reason to link this metaphor with its use in Plato's *Theaetetus* (150E) apropos Socrates' maieutic techniques as 'midwife' to other people's ideas – it is there applied to those who leave Socrates' company too soon: but I think Dover underestimates the extent to which Aristophanes in the *Clouds* deliberately parodies verbal usages or imagery subsequently attributed to Socrates by

Plato (see above for several such instances: they could be multiplied tenfold).

Sometimes Strepsiades gives mere juxtaposition a causal significance it does not possess, as when he concludes (167-8) that knowing which orifice in a gnat produces the hum will help him to gain acquittal in a lawsuit. More often the *malentendu* is verbal, a phrase acquiring limited concrete significance in Strepsiades' mind. When told that students are studying 'things underground' *(ta katà gēs)* he at once assumes they must be truffle-hunting (188-90). His entire introduction to the Cloud-Chorus hinges on an inability to make the slightest concession to the Clouds *as concepts*: for Strepsiades they are either real clouds or real women, and his mind seesaws doggedly between the two. To begin with (267-8, 329-30) he is dealing in clouds and mist, things with which a farmer has close acquaintance. At 335 f. the idea of clouds-as-goddesses briefly touches him: but by 341 he has to reconcile the Chorus in the theatre with actual clouds in the sky, and is lost again. Why, he asks plaintively, do they look like women? Why, above all, do they have *noses* (344)?

Metaphorical usages always take him aback. When Socrates talks of bringing 'new devices' *(kainas mēchanàs)* to bear on him (a favourite Socratic term: cf. Plat. *Crat.* 415A and elsewhere), Strepsiades at once has nervous visions of the machines *(mēchanai)* used in siege-warfare (478-81). Socrates, in another characteristically homely image (cf. Plat. *Crat.* 407D 8, *Rep.* 536D 7, etc.) talks of 'throwing' him an idea, which he must 'snatch up' instantly. Strepsiades, literal as always, his mind clearly running on bones (cf. *Wasps* 916), complains that he is being made to eat cleverness 'like a dog', thus provoking the retort that he is an ignorant savage (489-92). When told by his mentor (634) to pay attention – literally, 'turn your mind here' – he replies 'look, I am', obviously identifying mind with head and thrusting the latter forward. Similarly, when asked (733) 'Is something the matter?', he at once takes the question to mean (which it could) 'Have you got hold of something?' in a physical sense, and makes the characteristically Aristophanic reply: 'Nothing except my cock in my working hand' (734).[15]

More revealing still are Strepsiades' reactions to the educational methods of the Think-Tank. These sometimes depend on verbal confusion: but the confusion always has a point. On being instructed to 'slice his thought thin' (740) he exclaims 'Woe is me!', clearly convinced that Thought, like Mind, is in some way a physical part of him, if not winged, as Theognis and others supposed. The mode of thought is familiar and archaic, and R.B. Onians has pointed out that to early Greeks 'emotional thoughts . . . were living creatures troubling the organs in one's chest'.[16] Strepsiades is not a plain fool: he is fundamentally *old-fashioned,* and as such evinces archaic thought processes which tend, inevitably, towards the specific, concrete and physical. When any verbal ambiguity arises, Strepsiades will always pick a practical interpretation, preferably – since he is also a country peasant – connected with food, money, or sex. This emerges with great clarity in the long passage on metrics, rhythm and gender (636–93). When Socrates mentions *metra* (a hold-all term covering 'measures' of every sort), Strepsiades' immediate thought is for measures of *dry capacity*, used when handling grain. With the dealer's swift practical arithmetic he instantly converts the intellectual's prosodic 'four-measure' (in metrical parlance a tetrameter) into a *hemiekteon* or half-*hekteus*, the sixth part of a bushel – logically, on his own terms, since it contains precisely four quarts *(choinikes)*.

The mention of *rhythmoi* (648 ff.), again in a prosodic sense, at once – probably by verbal association – turns his mind to sexual intercourse: one stock definition of rhythm was 'the ordering of movement'[17], and the word for 'movement', *kinēsis*, was also commonly used to suggest the act of sex. Equally unmistakable puns follow on terms such as *synousia* ('congress': English has the same ambiguity) and *katà dáktylon* ('dactylic': literally, 'by the finger'). For once the sexual lead-in has an ulterior purpose: to set up the basic misunderstanding over problems of gender that follows. To the concept of language with its structural metaphors Strepsiades is wholly oblivious. Such terms as 'masculine' or 'feminine' mean to him physical distinctions of sex in living creatures and nothing more. The entire passage plays with great skill and subtlety on this failure of communication. Strepsiades, for instance, is wholly baffled by the notion of feminising an inanimate object such as a kneading trough (670 ff.), but finds no difficulty in applying the same tag to an effeminate homosexual, Cleonymus. Similarly, when Socrates demonstrates the feminine-sounding vocative *Amynia* and suggests that this is to call Amynias a woman, Strepsiades undercuts his mentor's irony with the retort (692): 'Quite right too, since he's a draft-dodger.'

This world of concrete objective correlatives possesses its own archaic logic, strongly tinged, as we might expect, with magical beliefs. One solution Strepsiades proposes to avoid being dunned for debts in court is to melt the wax tablet on which his indictment is inscribed (and which for him constitutes its sole legal reality) by focusing a burning-glass on it (764–72). Even more suggestively, he also equates his own verbal proposal on this score with factual accomplishment: to say and to do are, in his world, virtually identical. Two lines later, indeed (773–4), he is congratulating himself because his five-talent debt *has been* wiped out (*diagegraptai*). That Alcibiades had recently done something very similar[18] adds to the joke but does not modify its essential nature. The same logic can be detected in yet another payment-dodging device of Strepsiades (749 ff.). He will buy a Thessalian witch and make her call down the moon, which will then be shut in a box. Since interest (*tokos*) is collected monthly, he reasons, and calculated by the phases of the moon, the latter's absence will put a moratorium on interest payment. This is a remarkably percipient parody of archaic thought processes and of sympathetic magic.[19]

But the best and most striking demonstration of the conflict between Strepsiades' mode of thought and the new intellectualism, between logical and non-logical symbolism, occurs in his discussion with the student-doorkeeper concerning the map on display in the Think-Tank (206-16). Anaximander had constructed a map of sorts, which Hecataeus improved: Herodotus twice mentions *periodoi* of the world: and lately an excellent relief map of the hinterland behind Ephesus has been identified on the reverse of an Ionian silver tetradrachm.[20] We may therefore assume that in 423 an Athenian audience would be aware of at least the basic principles governing cartography: indeed, such knowledge is predicated by Aristophanes' joke. Strepsiades, on the other hand, cannot conceive representational symbolism at all. When told 'This is Athens', he doubts the statement because he sees no dicasts in session, and then proceeds to search the area of his own deme for his fellow-demesmen. Characteristically, and in line with the old Greek tag that 'men make the city', he equates a place with the people in it. His thinking is conditioned, here as elsewhere, by a respectable archaic cliché. When the student identifies Lacedaemon, Strepsiades, treating the map as concrete reality – or perhaps as a powerful instrument of magic – says: 'How near it is: we ought to shift it further off.' It is no accident, given his mode of thought, that when Strepsiades *does* use an image, it is more often than not that pregnant and quasi-magical form of archaic poet's metaphor, the pun: there is a neat instance in this very passage.[21]

Strepsiades, then, is intellectually mocked for his failure to grasp notions or symbolic logic. This should make us look more carefully at his attitude to the Think-Tank and its educational dialectic (Aristophanists familiar with modern Greece should get a certain ironic pleasure from the fact that today a *phrontisterion* is a night school). Editors commonly suppose that Strepsiades' function was 'to caricature the genus "intellectual"'[22], and up to a point this is true. It is, however, significant that the most obvious nonsense comes not from Socrates but from the student-doorkeeper: it is the latter who retails the story of the jumping flea (144-52), the gnat's trumpet (156-68) and the experiment in geometry designed for the ulterior purpose of filching clothes (177-79). For the bulk of the play Sophistic methods in dialectic, linguistics or rhetoric are described rather than parodied (see, e.g. 314 ff., 340 ff., 369 ff., 398 ff., 478 ff., 489 f., 741 f., 757 ff., 775 ff.). What is more, they work. When it comes to debate, the Unjust Argument wins hands down. After a quick crash course, Pheidippides can run intellectual rings round his father (1171 f.), much as Alcibiades is said to have done with Pericles (Xen. *Mem.* 1.2.40-46: 'Ah, Alcibiades,' Pericles is represented as saying, 'at your age we were very smart at this sort of thing too', to which his pert ward replies: 'If only I'd known you well when you were really on form'). In the set-piece of the Agon it is the Unjust Argument that emerges victorious (1103), and Strepsiades' sole final recourse is to the mindless violence of arson (1490 ff.) [23] – ironically, since he had been only too willing at first to exploit the New Dialectic for his own questionable benefit (243-45, 433-34, etc.).

That Aristophanes objected to what he thought of as the immorality and atheism of the Sophists [24] seems certain: but he had no illusions about their effectiveness, and indeed would appear to have been covertly fascinated by many of their arguments – one reason, perhaps, for Cratinus' famous charge against him (fr. 307) of 'euripidaristophanising'. When we re-examine the play with these criteria in mind, Aristophanes' *intellectual* criticism of the New Learning reduces itself virtually to nothing once the pseudo-scientific student-doorkeeper and his fellow experimentalists are off-scene. (Humanist critics in all ages have an unfortunate tendency to fear or mock scientific development (cf. above, pp.25ff.). With the opening of the *Clouds* we may compare the chapter entitled 'A Voyage to Laputa' in Swift's *Gulliver's Travels,* especially the passage (§5) describing the Academy of Projectors. A more modern example would be the literary Luddism of D.H. Lawrence, sedulously propagated by F.R. Leavis and brought to the attention of a wider public through Leavis' acrimonious debate on the 'Two Cultures' with C.P. Snow.) There is surely implicit satire in Socrates' treatment of Air, Aether and the Clouds as deities (263 ff.), and the symbolic potential of clouds (*nephelai*), smoke (*kapnos*), and mist (*omichlē*), in conjunction, as what we would term 'hot air' is brought out at 331-4 with the list of intellectual fakes and parasites who batten on them. Yet we would expect far *more* of Aristophanes' attack to be directed against the bogus intellectual, whose false images and pretentiously vapid abstractions have always done so much to reinforce the common man's prejudice against all manifestations of higher thought, whether genuine or not.

The first two hundred lines of the play suggest that this is, in fact, the target being lined up. But from the moment Socrates descends from his basket (*tarros,* 239) the idea is shelved. It is as though by coming down to earth he automatically abandons his airier pretensions. The Clouds, too, turn out in the end to be all-too-orthodox supporters of conventional religion and morality – a characteristic latent in their pronouncements *ab initio,* and thus unlikely to have been the result of post-423 revision by the author. This brief excursus into the higher nonsense is as penetrating as it is witty: few readers can have studied it without regretting Aristophanes' subsequent change of tack. For one brief speech (225, 227-34) Socrates talks the most splendidly contrived gibberish, mixing pseudo-physics, pseudo-biology and psychological theory in the kind of plausible metaphorical stew that F.A. von Hayek spent so much time demolishing in *The Counter-Revolution of Science.*[25] To understand 'lofty matters' (*ta meteóra*), he explains, he had to suspend his thought aloft, mingle it with equally rarified air. Had he confined his efforts to ground level, he would have got nowhere, since 'the earth draws into itself the moisture of thought' – and the same, he adds as an afterthought, is true of watercress. We laugh at the pretentiousness of it all – not least when Strepsiades, his mind dazed, replies: 'What? Thought draws the moisture into cress?', and tells Socrates in the same word (*katabēth'*) to come down and come off it.

It is possible that this homely instance was deliberately inserted – like many other turns of phrase in the *Clouds* – to catch the characteristic flavour of Socrates' speech. Alcibiades in Plato's *Symposium* (221E) describes his conversation as being full of 'pack-asses, coppersmiths, cobblers, tanners', a remark which suggests not merely surprise at the *outré* but a gentleman's cheerfully snobbish contempt for the lower classes and all their works. But then we remember that Aristophanes was, once more, not so much parodying as citing a genuine philosophical theory, that held by Diogenes of Apollonia, in which the words for moisture (*ikmás*) and drawing-in (*hélkein*) used by Aristophanes [26] play a key role. With such theories on hand, what need of parody? As students of Pythagoreanism – indeed of all archaic Greek thought – must be uncomfortably aware, the dividing line between magic and science, intellectual discovery and pseudo-mysticism (both constantly involved, without apparent distinction, in the process of intellectual enquiry, *historia*) is a narrow and perilous one. Even in the mid–fifth century BC, as Dodds [27] has made us all too well aware, the old and new modes of thought still coexisted, side by side and not always uneasily. It is much to Aristophanes' credit that he had the insight, both intellectual and psychological, to diagnose this double condition. That the Athenian jury relegated the play to third place at its original performance need surprise no one.

VIII

DOWNTREADING
THE DEMOS

IRST, APPROPRIATELY ENOUGH, some statistics. Geoffrey de Ste Croix's *magnum opus, The Class Struggle in the Ancient Greek World,* contains over seven hundred closely printed pages, and weighs, in the hard-cover edition, more than three pounds. The notes alone run to some 107,000 words, and the total word-count is not far short of half a million. As a development of what began as three J.H. Gray lectures, this represents inflation on a truly monumental scale. At first sight only the appendixes show restraint: four in thirty-three pages, where *The Origins of the Peloponnesian War* had forty-seven in 109. Closer inspection, however, reveals other economies, of an unexpected and paradoxical nature. *The Class Struggle in the Ancient Greek World* finds room for little more than twenty pages on the archaic and classical periods, from Hesiod to Alexander the Great (though incidental allusions occur elsewhere): the rest is divided between the Hellenistic kingdoms and Roman imperialism, with a bloated preliminary excursus on 'proper Marxist definitions' (not always Marx's) of class and the class struggle and cognate matters, plus a drawn-out coda describing the fall of the Roman empire in terms of class exploitation. The book comes bound in the appropriate liturgical colour ('red for the Feastdays of the Apostles and the Martyrs, who shed their blood for the Faith out of love for the Redeemer'), and adorned with a symbolic icon, Van Gogh's 'The Potato Eaters', reproduced in the authentic sickly-green tones of want and despair.

Several of these features are instantly disturbing. At the risk of being relegated by Ste Croix to that stooge-chorus of bourgeois colleagues who (by his account) reacted to each successive phase of his work, circulated in draft, with shock, obtuseness and predictable capitalist cliché, I think it is important to ask ourselves why. The Van Gogh frontispiece is a good starting-point. 'These', Ste Croix tells us, 'are the voiceless toilers, the great majority . . . of the Greek and Roman world', and so on. In fact they are nothing of the sort, and Ste Croix's correlation between the ancient and modern worlds remains, at best, disingenuous. Eating potatoes and drinking coffee (to get which, at affordable prices, they did some indirect exploitation of their own), these northern Dutch labourers, malnutritional victims of the Industrial Revolution, have little in common with the peasant of the Hellenistic *chora,* and even less with the *thes* or *zeugites* of Attica. The obvious question is why Ste Croix did not utilise a genuine icon from antiquity. His answer would doubtless be: because no suitable icon existed. The operative word here is *suitable.* In fact, since he includes the Roman Empire in his survey, Ste Croix had an ideal – indeed, unique – work to hand in the great agricultural mosaics from Cherchell (Caesarea) in North Africa, praised by Bianchi Bandinelli (himself a Marxist) for their 'easy, realistic accuracy'. The trouble, of course, is that not only are these workers working (rather than sitting about indoors as deprived consumers), but looking healthy, if not happy, and actively involved in their work. Better, clearly, an irrelevant icon that produces the correct emotional effect. The end justifies the means.

It is also symptomatic that in a book ostensibly consecrated to the Greek peasant (Ste Croix repeatedly, and with justice, stresses the primacy of agriculture in the ancient economy) so little effort should have been made to study the breed at first hand, *in situ.* No use whatsoever is made of the rich comparative material assembled in recent years by Mediterranean anthropologists: Peter Walcot's *Greek Peasants, Ancient and Modern* (1970) is conspicuously absent from Ste Croix's vast bibliography, along with the related work of scholars such as Campbell, Friedl, Sanders, and Peristiany. The continuous emphasis on theory (Ste Croix is contemptuous of scholars who do *not* work from *a priori* models) lends an unexpectedly arid tone even to the deployment of specific literary sources – in which area, it must be said, this book exhibits a truly formidable breadth and expertise. Worse, the suspicion arises that Ste Croix's offhand treatment of the three most vital centuries in Greek history is dictated not so much by a shortage of evidence – Andrew Lintott's scrupulously documented *Violence, Civil Strife and Revolution in the Classical City* would alone suffice to disprove such a claim – as by the obstinate refusal of the material to demonstrate Ste Croix's general thesis of class exploitation. Like the Fat Boy in Dickens, he wants to make our (bourgeois) flesh creep; and for this purpose the habits of Ptolemies or, *a fortiori,* Roman provincial administrators, are more to the point than the stubborn, outspoken and ultimately self-defeating egalitarianism of the post-Periclean Athenian Assembly. Even so, an account of the Greek class struggle which devotes no more than a short paragraph to the Thirty Tyrants, glosses over Thucydides' lethal account of *stasis* on Corcyra, and makes no reference at all (among other interesting omissions) to Melos, Hesiod's fable of the Hawk and the Nightingale, or that fascinating if unsavoury right-wing intellectual ultra, Critias, might be thought, to say the least, something more than idiosyncratically lopsided.

To find possible ideological motivation for what might otherwise seem mere perverse eccentricity, we need to take a very careful look, in the first instance, at Ste Croix's definitions, and application, of those elusive concepts 'class' and 'class struggle'. Normally he is not at all shy about second-guessing, or improving, either accepted Marxist or, indeed, traditional Christian tenets: in both cases he displays an arrogant confidence – laced with the caveats of mock-humility – that *his* version of the Founder's creed comes closer to the *Ur*-truth than the institutionalised and corrupt public dogma which ousted it. (I suspect that few things would annoy him more than being accused of anti-Christianity: his own version of Christ seems to be, as one might expect, about midway between Brecht's and Pier Paolo Pasolini's.) Other critics have noted his avoidance of many Russian, East German, and Italian Marxist sources: I suspect an implicit judgment here on his part. On the other hand, perversely, he hampers his definition of 'class struggle' almost past belief by a determination to reconcile it with the opening sentence of *The Communist Manifesto*. Hedging carefully (for reasons that will emerge below) he writes at one point: 'A class (a particular class) is a group of persons in a community identified by their position in the whole system of social production defined above all according to their relationship (primarily in terms of the degree of ownership or control) to the conditions of production (that is to say, the means and labour of production) and to other classes.'

Conventional, if nervous. But then Ste Croix later produces a second, and for him more important, definition: 'Class', he tells us, 'is the collective social expression of the fact of exploitation', while 'class struggle is the fundamental relationship between classes . . . involving essentially exploitation, or resistance to it'. Class, he concedes, is not the only category needed for analysis of Greek or Roman society, but it remains 'the fundamental one, which *over all* . . . and *in the long run* is the most important'. He seems to understand that there need be 'no necessary connection between the existence of a surplus and the exploitation of man by man'. However, since exploitation remains for him (as for Marx) a fundamental *constituent element* in all transactions involving the employment of labour, rather than a frequent *incidental attribute* of such transactions – did he, I wonder, regard himself as exploited by New College during his teaching career there? – he is committed to discovering, throughout the ancient world, not only exploitation *tout court*, which would be easy enough, but *class* exploitation, quite another matter.

To complicate the situation still further, though no one would doubt Marx's preoccupation with the class struggle (in an 1868 letter to Engels he described it as the thing into which 'the movement of the whole *Scheiss* is resolved'), he never formally defined it, while in his crucial *Preface to a Contribution to the Critique of Political Economy* (1858-59) he did no more than glance at the problem of class, and made no reference at all (because of Prussian censorship, it has been argued) to the class struggle. Nothing daunted, Ste Croix hammers out his own definition, reassuring us that if Marx *had* produced one himself, it would have been 'not very different from the one I have given'. (No danger, if the militant atheists are right, of Marx's ghost rising from Highgate Cemetery to correct him, though some of us might have relished the exchange.) As Bernard Knox saw, there is something verging on the metaphysical about the term 'class struggle' being used for (in Ste Croix's own words) 'situations in which there may be *no explicit common awareness of class* on either side, *no specifically political struggle at all*, and perhaps even *little consciousness of struggle* of any kind'. Some Marxists, as Ste Croix well knows, insist on class-consciousness and active political conflict as essential ingredients in any definition (a view with which I have some sympathy). But to do this, he argues, 'makes nonsense not merely of *The Communist Manifesto* but of the greater part of Marx's work' – a consideration which, as Knox demurely observed, 'will have more force in some quarters than in others'.

It also (perhaps more seriously) puts severe limitations on anyone attempting to interpret the ancient world in Marxist terms. Both Ste Croix and Lintott correctly dismiss as moonshine earlier attempts by Ure and Wason, or a favoured Stalinist such as George Thomson, to posit a powerful *tiers état* of merchant-princes, a *Kaufmannsaristokratie* between the old nobility and the *demos*. (Ste Croix's notion of Solon and Plato trading only to pay for their tourism goes, perhaps, too far in the other direction.) What they do not ask themselves is why such a theory should have arisen in the first place. The truth of the matter is that in a class struggle it takes two to tangle: and the kind of *stasis* for which evidence exists in archaic Greece has proved singularly resistant to Marxist analysis. There was no labour market in the modern sense; indeed, as Lintott observes, there was not even 'a separate sector of economic activity, in which men could confront one another as employers and employees'. The free poor smallholders, as a class, outnumbered by far not only those landed aristocrats who would qualify, in Marxist terms, as appropriators of labour (and the surplus that it produced), but also, at least till well on in the fifth century BC and possibly longer, the slave population. Their chief aim, moreover, as Lintott says, was not 'to improve the conditions for selling their labour but to avoid that kind of labour altogether', so that we are faced with the paradox of a state which, far from evolving towards the subjection of its producing class, instead used democratisation as a weapon for freeing that class from its would-be exploiters.

Where, then, was the class struggle? Small wonder that Ure and Thomson chose to retroject a group of hard-faced proto-industrialists into this pre-industrial situation – the only way (as they saw it) in which orthodox Marxism could extrapolate a class conflict from such recalcitrant material. Ste Croix, who has far greater respect for awkward facts, salvages what he can from the mess by simply arguing, without stressing comparative figures, that the land-owning class appropriated its surplus by exploiting unfree labour (never mind that this phenomenon represented only a small percentage of the total turnover in archaic Greece); that in certain circumstances the free producers would be indirectly exploited themselves; and that therefore, though Greek and Roman civilisation was not technically a slave economy, he would not 'raise any strong objection if anyone else wished to use that expression'. At this point non-ideologues may find their patience wearing a little thin.

The whole concept of slavery, indeed, raises thorny and controversial issues that can hardly fail to embarrass any orthodox Marxist. Whether 'orthodox' is an apt label for Ste Croix I rather doubt (though I'm quite sure *he* would think so, having a rare knack for treating all Marxists who disagree with him as mere misguided heretics); but the embarrassment is palpable. Discussing the short supply of free hired labour, and the availability of cheap slaves, he asserts: 'I do believe that slavery increased the surplus in the hands of the propertied class to an extent which could not otherwise have been achieved *and was therefore an essential precondition* (italics mine) of the magnificent achievement of Classical civilisation.' This is tendentious to a degree: it gets its effect not only by treating a minority as a monopoly, but by carefully fudging a crucial time-sequence. The expansion of slavery at the expense of free labour was an undoubted fact (Solon's reforms being the original factor that set the long-term process in motion), but its full impact was not felt until the Periclean age was over, and that age's achievement fixed for all time. (For once, dogma has led Ste Croix, by implication, to criticize Athens: in the ordinary way he is only too eager to find excuses for any manifestation of Athenian imperial hubris.)

In any case the status of slaves remains, for a Marxist, full of inconsistencies. They frequently turned up in managerial roles, as bankers or businessmen (even, as Ernst Badian has pointed out, themselves owning slaves), in which capacity they functioned as large-scale producers and consumers rather than as sources of exploitation. Ste Croix is, understandably, shy of servile success stories: he does not enlarge on the Athenian millionaire banker Pasion, and he regards Trimalchio as a mere grotesque fiction. What seems clear is that in Greece no less than Rome a slave's degree of freedom, and indeed his relation to the means of production, could vary very considerably. That abrasive anti-populist pamphleteer of the Periclean era, known to scholars (since his identity is in doubt) as the Old Oligarch, complained that in Athens it was impossible, on the street, to tell a slave from a free man, and this fact is of more that merely social importance. At the other end of the scale Ste Croix, surprisingly, challenges the notion that slavery was a factor holding up technological development. Such a dedicated gadfly of institutionalised Christianity can hardly have failed to notice that strong moral objections to slavery emerged only when the Industrial Revolution offered a cheap substitute for the 'animated tool' (thus proving, in an unexpected way, Aristotle's argument about total automation as the only viable alternative to slavery).

What Ste Croix prefers to stress is 'exploitation as the hallmark of class', 'exploitation' being – a point not lost on Ste Croix's Weberian bugbear Sir Moses Finley – a usefully vague, and hence elastic, conceptual holdall. While

Marx's concept of the class struggle was (as Ste Croix admits in his more candid moments) largely defined by, and thus limited to, modern industrial society, exploitation, of one kind or another, has been going on since the dawn of history, and can, with a little ingenuity, be adapted to almost any theoretical model. The trouble remains that the Greek, and in particular the Athenian, *polis* was so intractably different from all other Near East systems, even from the earlier Minoan or Mycenaean palace economies, all of which operated along lines far more congenial to any Marxist exploitation–spotter. Here, as Ellen and Neal Wood have stressed in their *Class Ideology and Ancient Political Theory* (1978), the state *was* essentially 'a means of organising and extracting labour from largely dependent labouring populations, a means of maintaining a fundamental division between producers and appropriators, an instrument for the exploitation of the former by the latter'. Similar conditions were to recur in the great Successor Kingdoms of the Hellenistic Age: the pattern of administrative exploitation was taken over and developed still further by Rome.

It should by now be tolerably clear why Ste Croix devotes the bulk of his book to these later periods, analysing with skill and (it seems to me) a certain angry ideological relish, just how the Greek propertied classes combined with their Macedonian and Roman overlords to stamp out the last sparks of true Greek democracy – a fortunate participation, from the dogmatist's viewpoint, since it enables Ste Croix to treat as *class* exploitation what might otherwise appear as simple colonial imperialism exercised over a subject race, rather akin to the Spartan exploitation of Messenia.

The road of the true party-liner through ancient Greek civilisation is beset with innumerable pitfalls. To his credit, Ste Croix tries to come to terms with most of them, though in the process he increases his own vulnerability. Honesty will keep breaking through the dogma, and the ideological restrictions he forces himself to accept give him the air of a fighter with one hand strapped behind his back, while the other jabs away heroically at all comers. Take the relation of the individual to the means of production as a decisive factor in defining his class. Ste Croix has to describe this, despite its antecedents, as 'a rather too narrow conception': about twenty pages later we see why, when he admits that it would involve our treating the slaves of the Greek world, 'absurdly, as belonging to the same class as free hired workers and even many poor free artisans and landless peasants'. His old bottles, even when refurbished, cannot always contain the heady new wine he wants to put in them.

Here, of course, Lintott, who has no detectable ideological preconceptions, and a healthily pragmatic attitude to evidence, stands at a great advantage: the reader who wants to supplement Ste Croix's brief and in many ways unsatisfactory account of the archaic and classical periods could not ask, on the whole, for a more sensible or less tendentious survey. Lintott has his quirks (e.g. a conviction that the Solonian crisis arose from 'debt viewed as a legal deficit' rather than a general dependence of the poor on the rich); but he is alert to the crucial tensions between old tribal and new civic thinking that furnished the classical *polis* with its dialectic, and realises that 'from about 500 onwards it was war between cities which was the greatest stimulus to fighting inside cities', an element of city-state *stasis* that Ste Croix almost wholly ignores. To *stasis* as such Lintott rightly assigns a central position in Greek political development, granting (as did Aristotle) the tensions created by fundamental inequalities between rich and poor, giving due – but not exclusive – weight to aristocratic factionalism, and concluding, convincingly, that genuine class conflict was comparatively rare. Nevertheless, he contrives to dig out some nice early instances ignored by Ste Croix (Croton, Cumae, Syracuse), complete with land redistribution and cancellation of debts, things which, as he says, 'appear more commonly as bogeys in the writings of philosophers and orators than in fact'.

Ste Croix's commitment, wherever possible, to explaining classical Greece, Athens above all, in terms of a landed elite appropriating the labour and surplus of the exploited unfree makes it hard, at times, to understand what was really going on. Here, again, Lintott is far clearer. Even Ste Croix has to admit that, for a while at least, political vigilance by the *demos* held up the inexorable march of economic necessity (though he then tries to have it both ways by asserting that Marx was no economic determinist). Paradoxically, he makes less than he might of the Solonian confrontation, rightly described by Lintott as 'the earliest evidence of class conflict between citizens in Greek history'. But then the main result of Solon's reforms was to give free agricultural producers (who constituted, then, the bulk of Attica's population) extra protection and clout against their former oppressors. At least from Cleisthenes' time all adult free males, landless or not, were citizens. This, as the Woods stress, 'gave the labouring class a freedom and power that it had never possessed before and in many respects has never regained since'. Democratic elitism was the name of the game. Did you work for a living, and, if so, at an employer's beck and call (the ultimate degradation), or did you command the labour of others? Ample evidence shows that this last was the ideal, not of a privileged few, but of *the entire citizen body,* rich and poor alike.

It follows that Athenian imperialism came as no accident: it was built into post-Cleisthenic (and, *a fortiori*, post-Persian Wars) Athens as an ultimate inevitability. Someone, somewhere, outside the charmed circle had to foot the bill for Athenian autarky. Some animals were indeed to become more equal than others. Just as Sparta's 'Equals' (*homoioi*) were sustained by the serf labour of the Messenians and Helots, so – as the Old Oligarch so clearly saw – the cities of the empire supported the Athenian *demos* in the state to which, by the time of the Periclean ascendancy, it had become accustomed. Democratisation, by protecting free labour, had meant, *inter alia,* the increased acquisition of slaves, by war or purchase – non-Greek *barbaroi,* hence fair game – as a source of manpower. Nevertheless, free producers continued to work their own farms (a tough job, as is clear from Xenophon), and in the matter of employment resident alien and citizen stood on an equal footing. The real exploitation in the Athenian democracy was carried out, in effect,

********* **********************
Grove Branch Library

710-798-8…
…hollibrary.org
… Request Slip
****

e-Mail …

…2010

…homas, George
Herman

…iss, at the expense of foreign slave …ean thalassocracy. Ste Croix, in a …as I believe, that the supposed …very (*douleia*) was a myth invented …as to show just what a latter-day …ic imperialism). While a democratic …s if that involved loss of *demokratia*, …ind keep its political constitution it …ver losing Athenian overlordship'. …as not the monopoly of the major

…its elitists, its snobbery and class …pervasive kind, as careful study of …s clear). But two points are worth …reformers showed a skill amounting …irianism in the citizen body while …intact. Foreign ancestry or a menial …ipposedly selling vegetables in the …ng laugh. As both Lintott and Ste …class-slanted terminology exists in …ing, on the one hand, the wealthy, …ent; on the other, the poor, stupid, …ets in each cluster seem to have been …point is the remarkable degree to …ian *demos* prevailed against subversive

which, despite such … efforts by the ultras, not only in the fifth century but well towards the end of the fourth. If the 'propertied classes' had been united in a determination to exploit the citizen body, they had their chance in 411, and again in 404. Both attempts failed ignominiously, and after a very short time, through internal dissension and a strong, determined, democratic opposition. Though encroachment by the propertied began almost immediately thereafter – protection of the wealthy was (as indeed it had been for Solon) a cornerstone of the restored democracy, and the oath included a refusal to countenance debt abolition or land redistribution – there were still no really significant episodes of class conflict in Athens till the Lamian War that followed (322) Alexander's death. It is a heartening record against odds, and I wish Ste Croix had made more of it.

Still, his business is the class struggle, and he must hunt that down where best he can. By far his finest achievement in this massive, and massively discursive, work is the grim analysis he offers, at length, of the reversion to authoritarian plutocracy that followed the collapse of city-state freedom, the progressive betrayal of Greek democracy by the ever more powerful Greek propertied classes, hand in glove with Macedonian and, subsequently, Roman imperialists. (His explanation for the fall of the Roman Empire, through a 'most intense and ultimately destructive economic exploitation of the great mass of the people, whether slave or free', I do not feel competent to discuss.) The thesis he presents is as convincing as it is depressing, being argued with meticulous scholarship and a stunning mass of apt, and often unfamiliar, illustrative material. The seeds of this corruption had been sown early, by an intellectual minority influential out of all proportion to its size. Whereas in Pericles' day the *apragmones* (do-nothings) and *idiotai* (individualists) had earned nothing but public contempt, from Euripides onwards, as the hold of the *polis* on its members loosened, self-interest and solipsism took increasing toll of *engagé* democratic loyalties. The citizen now preferred to cultivate not merely his garden but also his soul and his capital reserves. Political impotence bred a taste for money-making and social trivia. Thinkers from Plato onwards showed increasing alienation from democracy as such. Authoritarian government, explored with imaginative sympathy in *The Republic* and *The Laws,* soon became all too real a phenomenon. Demetrius of Phaleron showed Athenians, to their cost, what a philosopher-ruler could be like in action, while the Ptolemaic and Seleucid dynasties revived absolute monarchy on a hitherto unimagined scale.

Plato, of course, offers a natural target for Ste Croix's scorn (though others have been ready to see him as a proto-Marxist, and Books VII and IX of *The Republic* as the source for Marx's concept of the class struggle). Ste Croix scourges this aristocratic elitist as 'anti-democratic in the highest degree', with an 'arrogant contempt for all manual workers', in short as 'one of the most determined and dangerous enemies that freedom has ever had' (amusing to find Ste Croix, however briefly, in Sir Karl Popper's camp). On the other hand, Marx eulogized Aristotle, in particular the Aristotle of the *Politics*, so Ste Croix must eulogize him too, forgetting the awkward fact that the *maestro di coloro che sanno* was at least as anti-banausic as Plato, and no less capable of justifying authoritarian rule, in his case monarchy, with one sedulous eye to his (presumably exploitative) employer, Philip of Macedon. Ste Croix finds Aristotle 'closer to Marx than any other ancient thinker I know', which is not in fact all that close. He was little concerned with the forces of production, not at all with slaves as producers; though admitting inequality of property as a cause of *stasis*, he thought legislation to remedy such conditions futile, and identified the prime impulse to revolution under a democracy as, in Lintott's words, 'the insolence of demagogues in harassing the nobility'. His famous distinction between acquisition or production for use and for profit was in fact made as an argument in favour of old-fashioned aristocratic agrarian rule. It was Marx who changed it, as the Woods remind us, into 'a conceptual weapon to attack capitalism and to provide the theoretical basis for the idea of a non-exploitative society'. Nothing, in the end, hampers Ste Croix so much as his ideology.

This is a great pity, since it skews too much of what still remains, in so many ways, a superb and – dare one say it? – Stakhanovite achievement: few scholars could match Ste Croix's close familiarity with so wide a range of *testimonia* and modern scholarship, perhaps none could organize this mass of material with such sure control, or offer so many brilliant incidental insights into vexed historical problems. Yet the great historian in Ste Croix is constantly being elbowed aside by the quibbling theologian, sometimes with regrettable effects on his historical judgment. In particular, his credulity seems to run rampant over the iniquities of exploiters, whether Greek or Roman. Thus he will, legitimately, query the figures given for Mithridates' slaughter of Romans during his 'night of the long knives' in 88 BC, but accept unquestioningly the (no less inflated) numbers associated with L. Aemilius Paullus' mass killing of Epirotes, or Belisarius' pogrom after the Nika Riot; while he is so anxious to believe the rhetorical horror story about P. Vedius Pollio ordering slaves thrown into his fish-pond to be devoured by ravenous lampreys, that he has failed to do his homework on lampreys as such, which, though modest blood suckers, do not, alas, possess jaws. On the other hand, he seems ready to excuse the fifth-century imperial depredations of Athens by the delightful argument that Rome did the same thing on a far larger scale, which reminds me of the housemaid's apologia for her illegitimate baby: 'Please, mum, it was only a very small one.'

When modern parallels are in question, we hear about Hiroshima and Dresden, but not a word on Cambodia or the Gulag Archipelago. Professor Badian has paid Ste Croix a handsome compliment when describing his 'boiling rage at man's inhumanity to man'. But for me the thing that really raises Ste Croix's blood pressure is *odium theologicum* at a high theoretical level, and I would be far more inclined to believe in his real concern for man's inhumanity to man if he were a little less selective in picking examples of it. (I suppose the kindest way of describing his remark about organised Christianity constituting 'a persecuting force *without parallel* (my italics) in the world's history' would be as a case of barefaced ideological *chutzpah*.) His *magnum opus* is a monumental masterpiece that scholars will continue to quarry for decades. But it remains a flawed masterpiece, its marvellous insights and truly chalcenteric learning cramped, too often, by the ideological straitjacket that its author wears like a Church Father's penitential hair shirt.

IX

SEX AND CLASSICAL
LITERATURE

THE OPERATIVE WORD, of course, is *literature*: signpost, definition, and, to the wary, warning. We are not primarily concerned with sex, as such, in antiquity, a topic for which the evidence – partly by the nature of the activities involved, partly on account of natural attrition over the centuries – is both minimal and ambiguous. Sex in literature (and, for that matter, in the visual arts) may, at times, be roughly congruent with the actual sexual habits of the society in which the writers or painters or sculptors lived and worked, but the equation remains at best intermittent. What we are dealing with here – and the rule is not restricted to Greek and Roman civilisation – is not so much sex *per se* as sexual fantasy and propaganda: sex in the head, sex as the creative spirit may idealise or demean it, sex as society would like to believe it is or ought to be, private taboo-breaking orgies, surrealistic mythological sex (showers of sub-Freudian gold, cycnean or taurine miscegenations), sex as political camouflage or rhetorical *topos,* as lyrical comforter, as marital advertisement, as creative revision of personal inadequacy. For sheer compulsive ingenuity *l'esprit de l'escalier* runs a very poor second to *l'esprit du boudoir,* and the raw meat of a poet's or novelist's love affair tends to get cooked in ways that might surprise Claude Lévi-Strauss by the time it is served up for public consumption. To discuss sex in classical literature, then, is to analyse, tentatively, what, at various periods, segments of Greek and Roman society thought about themselves, the image a minority – often a minority of one – aimed to project. Any resemblance between that image and practical reality is not only coincidental, but in most cases quite impossible to detect.

If this sounds like a bad case of nit-picking academic particularism, blame the methodological inanities which, till very recently, characterised almost all investigations of sexual phenomena in the ancient world. Since the subject was sensitive, indeed largely taboo,[1] those who dabbled in it – unless they went anonymous, like Paul Brandt, the Ovidian scholar, who as 'Hans Licht' was responsible for *Sexual Life in Ancient Greece* (Eng. trs. 1932), or, like A. E. Housman, wrote in Latin – tended to be amateur *littérateurs,* often with a sizable obsession of their own to work off. If there is still a vague belief among Western progressives that the ancient world was an indiscriminate paradise for homosexuals and orgiasts, the myths disseminated by these purveyors of *haute* (or, in many cases, *basse*) *vulgarisation* are largely responsible. Sex, like death, does not tend to bring out either logic or a sense of history in those who write about it. Above all, what got lost was the changing, evolutionary quality of sexual beliefs and fashions. Evidence to make a point would be culled indiscriminately from Greek or Roman authors over a thousand years and more, from Homer to Lucian, as though the civilisation under review were one and indivisible: this would be rather akin to juxtaposing *The Miller's Tale* and *The Waste Land* as generic evidence for the sexual proclivities of middle-class Englishmen. The result – until collapsing taboos brought some first-class scholars into the field[2] – was a dubious mass of romanticised, and profoundly unhistorical, generalisations. Diachronic rather than topological treatment is called for as a corrective.

It might be tempting to follow the rhapsode's example and 'begin with Zeus', but this route bristles with more pitfalls than usual for the unwary. Nowhere do we find a more chaotic situation than in the field of religion and mythology, which both tend, by the nature of the case, to be treated *sub specie aeternitatis,* a practice unconducive to good social history: worse, the subject's current trendiness, in universities and elsewhere, has further contaminated it with a foggy blanket of modern theorising, structural or Freudian.[3] Since the gods were unshackled by human restrictions, and in many ways clearly embodied projections of the psyche's unfulfillable aspirations, the degree to which erotic motifs proliferate in Greek and Roman myth should come as no surprise. Yet the nature of these fantasies, and their impact on social awareness, varied considerably with the progress of time. The emergence of a middle class, for instance, endowed – as always – with that genteel morality which forms its most characteristic feature, produced great embarrassment over traditional archaic-tribal tales of the gods' insatiable, and indiscriminate, sexual adventures. Yet we continue to treat evolving myths as timeless *contes drôlatiques,* cobbling together our evidence, virtually at random, from a range of witnesses that begins with Homer and Hesiod in the eighth century BC and progresses, by way of the Greek tragedians, Ovid's *Metamorphoses,* and various late mythographers both Greek and Roman (Apollodorus, Hyginus, Antoninus Liberalis), to the browsings of that antiquarian Byzantine archbishop Eustathius, who died only just before the Fourth Crusade of AD 1204.

Myth and literature, then, both insist that we should begin at the beginning: that is, with the *Iliad* and *Odyssey.* The evidential layer cake *can* be made to yield much intriguing information – but not if all its layers are lumped together indiscriminately across cultures and centuries, nor if fiction, drama, lyric poetry, courtroom speeches, letters, inscriptions and biography are treated *in pari materia* as direct, factual sources of sexual information, and that information is then assumed to represent actual practice, rather than literary artifice which may or may not approximate to real life. What I propose, then, is to follow significant *changes* of literary emphasis and fashion in the sphere of sexual mores, from Homer's day (eighth century BC) to that of Juvenal (second century AD), and, where possible, to suggest explanations for them. The human sexual instinct is powerful but, as such, both simple and uniform the world over. What makes it so complex – in Greece, Rome, or anywhere else, during the Dark Age or under the Empire – is that wide spectrum of moral sanctions, social programming, and religious taboos employed to direct, encourage, or repress it, and reflected – whether in opposition or conformity – by the literature and art of each period.

HOMER IS A TRICKY WITNESS on whom to start, because of course the *Iliad* and the *Odyssey* are themselves layer cakes, preserving much from Bronze Age Greece, but recombining this material with assumptions that more properly belong to eighth-century BC Ionia – when Homer himself, and other oral poets like him, made a living by recalling the 'great deeds of heroes' at the courts of petty princelings who took pride in their supposed descent from Agamemnon or Nestor. Presumably Homer reflects the social outlook of his patrons. His attitude to sex is familial, civilised, domestic, and in many ways more modern than anything which succeeded it until Plutarch's day. Despite the electric charms of that *femme fatale* Helen it is the wives – Penelope, Andromache, Arete – who stick in the mind. Even flirtatious Nausicäa has her mind as solidly set on marriage as any deb. As Murray long ago saw, the poems show evidence of having quietly expurgated such traditional barbarisms as human sacrifice, mutilation of corpses, incest, and – in the case of Achilles' relation to Patroclus – homosexuality.[4] Bourgeois values were stirring in Ionia. A clear measure of how far, and fast, these developed is the famous attack upon Homer made, less than two centuries later, by Xenophanes of Colophon, who objected that the poet 'attributed to the gods everything that is a shame and reproach among men, stealing and committing adultery and deceiving each other' (fr.169 Kirk-Raven). The charge was fair enough. What Homer in fact still preserved – on Olympus if not among more self-conscious mortals – was that old, basically aristocratic attitude to sex, which believed in the *droit de seigneur,* found intercourse pleasurable but not emotionally significant (Zeus' enthusiastic bout with Hera on a mist-clad mountain-top demonstrates this to perfection), and was prepared to treat adultery as a great joke provided – as in the case of Ares and Aphrodite – it was a social inferior, here lame Hephaestus, who wore the horns.

The contrast between Homer's sexually irresponsible gods and his human protagonists – whose ideal (however often they may fail it along the way) is that fine old bourgeois institution, a stable marriage – has more than casual significance. The conservatism of religious traditional beliefs was counterpointed, in the Greek psyche, against a quite unusually rapid social evolution from tribal to civic standards of behaviour. Thus not only in Homer's day, but throughout the Archaic and Classical eras, reason tended to get in advance of instinct, heart and head worked against each other. This dialectical tension lay behind many themes predominant in Attic drama (e.g. the head-on clash between familial and socio-political beliefs in Sophocles' *Antigone*), and it certainly explains why, as early as the *Iliad,* the old patriarchal ethic, still valid on Olympus, was slowly being replaced on earth – despite the heroic tradition – by a middle-class social code based on the nuclear family and a system of largely cooperative or defensive values. Hector dies for Troy, but also for his wife Andromache, his child, his home: he is the most uxorious of heroes. Odysseus may spend much of his homeward wanderings from Troy bedding nymphs and goddesses, who are fair game in every sense,[5] but his mind, ultimately, is set upon Penelope and Ithaca, upon that symbolically immoveable marriage-bed, with its still-living olivewood post (*Od.*23.183ff.). Nor has there ever been a more moving tribute to the marital condition than that which Odysseus, again, pronounces – quite gratuitously – to the Phaeacian princess Nausicäa, a *jeune fille en fleur* buzzing with delightful dreams of marriage, who could be relied on to appreciate it at its true worth: 'For nothing is greater and better than when a man and a woman keep house with one mind together: much grief to their enemies, great joy to their friends, but they themselves know it best of all' (*Od.*6.182-5). This is, among other things, a testament to *equal partnership*, something we will not meet again for a very long time: and indeed one striking feature of Homer's women is their dignity, their independence, their freedom of action. This exists quite apart from those matrilinear hints that anthropologists have picked up among the Phaeacians and on Ithaca (e.g., why were suitors courting *Penelope,* clearly with an eye to the kingdom, while Laertes and Telemachus were both still very much around?). Victorian scholars were shocked to find Homeric kings' daughters not only doing the laundry, but unconcernedly bathing and rubbing down male guests, with no hint of impropriety, but rather that asexual casualness sometimes found today in a sauna. Wives, moreover, got Homeric consideration in that area often declared a product only of modern romanticism (understandably, when we look at some of the later evidence) – the lordly importation of concubines into the home. When Laertes first bought Eurycleia as a young maid, he 'treated her with as much respect as if they had been married, but never slept with her, to avoid offending his dear wife' (*Od.*1.432-3). Agamemnon was not so sensitive, and paid for it with his life: but the principle, even if later generations chose to forget it, had been established.

And sex? Homer's men and women both get great satisfaction from it, as do his gods: its power, sometimes personified in the moving force of

Aphrodite, is recognised, but not over-venerated when it comes into conflict with more fundamental social values. Helen, after all, is the symbol and embodiment of what blindly ruinous passion, the pure gonadic urge, can do to a man.[6] Paris abused the laws of hospitality, stole his host's wife, and started a ruinous war in consequence: after nearly ten years of indecisive fighting (as Homer stresses) he can *still* be dragged from the battlefield, *coram publico*, and into Helen's bed, by his ungovernable urge to fuck her, an urge even more violent than at the time of their first incendiary coupling on Kranäe (*Il*.3. 380-448). It is remarkable, and seldom stressed, that the only other *grande passion* in the *Iliad* – with nice symmetry, it belongs on the Achaean side – is that between Achilles and Patroclus. Though this relationship is not delineated in crudely sexual terms, the mythic tradition was well aware of its motivation,[7] and Homer himself abundantly and repeatedly stresses the intensity and closeness of the two heroes' feeling for one another: if not homosexual in presentation, it is most certainly homoerotic. Aeschines was right to interpret this reticence not as an indication that Homer shrank from conceiving the relationship in erotic terms, much less that he disapproved of it, but rather as a pointer to his cultivated sensitivity. There is a nice blending here of aristocratic tolerance and middle-class restraint.[8]

THOSE WHO USE THE CULTURES of Greece and Rome as arguments against the Puritan ethic (whether Christian or secular), praising their alleged encouragement of guilt-free sexual pleasure, whatever form it may take – old myths, alas, die hard – never, I feel, give enough weight to the highly significant Greek and Roman terms for the sexual organs. *Aidoia* and *pudenda* both are to be construed as those parts concerning which one should feel shame or modesty (not always quite the same thing). There can be a considerable slide here in semantic emphasis, ranging between 'respect' at one end of the scale and 'disgust' at the other: the position of the indicator, so to speak, is often a very useful guide to a culture's social and psychological health. One reason why I have placed such emphasis on the Homeric poems is because the social and sexual tenets they uphold are, by modern standards, quite exceptionally adult, sane, and well-integrated. This fact should be kept in mind when examining the sexual conventions described by Greek city-state writers during the next two centuries, the so-called Archaic Age, since *polis* society is commonly held to be progressive, whereas Homer's world often gets written off as a backward-looking and feudally ossified hangover from the Bronze Age. Comparison, however, as we shall see, would appear in many cases to indicate regression rather than enlightenment. One of the more piquant paradoxes (as a modern student sees it) about the ancient world is that Greek and Roman intellectuals – thinkers, playwrights, poets, historians, pamphleteers – were associated neither with political nor with sexual radicalism, both of which, indeed, they more often than not actively opposed, being generally lined up, as good *rentiers*, with the ruling class, the forces of law and order. Those who attack governments, from Hesiod to Juvenal, tend to have purely personal reasons for doing so: and I cannot think of any ancient author – Aristophanes included – who argued a case for greater sexual freedom.[9]

Though Homer continued to command respect throughout antiquity. Homeric mores are largely conspicuous by their absence from subsequent Greek literature. The characteristics of the period between 750 and 450 BC, the pre-classical or Archaic Age, are radically different. These centuries saw the spread of alphabetic writing, and the consequent establishment of law codes; a great colonising movement from Spain to the Black Sea; pioneering scientific and philosophical exploration in Ionia and south Italy; and the evolution of the city-state (*polis*), with which democratic institutions were so closely associated. It was an age of ferment, of intellectual discovery and organisation, culminating, appropriately enough, in the Persian Wars, which found Greeks standing off an authoritarian regime in the name of freedom. Socially, it was remarkable for the skill with which a tenacious aristocracy managed to adapt itself to new democratic political rules, while at the same time preserving intact its own code of manners, not least as regards sexual relations. The Athenian upper classes never entirely capitulated to *polis* respectability. Various apparent anomalies in our evidence all spring from this persistent conflict. We find, to begin with, a sudden upsurge of individualism in our literary sources: poets are now talking about themselves and their emotional affairs, cracking the old shell of bardic anonymity. They analyse the psychology of the heart, they cultivate unruly passions, they anatomise private sex in a way quite alien to Homer. The swing is away from heroics or familiality to non-socialised, and very often homosexual, relationships. At the same time, our sources also suggest a widespread, and oddly intolerant, depreciation of women, which persists into the classical period. Misogynistic contempt and fear flourish in a new, non-Homeric world peopled by faceless kitchen drudges or cheap whores. Taboo words are on occasion employed, taboo activities described. At the same time, as we have noted, genteel middle-class objections begin to be raised against the behaviour, in particular the sexual behaviour, sanctioned by Homer. (This is not such a paradox as might be thought; pornography always flourishes best in strict Bible-belt areas). It is clear that what the Greeks – or, more specifically, the Athenians – went through now was a lengthy conflict, largely class-based, over sexual values, between the old aristocratic code and those new bourgeois conventions which the *polis* made peculiarly its own. In the end, the *polis* might be thought to have won: by the time Aristophanes wrote *The Clouds* (423 BC) many aristocratic conventions recognisable from Archaic art and literature had become mere historical curiosities. Yet the legacy they left was both persistent and pervasive, surviving not only in the works of Plato and Aristotle, but also being taken over by Rome.

All this, of course, very clearly demonstrates the perils of generalising from inadequate or partial evidence. When we turn from Homer to his immediate literary successors, it looks, on the face of things, as though a rapid social revolution has taken place; and though such a possibility can't be entirely discounted, it is far more probable, first, that the mores we meet in Homer are, as it were, preserved only in epic aspic, and had been largely obsolete for centuries – during the whole of the Greek Dark Ages, in fact (*c.*1100 to *c.*850 BC), – when Homer himself came to compose the *Iliad* and the *Odyssey;* second, that the aristocratic-homosexual tradition, as we meet it, variously, in writers as diverse as Sappho, Theognis, Pindar, or Plato, represented only a tiny elitist minority at any time, deceptive through its intellectual force and articulate creativity; and third, that the surly misogynistic chauvinism which crops up in Hesiod and Semonides of Amorgos was a far more deeply rooted, and perennial, element in the Greek social structure than it has hitherto been fashionable to admit. We often forget that Greece was, and to a remarkable extent still remains, an agrarian peasant culture.[10] Hesiod's basic farm equipment is a homestead, a plough-ox – and a woman to do the ploughing (*Works and Days [WD]* 405-6). He assumes that if a woman shows interest in a man, what she's after is his barn (*WD* 373-5). A wife is simply a chattel, to be worked like a slave; yet her sex also makes her an object of unease and alarm.[11] Despite refrigeration, TV, and the transistor radio, things have not changed all that much in the Greek countryside to this day; as Walcot rightly says (pp.66-67), 'Hesiod is only a misogynist in the sense that all Greek males, whether ancient or modern, are misogynists when measured by the standards of sophisticated Western Europe and North America . . . His mistrust of women is an expression of the prevalent attitude towards women in Greek society.' This attitude is distilled in the famous poem by Semonides (seventh to sixth century BC), comparing various types of women to animals: the sluttish sow, the wicked vixen, the yapping bitch (who won't shut up even if a man 'knocks out her teeth with a stone'), the greedy, promiscuous ass, the sex-mad ferret, the lazy, extravagant mare, the ugly monkey ('oh the poor man who gets an armful of *that* disaster'). Only the hard-working, sexually aseptic bee wins a clean bill of health. '*Women!*' Semonides snorts, 'the biggest evil Zeus ever made!'[12] The Pandora legend should be read with these strictures in mind. Even today, when the Olympian religion is no longer in favour, a woman who bears a daughter tends to receive sympathy rather than congratulations: and only a male child can be taken behind the *eikonostasis* (rood screen) and there blessed by the Orthodox priest.

A society that depreciates its legitimate wives almost invariably compensates by creating a special niche for courtesans, and Greece was no exception to the rule.[13] From now on we hear a good deal about the *hetaira* (a nice euphemism: its literal meaning is 'female companion') who became a standard fixture – well illustrated by Attic vase painters – at Greek drinking parties, prostitute in essence but, as time went on, acquiring, geisha-like, various ancillary social graces, from dancing and musicianship to the art of good conversation. The rough uncertainties of a colonist's life, as we know from Archilochus, encouraged the usual camp followers and campaign whores. Archilochus himself (?715-?650 BC), who spent his life, as he tells us in numerous surviving fragments, fighting, drinking, and fornicating,[14] mostly in Thrace or on the newly-settled island of Thasos, was just as ready to seduce respectable ladies as tarts: a recently discovered fragment describes his conquest of his ex-fiancée's sister in strikingly graphic terms ('and let the white strength of me come/ while stroking her yellow hair'). While the tradition that both girls hanged themselves for shame because of his attacks is probably untrue, to have such kiss-and-tell ballads hawked round a smallish island must have been, in that tight-knit village society, something worse than embarrassing.

Some erotic activities, however, were not to Archilochus' taste. In particular, he exhibits the kind of guffawing revulsion from homosexuality that marks the macho male in any age; if he were alive today he would be laying down the law about fruits and pantywaists like any locker-room pundit. There are two interesting points to notice here: first, that in that rough colonists' world the phenomenon not only existed, but was visible enough to attract notice: and second, that what it aroused in Archilochus was derision and contempt. Significantly, those he accuses of it seem to have been aristocrats, cavalry officers, members of an elite. This should not surprise us. Throughout the whole period during which homosexuality was most openly and approvingly represented, both in literature and art – that is, during the last two centuries immediately prior to the Persian Wars (490-479 BC) – we always find it closely bound up with notions of inherited excellence, pedigree, and privilege, with the politics and responsibilities of blood. It stands in direct opposition to that progressive political democratisation which distinguishes sixth-century Athens: and this is an important clue to understanding its later manifestations.

For example, Theognis of Megara (*fl. c.*540 BC), who preached Spartan-style moral uplift to his beloved Kyrnos – and whose vigorous, not to say earthy, erotic verse employed much imagery drawn from that perennial elitist occupation, the breeding and training of horses – was a passionate reactionary, exiled for his anti-populist politicking.[15] Sappho and her contemporary Alcaeus of Lesbos were both similarly exiled, again because of involvement in, or sympathy with, aristocratic coups of some sort: Sappho may have ranked affairs of the heart above naval or military glory (fr.16.1-4 Lobel-Page), but socially she too aligned herself with the Best People, while Alcaeus, a more activist poet, like Theognis cultivated a pederastic image (Cic. *Tusc.Disp.*4.71: Horace, *Odes* 1.32.9-11). Solon (fr.25) not only acknowledged the pleasures of pederasty, but also (Plut. *Sol.*1) passed a law forbidding slaves 'to have a boy-lover, so that his intention was evidently to class this as an honourable and dignified practice and thus, in a sense, to recommend it to reputable men by the act of forbidding it to the unworthy'.

The class emphasis is unmistakable. Pindar (who died in the arms of his lover Theoxenos) reveals an identical atmosphere, which numerous more or less explicit representations on high-quality black-figure vases[16] only serve to confirm. The sixth-century cult of homosexuality, at least as revealed in our surviving evidence, was indissolubly associated with aristocratic values and politics. (This is not, of course, to suggest that homosexual practices were in fact restricted to an elite: Eros is no respecter of parties. What it *does* mean is that pederasty, in its more public aspects, did carry elitist connotations for the Athenian man-in-the-street.) The subsequent triumph of democracy through Salaminian sea-power – nothing elitist about the 'naval rabble' that rowed the triremes – together with the establishment of a middle class based on wealth rather than blood, forced the traditional peasant and elitist values of Attica's old two-class society into a fresh confrontation, and compromise, during the so-called Periclean Age.

IT IS WORTH NOTING that neither Theognis nor Sappho regarded their homosexual proclivities as in any way incompatible with marriage. They were both married themselves, and Theognis tells Kyrnos (*Theog.*1225-6) that 'nothing is more delectable than a good wife'. He can testify to this from personal experience, he says, and advises Kyrnos to follow his example. This attitude highlights one fundamental difference between ancient and modern homosexual mores: with certain special exceptions (Plato, as we shall see, is atypical in the extreme), neither Greeks nor Romans professed to find any kind of psychological or moral barrier between heterosexual and homosexual experience. Some practices earned their contempt (e.g. an adult male who cultivated the passive, feminine role), and various formal restrictions (see below, p. 142) were imposed on the type of homosexual relationship sanctioned by society: but it was taken for granted, by Greeks and Romans alike, that any person was liable to be erotically aroused by members of either sex, and that susceptibility of one sort did not preclude the other. Kritoboulos, who in Xenophon's *Symposium* (4. 12-16) so enthusiastically praises the charms of his boy-lover Kleinias, is represented as being newly married at the time (ibid. 2. 3). Generalisations about sexual patterns in antiquity are dangerous, but the assumption of bisexual excitability does seem to have been virtually universal, at all periods, and this is something to bear in mind, since our own moral conditioning on the subject tends to be so very different.

On the other hand, though bisexualism may have been an unquestioned fact of life, its mere existence does not in any way imply universal sexual permissiveness. *Tout comprendre* was by no means *tout pardonner* in the ancient world, and nothing could be further from the truth than to treat, say, Plato's Athens (which was not most people's Athens), or even the Rome of Petronius (which, equally, was not most people's Rome), as a beautiful playground for highminded or socially endorsed *amitiés particulières*. The period from the

Persian Wars to the death of Alexander (479-323 BC), including the Periclean Age, marks the zenith and initial decline of the city-state: we can understand neither the social evolution of sexual mores during this period, nor the way in which these mores were reflected in art and literature, if we assume that their general underlying attitude was a kind of indiscriminate anti-Christian sensualism. Sexual abstinence was a prominent feature of religious ritual long before thinkers such as Plato made a moral or philosophical virtue out of it. To copulate in a temple was unthinkable: no one could enter any shrine after intercourse until he had undergone ritual purification.[17] Such provisions, like the names for the private parts (above, p.134), hardly suggest a total absence of shame or guilt.

It is also significant that only one or two specific literary genres – e.g. iambic raillery in the tradition of Archilochus and Hipponax, or Attic Old Comedy, typified for us by Aristophanes – were permitted overt sexual or scatological allusions, much less the use of 'four-letter words'. Tragedy, even the work of an 'advanced' playwright like Euripides, remained circumspect almost to prudishness in its language and subject-matter, though euphemistic metaphor (then as always) was a great standby: a serious Greek poet was not allowed to call a cunt a cunt, but he could, and did, talk about 'the split meadow of Aphrodite'. Euripides had to rewrite the original version of his *Hippolytus* because Athenians found a play that showed Phaedra directly propositioning her stepson on-stage shocking to their sense of decorum.[18] If sex was taboo, so was violence: Clytemnestra could not murder Agamemnon, nor Medea her childern, in full view of the audience. It is not hard to deduce, from Aristophanes' ceaseless taunting of Euripides over his 'shocking' characters – and indeed, by contrast, from the violent obscenities that came cascading out on occasions of licensed buffoonery: compare Carnival in the Mediterranean and Latin America today – just how rigid a standard of sexual restraint was normally imposed. Decorum, indeed, was a major factor in all public art.

Yet at the same time there can be no doubt that the actual range of sexual or excretory topics to which explicit reference could be made in literature or art shrank very considerably between the mid-sixth and the late fourth centuries BC. This may have been in part an egalitarian reaction against aristocratic mores: the disappearance of homosexual vase-paintings and poetry certainly could be interpreted this way. But the artists, with Rabelaisian enthusiasm, had portrayed other activities it would take some ingenuity to define as elitist: intercourse *a tergo* (the most frequently represented position), group orgies, parties where everyone seems to be either masturbating, defecating, or throwing up, for the most part in full public view. What was the market for these cups and jolly jugs, and just why, about the mid-fifth century, did the bottom (so to speak) fall out of it? Whether the activities themselves went on or not (and there is some evidence that they did), there was clearly a new social unwillingness to publicise or describe them. Why? The answer would seem to be an upsurge of middle-class urban *pudeur*, a familiar phenomenon in any rapidly developing bourgeois society, and one for which Periclean Athens could provide all the necessary ingredients.

As we have seen (above, p. 132), intellectual criticism of sexual laxity in the traditional myths concerning the gods began as early as the sixth century, and was closely bound up with the new secular, rational morality of the *polis*. This not only laid the foundations for a progressive movement away from archaic tribal values, but by its very nature emphasised civic (i.e. in a modified sense, urban) centralisation at the expense of the rural outback, with its local cults, its patriarchal landed gentry, and its outspoken, earthy, old-fashioned ways. Now urban intellectuals of any age, being brought up in the relatively artificial circumstances of the big city, away from midden, byre and barnyard, very soon lose that intimate acquaintance with, and respect for, the raw facts of life that mark the country squire or stockbreeder. Inexperience is the mother of distaste. The capacity for abstraction not only induces a sense of moral superiority over lesser breeds still rooted – and, pig-like, rooting – in the concrete vulgarity of brute facts, but also generates a self-protective cocoon of genteel euphemism to insulate thinkers from reality's more unpleasant edges. This at once suggests an explanation not only for the increasing inhibition in sexual matters that marks the later fifth century, but also for that special intellectual enskyment of pederasty most familiar to us from Plato's *Symposium* and *Phaedrus*. Heterosexual eros, for such thinkers, lacked uplift because of its inevitable association with the mindless coupling of the farmyard: it was animal, sub-rational, a matter of mere instinct, creative only in the physical sense, and to be transcended (as Diotima revealingly observes) by those who are 'fertile in soul'. It is no accident that Plato reveals so profound an ignorance of animals. He personifies the aristocrat, not as working landowner, but as a relatively new phenomenon, the urban intellectual living *in absentia* off inherited wealth or the profits of his estates, and whose preoccupation with (theoretical) eros has, in Plato's case, to be offset against a marked, and characteristic, distaste for actual sex.[19]

The older aristocratic tradition of stylish and luxurious hedonism is exemplified to perfection by that elegant anachronism Alcibiades (?451-404 BC), a man, if ever there was one, born out of his time, with his chariot victories and racing debts, his high living, good looks, and indiscriminate sexual conquests, his intellectual brilliance, his casual indifference to the social disapproval of inferiors and equals alike. (His parties were notorious, suitable material for the world of the black-figure vase-painters.) *Polis* loyalty was only one of the middle-class civic virtues that he discarded whenever it suited him. He moved in the Socratic circle, which he seems to have held spellbound with his eternally adolescent charms: the perpetual *eromenos,* or teenage love-object, flirting with an older lover (*erastes*), in that formal sexual quadrille of pursuit and elusiveness that constituted the socially acceptable homosexual relationship at Athens.[20] Even Plato was clearly fascinated by him, though their attitudes were about as diametrically opposed as they could be, since Alcibiades saw no virtue in sexual self-denial, and indeed, if we are to trust Plato (*Symp*.218c-219d), made at least one spirited attempt to seduce Socrates himself. Alcibiades and Plato shared a common aristocratic background (including a marked distaste for democratic institutions), and indeed a common intellectual heritage, that of the philosophers and Sophists: where they differed, fundamentally, was in their social and moral assumptions. Plato's abiding concern was with the eternal verities behind the flux of appearances. But from the time when, as a precocious boy, he ran dialectical rings round his guardian Pericles (Xenophon, *Memorabilia* 1.2.40-46), Alcibiades' only concern with the truth – as with a political situation – was to manipulate it to his own best advantage. If we treat him as a latterday throwback to the sixth-century Attic or Ionian aristocrat, we will not go far wrong.[21]

Equally symptomatic of the old ways, but at a quite different level, is the cheerful, lowbrow countryman who plays such a prominent role in several of Aristophanes' early plays: e.g. Dicaeopolis in *The Acharnians* (425) and Strepsiades in *The Clouds* (423). Both are foul-mouthed, coarse, pragmatic, sensual, stridently anti-urban and anti-intellectual, moving in a world of simple appetites and grossly physical pleasures, attributing all their troubles to city bureaucrats and politicians, whom they describe, generically, as a bunch of dish-cooking bum-boys, *euryproktoi* (lit. 'stretched anuses'), the equivalent of such inferior creatures as women or foreigners (cf. Dover, *op. cit.* 103ff),[22] and, by implication, wholly alien to the procreative life of the countryside. When Strepsiades tries to shore up his tottering finances by learning sharp practice at the Socratic 'Think-Tank', he finds himself totally out of his depth in a world of (often bogus) abstractions.[23] Dicaeopolis, dismissing the war with Sparta as a profitable racket cooked up by demagogues and militarists, contracts out and makes his own private peace. Both are drawn as victims of that steady centralisation of government in Attica that had been going on since Solon's day, strengthening Athens' power at the expense of the rural demes, replacing local cults and squirearchies by the Panathenaic Festival and more controllable voting claques in the Assembly.

This concentration of administrative powers, coupled with the intellectual revolution pioneered by the Sophists, did more than anything else to undermine the old rural-aristocratic mores, sexual and social alike. Thus farmers and big landowners became natural allies against the new order: no accident that Strepsiades marries an aristocratic lady. There I was, he reminisces of his wedding, smelling of wine-lees, sheepskins, and *profits:* and there *she* was, smelling of perfume, deep-throat kisses, and *extravagance* (*Clouds* 49-52). He wants her class, she needs his cash: what they produce between them is a spendthrift son uncommonly like Alcibiades. These two deserve each other no less than the president's widow and the shipping millionaire. Yet both of them, though poles apart socially, subscribe to the values of the rural *ancien régime*. It is hard to imagine Coesyra, any more than her husband, embracing urban rule, abstract principles, middle-class values, or, worst of all, egalitarian demagoguery.

It should be stressed that there is nothing exotic or out of the ordinary about Dicaeopolis and Strepsiades: the characters who inhabit the Platonic dialogues are far rarer birds. Such countrymen remain, now as then, a major social factor in what has always been a predominantly agricultural economy. (Andreas Papandreou is no more typical of Greece outside Athens than was Cleon or Hyperbolus.) The interesting thing is that in the late fifth century, when rural conservatives were fighting a losing battle against City Hall, they happened to find, in Aristophanes, a passionate advocate who immortalised them in some of the finest political comedies ever written. This is one of the comparatively few occasions on which the urban intellectuals did *not* have it all their own way when establishing the literary and historical record for posterity. Yet even so, most of us, trying to visualise Athens' social, and in particular her sexual, mores, find Plato's dramatic special pleading obstinately uppermost in our minds. As Dover says (*op.cit.*13): 'Modern readers of *Phaedrus* and *Symposium,* which they may well have seen in the pornography section of a bookshop, are apt to believe that what they find therein is the quintessential doctrine of the Greeks on the whole topic of homosexuality, expressed in definitive terms by their acknowledged spokesman.' As should by now be clear, this is a complete illusion. Plato, far from speaking for all Greeks, spoke for no more than a tiny (and unpopular) minority of Athenians. By making adult homosexual eros the foundation of his ethic, rather than a transitional phase of prolonged adolescence between puberty and marriage, he alienated a large majority of his fellow citizens. By formulating a non-sexual (rather than a socially controlled, but sexually active) ideal, he not only emphasised his urban, non-agricultural position, but provided Aristophanic man – a far more typical representative of Athens than Plato and his circle – with a standing joke. Even today the phrase 'Platonic love', with its overtones of unreality and hypocrisy, is always good for a laugh and a flip definition (e.g. 'shooting yourself with a gun that isn't loaded'). Even as a philosopher Plato was challenged by other followers of Socrates.[24]

A less exalted, and for that reason probably more accurate, picture of the Socratic circle's quotidian activities is provided by another rural conservative, Xenophon (?430–?350 BC), a decent, unpretentious, and (fortunately for us) on the whole unimaginative writer, who in his youth cultivated Socrates, and had a retentive memory for what he heard. Xenophon also furnished a great deal of invaluable evidence concerning the kind of life led by an average Athenian-born country gentleman, well-read, but less intellectually and morally committed than Plato. We see him as a student of philosophy; as a cavalry commander and general; patiently and affectionately training a young wife in the intricacies of household management ('Ischomachus' is clearly a transparent mask for the author); hunting on his estate in the Peloponnese; writing treatises on horsemanship and elementary economics. As a testamentary counterbalance to the intellectual and social scene drawn by Plato his work is of immense value. He is altogether more relaxed about sexual relationships: though he too takes *paiderastia* in his stride, he is also capable – literally in the same breath – of portraying a husband and wife as passionately in love with one another (*Symp.* 8.3, cf.4.8.), which must have been a more common occurrence than we nowadays tend to assume. Marriage for Greeks – then as now – was not *solely* 'a mechanism for the inheritance of property'.[25]

The evidence of Xenophon and Aristophanes, then, together with the material to be gleaned from the fourth-century Attic orators (Dover *GPM passim*), comes as a welcome – and an unusual – offset to the more influential, more 'literary' picture projected by Plato's early dialogues. What these writers remind us of – and at times the reminder is very necessary – is how ordinary, how familiar to any European, ancient or modern, much of the classical Greek's day-to-day sexual conduct must appear. It reveals a pattern common to all Western cultures, a stockpot of social clichés as unremarkable then as now. No surprise to learn that stepmothers harboured designs (murderous or erotic) on their stepsons; that some husbands had it off with the maid, while others, more flamboyant, imported mistresses into their home; that some wives, like Deianeira, were jealous ninnies, while others hit the bottle, or sneaked out at night for assignations with lovers; that incest was at least well enough known to be employed as a regular smear-charge (like buggery against a medieval Pope); that adultery was a commonplace, masturbation a standing joke, and all the sexual variants, from cunnilingus to fellatio, in regular use,[26] despite the strict conventions governing their public discussion. In any society the range of sexual options is limited (marriage and fucking being universal constants), and most of the options will get taken up.

It is, of course, the atypical or socially significant case that attracts most attention. Plato is not the only example, though he remains the best known. Why, for instance, does Herodotus have such a weakness for mildly kinky anecdotes, involving variously voyeurism, necrophilia, anal intercourse (with a woman), and sexual mutilation?[27] Surely not just because of his cosmopolitan East Greek background? And what should we make of the evidence, largely drawn from Attic drama, that suggests, if not an Athenian feminist movement, at least an increasingly forceful, and vocal, pressure applied by strong-minded women in social, moral, even political affairs – and which contrasts so strikingly with Pericles' briefly patronising advice, in his Funeral Oration (Thuc. 2.45.2), that a woman's goal should be to have men talk about her as little as possible, whether in praise or reproof? (By a nice paradox Plato, in the *Menexenus*, 236B, suggests that this speech was actually the work of Aspasia!) Aeschylus' Clytemnestra is sexually as well as politically aggressive, a strong-willed, dominating, intelligent woman, a natural leader. Sophocles' Antigone – in her own way an aristocratic traditionalist – takes on the representative of a patriarchal *polis* bureaucracy with equal energy, brilliance, and arrogant contempt. Aristophanes' Lysistrata organises a sexual strike by wives against war; both she and Praxagora (the heroine of the *Ecclesiazusae*) aim to take over the Assembly and run Athens' politics. All these plays – which span a period between 458 and 393 BC – likewise reveal deep anxiety, in their male characters, at such reversals of traditional sex roles.[28] Euripides' heroines – even when, like Alcestis, they are given to self-sacrifice in the traditional and approved manner – still force us to take a very cool look at the (equally traditional, equally approved) Greek chauvinistic male, who remains with us to this day, in all his self-assertive, mother-fixated glory. As Pomeroy says (p. 110), Euripides 'shows us women victimised by patriarchy in almost every possible way'. Whatever the truth about women's status in Periclean Athens (a topic still hotly debated by scholars, not always on exclusively rational grounds), it is hard not to see, behind this dramatic obsession, a genuine – and unpopular – movement, encouraged by progressive opinion and the effects of a long and debilitating war, in favour of greater independence for women. It is the burning debates of the day that fill any theatre: if the dominant woman was not a problem, why does she so constantly reappear, in tragedy and comedy alike, taking her curtain-call, as it were, at the close of the Peloponnesian War, as Agave in the *Bacchae,* with her son Pentheus' severed head stuck on a thyrsus? Euripides, like Ibsen, only achieved real popularity after his death, when the causes he had fought for were won: and who, today, would argue that Ibsen was tilting at mere literary windmills?

SOON AFTER THE END OF the fifth century BC some fundamental changes in Greek – which here, for all practical purposes, means Athenian – social attitudes become apparent: changes that foreshadowed the more cosmopolitan outlook of the Hellenistic world, and the mixed Graeco-Roman culture that succeeded it. We here reach more familiar ground, since what Rome took from Greece was, in essence, not Athens' classical heritage, but the later internationalised culture of Alexandria and Pergamon: and what modern Europe rediscovered at the Renaissance was, similarly, an amalgam of imperial Rome and post-Alexandrian Greece as refracted through Roman eyes. This, if any, is the phase of ancient culture that a contemporary reader can explore with some sense of shared values and continuity: the landscape, though pre-industrial, is at least one that we recognise. To take a simple but striking instance, it is in the fourth century that we first come across the (to us) obvious notion of romantic individualism, the idea that erotic passion and psychological self-awareness are there to be cultivated for their own sakes. Yet up to that point the archaic and classical writers had, with some unanimity, presented the onset of passionate love as something worse than infatuation, as a dangerous lapse from reason, a temporary madness that one prayed to all the gods to be relieved from as quickly as possible.[29]

There are other significant pointers. In sculpture the ubiquitous male nude becomes less aggressive, its musculature appreciably softer (as we can see at once from the Praxitelean Hermes), and, even more significant, there now appear equally soft and sensuous female nudes – in competition, as it were – rather than those sexless, decorously draped figures previously in vogue. (The subsequent striking obsession with hermaphrodites looks like a compromise solution designed to give everyone the best of both worlds.) Ironically, while Plato was promoting homoerotic Eros and arguing for less physical sex all round, his fellow citizens seem to have been moving in precisely the opposite direction on both counts: they were certainly looking at women with new eyes. Plato's 'Heavenly Aphrodite' never really stood a chance against the 'Common Aphrodite' he so despised.[30] About the only thing the two Aphrodites had in common – in contrast to the old rural-aristocratic ethic – was a new genteel passion for euphemism: but then by now they were both very much urban ladies. No accident that at the same time the demand for Old Comedy's licensed ithyphallic horseplay dwindled and died, so that by Aristotle's day uninhibited sexual plain-speaking was condemned as 'dirty talk' (aischrologia), while a slave in Menander's Ghost (Phasma, vv.39–43) apologises, with prissy circumlocution, for using the word 'shit' – something it is hard to imagine Aristophanes doing. By the Hellenistic period commentators on Homer are tut-tutting about how 'unseemly' or 'inappropriate' it is for Thetis to tell her son Achilles (Il.24.129ff.) that going without sex and food is bad for him, in a context that makes the Homeric attitude crystal-clear: a good fuck and a square meal have the same therapeutic effect. Truism it may be, but the scholiast blushes regardless.[31] The new morality – middle-class, mealy-mouthed, romantic – has triumphed over peasant earthiness and aristocratic insouciance alike. In essence it is what has survived, with Roman accretions and Christian modifications, to the present day.

There is a striking – and, for some, alarming – sense of déjà vu about the Hellenistic era for a modern reader. The polis – already under centrifugal pressure from growing individualism and commercial interests – was dealt a fatal blow by Philip of Macedon at Chaeronea (338 BC), and finally succumbed, as an institution, to the vast bureaucratic kingdoms established by Alexander's successors and then absorbed piecemeal in the Roman empire. The teeming, polyglot cities of the third and second centuries BC – the Alexandria of Theocritus' affluent, concert-going, vapid suburban housewives (Idyll 15) – generated a new social pattern, characteristic and enduring, what Lewis Mumford has stigmatised as Megalopolis in decline: Rome itself offers the most aggravated example of it. The main features of this pattern[32] are large-scale capitalism and free enterprise, authoritarian government, the standardisation of culture, the encyclopedic tabulation of science and scholarship, an obsession with mere size and number – the tallest buildings, the vastest food supply – and, for the individual, an increasing sense of alienation, the determined pursuit of affluence, the retreat from political involvement to a private world of social and domestic trivia, a growing preoccupation with chance (*Tyche*), magic, astrology, exotic foreign cults, and, above all, sex. Hellenistic literature emphasised technique and artifice, obscure mythology, arcane scholarship, the psychopathology of character, books made out of books. In poetry and art alike, idealism was out, and realism in – or, more often, the seductive (and at times grotesque) pseudo-realism of kitsch, pastoral, and pornography. The romantic picaresque novel made its appearance, and proved vastly popular (it took the upper-crust Roman genius of Petronius to put a satirical pill inside the sugar). Small wonder, then, that the past few years have witnessed an unprecedented upsurge of interest in Hellenistic culture: for this troubled age of ours it offers, even more than the fourteenth century AD, that 'distant mirror' so brilliantly formulated by Barbara Tuchman. It shows us our own flawed humanity.

The most immediately striking phenomenon is the enormous increase of heterosexual passion – whether with marriage as its prime object or not – as a motif in our surviving literature, and the regular assumption that its natural and desirable end is physical fulfilment: on both counts a flat reversal of Plato's attitude. 'Sweeter than ice-water in summer', wrote Asclepiades (*Anth. Pal.* 5.169), 'it is when one cloak covers two lovers.' Characteristically, there is no indication of the lovers' sex in this epigram, and in fact Asclepiades, like many other ancient poets, wrote love poems, with fine impartiality, to girls and boys alike. We should not assume a swing of opinion against *paiderastia*: there is ample evidence (including Book 12 of the Greek Anthology, exclusively devoted to homosexual themes) which suggests that boys were not only as popular as ever, but cooperated with their pursuers a good deal less coyly than they had done in the fifth century. Heterosexual activities did not supplant *paiderastia,* but simply supplemented it: variety, now, was the name of the game.

Antimachus and Philetas established the convention of writing volumes of love poetry to one's mistress, a formula later taken over by Roman elegists from Catullus to Ovid, who exploited the idea of servitude in love to a dominant, capricious mistress with masochistic (and decidedly un-Greek) fervour. The concept of the *grande passion* was popularised, with incalculable effects on subsequent European literature: the Medea drawn by Apollonius Rhodius (*fl.* third century BC) in his *Argonautica* – heart a-quiver for Jason like the flicker of sunlight on water, speechless, rapt, the original *jeune fille en fleur* – is the ancestor of too many star-crossed heroines, not least Virgil's Dido.

It is also in the *Argonautica* – which found a far wider public than the poems of Asclepiades – that the cliché of Cupid's arrows, the fiery darts of love (Ap. Rhod. 3.275ff.), really gets launched on its long literary career. Romantic passion, as a concept, spread with the speed, and heat, of the proverbial bush fire. Countless epigrams testify to the agonising pains of unrequited desire, the heaven-on-earth of attainment. *Carpe diem*: a girl's concern for her virginity draws the brisk rebuttal that in Hades we're dust and ashes, no sex there, you can't take it with you (*Anth.Pal.* 5.85). Lovers from Asclepiades (*Anth.Pal.* 5.189) to Ovid (*Amores* 1.6) pine all night outside their beloved's door, or at least write stylised outside-the-closed-door poems (*paraklausithyra*) claiming that they did: *chagrin d'amour* really does seem to be a more potent emotion than *plaisir d'amour*, besides lasting longer. If this literature is what most encourages the delusion that the Greeks, to quote Sir Kenneth Dover (*Greek Popular Morality* 205: cf.n.25 above), 'lived in a rosy haze of uninhibited sexuality', it also abounds in poetic artifice, *topos*, and convention.

There is a nice paradox here. As the erotic experience in literature shifted from the public to the private domain it became less, rather than more, in touch with life as actually lived and loved: graffiti, epitaphs, and nonliterary documents on papyrus (wills, marriage-contracts, private letters) reveal a far more stable world of touching, if humdrum, relationships. 'She loved her husband with her whole heart' and 'was charming in conversation', declares the sepulchral inscription of a Roman wife named Claudia. In one Hellenistic marriage-contract it is specified that the husband shall not insult his wife by bringing home a mistress, or have children (on pain of forfeiting the dowry) by other women. 'I bequeath to my wife', wrote Acusilaus of Oxyrhynchus in Egypt, 'whatever I may leave in the way of furniture, utensils, objects of gold, clothing, ornaments, wheat, pulse, crops, all my household stock . . . ' Hilarion, in 1 BC, writes to his wife Alis: 'I beg and entreat you, take care of the little one, and as soon as we receive our pay I will send it up to you . . . You have said, "Do not forget me." How can I forget you?' 'Good luck, Valens,' reads one Pompeian graffito, scribbled on Valens' house wall, 'I wish it had been me marrying you.'

Humankind, as Eliot shrewdly remarked, cannot bear very much reality, an apothegm which the literary portrayal of sex tends to bear out in unexpected ways. One of the sillier judgments from antiquity was that which claimed not to know whether Menander (342/1-*c.*290 BC) had imitated life, or life Menander. In fact he spent his entire career avoiding the realistic portrayal of contemporary life, and with good reason. Living as he did in an Athens reduced to political insignificance, caught between the fierce struggles of Alexander's power-hungry successors, Menander, who was writing to please his audiences, concerned himself exclusively with domestic trivia and artificial romance, stock types (the pimp, the parasite, the braggart soldier), and far-fetched happy endings. The world of pirates, foundlings, kidnapped heiresses, and long-lost siblings he portrays, however tricked out with shrewd characterisation and peppy moral aphorisms, belongs to folklore and popular mythology: social realism has little part in it.

This, clearly, did not bother Menander's audiences, who, we can imagine, had no great liking for the world in which they found themselves, and preferred fantasy to unpalatable facts, a psychological addiction which the Roman playwrights Plautus and Terence (who both adapted Menander's material) found as flourishing in their day as Samuel Goldwyn or Norman Lear have done in ours. Cunning slaves, manipulative pimps and bawds, irate fathers, wastrel sons and the rest no doubt did, and do, occur in real life: but for Menander (or Sheridan, or Noël Coward) they were no more than humours, cardboard cut-outs from a perennial pantomime. Sex and money remain the eternal prizes, but the girls, though constantly exposed to the regulation fate worse than death, all come through in the end as triumphantly inviolate as any Barbara Cartland heroine, getting Mr Right *and* his father's cash at the very end of Act V.

Greek novels explore this world of sexual fantasy in an even more grotesque manner: *Daphnis and Chloë,* for instance, depends on the notion of a young country couple too innocent to know about intercourse, the ultimate improbability to anyone brought up within reach of a farm. This gap in understanding between city and country is represented to perfection by what was perhaps the most characteristic literary development of the Hellenistic age: the pastoral idyll. Its ideals prettify the bucolic. The rural effusions of Theocritus, Bion, or Moschus, with their piping and waterfalls, their leisurely serenades of Amaryllis and other equally unreal country maidens, their sanitised goats and sheep, their abundant and largely effortless harvests, their perfect weather and formal landscapes, consciously romanticise the shepherd's life almost past recognition. Their mythical Arcadia (the real Arcadia was, is, remote, backward, mountainous) could only have been invented by nostalgic urban intellectuals who had never herded sheep, much less milked cows, in their lives, but were hooked on the seductive dream of a lost rural Golden Age. Theocritus' herdsmen retain at least some semblance of earthiness: they bugger each other *al fresco* when bored (*Idyll* 5), carve wood, chase girls. But Polyphemus' outsize and milky devotion to Galatea (*Idyll* 11.19ff.) hints at the stylised sentimentality inherent in the genre. These shepherds are fair poets, but no one believes in their sheep or goats. Virgil's blandly pederastic Corydon is a mere literary humour: the way is being prepared for Marie Antoinette and her idiot Court milkmaids.

Unreason and fantasy are compounded by those implacable demands for instant gratification that stamp a consumer culture, and were directly responsible, throughout the Graeco-Roman period, for a quite startling explosion of erotic magic, reflected equally in the literature and in spells or curses surviving on lead tablets or papyrus: spells (*katadesmoi, defixiones*) to compel desire in cooled-off lovers (Theocr. *Idyll* 2), to punish infidelity, prevent impotence, and generally to bend universal laws for the attainment of private pleasures.[33] There is, of course, a nexus between magic and pornography, which, again, seeks to reshape nature as *ad hominem* (or *ad feminam*) wish-fulfilment, by projecting fantasies of stakhanovite yet reductionist sexual athletics, all parts and no whole. Though true pornography was rarer in antiquity than we might guess from some modern bookshops, such beady-eyed practitioners as Sotades, Herodas, or, later, Martial, with their dildoes, scatology, and bisexual couplings, suggest that the formula has stayed fairly constant down the ages.

Urbanity, in every sense, reached its apogee in antiquity with that witty and polished Roman elegist Ovid (43 BC to 17/18 AD), who spent almost forty years of his life writing erotic verse: one alleged reason for his exile by Augustus in AD 8 was his notorious spoof-didactic manual of seduction, *The Art of Love*. Ovid was the last in a sequence of Roman love poets – Gallus, Catullus, Tibullus, above all Propertius – who developed a virtually new genre, the erotic elegy, keying it to an overmastering, hopeless passion for some always exacting and more often than not cruelly elusive mistress. Catullus was tortured by his love-hate for 'Lesbia' (pseudonyms remained *de rigueur* for these ladies, and their social status has been the subject of much debate); Propertius, with masochistic relish, described the humiliations inflicted on him by 'Cynthia' and her ominous-sounding successor, 'Nemesis'. All that remained for Ovid to do, by way of innovation, was to poke poetic fun at this solemn obsessionalism, which he duly did, equating the pursuit of sex with military service, in a sparkling display of ironic parody and tongue-in-cheek self-deflation. His erotic verse is so allusively literary that some scholars have suspected – wrongly, I think – his own pseudonymous mistress, 'Corinna', of being a mere literary fiction.

In any case, Ovid's sophisticated *reductio ad absurdum* of his predecessors' high and Werther-like passions finished off Roman erotic elegy as a viable genre. He remains by far the most modern poet to survive from antiquity: and one of the most modern things about him is the fact that he found the battle of the sexes irresistibly comic (I still regret that no editor ever commissioned Thurber to illustrate *The Art of Love*). He might claim, with one eye on Augustus' new moral legislation, that he was writing exclusively for courtesans and *demi-mondaines*, fair game for the gallants who hung about Rome's theatres and arcades in the hope of a quick pick-up: but his own poems make it all too clear that what he really had in mind was the world, so familiar to us today, of well-heeled wife-swopping and discreet, if perilous, adventures in social adultery. Ovid's erotic poems, together with the lurid revelations of Tacitus and Petronius, were between them largely responsible for that persistent myth of Rome having fallen through her own fatal moral decadence (cf. below, pp. 256ff.)

Yet it would be a mistake, again, to suppose that Graeco-Roman civilisation evolved as an increasingly permissive culture which only Christianity, in the end, could control or change. The sense of restraint, of social decorum, as at Athens, was always there: the extent of its influence varied, but it was never a negligible force. The age that produced Catullus also threw up that stupefyingly respectable bourgeois politician Cicero: of the two, Cicero was by far the more typical. The *Meditations* of Marcus Aurelius remind us that, at the very close of classical antiquity, a chaste Stoic spirit was not quite such an anomaly as we might suppose from skimming the racier anecdotes of Suetonius or Juvenal's rebarbative satires.

We hear a good deal about the sexual puritanism supposedly imposed on a cheerfully guiltless pagan culture by St Paul's tight-lipped disciples: the monastic exodus to the Egyptian desert, the dirt, the fasting, the self-flagellation, the graphic temptations of St Anthony. Yet none of this killjoy ethic was new, or even specifically Christian. The instinct had been there from the beginning. Paradoxically, it reaches its anti-romantic apogee almost a century before Christ in a passionate atheist, Lucretius (94-55 BC), who devoted a long section of his philosophical poem *De Rerum Natura* (4.1058ff.) to sex, piling detail on sickened and sickening detail, harnessing the rhetoric of disgust to biological exegesis, the 'cold friction of expiring sense'. Juvenal by comparison is mild: the old satirist may find women either bores or bitches, but his pragmatic solution is to sleep with a boy instead (*Sat.* 6.34ff.; cf. p.251 below). The literature of sex in antiquity is full of these paradoxes: its very unpredictability is what makes it so intriguing. We should, as I hope I have shown, be cautious of over-indulging our uneasy sense of self-identification with cosmopolitan Hellenistic and Roman attitudes: this does not mean that the striking parallels they provide are all illusory. Sex *is* the ever-interesting topic (for once the cliché is right), not least because, in a matter of vital concern to each and every one of us, no consensus is attainable, by historians or anyone else. That, of course, does not relieve us of the responsibility for trying.

X

THE MACEDONIAN
CONNECTION

FTER TUTANKHAMUN, ALEXANDER. In late 1980, with an explosion of publicity, yet another spectacular venture in museum
promotion was launched. It was fitting, and historically ironic,
that Time Inc. and the National Bank of Greece, co-sponsors of
the exhibition, should have patented as its trademark the so-called 'royal
Macedonian starburst'. Ironic, because it is clear from recent research[1] that
this emblem occurred in many different places and periods, and, despite
Herodotus' anecdote (8.137-140) about an ancestor of Alexander I symbolically
encircling a shaft of sunlight for his wages, was in all likelihood neither royal,
nor Macedonian, nor even beyond all doubt a starburst. Fitting, because the
major exhibits of the display, and *a fortiori* the claims made about them, all
depended on a concatenation of tenuous hypotheses and obstinately ambivalent
evidence, remorselessly touted as proven fact in the interests of national pride
and publicity. But then 'The Search for Alexander' – was ever a title more
misleading? – had little time for the still small voice of historical doubt.
Regally packaged and presented, it toured the cultural centres of the USA –
Washington, Chicago, Boston, San Francisco, New York – to the accom-
paniment of media superlatives and the most lavish social enhancement.

There were black-tie celebrity dinners, with politicians, archaeologists, art
collectors, historians, diplomats, and glitzy Beautiful People thrown into
rather uneasy proximity. A two-day academic symposium was held in
conjunction with the opening of the exhibition, on the theme of 'Art and
Architecture in the late Fourth Century and Hellenistic period in Macedonia
and the rest of Greece' (those last six words, as we shall see, are politically
loaded). A series of Sunday lectures was inaugurated by Professor Manolis
Andronikos, speaking about his now famous discoveries in the royal burial
ground at Vergina (ancient Aegae), complete with new slides of low-relief
miniature ivory sculptures and a superbly restored ceremonial shield. Special
films were scheduled on the Vergina finds, on Alexander's life, on Greek art and

architecture, and on ancient Greek history. A popular biography by Robin Lane Fox, also entitled *The Search for Alexander*, was brought out to coincide with the exhibition. The usual museum reproductions, from Hellenistic costume jewellery to plaster busts of Alexander, sold briskly and probably made someone a small fortune.

When the exhibition was in its formative planning stage, between 1977 and 1978, huge crowds were flocking to one American museum after another, mesmerised by the fabulous gold of Egypt, pouring cash into the coffers of backers and subsidiaries, to make the Tutankhamun show (see above, pp. 77ff.) the greatest blockbuster on record.[2] It was inevitable that so heady a phenomenon should arouse extravagant hopes and ambitions in the group responsible for the Alexander project. Yet the plain truth of the matter is that, even weighing in the unique gold *larnax* (ossuary) and wreath from Vergina, this new museum joyride was simply not in the same league as its Egyptian predecessor. It neither stunned nor, except for brief moments, dazzled. It did contain some exquisite items – silver and bronze vessels, a spray of three golden wheatears, a double-snake bracelet: but these were exhibited along with one of the most fussy and vulgar artifacts, eclipsing even the Portland Vase, to survive from antiquity: the great bronze *krater* (a mixing-vessel or punchbowl for wine and water) found at Derveni, its lush romantic Dionysiac figures no advertisement for Macedonian quiet good taste.

With all the hype stripped away, what went on the road was, in essence, a small, low-key exhibition, admirably designed for teaching, of fine metal-work, jewellery, coins, and figurines from fourth-century and Hellenistic Macedonia, reinforced by one or two grave reliefs and an assortment of well-known marble heads of Alexander, including the Azara herm. It also included an audiovisual show that sketched a colourful montage of Alexander-influenced art through the ages, not without a certain streak of plummy pop sententiousness ('There was a horse called Bucephalas', the voice-over intoned as the credits began to roll). With certain exceptions, to which I shall return later, it was well and informatively captioned. But a four-star event, by any stretch of the imagination, 'The Search for Alexander' was not. There was thus a strong, and for the most part justified, feeling among academics and others that the advance fanfare had been out of all proportion. In particular, the exhibition's title was regarded as little short of wilful misrepresentation. Whatever the exhibitors were bent on discovering, it was not Alexander, whose relation to the artifacts on display was at best tangential, being expressed for the most part through that Macedonian heritage which he spent so much of his short life trying to jettison in favour of more grandiose, Oriental concepts of kingship.

Reliable insiders I spoke to suggested that the title originated with Time Inc. as a marketing device aimed at selling the show, a slogan that would appeal to the popular imagination, and was easily transferable to other products, such as Robin Lane Fox's book, the museum catalogue, and commercial art-reproductions – all three, as it happened, put out by Time Inc. subsidiaries. It became clear, too, on further investigation, that the aims of the museum authorities, of Time Inc., of the archaeologists and historians, and (last but by no means least) of the Greek government had not always coincided. Their stresses and divergences – the intersection, as it were, of the timeless with *Time* – shed a fascinating light on that murky no-man's-land where scholarship, politics, and corporate finance manoeuvre for advantage.

The genesis of the Alexander show goes back to 1966, when Zachary P. Morfogen, a Greek-American then working for the international division of Time-Life Books, discussed with his friend the Greek politician Takis Lambrias plans to promote a big book and perhaps a film or a TV programme about Alexander.[3] Thus both Time Inc. and the Greeks were involved, however fortuitously, *ab initio*. The scheme was shelved during the Colonels' regime, but revived again in 1974, when Lambrias became Karamanlis' minister for press, information and television. At the same time both Carter Brown, director of the National Gallery in Washington, and Thomas Hoving, then director of the Metropolitan Museum, were exploring the possibilities of mounting a loan exhibition from Greece. Brown discussed the problem with Nicholas Yalouris, then director of Greek antiquities, but ran into what seemed an insuperable obstacle: a Greek law prohibiting the export of museum antiquities, even on temporary loan. Despite strenuous efforts by Morfogen and Brown, the sympathy of Yalouris, and the helpful fact that Karamanlis himself happened to be a Macedonian from Sérres, between 1974 and 1977 no real progress was made in breaking the deadlock. Some extra inducement, clearly, was needed at the Greek end.

Then, in 1977, Manolis Andronikos attracted international attention with his extraordinary discovery of an unrifled royal Macedonian tomb in the great tumulus at Vergina. It was not only the splendid gold wreaths and ossuaries, the unparallelled fourth-century frescoes and the ceremonial armour that caught the public imagination, but also Andronikos' provisional identifi-cation of the burial as possibly that of Philip II, Alexander the Great's scarcely less famous father. Andronikos, to begin with at least, as an experienced archaeologist was, very properly, cautious. With the Greek political authorities it was quite another matter. They at once saw what an immense amount of political and nationalist capital could be made out of the find. Ever since the late nineteenth century the conflicting claims of Greeks, Bulgars, Serbs, Montenegrins, and Turks on the ill-defined region of Macedonia – so ethnically confused that it provided the French language with the term *macédoine* for a fruit salad[4] – had produced constant trouble of a more or less violent nature, culminating in the Balkan Wars of 1912 which terminated five centuries of Turkish overlordship.

After the Smyrna debacle of 1922 thousands of Greek refugees from Asia Minor were relocated in Macedonia: both Yalouris and Andronikos, it is worth noting, were thus uprooted as children, from Smyrna and Prusa respectively. For the Greeks, moreover, the recovery of Macedonia formed an essential step in the implementation of the 'Great Idea' – that is, the gradual reabsorption of all territories that had formed part of the Byzantine Empire, including Constantinople itself. The Greco-Turkish war of 1922 dealt a major blow to this dream. But the dream itself remained intact, and persisted. Both before and during World War II the Greek Communist Party (KKE) incurred enormous hostility by dutifully backing the Cominform line advocating an autonomous Macedonia as part of a Balkan federation (though this, ironically enough, would in effect have been to turn the clock back to the fourth century BC). Much Greek blood had been spilt for that territory: the very thought of ceding it was regarded as rankly unpatriotic, an insult to those unforgotten heroes who had died in the struggle for what was regarded, rightly or wrongly, as the land of their fathers.[5]

No Greek, however scholarly, could be expected to remain altogether impervious – even if only subconsciously – to these potent political, ethnic, and emotional issues when considering the status of ancient Macedonia. Above all, there was, and still is, bound to be a strong predisposition, encouraged by some over-credulous if *prima facie* plausible ancient evidence, towards identifying Macedonia as far as possible with Greece, and not only on political grounds. Though the area contains most of Greece's heavy industry, and some of her richest farm land, it has also retained its ancient reputation for a certain 'un-Greekness', a comparative lack of culture. It will follow that Philip and, above all, Alexander, royal Macedonians *par excellence*, must likewise be shown to have possessed the strongest possible Hellenic antecedents and connections. But here an awkward fact intrudes. In the fourth century BC the Greeks of the city-states regarded Macedonians as alien *barbaroi*, not even Hellenic by speech, who after Philip II's victory at Chaeronea in 338 had imposed their detested rule on Greece by main force. Alexander himself had continued this tradition and, worse, earned the Greeks' undying enmity by the savage destruction of Thebes, as an object-lesson in the fate of would-be rebels, before departing on his career of world conquest in the East. Whether the Macedonians were or were not Greek-speaking (not necessarily the same as being Greek) remains a much-debated point among linguists, and for the purposes of this argument is relatively unimportant. As Ernst Badian insisted, during the Washington seminar, 'what is of greater historical interest is the question of how Greeks and Macedonians were *perceived* by each other'.[6] But for modern Greek politicians and propagandists, for whom Alexander was a national hero held up as a role-model for army recruits, and Macedonia itself a much-cherished part of the fatherland, such distinctions were a mere historical embarrassment, to be ridden over with ringing patriotic rhetoric. Best to forget the equally fervent hate-tirades of Demosthenes, and, *a fortiori*, the gut reaction of another

Athenian orator, Demades, who on learning of Alexander's death at Babylon in 323 exclaimed: 'Alexander dead? Impossible: the whole world would stink of his corpse.'[7]

Indeed, in Alexander's case this problem is exacerbated by the fact that the world-conqueror was virtually the only figure from antiquity to survive, however mythicised, in the folk-consciousness of medieval and modern Greece. As Professor Yalouris reminds us in the exhibition catalogue,[8] Alexander 'became the symbol that embodied the desire for a national uprising' immediately before the Greek War of Independence. Rhigas Pheraios, the revolutionary Greek poet later shot by the Turks, and a passionate promoter of the 'Great Idea', featured the bust of Alexander on the clandestine broadsheet that he circulated in 1797. Alexander, in Constantine Karamanlis' own words, 'has served, as no other man has done, the dreams of the nation as a symbol of indissoluble unity and continuity between ancient and modern Hellenism'. The notion of Alexander, who distrusted the Greeks and was cordially detested by them in return, as a kind of patron saint for, of all people, Greek freedom-fighters may strike non-Greek historians as ironic, to say the least: but it remains true that with the discovery of the royal burial at Vergina, any scheme for the promotion of an international exhibition featuring Macedonia at once acquired considerable political importance.

This fact was clearly not lost on the Greek government, in particular on Karamanlis himself, then still Prime Minister. He at once made extensive public funds available for further excavation – the dig had hitherto been financed by the University of Thessalonike [9] – and thereafter took a continuing personal interest in the project. He gave a much-publicised speech at the opening of the exhibition in Thessalonike (then entitled, rather more accurately, 'Alexander the Great: History and Legend in Art'), during which, inter alia, he referred to Alexander as 'the representative of all the Greeks' in whose person 'a now mature Greek civilisation found the suitable medium by which it could extend itself beyond the boundaries of the ancient Greek world': arguments, from Plutarch to Tarn, justifying the pursuit of empire by the dissemination of Hochkultur had clearly not been lost on him. Through Karamanlis' energetic personal lobbying the law banning the export of Greek antiquities was rescinded in 1978, thus opening the way for Time Inc., the National Gallery, the publicity firm of Ruder and Finn, and a number of Greek agencies, headed by the National Bank of Greece, to set up a deal that would, it was hoped, satisfy everybody.

In fact these volatile partners found it hard to combine, and the main victim, inevitably, was the exhibition itself. Despite a publicity handout stressing its support of the arts ('Time Incorporated believes that its business is the total society in which we live, and it recognises man's necessity to enrich the soul as well as the body', etc.), it seems clear that Time Inc.'s main interest was by no means exclusively cultural. Early draft contracts caused a considerable outcry in the museum world, and though Time Inc. claimed not to expect to make money on the final deal, it was originally accused in the press[10] of 'using museums as outlets for its own marketing projects'. In any case, the mere fact of their sponsorship provided Time Inc.'s directors with some first-rate publicity. As far as the exhibition itself was concerned, what Time Inc. and Zachary Morfogen – later reported to be working on a musical called *Alexander* – stressed throughout was Alexander himself and the Alexander legend: an excellent formula for selling the package to Americans with only the haziest notion of, or interest in, Macedonia as such, whether as ancient imperial kingdom or modern Greek province and bone of Balkan contention.

On the other hand, the emphasis on Alexander was at odds not only with the museum's approach to the artifacts in the exhibition, but also, in a more subtle way, with the aims of the Greek government. Apart from some unexciting historical wall-displays and a few heads and coins, the exhibition had no functional connection with Alexander at all: what it demonstrated were, rather, select aspects of Macedonian culture, much of it Hellenistic. Katerina Rhomaiopoulou, then the director of Thessalonike's archaeological museum and curator of antiquities for Central Macedonia, was defensive about such charges, insisting that 'the Vergina items belonged to Alexander's father' – a debatable point, as we shall see – and that 'Alexander lived with these items when he lived with his father'.[11] Including the funeral *larnax?* It is a pretty thin defence. Such inconsistencies, of course, are part of the price that not only Greek archaeologists but also Carter Brown and the National Gallery had to pay for corporate sponsorship. Highly publicised spectacles with romantic titles attract visitors and revenue (cf. above, p. 152), but they also, as we are often reminded, cost the earth in overheads. Thus Time Inc.'s support became crucial. (The National Endowment for the Arts apparently turned down an application from the Gallery for support on the grounds that it was already being heavily backed by private business!) It remained true, though, that an unwitting visitor to 'The Search for Alexander' could, and in many cases did, emerge feeling that he had just seen *Hamlet* without the Prince – or, to take a closer parallel from the ancient world, the Mausoleum minus Mausolus.

However, it is the attitude of the exhibition's Greek backers and organisers, from the government and the National Bank of Greece to the archaeologists who came to Washington as official consultants, that was in the long run significant, especially for scholarship. Almost every recent major foreign exhibition, including those from China, Egypt and East Germany, has had some sort of political angle. What, to put the matter bluntly, was in it for the Greeks? 'To put Macedonia on the map' was the prevailing view,[12] but that, surely, is an over-simplification. Karamanlis' Thessalonike speech quoted above suggests a more complex scenario. Again and again what we find emphasised, just as we might expect, is the *Greekness* of Macedonia, to the point where Dr Rhomaiopoulou could publicly declare her preference for the term 'Northern Greece' as opposed to 'Macedonia': the two were to be treated as synonymous.

Justifiable, up to a point, in modern political terms, this practice becomes, as we have seen, highly misleading if applied to antiquity, when Macedonia, far from being even partly incorporated in a united Greek republic, was an independent (and under Philip II aggressively expansive) kingdom that ultimately destroyed Greek city-state independence in any meaningful sense. As Professor Badian pointed out, with relentless objectivity, whether the Macedonians were or were not Greek by speech and origin is altogether irrelevant to this issue. The point is that their Greek contemporaries, rightly or wrongly, regarded them as barbarians and foreigners, in a sense that they could not have applied, even for purposes of propaganda, to people such as the Thessalians. Indeed, when Thessaly, late in the fifth century, was attacked by a Macedonian king, Archelaus, a speech *On Behalf of the Larissaeans* composed by Thrasymachus contained the sentence: 'Shall we be slaves to Archelaus, we, being Greeks, to a barbarian?'[13]

Like Karamanlis, Professor Yalouris is on record as favouring the establishment of historical truth: 'Since Thucydides,' he declared in an interview at the time of the exhibition,[14] 'historical accuracy has been *sine qua non'*, and I have no doubt of his sincerity. Nevertheless, the article he contributed to the museum catalogue, entitled 'Alexander and his Heritage', offered some interesting glosses on that principle. Alexander I, he claims, took part in the Olympic Games 'after he had personally argued the case *that the Macedonians shared a common ancestry with the other Greeks'* (italics mine). Can he actually have read the passage in Herodotus (5.22) on which this claim rests? All Herodotus in fact says is that *Alexander himself* demonstrated his Argive ancestry (in itself a highly dubious genealogical claim), and was thus adjudged a Greek – against angry opposition, be it noted, from the stewards of the Games. Even if, with Professor N.G.L. Hammond, we accept this ethnic certification at face value, it tells us, as he makes plain, nothing whatsoever about Macedonians generally. Alexander's dynasty, if Greek, he writes, 'regarded itself as Macedonian only by right of rule, as a branch of the Hanoverian house has come to regard itself as English'.[15] On top of which, Philip II's son Alexander had an Epirote mother, which compounds the problem from yet another ethnic angle.

After this it comes as no surprise to find Professor Yalouris claiming that fourth-century Macedonia was 'the main meeting ground for all the great scholars as well as for the intellectual pioneers of the period' (an interesting distinction), and citing Plutarch (*Vit. Alex.* 4), erroneously, for the statement that literary and musical competitions were frequently organised *in Macedonia*. Even if we take with a grain of salt Demosthenes' dismissal of Philip (*III Phil.* 9.30 f.) as an uncouth product of a non-Greek country 'where it used to be impossible even to buy a decent slave', the King was not noted for his cultural interests.[16] When Dr Rhomaiopoulou, in the article following that by

Professor Yalouris, dates King Archelaus 412–359 BC, thus extending his reign for forty extra years to the beginning of Philip's, and sliding over some of the most lurid and disreputable decades in Macedonian history, one can only hope that '359' is in fact a misprint for '399', especially since the intervening years are skipped without discussion.

The general drift of such aberrations is all too clear. It is also in a very old and well-established Greek tradition: *polis* patriotism and ethnic loyalties have always exerted strong claims on the Greek historian. He has regularly been expected, as a matter of course, to give his country rather more than the benefit of whatever doubt may be going. Herodotus and Thucydides, with their comparative objectivity, their readiness to face unpleasant truths and unpopular or foreign viewpoints, constitute the exception rather than the rule in Greek historiography. Far more characteristic is a writer such as Dionysius of Halicarnassus, who (*Thuc.* 37 ff.) was shocked to the core by the Melian Dialogue, in which 'the wisest of the Greeks' (i.e. the Athenians) are made to 'adduce the most disgraceful arguments and invest them with the most disagreeable language'. Similarly with Plutarch, who in a savage essay[17] excoriated Herodotus for avoiding polite euphemisms, inserting discreditable facts not strictly 'relevant' – how history repeats itself! – to the issue, preferring the 'less creditable' version of an event, querying nobility of motive, being (horrors!) pro-barbarian (*philobarbaros*), and so on. 'We must not be tricked,' he concludes, 'into accepting unworthy and false notions about the greatest and best cities and men of Greece.' Dionysius, like Premier (later President) Karamanlis and Professor Yalouris, also claimed to regard history as 'the high priestess of truth' (*Thuc.* 8). I do not get the impression that he, any more than they, had his tongue in his cheek when he wrote this.

It is against such a background, and historiographical tradition, that we should consider the complaints, among non-Greek participants in the organisation of the exhibition, that various Greek officials, including some from the Ministry of Culture and Sciences, had been putting pressure on them to tone down, or omit, statements that did not accord with the official Greek line. (The academic symposium organised for the exhibition, it is only fair to say, remained largely free from such troubles, except for one glaring omission to be considered in a moment.) This applied particularly, as might be expected, to the interpretation of Alexander himself. Professor Eugene N. Borza, as historical consultant to the exhibition, found himself faced with some surprising objections. Alexander, he was told, could not suffer a 'disaster', even in the Gedrosian Desert. The mutiny at the River Beas (which forced him to abandon his march to the world's end) was reduced, in the final wall caption, to a mere hesitation on the part of some of his officers, a stumbling-block to Alexander's exploration of the Indian sub-continent. When Professor Borza stressed that the only master he served in advising the exhibition was historical truth, his Greek opposite number retorted: 'I have to serve three masters, and they're all in Athens.'

Robin Lane Fox, during the preparation of his new, heavily illustrated biography to coincide with the exhibition, was at first subjected to similar propaganda: no suggestions, please, that Alexander was homosexual (rather like Soviet officialdom defending Tchaikovsky), or – a more recognisably political angle – that Cyprus had ever been inhabited or ruled by non-Greeks. To his credit, he resisted such approaches: both Hephaestion and Bagoas are mentioned, with proper caveats, as Alexander's possible lovers (after the uninhibited sexual omnivorousness with which he credited Alexander in his earlier study he could hardly have done otherwise), while the princelings of Cyprus appear, in inverted commas, as *soi-disant* 'Hellenes of the Hellenes'. Perhaps because of this the Greek authorities apparently refused to give the book their official imprimatur, and washed their hands of its author. From their own point of view this was surely a mistake. It should have been clear, to even the most obtuse reader, that Lane Fox's Alexander was romantic enough for any Greek nationalist. His topographical photographs, in full colour, could not fail to impress. He might have held firm on sex, but he had backed off from some other of the more provocative positions (e.g. on the value of the non-Arrianic historical *testimonia*) that he previously held. Above all, he firmly believed that Tomb II at Vergina held the bones of Philip II. On the other hand, this volume shows every sign of having been thrown together at short notice, and is written in a clotted, staccato prose in striking contrast to the lush, rolling periods of his earlier study. I would like to think that the Greek Ministry of Culture withdrew its backing because it found the book largely unreadable: but that would be too much to hope for from any government ministry, even a Greek one.

LIKE THE EXHIBITION, the accompanying symposium largely avoided a direct confrontation with Alexander, even in the historical section (a late addition to the programme). In view of the course taken by Alexander studies since World War II, it is not hard to see why. World conquest has gone decidedly out of favour, and Alexander's very considerably activities in this area get short shrift from unromantic realists, some of whom had suffered from the grandiose ambitions of his modern imitators. Both Yalouris and Andronikos found themselves put very much on the defensive by reporters who suggested – getting rudely to the heart of the matter – that Alexander was 'a willing, even enthusiastic, leader of slaughter and pillage'.[18] Both argued that during a war (however occasioned) atrocities are inevitable, and that in any case Alexander's positive achievements outweighed anything else. One could hear, in the background, all those Eastern eggs being broken to make cultural Greek omelettes. Their Alexander, like that of Plutarch and Sir William Tarn, was a beneficent conqueror, with a mission to spread sweetness and light, the *beau idéal* of Greek highschool students and worshippers of T.E. Lawrence: he had to be handled gently.

So, of course, did the vexed Macedonian ethnic problem, though that did at least get on the programme. Even so, the toughly worded abstract of Professor Badian's paper, circulated in advance, brought almost every Greek attending the symposium to a fine pitch of nationalist fury: unjustifiably in the event, but then reason and scholarship played very little part in the matter. For the most part speakers concentrated, very profitably, on less controversial topics: Macedonian jewellery and vases, painting, sculpture, architecture, coinage, arms and tactics. But one crucial problem, uppermost (it's safe to say) in the mind of every scholar present, the subject of ongoing academic debate (which continues to this day), and central to the interests of exhibition and symposium alike, got no official airing at all. Whose, in fact, *were* the bones in Tomb II at Vergina? A royal burial, all agree – but which king? Alexander's father Philip II, or his epileptic, mentally defective elder half-brother, Philip III Arrhidaios? Under discreet indirect lighting the exquisite gold *larnax* gleamed bright, and kept its counsel.

The world is very much in Professor Andronikos' debt. His exemplary excavation of the great tumulus at Vergina has resulted in what is arguably the most valuable historical discovery – certainly by far the richest tomb – in the annals of Greek archaeology. Vergina is now identified, beyond any doubt, as the site of Aegae, the old Macedonian capital and burial ground of the Argead kings: splendid confirmation of an identification first proposed by Hammond as long ago as 1968.[19] Finally, from the very moment of his great discovery, Professor Andronikos has responded to the immense public interest it generated with a more or less continuous flow of articles and interviews, culminating in the splendid and sumptuously illustrated book he produced covering every aspect of the find.[20] These clearly reflect his evolving ideas about the royal burials. At the same time he has argued from the start that until he has published the formal excavation report which will present his mature conclusions, among other things on the identity of Tomb II's occupant, he is not willing to engage in scholarly debate on the matter.[21] This is understandable, and indeed normal academic practice: but in view both of his widely published views and of other scholars' reactions to them, perhaps a trifle disingenuous. He has never made any secret of his inner conviction, which could indeed be right and has won much serious support,[22] that the main burial is that of Philip II. That view has, nevertheless, been seriously challenged.

Hence Andronikos found himself in a difficult position, with non-academic considerations, for the most part ethnic and political, putting enormous pressure on him to stick with his original thesis, while much new circumstantial evidence pointed increasingly in the other direction. The political value, as a reinforcement for neo-Macedonian propaganda, of firmly labelling the burial as Philip's is both potent and obvious. Looked at in these terms, poor Philip Arrhidaios – unheroic in life as in death, epileptic, weak-minded, unfit for active service, shunted off into the noncombatant job of minister for religious affairs while his wife Eurydice was trained as a warrior in his place – could hardly be regarded, by historians or statesmen with the public image of a Greek Macedonia at heart, as an adequate or indeed desirable candidate. Arrhidaios, in short, was an embarrassment. Yet there were at least two awkward facts that had, and still have, to be faced. First, this apparent nonentity was endorsed, with enthusiasm, as Alexander's successor by the Macedonian infantry in Babylon;[23] and secondly, he and his warrior-wife Eurydice were given a splendid royal burial, in Aegae, by Cassander.[24]

The trouble is that our final verdict in this matter, now and probably for ever, must remain a non liquet. No irrefutable and clinching evidence has turned up – though there have been one or two suggestive pointers – and if Professor Andronikos is keeping the case open, it may well be in the forlorn hope of an eventual miracle. Of the three royal tombs, it is Tomb III that offers best chance of an identification. Andronikos has several times stated [25] that the bones in this tomb are of an adolescent boy between twelve and fourteen. The only boy between twelve and fourteen eligible for royal Macedonian burial in the second half of the fourth century was Alexander IV, Alexander's son by Roxane, murdered in prison by Cassander in 311/10.[26] Tomb I offers a greater mystery. As is well known, it was robbed, leaving only some bones, some pieces of pottery, and murals – a seated woman, the Rape of Persephone, possibly the three Fates – the iconography of which, taken together, suggests a young girl cut off in her prime. As is, or was, not so well known, the bones were identified as those of a woman in her twenties, a baby, and a large man.[27] As I saw at once in 1980, without being entirely willing to draw the obvious conclusion from it, one candidate for this cist-tomb, significantly earlier than II and III, which were both vaulted, would be Philip II's wife, Cleopatra/Eurydice, murdered (or made to commit suicide), along with her newborn child, by Olympias, some months after Philip's assassination.[28] But then the 'large man' would, almost inevitably, be Philip himself: no wonder attempts were made to explain this intrusive and unsettling body as that of a grave-robber.

The trouble about this identification, which would make Philip III Arrhidaios and his wife Adea-Eurydice virtually certain occupants of Tomb II and its antechamber, has always been that, while supported by the archaeological evidence, it goes, as many scholars saw, right against the grain of our literary sources, which are far better satisfied by Andronikos' thesis, claiming Tomb II for Philip. When Cassander interred Arrhidaios and Eurydice, there was no need for a quick hugger-mugger burial, a vault roughly plastered, an absence of murals; whereas the circumstances of Philip's, and indeed of Cleopatra-Eurydice's death – assassination in the one case, execution in the other – would make both the disarray, and the surprising disposal of the female corpse in the ante-chamber, more than understandable. Yet, as Borza saw,[30] the natural allocation was for Philip, Eurydice and their child in Tomb I, Arrhidaios and his warrior-queen in Tomb II, and Alexander IV in Tomb III, the interments to be dated 336, 316, and 311/10 respectively. Chronologically this suited the shift from cist to vault, as well as certain other evidence, drawn from the pottery, to be discussed below. But, as Borza concluded, 'the expression of these views does not affect my belief that the evidence of the ancient texts and our general understanding of the events of later fourth-century Macedon point to an interment of Philip II' in Tomb II. The severe internal contradictions of the case have yet to be satisfactorily resolved.

That the burial was royal, not earlier than 340 and not later than 300, is just about certain: this at least in effect limits the field to the two main candidates. Everything else remains debatable. Andronikos claims that the bones from the Tomb II burial are those of a man in his forties, while those from the antechamber (also given royal honours) belong to a woman in her early or middle twenties. This would suit either Philip (and indeed either Eurydice) equally well. (Some physical anthropologists feel, however, that even this is over-confident, that the bones require further expert outside examination, that the ages may be wrong or even, because of heavy cremation-induced shrinkage, ultimately indeterminable.) Between 336, the date of Philip's murder, and 316, when Cassander gave Philip III and Adea-Eurydice a delayed burial in the royal necropolis at Aegae, is only twenty years: far too short a period, one might have thought, to get a decisive verdict from the scanty pottery or the style of the silver vessels found in the tomb. Yet there are, as I said, pointers. Perhaps the most significant is Susan I. Rotroff's dating of three spool saltcellars found in the Athenian Agora, and exactly comparable to others from Tomb II at Vergina, to the period between 325 and 295, now further confirmed by numismatic evidence.[31] Philip was assassinated in 336, and grave-goods tend to *pre*date the tomb in which they are placed.

Advocates of Philip Arrhidaios [32] have argued, *inter alia*, that the barrel vaulting found in the tomb was first brought back to Greece from Mesopotamia by Alexander's engineers; that the royal golden diadem among the grave goods was likewise an Oriental import first affected by Alexander; and that Alexander himself was unlikely to pay funeral honours to his father's last wife, especially after the bride's uncle had accused him, at the wedding feast, of being illegitimate. These arguments, too, remain inconclusive. The claim that the barrel-vaulting of Tomb II could not have predated Alexander's opening up of the East – where such vaulting abounded – rests on an *argumentum ex silentio* which fresh discoveries could at any time refute; it also assumes a quite astonishing lack of prior communication between East and West. All we can say for certain is that the tomb appears to be, with the vaulted stadium tunnel of Nemea discovered at about the same time, the oldest example of this type so far found. Plato, it is true, writing about 350 in the *Laws* (947D-E), mentions an underground vaulted tomb of some sort; but Boyd's distinction between corbelled and voussoired (barrel) arches may well explain this, so once again the question is left tantalisingly open-ended.[33]

The assertion that the diadem does not predate Alexander's orientalising phase remains highly debatable, and much evidence has been brought against it.[34] Lastly, the supposition[35] that Alexander would never have accorded Philip's wife Cleopatra royal burial honours out of respect for his mother Olympias is mere speculation, and in any case implicitly contradicted by Plutarch, who says that Alexander was, understandably, 'infuriated' by Olympias' murder of Cleopatra and her child the moment his back was turned (Plut. *Alex.* 10.4). Better, at that tricky early point in his reign, to offend his mother than a powerful group of old-guard Macedonian barons.

Most of the other evidence adduced in the case – e.g. the *larnaces* and the miniature ivory heads – however interesting *per se*, adds nothing to a solution of the central problem (though at times misrepresented to this end by the *parti pris*),[36] and no point would be served by rehashing the arguments here: though it is perhaps just worth observing that *if* the ivory with the upturned gaze and 'Lysippan' twist to the neck does represent Alexander, we have one more argument in favour of a later burial, since in 336 Alexander was barely twenty, and certainly not yet in any position to appoint Lysippus his royal portraitist. We can, fortunately, eliminate for good at least one piece of evidence: the shortened and distorted greave that (it has been argued) got that way because Philip II was its owner, and had been lamed by a spear-thrust through the thigh.[37] We do not even need to argue, with Lehmann and Adams,[38] that such a wound would not shorten the leg. Especially since Philip sustained a further wound, in the shin, which might otherwise have clinched the case for Philip (but which neither Andronikos nor anyone else cites), it is in a sense frustrating to have to report that Philip's wounds cannot possibly have had any connection whatsoever with the ceremonial greaves in the antechamber of Tomb II. Our best source in general for those wounds, Didymos Chalcenteros,[39] reports spear-thrusts through the thigh and shin of the right leg, just as we might expect from normal cavalry encounters. Yet a glance at the greaves themselves, as Andronikos was well aware from the beginning,[40] shows that it is the *left* one that belongs to a shorter and in some way deformed limb.

We are thus forced to the conclusion that, if these greaves *do* belong to Philip II, not only was his right leg virtually unaffected – except for the lameness Plutarch records (*Mor.* 331B) – by two major wounds, but, in addition, his left leg was malformed, perhaps congenitally. This possibility cannot be ruled out, but it remains, if true, a striking physical trait mentioned in no surviving source. The opinion of an orthopaedic surgeon who examined photographs of the greaves is that their owner may well have suffered from the effects of a clubfoot or, more probably, poliomyelitis, in the left leg.[41] In 1980 I had the opportunity to make a close personal examination of the greaves: the left one almost completely lacks that strong muscular 'swell' so prominent in the right one, which would seem to offer support for the polio theory. It is an interesting thought that if the occupant of Tomb II was Philip

III Arrhidaios rather than Philip II, he must have been, not only epileptic and weak-minded, but also congenitally lame.

For virtually every point a counterpoint can be found. The Alexander Romance, not on most things the best of evidence (to put it mildly) but not on that account to be dismissed out of hand as regards details, asserted that Alexander built some sort of temple or shrine close to his father's tomb. Andronikos found what he claims[42] to be such a shrine, or heroön, a small marble edifice (destroyed except for its foundations), duly situated close to the three royal tombs. As Hammond reminds us, only two fourth-century Argead kings – apart from Alexander III – were paid divine honours: Amyntas III and Philip II. If we could be sure of this building's function, it might strengthen the case for Philip; but Andronikos' identification of it rests, at best, on the flimsiest foundations. It could have been any kind of shrine. Andronikos excludes, without explanation, the theory that 'it is a temple or other sacred building not associated with the graves', and asserts bluntly: 'The only possible explanation is that we have to do here with a "heroön" in connexion with the cult of the dead who are buried here.' A possible explanation indeed, but the *only* possible one? Elsewhere[43] Andronikos uses this identification to attack the likelihood of Philip Arrhidaios being buried here, on the grounds that he (as opposed to Philip II) would not receive divine or heroic honours. But the argument remains obstinately circular.

Five years ago I wrote that 'while the case for Philip II is circumstantially stronger than that for Philip III Arrhidaios, it cannot, yet, be regarded as proven'.[44] Today I am less sure of the circumstantial strength of that case than I was. Though the literary evidence, as we have seen, indeed fits the known facts of Philip II's death better, there has been a steady accumulation of archaeological data all pointing to a date perhaps two decades later than 336. Against this trend we can only set, in the way of physical testimony, the later construction of the antechamber to Tomb II (which would fit the facts of Cleopatra's demise, but not those of Adea's), and the presence in Tomb II of a silver strainer, inscribed on the rim with the name MACHATA, i.e. Machatas, which is rare: before the second century BC, in fact, the only known holder of it was the brother of Philip II's wife Phila. Even so, it would not be hard to explain the presence of this strainer in Arrhidaios' tomb; for so late a reburial Cassander would have collected family heirlooms where and as he could. A *non liquet* verdict still remains the only possible one. We can only hope that if, by some miracle, an epigraphical text should turn up from the site naming Philip, it makes unambiguously clear just which *Philippos Basileus* is in question. One ends by sympathising with the museum curator who remarked: 'This show is called "the Search for Alexander", but we've finally found Philip II instead, and we're not even sure about that.' *Verb. sap.*

XI

AFTER ALEXANDER: SOME HISTORIOGRAPHICAL APPROACHES TO THE HELLENISTIC AGE

[Note: *Ever since the early 1950s I have taken a strong interest in the history, literature, and culture generally of the Hellenistic Age. This concern, at first dismissed by my Cambridge friends as a characteristic aberration of taste and judgment, has now – to my satisfaction but not to my surprise – come to reflect a mainstream, and crucially important, preoccupation among classicists, while the numerous and striking resemblances between that age and our own have drawn the attention both of scholars outside the classical field, and, increasingly, of intelligent general students of Western civilisation.*

In the mid-1970s I began preparing a lecture course on the Hellenistic period, and in 1981 I started work on a long and wide-ranging book based on these lectures, entitled Alexander to Actium, *with the programmatic sub-heading 'An essay on the historical evolution of the Hellenistic age'. This study is today (1989) in the process of publication. Thus over a period of some three decades my perennial concern with the period has continued to develop and, I hope, mature, just as the period itself has attracted increasing, and evolving, interest from the scholarly world at large. I thus feel it may be illuminating, on both counts, to reprint here, largely unchanged, four review-articles which I wrote in 1957, 1973, 1981 and 1985 respectively. The first appeared when I had recently discovered Polybius (on whom my views have changed somewhat since); the second reveals the influence of that remarkable book on Hellenistic* Athens *(1911) by W.S. Ferguson, and was written about the time that I first began to do serious research in the Hellenistic field; the third coincided with a series of structural and methodological problems I faced in composing my own full-scale study; and the fourth, appearing when that study had already been accepted for publication, embodies my current thinking, on both method and substance, about the history (in the widest sense) of the Hellenistic age.]*

THERE ARE CERTAIN WRITERS, philosophers or historians for the most part, whose thought exercises a widespread and enduring influence entirely disproportionate to the limited public that actually reads their books. Polybius provides an early and striking instance of this phenomenon. He was probably the first universal historian, as we understand that term, and thus in a sense the direct, if remote, ancestor of Arnold Toynbee. He was a pioneer in the conscious evaluation of historical purpose and method. We may quarrel with his utilitarian aims no less than with his dangerous, if seductive, assumption that the future is predictable from an examination of the past; but most of the main principles he laid down for historical research still hold firm today. It was, too, his version of the famous 'mixed constitution,' with its protective system of checks and balances, which was taken up by Cicero [who could sidestep Polybius' grotesque assumption that the Roman system offered an example of it], and from him, via More, Machiavelli and Montesquieu, passed into the blood-stream of eighteenth- and nineteenth-century European diplomacy. But perhaps most relevant for our own times is the fact that it was Polybius who popularised (though he certainly did not invent) the cyclic theory of revolution – a theory that was to be taken up by Vico and Spengler, and which is implicit in Marxist historiography.

Yet Polybius himself is little studied or read, and surprisingly few books have been devoted to him [less true now than in 1957, in great part due to Walbank's efforts, not only in the completion of his *Commentary* (1967, 1979), but also in his Sather Lectures, *Polybius* (1972); other major studies by K. Ziegler, G. Lehmann, P. Pédech, and K.S. Sachs]. In spite of the tributes of scholars such as Mahaffey or Mommsen (who praised the completeness, simplicity and clarity of his narrative) he has all too often been dismissed as a second-rate scissors-and-paste historian, useful to supplement the lacunae in Livy, but lacking in that literary style and rhetorical warmth which classical scholars tend to demand from their prose authors, the exponent of what German scholars dismissively labelled *Kanzleisprache*. It is symptomatic of the professional esteem in which Polybius (and, indeed, ancient history as a serious discipline) was till recently held that the only complete commentary existing prior to Walbank's was Schweighäuser's, compiled during the French Revolution and largely concerned with scholarly minutiae. [Arrian, despite the vast interest in Alexander, has been even more neglected: Professor A.B. Bosworth's historical commentary, the first volume of which appeared in 1980, is, incredible though this may seem to those who think of classics as a worked-out vein for research, the first to appear in any language.]

During the past few decades there has been welcome evidence that ancient historians are widening their field of reference to embrace the larger and more perennial issues. [To the corpus of M.I. Finley's work in social history and economics we might add, now, such important studies as S.C. Humphreys' *Anthropology and the Greeks* (1978).] Contemporary world events have proved, time and again – and often in a distressingly personal way – that philosophies of history, however dismissable as fallacious intellectual aberrations, can still charge, indeed on occasion overcharge, the batteries of human action and purpose. In this sense Polybius has become, at one stroke, modern, relevant, and important: a fact abundantly demonstrated by the appearance in 1954 of Kurt von Fritz's masterly work, *The Theory of the Mixed Constitution in*

Antiquity [a study that stimulated even when, as so often, one came to disagree with its conclusions]. Professor Walbank's new commentary [on which, in 1957, he had already been engaged for twelve years] thus comes at an opportune time: but its aims no less than its achievement are conditioned by the old, limited view of what such a work should be. [Three decades later, with well-thumbed copies of all three volumes on my desk, I feel I seriously underestimated Walbank's overall achievement in this monumental undertaking, a change of heart already noticeable by 1981 (see below, pp.179–80): but those early criticisms did have some substance, and on reflection I am inclined to let them stand.]

The first volume [of two originally planned: in the end three proved necessary] covers Books I–VI of Polybius' narrative, from the first Punic War to the important excursus on the Roman constitution. Out of 746 pages (excluding marginal matter such as indexes) Professor Walbank devotes about thirty to the Mixed Constitution and the theory of *anakyklosis*; thirty-seven to an introduction recapitulating Polybius' life, his views on history, his concept of *Tyche* (Fortune), his chronology, and his sources: the remainder is almost entirely given over to detailed notes on military, topographical, and constitutional matters. Such proportions speak for themselves. So far as it goes, Professor Walbank's work is thorough, accurate, and comprehensive; it is well documented with the findings of recent scholarship, and makes its points succinctly and without fuss. But does it go far enough? Philology has indeed been largely thrown overboard in favour of historical exegesis (which may explain the absence from the bibliography of Lipsius and Casaubon), but it has still left its methodological legacy behind. One gets the uneasy feeling that Walbank is so involved with the details of his mosaic that he never stands far enough back to survey the picture comprehensively [no longer true today].

Major judgments are not this scholar's habitual stock-in-trade: nowhere in these learned pages will the reader find so illuminating an opinion on Polybius as that thrown off, almost casually, by R.G. Collingwood in *The Idea of History* (1946, p.36) while discussing *Tyche* and the 'new element of determinism' in the post-Hellenistic era:

As the canvas on which the historian paints his picture grows larger, the power attributed to the individual will grow less. Man finds himself no longer master of his fate in the sense that what he tries to do succeeds or fails in proportion to his own intelligence or lack of it: his fate is master of him, and the freedom of his will is shown not in controlling the outward events of his life but in controlling the inward temper in which he faces these events. Here Polybius is applying to history the same Hellenistic conceptions which the Stoics and Epicureans applied to ethics.

[Nor, I might have added, did Walbank then show the kind of acute instinct for Polybian moral or political inconsistencies that von Fritz displayed throughout *The Theory of the Mixed Constitution in Antiquity*, though he has since to some extent rectified this. To the argument, often brought, that in a commentary one is concerned primarily with the trees rather than the wood, I would still reply that without a full understanding of the wood's structure and rationale, the individual trees make very little sense.] Professor Walbank's commentary will be an invaluable foundation on which future historians can build; but students of political theory or the philosophy of history will find it somewhat barren sustenance.

The pattern which Polybius' work assumed is inextricably bound up with the events of his own times and life. He was born between 208 and 200 BC, an Arcadian from Megalopolis. His family included distinguished public servants: Polybius himself, like his father Lycortas, was a prominent statesman in the Achaean League. Though Rome was not to bring Greece finally and openly to heel till 146, the inescapable shadow of Roman power hung over the League's deliberations long before that date. Though technically autonomous, League members had little doubt where the real authority lay. Polybius himself, throughout his official career, consistently advocated the acceptance of Rome's *de facto* supremacy in Greece [here I have changed my mind considerably: Polybius' recommendations were grudging, hedged with caveats, and often made in a parochial spirit without reference to Rome at all: there were solid reasons for his deportation to Italy]. Others, understandably, were not so realistic. Frustration bred intrigue, and Roman suspicions were aroused. The Third Macedonian War between Rome and Perseus (172-168/7) provided an excuse to deport a thousand leading Achaeans, Polybius among them, to Italy, to be tried on charges of political disaffection. The trials never took place; but one of the victims, through this accident of fate, this *ad hominem* instance of *Tyche's* unpredictable malevolence, came to discover his true métier in life.

Polybius endured exile with some equanimity, since his treatment was exceptionally privileged. He was taken up by the Scipionic circle in Rome, and allowed very considerable freedom of movement. He studied Roman institutions with ever increasing admiration, though with something less than complete understanding, and what he saw offered him a unifying theme for the history he contemplated writing – the astonishing rise to world domination, in a mere half century or so, of the Roman people. It is fascinating to speculate how far his personal circumstances conditioned the views he held. To what extent were his utilitarian criteria and his insistence on practical experience in the historian dictated by his own career as an Achaean statesman? Were his obsessional pursuit of the truth and his angry denunciation of bias partly a public persona to mask pro-Achaean prejudice, partly to compensate for the fact that he lived 'in a self-conscious age, when criticism was mostly captious and destructive, and standards of right and wrong, of truth and falsehood, were unsteady and uncertain'? Were his inconsistencies over Fortune's role in human affairs connected in any way with the final humiliation which Greece had suffered during his own lifetime? These questions, as von Fritz pointed out, have seldom been asked, and few others beside himself have made a serious attempt to answer them. His analysis shows how deeply Polybius' theories were in fact affected by specific contemporary events: in this unconscious equation of the particular with the abstract concept lies the special fallacy that can wreck every philosophy of history.

Like most utilitarians, Polybius was also didactic. He aimed – like his great predecessor and model Thucydides, also an exiled general – to instruct rather than amuse, and severely criticised the 'dramatised' history and lurid bio-graphies which too often passed for scholarship in his day as in ours. He was more concerned with analysing the underlying causes of events than describing those events for their own sake:

If we take from history the discussion of why, how and wherefore each thing was done, and whether the result was what we should reasonably have expected, what is left is a clever essay but not a lesson, and while pleasing for the moment of no possible benefit for the future (3.31.12-13).

As a practical and experienced statesman-cum-commander, he had a ferocious contempt for armchair historians like Timaeus, who relied entirely on documents and made no effort to obtain and sift first-hand information. He remarked (and the criticism still has pertinence today, not least among students of Graeco-Roman papyri) that over-specialisation in history tends to corrupt the writer's general judgment by exaggerating the importance of events trivial in themselves. [His criticisms of others, e.g. of Phylarchus, for over-dramatised sensationalism would carry more weight if he were not more than ready, e.g. over the mutiny in Alexandria after Ptolemy V's accession, to pull out the rhetorical stops himself when it suited him.]

Polybius' prejudice against partisan bias (perhaps, too, his Hellenocentric, even Achaeocentric, world-outlook) was strong enough to rein in any temptation he might have felt, as a privileged exile, to disseminate uncritical pro-Roman propaganda. He always tried [though not invariably with success] to give both sides of an argument. He openly favoured Hannibal at some points during his narrative; he duly set down [though carefully sandwiched between less inflammatory material] the statements of those who 'accused the Romans of the basest treachery and perfidy' before the Third Punic War (149-146 BC); and he himself criticised Rome severely for her brutal policy in Greece during and after Mummius' sack of Corinth in 146. 'Truth is to history', he proclaimed more than once (1.14.6, 12.12.3; cf. 34.4), 'what eyesight is to the living creature.' It is characteristic of this Romanised Greek that what detectable bias, and animus, he has should be primarily directed against his former political enemies in Aetolia, Boeotia, or the Peloponnese. The generalisations, as with Thucydides, rest on an all-too-local basis of fact, remain incurably parochial. As Professor Walbank justly observes (p.16):

A slight concession (in principle) to politic piety and (in practice) to local patriotism, a limited success in retailing the real contents of some of his reported speeches, a readiness to embrace the terminology (but not the emotional attitudes) of 'tragic' history in the interests of *to terpnon* [the pleasurable] or moral edification – these probably represent the sum of what a critic of Polybius' truthfulness can assemble. What contemporary historian could claim more for his sense of objectivity than that? [I don't know about modern objectivity, but I think Professor Walbank would probably agree with me now that in 1957 we both let Polybius off a good deal more lightly than he deserved.]

It is important, when criticising Polybius, to distinguish between his methodology, which was for the most part remarkably sound, and his declared purpose in writing, which to a modern historian may appear irrelevant where it is not positively misleading. The one does not automatically vitiate the other. It is easy to point out (as, for instance, von Fritz has done) that the 'cycle of revolutions' is demonstrably false, and had been shown to be false by Aristotle long before Polybius ever set pen to paper. But this does not affect (to take an obvious example) the validity of Polybius' argument about how the historian should select and sift his evidence: nor does it alter, or explain, the enormous influence which a view repudiated by every serious historian may still command with the public or with posterity. If the public wishes to believe in a cycle of revolutions, or the Spenglerian cosmos, or a universally beneficent Alexander, it will do so regardless; and sufficient belief has, before now, converted many a myth into reality. (As Shaw remarked in *St Joan*, a miracle is that which creates faith.) The same applies to the notion that historical method, *scientific* method, can be applied to the prediction of future events, a proposition to which Stoicism and the astrological *mathematici* gave a considerable boost. However often hard facts give prophecy the lie, hope and desire still mingle in the theorist's breast, and a little special pleading will always wipe the slate clean of past miscalculations.

It is interesting, in this connection, to examine more closely Polybius' ambivalent, not to say labile, attitude to the element which he describes as *Tyche* and which for us is, at various times, roughly equivalent to Fate, Fortune, happenstance (the unpredictable random factor), or an Act of God, according to our mood or individual preconceptions. His inconsistencies in this awkward historical Tom Tiddler's Ground (inconsistencies which, however, as Professor Walbank justly observes, are also liable to affect even the most hardheaded of modern writers) have worried Polybian scholars considerably, to the point where they were prepared to suggest not only that he changed his mind completely several times while composing his *Universal History*, but was also, apparently, too careless or too plain idle to correct his earlier opinions. (Neither von Fritz nor Walbank, happily, has any time for this moonstruck theory). The point at issue is simple. Sometimes Polybius regards *Tyche* as Fortune or Fate semi-personified, an overriding force that invalidates human actions no less than human predictions; on other occasions – sometimes very nearly in the same breath – he treats such a concept as the last refuge of a lazy historian stumped for a convincing rational motive.

Now it is true that if one's own assumptions are sceptical, Polybius might appear to be using *Tyche* as a convenient escape clause or *deus ex machina* whenever it suited him, irrespective of circumstances. But Polybius himself (36.17) gives an explanation which virtually reconciles the inconsistencies:

> As regards things the causes of which it is impossible or difficult for a mere man to understand, we may perhaps be justified in getting out of the difficulty by setting them down to the action of a god or of chance (*Tyche*), I mean such things as exceptionally heavy and continuous rain or snow . . . or a persistent outbreak of plague or other similar things of which it is not easy to detect the cause . . . But as for matters the efficient and final cause of which it is possible to discover, we should not, I think, put them down to divine action.

In other words, while it is the historian's duty to search for a rational explanation of phenomena which can be rationally explained, he is at liberty (in the pursuit of truth) to identify as irrational, or due to *Tyche*, those events which are manifestly beyond human control. As von Fritz pointed out, it was for Polybius the *results* of human wisdom or folly that were due only to that wisdom or that folly; the states of mind which provoked action, on the other hand, might be of such a sort that they could only be explained by divine intervention.

Yet behind *Tyche*, as behind all Polybius' major assumptions, lurks the shadow of immediate events:

> Both after the conquest of Greece by Alexander [von Fritz p. 394] and later after the conquest of Greece by the Romans, many Greeks tried to console themselves and to escape a feeling of humiliation by the assertion that these events were entirely attributable to luck.

Though Polybius' rational training revolted against such foolish escapism, the concept invaded his own mind in subtler ways. Would he have discovered such peculiar excellences in the Roman constitution, or even (*pace* Schwartz) have tried to fit it into his general constitutional theory, if he had remained a free Achaean statesman in a Greek world where Rome had no place? Might it not be said that his whole notion of universal history was a rationalisation of defeat, a concept which absolved his impotent countrymen from moral failure by preaching the inherent, unarguable supremacy of Rome? It made no difference in the end: as always, it was the ideas that endured. But these ideas, in the last resort, sprang directly from the events engendering them, a fact which contributes signally to Polybius' uniqueness. He was a man, an historian, at the crossroads between two worlds, the first of many *dépaysé* cosmopolitan writers who diagnosed an alien empire's condition, the spearhead of those Greek thinkers who were soon to leaven and disrupt the Roman traditionalism which they both despised and envied (an attitude that the Romans reciprocated in full measure). He was the forerunner, the characteristic prototype, of that multifaceted hybrid growth, Graeco-Roman man.

IF IT IS NO LONGER TRUE that the average humanities graduate – let alone the ordinary educated reader – thinks that Athenian and, *a fortiori*, Greek history came to an abrupt halt at the end of the Peloponnesian War, there nevertheless still [1973] remains considerable vagueness, and indeed a massive residual indifference, concerning Greek affairs after the death of Alexander. Standard histories, e.g. those of Hammond and Bury, only encourage such an attitude by making 323 BC a kind of terminal watershed, after which, in due course, as Louis MacNeice put it in *Autumn Journal*,

> . . . Athens became a mere university city,
> and the goddess born of the foam
> became the kept hetaera, heroine of Menander,
> and the philosopher narrowed his focus, confined
> his efforts to keeping his own house in order
> and keeping a quiet mind.

Even the first half of the fourth century gets far less attention than it deserves. Between Socrates' execution in 399 and Philip II's accession to the throne of Macedonia forty years later, comes what Hammond, with orotund but accurate relish, terms 'the period of transient hegemonies': mainly those of Sparta and Thebes, with Athens, somewhat in the background now, busy rebuilding her old thalassocracy, but minus all those special cultural trimmings which took the sharp edge off Periclean (as opposed to Spartan) imperialism, and provide it with much of its central attraction today.

There was, of course, Plato; but we need only study some of the Athenian Stranger's speeches in the *Laws* to know what Plato thought about Athens' populist naval machismo (nowhere do his aristocratic prejudices emerge more clearly), and in any case Plato's admirers have seldom been much more concerned with mere vulgar historical accuracy than was the Master himself. The Attic orators, then? Ploughing through the speeches of Demosthenes has never been a very popular chore, and Isocrates (to look a little further afield) must be, with the possible exception of Isaeus, about the most consistently neglected major author of the classical period in the entire Greek corpus. Xenophon's *Anabasis* and *Hellenica* have their adherents, but how many casual readers are familiar with the *Ways and Means* or the *Memorabilia*? Even students who can, at a pinch, write essays on Philip II's foreign policy or the Peace of Antalcidas are liable to flounder or look blank when quizzed on such fourth-century Athenian figures as Callistratus, Eubulus, or Lycurgus (the last-named being sometimes hopefully identified as 'that mythical Spartan'). Yet all three played immensely important political roles in Athens; and Athens was still the same violet-crowned city, still endowed with all its fifth-century, but now illusory, ambitions, one characteristic of the Athenian *demos* throughout its long history being a quite remarkable disinclination to learn from experience.

What is the reason for this neglect? Why should Athens and Greece mysteriously lose their prime attraction after 404 BC? The problem becomes even more baffling when we take into account the fact that, for professional scholars at least, Hellenistic and Graeco-Roman culture has, over the last few decades, been enjoying an unprecedented boom. Ever since the Twenties – in some cases even earlier – a flood of major works by such specialists as Bevan, Tarn, Berve, Wilcken, Walbank, Will, Préaux, Welles, Fraser and many others has testified to the enormous potential of a period in many ways far more richly documented than classical Greece, and of at least equal fascination as regards the arts. Yet popular enthusiasm has (despite the obligatory crop of paperbacks) been slow to kindle. Abundant *testimonia*, from statuary to papyri, from mosaics to architecture, are, it seems, not enough. Even Athens, for most people the focal point of Greek culture, excites little curiosity in those centuries between Aegospotami and Actium, even though it is the subject of at least one brilliant study in English, W.S. Ferguson's *Hellenistic Athens* (1911, repr. 1969), and several in France by P. Graindor. Art-enthusiasts, significantly, tend to show more interest in Pergamon or Alexandria during this period. Why is Lycurgus not as eagerly studied as Pericles? Why above all, if the concept of *eleutheria*, freedom, can stir every Hellenophile heart, have nine people out of ten who profess a love for Greece never even heard of the Chremonidean War?

Various explanations have been attempted. It is still sometimes asserted that there was a falling-off in cultural achievement, but this is a value-judgment that goes soft on detailed investigation. It is true that the *nature* of the achievement changed, turning more towards scholarship, medicine, science, philosophy and history, while literature – poetry in particular – became more selfconsciously mandarin. But only the kind of bigot who identifies culture exclusively with Attic drama, High Classical sculpture, and the architecture of Ictinus and Pheidias could talk in terms of 'decline'. It would be about as illogical to claim [as is beginning to happen: 1987] that the fifth century showed a sad falling-off from the sixth because its pure lyric impulse had been diverted to drama, because Ionia no longer bred physicists or moralists like Anaximander or Xenophanes, or because Athenian democrats had failed to come up with something better than the Solonian-Cleisthenic political system. The culture was there: the trouble was, it was culture of a sort which modern romantics tend to find unattractive. In just the same way (to take an example near to my heart) the Roman poet Ovid, so popular until the eighteenth century, then entered upon a period of neglect and disparagement – more or less coincident with the Romantic Revival – from which he is only now emerging.

More suggestive is the complaint (seldom voiced publicly, but omnipresent among students, who have no *pudeur* about admitting what their professors prefer to hide, e.g. being bored to death by Menander or depending on Loebs in an emergency) that fourth-century and Hellenistic history, especially in its political and military aspects, is a bewildering, meaningless sequence of complex but fundamentally unimportant events, from which no clear-cut, significant, or, above all, *morally valuable* pattern emerges. This is a disturbing phenomenon – disturbing especially because of its historiographical implications – which deserves a good deal more attention than it normally gets, not least when we reflect on the exceptions that are so often made to it: the reigns of Philip and Alexander, Rome's expansion after 220 BC. Does it, perhaps, take great events (and of what sort?) or, more alarmingly, great *historians* to give shape to a period? And is what we see then in essence their vision, their creation? How far, for instance, is our understanding of the Persian or the Peloponnesian Wars and their background predetermined by the *Weltanschauung*, the idiosyncratic interpretation of these events, of Herodotus and Thucydides? To what extent does our whole moral picture of the years between Philip V's accession and the destruction of the Achaean League depend on Polybius (only marginally offset by the later books of Livy)? Is it not true, in the last resort, that the last few years of the Peloponnesian War, from 411 onwards, lose considerable lustre, clarity and significance because our main historical source is no longer Thucydides but Xenophon – and should this fact not worry historians as regards the veracity of the former rather than the latter? It is over seventy years now since Cornford accused Thucydides of reshaping the Sicilian Expedition as an Attic tragedy: the claim has never been effectively refuted.

On these terms it would not be hard to explain lack of interest in the Chremonidean War, since when studying it we are reduced (epigraphical evidence apart) to reliance on such late and minor authors as Justin, Polyaenus, and Pausanias. The thought that historical credibility could be dictated, even subconsciously, by the literary quality of the source is something one faces with considerable reluctance [though I did know one doctoral candidate in literature who, as Housman said in another context, formulated the rule without misgiving, and practised it with conscious pride]. On the other hand there is more to the problem than historiographical inflation, an argument which anyhow cuts both ways: if great historians 'create' a period, it may be equally true that a culture at its apogee calls forth the great historian. Even today, when the 'Great Man' theory of history is at an official discount, historians no less than laymen still seem to fasten on great historical figures with uncommon avidity. And do we not respond by instinct to an exceptional *élan vital* in any society, be it centred in one man or the *polis*, and directed towards world conquest or artistic creation? Is it not true that this remains the one force capable of inspiring men to meaningful action, and of eliciting a clear pattern, discernible by later generations, from that mundane, self-motivated muddle of diurnal events which makes up the greater part of what we term human history?

Viewed in these terms, is not the moral judgment implicit in the title of Claude Mossé's *Athens in Decline* (1973) arguably justified? The chapter in

Athenian history that Professor Mossé unfolds is not, one has to admit, a particularly inspiring one; nor is it enhanced by the fact that, at least from the mid-fourth century onward, Athens begins to lose her hitherto unquestioned primacy – creative as well as political – among the various centres of the Greek world. This unpalatable truth has produced two contrasting reactions among scholars. On the one hand there are those who argue, from the fact that Greek city-states continued to go through all the traditional forms of democratic municipal hoopla, despite their underlying political impotence, that the institution actually enjoyed a revival during the Hellenistic period (cf. below, p. 184). These are the local-council meliorists. On the other, there are those who accuse the *polis* of being, *ab initio*, a horrible, unworkable, disruptively populist Greek mistake, stasiotic and sclerotic in about equal degrees. These are the authoritarian pejorists. Both views remain distorted and partial. Given freedom and self-respect, the system worked surprisingly well. Without them, what emerges is a bunch of oligarchs and businessmen going through the motions.

The long death agony of the *polis*, and the tell-tale social symptoms that accompanied it, evoke surprisingly little sympathy, except for a series of desperate revolts against authoritarian rule (cf. below, p. 185) that were doomed before they began. (Even here the failure of the hoplite tradition tells its own story.) We see the agricultural crisis of the early fourth century polarising social groups in a hunt for quick profits, the urban *demos* and the generals (*strategoi*) favouring war, the peasantry and the middle classes preferring retrenchment. We watch the dizzy increase of litigation, till Athens becomes a lawyers' republic such as Peithetairos and Euelpides in Aristophanes' *Birds* never dreamed of. The rapid growth of specialisation soon put paid to the ideal of a homogeneous citizen assembly, and *a fortiori* to that of a citizen army. Mercenaries were now hired to do much of the fighting, orators no longer (so to speak) put their sword-arm where their mouth was, generals became quasi-professional guerrilla leaders (Iphicrates is a good example of this trend), symbolic statue-groups of Peace and Wealth (*Eirene* and *Ploutos*) now replaced images of Victory (*Nike*). Civil and military functions, in short, were being radically separated, while (perhaps partly as a result of this) Assembly decisions took on an increasingly arbitrary, not to say demagogic, tinge as the century proceeded. New Comedy, a sign of the times, came to exemplify what Professor Mossé calls the 'withdrawal of the bourgeois class from any real political activity' – a view confirmed by Theophrastus' largely non-political *Characters* (though his portrait of the Authoritarian offers a nasty glimpse of post-Crannon oligarchs in action).

Raphael Sealey may have exaggerated slightly – *c'est son métier*, after all – when he claimed that Athenian political life in the fourth century never rose above mere factional conflict; but on the evidence here presented it is hard not to sympathise with such a view. Sixth-century diehards such as Theognis, already voicing that perennial complaint, 'Money's the Man', would have suffered a severe shock had they come back to earth and seen just how much worse things had got a mere two hundred years later. The one scheme capable of uniting almost all factions in the 380s was a commercially profitable rerevamping of Athens' old sea-empire. But Isocrates, blind as always to economic trends, argued that Athens must renounce her control of the sea – a stance in which he could at least count on the enthusiastic support of ultra-conservative landowners, and one which became immensely popular a decade or two after his death, when trade, agriculture and mining concessions once more began to show handsome profits. Private luxury now began to proliferate at a stupendous rate. Incentives to affluence multiplied. The state still imposed only moderate taxes on business transactions, and much trade remained in the hands of resident aliens, who were not liable for 'liturgies' (*leitourgiai*), those cripplingly expensive public chores required of all Athens' wealthier citizens. It is significant that Athens' main objection to Philip of Macedon, at least to begin with, was that his depredations in Thrace and the Chersonese threatened her crucial Black Sea grain route. Shortage of wheat is a leitmotif that runs in the background throughout Athens' history, and is duly reflected in this book.

Professor Mossé is excellent on the subtle shades of opinion dividing pro- and anti-Macedonians in Athens. She is perhaps a little over-emphatic about not identifying the oligarchs with the Macedonian party: as she herself correctly states elsewhere, there had not been an oligarchic party – if one may use that term – in Athens since the democratic restoration of 403, so presumably in the mid-fourth century the ultras were out on a limb, and thus the first people, in all likelihood, to whom Philip's agents would have appealed. While it remains true that the struggle against Macedonia could unite a moderate such as Lycurgus with Demosthenes and his fellow-extremists, it is perhaps even more significant, in the long run, that 'men of wealth and property, the principal victims of the war effort, eventually envisaged peace with Macedonia as the guarantee of their security'. Professor Mossé's picture of Isocrates as a crypto-spokesman for the wealthy oligarchs has much to recommend it. There is, too, something richly symbolic about Athens later *buying back* Piraeus from a Macedonian garrison for 150 talents – an act which sorts well with the pursuit of affluence at the expense of dignity – and the extraordinary servile grovelling with which leading Athenians came, more and more, to acclaim powerful foreign monarchs, a habit which earned them a sharp rap over the knuckles from that Romanised Greek exile Polybius.

We get the whole sad sequence in less than two hundred pages: Lycurgus' hopeless attempt to turn back history and restore the Periclean Age (which had been provoking nostalgia among the *literati* at least since 412, when Eupolis produced his play *The Demes*); the devious, if ultimately patriotic, activities of men like Demosthenes or Demades during Alexander's campaigns; the defeat by Antipater at Crannon in 322; the Macedonian-backed ten-year 'philosophical tyranny' under Demetrius of Phaleron, followed by the somewhat different excesses of his namesake the Besieger, who turned the *opisthodomos* of the Parthenon into a harem, but at least had no time (as the Athenians noted with relief) for that Macedonian *condottiere* Cassander; the ill-fated Chremonidean War against Antigonus Gonatas, the failure of which 'meant the end of Athenian dreams of independence'; the increasing tendency of third-century Athenians – professional politicos, a small but powerful junta of wealthy landowners – to side with the highly undemocratic monarchs of Egypt or Macedonia or Pergamon against a 'wild man' such as Cleomenes III of Sparta, who advocated a species of communism [in fact a reversion to the military elitism that had flourished before Leuctra], and, unlike Aristophanes in the *Ecclesiazusae*, was in deadly earnest about it; the uneasy alliance with Rome against Philip V, and Flamininus' illusory declaration of Greek freedom at the Isthmian Games of 196; the fatal, desperate trucking with Mithridates VI of Pontus by anti-Roman Athenian democrats, which led directly to Sulla's terrible sack of the city in 86, when, according to Plutarch, all the Kerameikos inside the Dipylon Gate ran red with blood.

Attempts to regain independence were few, and more often than not (as in the case of the Mithridatic alliance) disastrous. The characteristic temper of third-century Athens is far better expressed by her leading politician Eurycleides, who, as Professor Mossé says, belonged 'to that wealthy middle class which had accepted Macedonian domination when it meant the maintenance of peace and internal order, but was ready to reject it as soon as it involved Athens in excessive expenditure'. So far was Antigonus Gonatas from being regarded as a *tyrannos* that we find the paradoxical (and ludicrous) situation of Aratus, the leader of the Achaean League, attempting to 'liberate' Athens from Macedonian rule, only to be repulsed by Athenians who preferred the status quo. Trade was largely going elsewhere, to Rhodes and the East; the Long Walls fell into disrepair. Only the philosophical schools – Peripatetics, Stoics, Epicureans – continued to flourish (nothing could stop an Athenian arguing two sides of a proposition, then or ever), though Professor Mossé is not over-enthusiastic about their achievements [times change: one of the most remarkable phenomena in the 1980s has been the upswing of interest in, and admiration for, Hellenistic achievements in philosophy]. Literature and art, except for a perfunctory description of Lycurgus' building-programme, and a stray reference to those of Demosthenes' speeches that describe 'a picturesque and colourful business world', she virtually ignores. This, we may assume, is a tacit value-judgment.

A survey of post-classical Athens for the student or general reader has been badly needed. W.S. Ferguson's *Hellenistic Athens*, though recently (1969) reprinted in America, first appeared as long ago as 1911, and is thus in many respects out of date; nor does it cover the crucial years of the early fourth century in any detail. By and large, despite a characteristic tendency to leave important details unexplained, and a more than usually rich crop of translator's *cocasseries*, *Athens in Decline* fills the need well enough. Professor Mossé's narrative is perhaps a little dry and over-compressed: some English readers might have preferred the ample sweep of her earlier work, *La Fin de la Démocratie Athénienne* (1962). The consistent eschewal of anecdote almost reaches Thucydidean levels, though I noted with pleasure that Demetrius of Phaleron's famous saliva-spitting mechanical snail rates a mention. The contemporary ancient historian's distrust of such vivid details can be overdone; a classical anecdote is not *by definition* fiction, exclusively concocted as propaganda or to illustrate character. Such incidents can be both true and revealing. A new edition, even if it does not deign to chronicle some of Demetrius Poliorcetes' more colourful erotic escapades, might at least give the text of that notorious hymn (see below p.181) with which he was greeted on entering Athens. Sedulous flattery, it might be thought, could scarcely go further. In Demetrius' case, all too symptomatically, it did.

THOSE THREE CROWDED and cosmopolitan centuries between the death of Alexander and Cleopatra VII's defeat by Octavian offer an eerie, and at times downright disconcerting, sense of *déjà vu* to any student of contemporary society. The resemblances are numerous and close. We find the same widespread reversion from democratic institutions to authoritarian regimes, the same sense of psychological and aesthetic fragmentation, the same anti-rationalist trends, the same social solipsism and self-absorption, the same active promotion of the critic at the expense of the creator (though mercifully without quite as much accompanying jargon as today: see above, pp.8-9), the same obsessive pursuit of affluence, exotic religious cults, fads in astrology and magic, offbeat eroticism, gourmet food; the same preoccupation with mere bigness (or, out of reaction, smallness: big book big evil), the same retreat from political involvement, the same cultivation of private inner gardens (Epicurean or other) at the expense of the public domain, the same tendency to treat scholarship as big business, to fuel academic development on governmental – most often military – or industrial patronage, the same cringeing sense of facelessness in Megalopolis, the depersonalised world of the Big City.

It is not, then, to be wondered at that, after years of comparative neglect, the study of Hellenistic institutions, long promoted, for their own ends, by professional papyrologists, should be today enjoying something of an incipient boom. What *is* surprising is the absence of a really good, penetrating, comprehensive synthesis of this extraordinary period in the English language. We have numerous excellent specialist studies, often on a massive scale, e.g. Rostovtzeff's *Social and Economic History of the Hellenistic World* (1941) and Fraser's scarcely less magisterial *Ptolemaic Alexandria* (1973). Such general studies as do exist in English (e.g. those by Ferguson, Peters, Bradford Welles, or Tarn and Griffith), though packed with useful material on a variety of topics, tend to be selective, ahistorical in organisation and, worse, confusing.

This fault is most glaringly apparent in the (for the most part wholly inadequate) attempts to deal with the admittedly complex political evolution and relationships of the Successor kingdoms. Tarn and Griffith offer a brief summary, but this is so concentrated as to be virtually incomprehensible to the layman for whom it is intended. Others largely ignore the political history as such and concentrate rather on broad general topics (one senses the malign indirect influence of the Ecole Annales here), thus giving the erroneous impression that the Hellenistic age was a static, consistent epoch during which no changes of real significance took place in the *oikouménē*. Such narrative as we do get is chopped up, for the sake of tidiness, between the various individual kingdoms, Ptolemaic, Attalid, Seleucid, Antigonid and the rest: the result is a kaleidoscopic mess, full of bewildering cross-references and repetitions. Rostovtzeff (a loner in this as in other things) was always acutely conscious that the Hellenistic world must be viewed as an interdependent whole, politically no less than economically, and studied in evolutionary terms.

This ideal seems to have been lost sight of in the English-speaking countries. We have nothing remotely comparable either to Edouard Will's *Histoire politique du monde hellénistique* (2nd ed., 2 vols., 1979, 1982) or to the late Claire Préaux's *Le monde hellénistique* (1978) for comprehensiveness, comprehensibility, and detailed documentation. Yet even in these excellent French scholars the approach is still more fragmented than one would like. At times (and more often as time goes on) I find myself turning back, with immense relief, to the old-fashioned (i.e. diachronically planned and paginally footnoted) narrative of Benedictus Niese's *Geschichte der griechischen und makedonischen Staaten seit der Schlacht bei Chaeronea* (1893), a work which may need updating in light of new epigraphical and papyrological evidence, and certainly breaks off far too early in the story, but is not nearly so far gone in obsolescence as some modern scholars would have us believe. Three fat volumes of clarity, sanity, chronological sense and respect for *testimonia*: those were the days.

F. W. Walbank's *The Hellenistic World* (1981), then, comes at the right time, and has a very visible gap to fill. I opened it with high hopes: its author has made Polybius his life's work, and, like Niese, has produced on him (also, as it happens, in three fat volumes) a work of equal clarity, sanity, chronological sense and respect for *testimonia*, among the best and (I would judge) most durable commentaries of this century. There is much in *The Hellenistic World* that arouses similar respect. Walbank's erudition is predictably wide as well as deep, his mastery of the essential documents assured: he quotes, frequently and with telling effect, from sources literary and non-literary, many of the latter in particular little-known. He is also commendably up-to-date on many vexed questions of interpretation, and it is perhaps as a résumé of current scholarly thinking that *The Hellenistic Age* has most value for the student.

Walbank is clear and perceptive on the 'shifting and uneasy relationship between the Greco-Macedonian ruling class and the native populations'; he is not overawed by residual propaganda about the supposed Hellenising mission of Macedonian veterans or Greek traders and bureaucrats. He knows that the gymnasia, theatres, temples and other evidence of Hellenism which crop up in the far reaches of the Seleucid empire were primarily for the benefit of the expatriate ruling class – ancient equivalents of the European Club in British India or the American PX abroad generally, perquisites of an ethnocentric enclave. Economically Walbank is also up to date: he presents the Ptolemaic system as a 'large-scale experiment in bureaucratic centralism and in mercantilism . . . concerned rather to prevent cheating than to secure the most efficient results', he reminds us that the Hellenistic era 'was not characterised by any substantial transformation of the forces of production', and he trots out all the currently favoured answers to the perennial question. 'Why is the Greek view of the possibilities open to technology so restricted?', from cheap labour to technical incompetence, from conservatism of investment to social contempt for the banausic.

So far so good, and Walbank has a great deal of value to offer. The trouble is that much of it will only (as so often with such books) be of real use to those who know something about the subject already: like too many experts, Walbank cannot always quite visualise what, for the layman, will be baffling, what a truism. He is also exceedingly dry: there are stretches of prose here in which the regrettable greyness of the paper used by Fontana seems to reflect an equal greyness of mind. It is, of course, hard to compress a complex subject without sounding either aphoristic or impenetrable, and Walbank obviously finds aphorisms as suspect as Polybius found the purple patches of Timaeus. What, for instance, were the issues at stake in Rome's showdown with Antiochus III (192–188)? John Briscoe, in his admirable commentary (1981) on Books XXXIV–XXXVII of Livy, offers, in just over three pages, a clear analysis. Antiochus wanted to reconstitute the Seleucid empire as it had stood at the death of Seleucus I Nicator, complete with a European toehold beyond the Bosporus. He had no plans to conquer all Greece, much less invade Italy; that did not stop him standing up for his supposed 'ancestral rights' in Thrace. Rome (with the examples of Pyrrhus and Hannibal to mull over) tended, as here, to overreact to supposed threats from the East, as from Africa, but had no original intentions of destroying the Seleucid empire. As Ernst Badian long ago argued (a view unconvincingly challenged by Briscoe) the two sides lurched into war without really meaning to, by a series of accidents and miscalculations. It would be hard to deduce *any* of this, however, from Walbank's ultra-brief reference (p. 237): I was left, as so often, with the feeling that his text, especially on major historical events, was rather more Delphic than considerations of space required.

This is partly the fault of the book's arrangement. Walbank begins well enough, with a crisp rundown on the sources, a glance at Alexander's career and subsequent influence, and a chapter on the chaotic period 323-301, during which Alexander's marshals, such as Perdiccas, Ptolemy and Antigonus One-Eye (Monophthalmos) manoeuvred and fought over the immense spoils of empire. But after Ipsus (301) he abandons his chronological survey altogether, and only picks it up again, somewhat haphazardly, to describe Rome's intervention in the Balkans. Thus the crucial third century is not viewed in evolutionary terms at all: the reader is forced to piece the period together as best he can from random, and at times repetitive, scraps of historical information flung out *en passant* during a series of general chapters on Ptolemies, Seleucids, and the Graeco-Macedonian homeland. Students on whom I tried the text as an experiment reported severe confusion. There are also brisk surveys of religion, exploration and geography, and 'Social and Economic Trends'; a chapter headed 'Inter-city contacts and federal states' that seems to have strayed out of some more specialised monograph; and a section on 'Cultural Developments' that whips through philosophy, science and technology in one quick conducted tour after devoting half of one casual paragraph (p. 177) to literature.

What does the concerned reader really want, in the last resort, from a study of this kind? Some kind of interpretative overview, I would think, tentative answers to large social questions. Walbank does, as I have suggested, come up with some of the current theories, and this is valuable; but I was struck, throughout his book, by the number of odd Hellenistic phenomena he seems to take for granted. *Why* did philosophers reverse the fifth-century credo of political involvement in order to pursue *ataraxia*, private freedom from worry? How much will an unglossed phrase like 'the diatribes of the wandering Cynics' mean to a non–classicist, and is there not a danger that the uninformed will take both 'diatribe' and 'Cynic' in the wrong sense? *Why* did an increasing emphasis on Ptolemaic ruler-worship mirror 'a decline in their real power and in their independence *vis-à-vis* the native priesthood'? What brought about the 'admission of political and perhaps spiritual helplessness' that Walbank detects behind that notorious Athenian hymn to Demetrius the Besieger ('The other gods are far away, or cannot hear, or don't exist, or are indifferent to us, but *you* are present, we can see you, not carved in wood or stone, but for real: so to you we pray')? This last question Walbank partially answers – three pages later – with a reference to the reduced power of the city-states and the decline in rationalism, but the connection would be less than clear to someone who was not already prepared for it. This is a useful interim report, but not the *vue d'ensemble* we need, much less a textbook for beginners. The field is still wide open.

ALEXANDER'S DEATH IN BABYLON (323 BC) was followed by a prolonged and ferocious struggle, between his senior officers, for the empire he had conquered. This division of the spoils produced, after some forty years, an uneasy balance of power in the so-called 'inhabited world'(*oikouménē*) of the Eastern Mediterranean and former Persian satrapies, between three competing dynasties: Antigonids in Macedonia, Ptolemies (or Lagids) in Egypt, Seleucids in Syria and the Orient. These 'Successors' (*diadochoi*) to Alexander proclaimed themselves kings; and monarchy, of a more or less absolute sort, became the preferred – indeed, given the circumstances, the only effective – mode of government. Popular though the Greek *polis* remained, its functions were now largely decorative and municipal: the true power lay elsewhere. Substantive exceptions, such as the maritime republic of Rhodes, were rare indeed. During the course of the first century BC, for reasons still fiercely disputed, the Hellenistic kingdoms were absorbed, one after the other, by Rome. The defeat of the last Ptolemy, Cleopatra VII, by Octavian at Actium (31 BC) is rightly seen as marking the end of an era.

Thus the Hellenistic age was, as several recent (1985) scholarly publications make very clear, in essence the poisoned imperial legacy of an inordinately ambitious, largely apolitical, military genius to posterity. As J.K. Davies observes in the new Volume VII of the *Cambridge Ancient History*, war and violence were the 'basic determining factors of Hellenistic experience'. Erich S. Gruen, in *The Hellenistic World and the Coming of Rome*, writes of 'the convulsive realignments that had characterised Hellenistic history since the age of the *diadochoi*'. Yvon Garlan puts it in a nutshell when he says: 'The Hellenistic states had their origins on the battlefield and that is where they met their doom' (*CAH* VII² 362): a predictable outcome, and one 'in line with the determining role played by violence in such societies'. It is sometimes forgotten how all-pervasive these antecedents were. Egypt, Syria and the East remained 'spear-won territory' (*doriktētos gē*), held down and administered, to a great extent for their own benefit, by Greeks and Macedonians, whose natural *de haut en bas* attitude to *barbaroi* had been strengthened through conquest, and developed unimpeded into that proprietorial imperialism which characterises not only the three great dynasties but also their lesser imitators, such as the Attalids of Pergamon. If the monarchies were, as Professor Davies claims, 'competitive, territorially unstable, and given to mutual spoiling', that must be reckoned no more than the logical outcome of their ingrained militaristic cast of mind.

Perhaps the most serious casualty of this reversion to brute force (now normally purchased, in the form of mercenaries) and authoritarianism (no longer creeping but blatant) was the longstanding trust in due process, the binding efficacy of law, and the prime importance of civic collectivism which had so clearly characterised *polis* activities in the fifth century. When legal sanctions were so patently vulnerable, in the last resort, to the will of the conqueror, their moral no less than their pragmatic strength could not but be seriously weakened. Alexander's request to be worshipped as a god might arouse sneers among intellectuals, but his cavalier treatment of the Greeks in

Asia Minor left no doubt in anyone's mind that civic statutes, juridical precedent, sworn treaties, special honours, boundary-lines, commercial contracts, and the rest of each city-state's official undertakings or traditional privileges had validity only insofar as Alexander himself was pleased to endorse them; and it soon became even clearer – *a fortiori* in the case of the Successors – that such endorsement was entirely conditional on doing the conqueror's will in all things. To cross him brought swift and condign punishment. *Sois mon frère ou je te tue.*

Philosophical precedent for this might-is-right attitude could be found in the pronouncements of fifth-century sophists such as Critias; the Athenians had given a notable, and notorious, demonstration of the thesis in their savage treatment of Melos during the Peloponnesian War: 'You know as well as we do,' they told the Melians (in Thucydides' words), 'that justice in human debate results from a balance of power, and that the strong exploit their advantage, while the weak must perforce yield.' Arguments of this type had not lost their force, or their popularity, with time. It is, however, worth noting that whereas in the fifth century such conduct had aroused a storm of disapproval, little more than a hundred years later it was virtually taken for granted: Alexander – after, characteristically, cutting the Gordian Knot rather than untying it – had driven the point home with ineluctable force. Gods (if Euhemerus was right) had been men, and now men were going the gods one better, had indeed become the measure of all things in ways Protagoras had never foreseen.

The full force of this militaristic ethic, and its ramifying implications for every facet of Hellenistic society, have not always been clearly recognised. That cherished human passion – strong especially in academics – for reason, order, law, due process, precedent, and their general acceptance in some version of the *contrat social*, can produce, on occasion, really bizarre delusions: e.g. Sir William Tarn's theory (wittily demolished by the late J.P.V.D. Balsdon) that Alexander required recognition as a god in order to give him the constitutional right to interfere with the internal affairs of individual cities in the League of Corinth – a right officially denied him as mere head (*hegemon*) of the League. Such touching faith in the binding force of law on a world conqueror with an army at his back is too extreme to be taken seriously; but more subtle variants of the instinct persist. In 1937 (of all years) Professor Alfred Heuss produced his *magnum opus, Stadt und Herrscher des Hellenismus*, of which the central, Weberian, thesis was the essential independence, in relation to the *Idealtypus* of king and *polis*, of the Hellenistic Greek cities: independence being in effect equated with constitutional continuity, while royal interference was written off as mere unimportant ad hoc tinkering. What mattered, as Heuss saw it, was the legal charter.

It might be thought that a magisterial rejoinder such as E. Bikerman's *Institution des Séleucides* (1938) would have sufficed to drive out this kind of *Idealismus* for good; or, failing that, that the events of the next few decades might have eroded historians' faith in the amenability of rulers to the human rule-book. Yet belief in the independence of the Hellenistic *polis* still flourishes. Even so sensible a scholar as Professor Davies can speak of its 'transformation and revitalisation', in a context which makes quite clear that what he has in mind is, on the one hand, royal recognition of urban municipal status, and, on the other, the spread of Seleucid or Attalid military and civilian foundations, which, he asserts, 'coincided so harmoniously [*sic*] with local aspirations, inside the kingdoms as much as in Old Greece, as to amount to nothing less than the renaissance and re-institutionalization of the *polis*'. This is really breathtaking. Municipal autonomy (to take the simplest point first) cost nothing, took a city's day-to-day administration off the shoulders of the ruling bureaucracy without depriving the monarch of any substantial power, and gave ample scope for those trumpery parochial honours which could be relied on to keep the local bigwigs happy. So much is obvious. But whose were the local aspirations with which the expansionist activities of an occupying power stood in such harmonious agreement?

Put like that, the answer is clear (even without reading S.K. Eddy's *The King Is Dead*), and would no doubt offer considerable comfort to, say, the Soviet-backed government of Afghanistan. Those who stood to benefit were the ambitious few determined to make a career in the service of the occupying power: history has found some unpleasant names for such people. The Macedonian dynasties in Egypt and the Near East were exploitative imperial regimes, ruling by military force for their own benefit, in the last resort massively indifferent to the indigenous civilisations with which they came in contact (Cleopatra VII was the first Ptolemy who ever bothered to learn Egyptian; there is virtually no trace of interpenetration between Hellenistic Greek and Pharaonic or Babylonian literature), and creating what were in effect ghettos of Greek *polis*-culture, complete with temples, theatres, baths, gymnasia, and the rest of the indispensable civic impedimenta, wherever they established a new outpost of empire. The whole notion of Hellenism as a missionary cult spread for the enlightenment of the heathen is a Victorian myth. Professor Davies mentions most of these facts – the settlers who wanted 'the sort of social structure that they were used to in the homeland', 'government by informal elites' in the cities themselves, the empty and meaningless ceremonial, the civic demilitarisation except for decorative upper-class cavalry squadrons – without ever coming squarely to grips with their social and historical implications. Professor Gruen, as so often, is more down-to-earth and realistic: he knows very well (a point we are never allowed to forget for long when reading his work) that 'the *poleis* of the mainland and of the Aegean had become political playthings, bounced around by the major powers and reduced to second-class status'.

At the same time, though he does not, like Professor Davies, suggest that the Greek cities were having a high old revitalised time, he knows very well that 'they had not lost a sense of their own identity and longing for independence, however shaky or restricted that independence might be' – a fundamentally different thing. No factitious distinctions between totalitarian and authoritarian governments for him. Indeed, one of the most striking phenomena about the whole period is the desperate against-the-odds belief in, balancing the cynical exploitation of, the slogan of 'Freedom (*eleutheria*) for the Greeks', which recurs again and again, long after one might have supposed that belief in its practicability would have been driven out of the Greek psyche. Historians, by the nature of things, tend to dwell more on the cynicism, the hollow manipulative pretensions: it is Professor Gruen who points out (correctly) that the 'removal of one overlord through the assistance of another was conventionally greeted as the restoration of liberty'. Yet the crowds who exploded in a delirium of joy when the Roman proconsul T. Quinctius Flamininus made his famous proclamation of Greek freedom at the Isthmian Games of 196 still, beyond any doubt, felt that *eleutheria* was truly within their grasp; and the desperate ventures fought for it against odds – Crannon and Amorgos, the Chremonidean War, the Mithridatic rising, above all the Achaean League's last-ditch stand against Rome's legions – prove, if proof were needed, that for those Greeks with memories of what true independence meant, freedom had not become a mere empty word.

As today, so in the Hellenistic world, authoritarian regimes could be, and often are, enlightened (not for nothing did at least two Ptolemies assume the title of Euergetes, Benefactor), while a technically autonomous state such as Sparta used its *eleutheria* for ends that sent shock-waves of panic throughout mainland Greece. Nothing better illuminates that universal conservatism so characteristic of Greek society, the passion for economic and social stability, as opposed to growth or development, than the hysteria which greeted such emergency measures in Sparta as the cancellation of debts, the redistribution of land, and the enfranchisement of second-class citizens (even, under Nabis, of numerous helots). The true object, it goes without saying, was to restore the Spartan *ancien régime*, to train a new model army in the old style, to reimpose, as Professor F.W. Walbank stresses in the revised Volume VII.i of *The Cambridge Ancient History*, Sparta's former dominance over the Peloponnese. Cleomenes' social measures 'were intended both to restore the kind of Sparta which had enjoyed domination in the past and to secure this once again in his own time'. In other words, Greek politics as usual: Professsor Gruen's telling phrase in this context (applied equally to the Achaean League) about 'new militancy and particularist aspirations' catches the mood to perfection.

Yet, ironically, not only did neighbouring states at the time firmly believe that the Spartan kings Agis, Cleomenes and, *a fortiori*, Nabis were social firebrands, intent on disrupting the fixed and stable order of society: their fantasies have found willing listeners among many modern scholars. It is fascinating, in retrospect, to study the attempts by progressive romantics, riding the initial wave of the Russian revolution, to present these ultra-reactionary military nationalists as progressive and enlightened reformers frustrated by the ancient equivalent of hard-faced capitalists. Naomi Mitchison's haunting novel *The Corn King and the Spring Queen* not only picks up this atmosphere but contrives to lace it with Frazerian symbolism as well: a juxtaposition, improbable in itself, that should not surprise those familiar with the later work of Jane Harrison. We have, fortunately, come a long way since then. If Professor W.G. Forrest and the late Alexander Fuks can still be counted among those who leave the door open, as it were, for the ghost of Spartan social idealism, Linda J. Piper's *The Spartan Twilight*, an excellent survey of Sparta in the Hellenistic and Roman periods, contrives to be at once politically realistic and sympathetic towards its subjects, in some cases a notable balancing act. Forrest thought a history of Hellenistic Sparta impossible: Professor Piper triumphantly refutes him.

In the last resort there is, after all, something inspiring, in the simple if unfashionable mode of *polis* patriotism (one of Arnold Toynbee's favourite bugbears), about the efforts by Sparta's Hellenistic kings to recover the old glories lost at Leuctra in 371, when Thebes smashed the myth of Spartan military invincibility and, worse, deprived her defeated foe of grain-rich Messenia, leaving Sparta 'cut down to the status of a provincial second-class state'. Professor Piper is, perhaps inevitably, a little in love with her protagonists, somewhat over-Phylarchan at the expense of Polybius (though many of her strictures on that *parti pris* Achaean activist are more than justified), giving Cleomenes, and even Nabis at his most brutal and desperate, the benefit of the doubt rather too often (could it *all* have been hostile propaganda?); but she charts Agis' slide into tyrannical illegality with cool if regretful objectivity. She is well aware that the Spartan revolution, so-called, was aimed at restoring Spartan militarism, and that with Cleomenes' defeat at Sellasia in 222 BC Spartan history degenerated, first, into a succession of petty tyrannies, and then into endless attempts, over fifty years, to break free from the stranglehold of the Achaean League.

All this she is right to stigmatise as a sad comedown from the days when Sparta 'remained free, paid no tribute, had no foreign garrison within her city, and, even in defeat, had suffered no shame'. *Eleutheria*, as Sparta's case demonstrates with uncomfortable clarity, is no guarantee of virtue in the free; but its absence, often in subtle ways, subverts the spirit, as too much of the Hellenistic world found out to its cost. The day of slavery, Homer knew, takes away half a man's worth (however we define slavery); and that it should have been the Spartans who provided the *casus belli* which brought the Achaean League into open conflict with Rome, and thus led to the final subjugation of Greece, remains the sharpest irony of all.

But the most shining example of obstinate and triumphant *eleutheria* in the Hellenistic period – in clear-cut contrast to all the servility, flattery, and authoritarianism – is provided by Rhodes: how curious, then, that Richard M. Berthold's *Rhodes in the Hellenistic Age* should be almost the only serious study devoted to this fascinating commercial republic in the past eighty years. Diodorus called the Rhodian state 'the best-governed city of the Greeks'; Polybius described the Rhodians as 'pre-eminent in maritime affairs'. Rhodes' famous code of maritime law passed down through Byzantium to Venice. The island might be governed, and its fleets commanded, by its aristocratic families, but these officers were freely elected, for not more than six-month terms. They also operated something very like a welfare state. In an age when military service elsewhere was largely undertaken by mercenaries, Rhodian citizens took pride (as Athenians once had done, but no more) in their service with the fleet. Rhodian shipbuilders were second to none, and their trade secrets jealously guarded. Swift Rhodian quadriremes kept down corsairs; Rhodes' merchant marine ranged from Egypt to the Black Sea. In 305 the island triumphantly stood off Demetrius Poliorcetes, giving an ironic twist to his title of 'Besieger'. The extent of Rhodes' commercial network may be gauged from the international roll call of states offering the island lavish relief after the great earthquake of 228/7, which, inter alia, brought down the recently erected Colossus.

It is an impressive success story: one, moreover, in which wealth and social responsibility advance hand in hand, something a great deal rarer. Professor Berthold tells the story crisply, and documents it well. The Rhodians' mercantile interests, as he points out, 'would determine the basic strategic objectives of the island in the eastern Mediterranean, specifically the suppression of piracy, the promotion of peace, and the preservation of a balance of power among the great monarchies'. (This attainment of aretē through trade was quintessentially Hellenistic, and must have had Plato turning in his grave.) If, because of her wheat imports, Rhodes had a special relationship with Ptolemaic Egypt, that did not stop her fighting an over-ambitious Ptolemy II during the Second Syrian War. She became involved in the Roman campaign against Philip V of Macedon mainly with a view to protecting her Pontic trade-routes, and took a less than glorious part (as Polybius and Livy both snidely point out) in the actual campaigning.

The truth of the matter is that with the entry of Rome, and Roman military expertise, on the Hellenistic scene, Rhodes' traditionally non-aligned foreign policy became increasingly hard to maintain. Even though the modern interpretation of this period in terms of pro- and anti-Roman factions is fundamentally mistaken (Hellenistic quarrels seldom took serious account of outsiders till it was too late), nevertheless the Rhodians found themselves forced more and more, as time went on, to abandon their evenhanded support for the balance of power and, however reluctantly, to commit themselves. 'Neutrality', as Professor Berthold remarks, 'was pointless once it was apparent that one side would gain a decisive victory.'

Even so, the Rhodians dragged their feet as much as possible, and it was this that finally proved their undoing. They got away with holding off until Antiochus the Great emerged as clear loser; then they declared against him, and did well in the post-war division of the spoils. Too well, in fact: not merely now the 'clearinghouse and banker of the eastern Mediterranean', but arrogantly independent – a quality which may have appealed to Cato, but did not please many of his colleagues. The crisis came during Rome's final confrontation with Macedonia. The Rhodians offered the SPQR no more than lukewarm support (including an ill-timed and disastrous promise of mediation), while at the same time revealing indiscreet public enthusiasm for the cause of Perseus and Macedonian independence.

Rome's treatment of Rhodes in 167, after the Macedonian phalanx had gone down before Aemilius Paullus' legions at Pydna, offers a useful starting-point for any discussion of Roman foreign policy in Greece and Asia Minor during the second century BC. The worst charge that could be brought against the Rhodians was that they had lacked positive enthusiasm over the Roman cause; but the Senate, apparently going on the principle of 'he that is not for me is against me', and determined to make an example of this proud would-be power-broker, stripped Rhodes of her profitable Lycian and Carian dependencies (granted by Rome herself under the Treaty of Apamea: what Rome had bestowed Rome could remove), set up the island of Delos, under Athenian supervision, as a free port, and, worse, left the island's application for a treaty of alliance (*foedus*) in limbo for several years, which did untold damage to Rhodes' commercial credit. Rhodian losses have been exaggerated: she still kept her lucrative grain trade (for which the harbours of Delos were unsuitable), and continued affluent after Delos was ruined; but Rome's reaction was, to say the least, highhanded, and we have to ask ourselves whether it can be seen – what has often been asserted – as merely one further step in a conscious policy of aggressive imperial expansionism by Rome into the Balkans and Near East.

As far as Rhodes herself is concerned, both Professor Berthold and Professor Gruen are in substantial agreement: Rome's patience was exhausted, the Senate was disturbed by 'Rhodes's tremendous reputation for pride and independence', the island republic was growing too big for its boots, was an untrustworthy ally, must be made an example of to discourage others. But that Rome had any conscious imperial designs on the Hellenistic world, even after Pydna, even with Magna Graecia, Sicily, Carthage and Spain telling a very different story, is something which Gruen is at elaborate pains to deny, and which indeed forms a key argument in his long, brilliantly argued, and impeccably researched *magnum opus*, *The Hellenistic World and the Coming of Rome*, which on every page offers the reader salutary reminders that it is as well to have such complete mastery of the primary evidence before evaluating the interpretations of that evidence made by one's predecessors in the field.

There have been various dominant theories to explain Rome's progressive involvement in the affairs of the Greek states: a militaristic appetite for conquest (Ferrero, De Sanctis, and, most recently, W.V. Harris' *War and Imperialism in Republican Rome*); commercial and mercantile greed (Colin, Rostovtzeff); the establishment of an international variant on the client-patron relationship (Badian). Gruen himself is most closely aligned with the 'reluctant and unplanned' thesis promoted, in various forms, by Mommsen, Tenney Frank, and, in particular, Maurice Holleaux. What distinguishes his work, above all, is a determination to see things always from the Greek rather than the Roman viewpoint, and a constant illuminating common sense. I think he may not give enough weight to the influence of the private sector, first in exploiting rich territories in Asia Minor, then in gradually bringing round the traditionally scrupulous senatorial class to a more acquisitive and less Catonic way of thinking; but there can be no doubt that *The Hellenistic World and the Coming of Rome* is a remarkable and original work of scholarship besides being (what scholarship, alas, so often is not) an exhilarating intellectual experience.

It is also, in the best sense, radically revisionist. I soon lost count of the occasions on which Gruen, marshalling his documents with precision and sure judgment, stood an *idée reçue* on its head. *Amicitia* was not, after all, a euphemism for clientship, nor had it been used to reduce communities to subservience: it was 'a presumption of cordiality, rather than an instrument of hegemony'. The Senate, in fact, did not apply the *clientela* model to overseas arrangements in the third and second centuries, much less exercise *patrocinium* over Hellenes. The worship of Roma originated on the Greek side: 'The practice was thoroughly Hellenic.' The modern notion of a senatorial lobby of Eastern experts is a myth: Gruen's analysis suggests that Roman proconsuls were no more appointed on the basis of local expertise than diplomats in the Foreign Office (like the Senate, long a bastion of self-styled amateur omnicompetence). Philhellenism, or indeed misohellenism (*pergraecari* = to lead a dissipated life), had little or nothing to do with State policy. Economics alone will not explain Roman slavery, and *publicani* did not dictate senatorial policy. There was no real Roman protectorate in Illyria, and Rome never played the kingmaker in Macedonia. The treaty of Apamea did not mean the establishment of Roman hegemony in Asia, any more than Rome in 200 undertook a species of guardianship (*tutela*) over the young Ptolemy V Epiphanes. The Sixth Syrian War did not turn Egypt into a client-state of the Republic. And so on. The general message is clear: Rome had no driving urge to annex or control Greece and Asia Minor; the Greek states were far more interested in their own quarrels and ambitions than in their relationship with this new and unpredictable military force from the West. *Barbaroi*, in the last resort, were not to be taken seriously.

This is all refreshing to a degree, and for the most part extraordinarily persuasive: Gruen's account of how the Senate and Antiochus the Great were pushed over the brink into war by their own escalating propaganda campaigns not only carries total conviction, but has (like so much Hellenistic history) an eerily modern flavour to it. His study certainly brings out, again and again, the perils of an excessively Romanocentric approach. One surprising fact that he stresses is the degree to which the Romans, far from imposing their own methods of administration on the Greek states, borrowed Hellenistic usages, both diplomatic and bureaucratic, with inevitable misunderstandings in consequence. The Romans tried to adapt the system, while the Greeks, as usual, were busily manipulating it, so that (for example) Rome's self-styled role as Greek liberator in the Hellenistic tradition simply drew endless embassies from warring parties, all eager to utilise Rome's support in the business of scoring off each other and crossly baffled when the Romans refused to behave as expected.

The Romans had no taste for direct rule as conquerors in the traditional Greek manner: the Hellenistic mask simply would not fit. Years of indifference would be punctuated by sudden bursts of violent punitive action, followed once more by inexplicable withdrawal. It is, as Gruen says, 'hardly surprising that Greeks found Roman actions maddeningly difficult to comprehend'. No more surprising, perhaps, than the modern urge to rewrite Rome's ventures into Greek diplomacy in strictly Roman terms. At times Gruen's robust common sense takes too cavalier an attitude to shaky sources; but overall he has done a magnificent job of reassessment that will, when assimilated, substantially modify our estimate of that fateful period when the destinies of Rome and the Hellenistic world first became interwoven, in the complex process which Polybius labelled *symplokē*.

Professor Walbank is, beyond a doubt, the most distinguished Polybian scholar alive; yet in his editing of the new Volume VII of *The Cambridge Ancient History*, *symplokē*, historiographically speaking, gets little more than a casual nod of recognition in his preface. Anyone who wants to see the Hellenistic world steadily and see it whole will have to look elsewhere. The confusing (but unfortunately traditional) practice of fracturing any academic study of the *oikoumēnē* into a series of discrete and most often artificially synchronous essays is still, for the most part, retained here. As a kind of concession, we are offered an account by Professor Edouard Will of the Successors' rivalries from Alexander's death to the battle of Ipsus (301): this, not surprisingly, conveys a certain sense of *déjà vu*, since (with one or two minor additions and corrections) it is a line-by-line translation from Volume I of Will's *Histoire politique du monde hellénistique* (2nd ed. 1979). And why draw the line at Ipsus? Because, seemingly, Antigonus One-Eye is regarded here as the last general who tried to lay hands on the whole of Alexander's empire: separatist politics breed separatist history. Quite apart from the fact that both Lysimachus and Seleucus I tried to scoop the pool after Antigonus (and Seleucus actually came within a hair's-breadth of doing so), is it mere captiousness to find such a methodology perverse?

Professor Walbank might, I suppose, argue, first, that the world of the Successor kingdoms is such a baggy monster, in the Jamesian sense, so heterogeneous and diverse, as to make a separatist approach inevitable; and, second, that since Polybius dates the onset of *symplokē* to 220–217 – which happens to be the date at which this volume technically closes – any 'interweaving of affairs throughout the whole civilised world' can be (as Xenophon said of Greek history after the end of his *Hellenica*) some other man's concern. Unfortunately it is not as simple as that. Granted the scope and variety of the subject, some degree of synoptic separatism is probably inevitable; but the interrelated overview should never be lost sight of. What we have here, to begin with, is the major, brutal dichotomy by which Part I of Volume VII describes the Hellenistic world, while Roman affairs are relegated to its not-yet-published successor, a division that would not, I suspect, win Professor Gruen's unqualified approval. It also leaves some irrational loose ends at the point of separation, i.e. Sicily and Magna Graecia. Thus while the present volume contains a useful essay on Agathocles by Professor Klaus Meister, anyone wanting to pursue Sicilian affairs through the reign of Hiero II will have to wait, since though Hiero comes within the official time-limit, he is adjudged more appropriate for inclusion in the Roman bin.

On the other hand, the essays on Ptolemaic Egypt and Syria (the first a brilliant *tour de force* by the late Sir Eric Turner, the second a handy rehash of Domenico Musti's monograph-length article 'Lo Stato dei Seleucidi', originally published in *Studi Classici Orientali* for 1966) range far beyond the onset of *symplokē*, into the second and even the first centuries. The wars between Seleucids and Ptolemies over Coele-Syria – a bone of contention then as today – get a chapter to themselves: this also, puzzlingly, includes a perfunctory round-up on the states of Asia Minor such as Bithynia, Pontus, Cappadocia, and (without apparent recognition of their far greater importance) Rhodes and Pergamon. Professor Walbank himself contributes a bland discussion on the theory and practice of Hellenistic monarchy, and reprises his work on Macedonia and Greece from the time of Antigonus Gonatas through to the Social War. G.E.R. Lloyd offers a predictably succinct and useful account of Hellenistic science (which, again, strays far beyond the third century). Other experts are allowed brief appearances only: Yvon Garlan on war and siegecraft, Dorothy Thompson on agriculture, F.E. Winter on building and townplanning. The result is a book packed with useful and up-to-date information for those who know what they are looking for, but bewildering as an introduction: its proper function is encyclopedic, it is for consultation, not to read.

It is also (as the alert reader will by now in all likelihood have deduced) remarkable both for what it omits and for the methodological, indeed the philosophical, assumptions which underpin these omissions. There is, to begin with, almost nothing about religion (except in relation to ruler-cults), or that fine flowering of Stoic cosmological pseudo-science, astrology, which may have been late, but was hardly Roman in origin. Further, and more important, Walbank argues editorially that 'it was not feasible to include a full critical account of the art, literature and philosophical speculations of the period'. No one would ask for 'a full critical account': the trouble is, we are not, except for incidental references, given *anything*. A whole block of crucial evidence has simply been ignored. The clear implication is that these cultural areas have no historiographical significance, and function in a sealed aesthetic enclave. A similar stance is adopted by Professor Berthold, who supposes that because he is writing a political history of Rhodes, this means he can afford a mere cursory sketch of the republic's social structure, treat economic problems only insofar as they refer directly to politics, and ignore cultural matters altogether. Perhaps that is why poor Professor Davies, whose contribution to *CAH* VII i is by far the liveliest, and who has a much clearer idea than most of what principles are to seek in his field, should have been given the impossible task, in a single chapter, of analysing 'Cultural, Social and Economic Features of the Hellenistic World', much as earlier historians, taking a break from the serious business of war and politics, used to churn out those perfunctory round-ups on art, philosophy, and literature. Excellent work – as all these studies demonstrate in their different ways – is being done today in every area of Hellenistic civilisation. What is crying out for revision (as they equally make clear) is the unreflecting adherence to an arbitrary, and constricting, set of historiographical guidelines.

CAESAR AND ALEXANDER: AEMULATIO, IMITATIO, COMPARATIO

❧

THE ELUSIVE HISTORICAL RELATIONSHIP between Julius Caesar and Alexander III of Macedon is something more often assumed than defined. Stefan Weinstock's treatment of the problem[1] is typical: 'There is no need', he asserts, 'to ask the question why Caesar wanted to become a successor of Alexander: every great conqueror, then and ever since, was by necessity following the path of Alexander.' The question is not asked; it is begged. *Did* Caesar in fact strive to emulate Alexander? On this point scholarly opinion is so divided that the dogmatism of the views expressed must strike any uncommitted investigator as, at best, paradoxical. At one extreme we find those, such as Meyer[2], or De Witt[3], who see in Caesar the natural inheritor of Alexander's alleged role as cosmocrator, civiliser of the *oikouménē* and unifier of mankind;[4] a similar attitude is taken by writers who accept the much-debated proposition that Caesar not only sought deification and monarchy in his own lifetime, but modelled his bid for both on Alexander's example. Lily Ross Taylor[5] and Dorothea Michel[6] are the most prominent scholars in this category – though the latter's claim that recent research has, almost without exception, confirmed Caesar's Alexander-*Nachahmung*[7] must be taken with a large grain of Attic salt. It was not true when she wrote it: even she had to concede Adcock's flat scepticism: 'The likeness between them', he wrote,[8] 'belongs to rhetoric rather than to history.' Since then further critical attacks have been launched against the whole idea of Alexander-*imitatio* on Caesar's part, most notably by Dietmar Kienast (in an article devoted primarily to Augustus),[9] and, above all, Otto Weippert, whose Würzburg dissertation[10] represents the most substantial contribution to this topic in recent years.

Yet anyone setting out to investigate the ancient evidence and its conflicting modern interpretations cannot get very far without being struck by the total absence, in a very vigorous ongoing debate, of any fundamental historiographical guidelines. One lone reviewer of Weippert[11] deserves credit for touching on this problem: 'Although giving some brief thoughts on the psychological phenomenon (of *imitatio*) he [Weippert] does not distinguish often enough between two quite disparate forms: (1) the report that a particular individual likened himself or compared himself with Alexander; and (2) the fact that some particular ancient source likened such an individual to Alexander.' This is a point of crucial importance, which can, and should, be refined considerably further. Hitherto no scholar involved in the controversy seems to have even been aware of it. Just why this should be so is hard to determine; but one contributory cause may lie in a prevalent academic attitude to *imitatio* as such.

With the possible exception of forgery, there is no characteristic that a modern scholar will so readily attach to any figure from the ancient world. When all due allowance has been made for the necessary pursuit of existing role models (particularly valid in education and scholarship, perhaps less so in the world at large), *imitatio* does seem to be too widely and uncritically accepted as a natural condition of mankind. Due allowance should always be made for significant exceptions. Though Alexander himself undoubtedly took Achilles as his exemplar,[12] the assumption that Caesar in turn must have imitated Alexander is highly questionable. It underrates Caesar's stubborn individualism; worse, it distracts attention from other sources of influence which may, in the long run, have affected him far more than the Macedonian ever did.

Thus it becomes abundantly clear, first, that the testimony relating to Alexander-*imitatio* must be sorted into several distinct categories; second, that the nature and scope of that *imitatio* require the most careful analysis; and third, that in all cases the motive involved is a factor of prime importance. Let us first attempt to establish the necessary categories. The major division, noted by J.S. Richardson,[13] is, as we have seen, that between *imitatio* described by, or attributed to, the imitator himself, and *imitatio* perceived or deduced by some third party. This latter function we may more properly term *comparatio*,[14] and it accounts for by far the greater part of our testimony concerning Caesar and Alexander.[15] More important, far rarer, and a good deal more tricky to analyse are claims made by, or on behalf of, the protagonist himself. Here we have to test both his own assertions and those statements or actions attributed to him for credibility and motivation. Within this category we should also make a sharp distinction between *imitatio* proper – that is, a conscious attempt to *copy* some model of excellence,[16] whether moral or practical – and *aemulatio*, an effort to rival or surpass that model, not necessarily by means of imitation.[17] There is, lastly, a difficult no-man's-land where it is hard to be certain which of these three main categories applies: in particular, where apparent *imitatio* may turn out to be based on sedulous flattery – or, alternatively, hostile propaganda – by some third party with an axe to grind. In all such cases the question of motive looms large. We can no longer assume that Alexander was a necessary or inevitable object of Caesar's emulation, any more than we can bracket him, for this purpose, with the very different cases – different from each other as well as from him – of Pompey and Mark Antony.[18]

When we break down the evidence for conscious *imitatio* or *aemulatio* of Alexander by Caesar it amounts to surprisingly little. In particular, Caesar's own works – which, we should not forget, consist exclusively of military narrative and apologia throughout – make no reference whatsoever, direct or indirect, to his great Macedonian predecessor.[19] Furthermore, neither Aulus Hirtius, nor the competent officer who reported the *Bellum Africum*, nor the charmingly illiterate centurion who, after his own fashion, did the same for the *Bellum Hispaniense*, nor – most surprising of all – whoever it was that put together that exercise in *opéra bouffe*, the *Bellum Alexandrinum*, ever once thought of promoting a comparison between the two commanders. This absence of testimony is in itself significant. Indeed, when we search for such testimony in other writers, there is one anecdote, and one only, which represents Caesar as consciously comparing himself, in fame and achievement, to Alexander. During his quaestorship in Further Spain, in 69 BC,[20] at the age of thirty-one, Caesar visited Gades, where in the temple of Hercules-Melkart he saw a statue of Alexander, perhaps set up there in 145 by Fabius Aemilianus.[21] At the sight he became greatly depressed, saying it was cause enough for sorrow that, at an age when Alexander had already subdued the world, he himself had achieved nothing worthy of note.[22] A variant on this anecdote[23] omits both temple and statue, and has Caesar instead reading an account of Alexander, after which he was lost in thought for a while, and finally burst into tears. It makes little difference which version we choose to follow: the essential point is that in 69, when, as Weinstock reminds us,[24] 'Pompey was the rising man in Rome', Caesar had yet to establish himself – and invoked Alexander as an emblem of the kind of success he hoped to achieve. Perhaps inevitably, this anecdote has been subjected to severe criticism by the sceptics, and Weippert's comments, that it looks uncommonly like *ex post facto* propaganda,[25] I find hard to gainsay. But it remains the only evidence of its kind that we possess.

Its authenticity becomes even more problematical when we consider the second anecdote with which Suetonius and Dio associate it.[26] About this time, they claim, Caesar had what we would now describe as an Oedipal dream of intercourse with his mother, which the soothsayers interpreted to mean that he would achieve great power. Dio places this episode, very plausibly, *before* the incident in the temple, and indeed suggests that it caused Caesar's reaction to Alexander's statue. The version adopted by Suetonius reverses this order of events, so that Caesar's dream now comes on the night following his experience in the temple. Presumably we are meant to regard the sight of Alexander's image as having triggered off in him, as De Witt inimitably suggests,[27] 'a psychological phenomenon that one might take the liberty of comparing to Saul's experience on the road to Damascus'. In

Suetonius, too, the soothsayers are far more emphatic and explicit: Caesar was, they said, fated to rule the world, 'since the mother whom he had seen subjected to him was none other than Earth, regarded as the parent of all mankind'. Plutarch, however (*Caes.* 32.6), with a nice sense of dramatic occasion, makes him have his dream in January 49, in Ravenna, just before crossing the Rubicon. What are we to make of this? Balsdon[28] dismisses the whole tradition out of hand. Strasburger[29] finds Plutarch's version more credible, because better adjusted to the historical march of events: who, he asks, would make such a prophecy to an unknown quaestor? But the quaestor in fact was far from unknown – his brush with Sulla alone would suffice to disprove this[30] – and in any case the prophecy was traditional and could have been given to anyone. Hippias before Marathon had an identical dream; and towards the end of the second century AD it turns up in the *Oneirocritica* of Artemidorus – each time with a similar interpretation.[31] It was simply a case of one cliché provoking another.

The specific literary evidence, then, for Caesar having consciously set up Alexander as his model is very slim indeed, something that should give us pause for thought. Equally suggestive is the fact that the Gades episode, however we look at it, clearly implies *aemulatio* rather than *imitatio*: what concerns Caesar is the idea of rivalry and achievement, not, in the first instance, the *modus operandi*.[32] His reaction to Alexander's career is instructive, also, in that it so clearly delimits those considerable areas where *imitatio* was impossible even if so desired. To begin with, we have the fact of Alexander's youth – the main contrast between them in the Gades episode, and regularly emphasised by Roman writers as an integral element of the Alexander legend. Cicero, for instance, stresses the fact that the Macedonian not only achieved greatness 'ab ineunte aetate', but also died ten years too young to qualify for the consulship.[33] Handsome in youth (Suet. *Div. Jul.* 45.1), Caesar came on the scene too late to compete with Alexander's boyish good looks. In middle age, to judge from his busts and coin-portraits,[34] he bore even less physical resemblance to his supposed exemplar than did Pompey. Progressive baldness is a fatal handicap when trying to cultivate the *anastolē*.[35] Further, while Caesar at a relatively early age claimed descent from both royalty and the gods,[36] and towards the end of his life may well have sought recognition, in some sense, of his regal and divine status,[37] he did not possess Alexander's greatest advantage: that of conducting his entire career, from the very first, as an acknowledged prince or reigning monarch. For this the prolonged commands in Gaul could, ultimately, be no substitute. Alexander might toy, in his more skittish or paranoid moments, with the notion of divine parentage,[38] but when it came to a crisis he was still capable of reminding his mutinous troops that he was Philip's son, an anointed king in whose veins there ran the blood of the ancient Argead dynasty.[39]

In several senses, then, Alexander was a dangerous, possibly an embarrassing, model for Caesar to emulate. Neither the danger nor the embarrassment would be lessened by the fact that Pompey, from adolescence onwards, had consciously modelled himself on the Macedonian conqueror, both physically and, in particular, as regards his military career.[40] *Imperator* at twenty-three, hailed by his troops as 'the Great' after a forty-day campaign in Africa – a title confirmed, whether ironically or in genuine admiration, by Sulla;[41] granted his first triumph shortly thereafter (12 March 81 BC), though he had never served as either consul or praetor; victorious in Spain, where, true to his exemplar, he erected an inscription commemorating the reduction of 876 cities; above all, the dazzling conqueror of Mithridates, the general who held the gorgeous East in fee[42] – Pompey had without a doubt exploited Alexander's military legend in a way that made him a difficult act to follow. Caesar at thirty-one might lament that he had done nothing; the same could scarcely be said about his great rival, a fact of which he was all too well aware. At the same time so astute an observer as Caesar must by now have noted various features of Pompey's character that were disquieting in an altogether different sense, and surely caused Caesar to face the future with greater equanimity than might otherwise have been the case. Despite his glittering successes, which reached their climax in the great triumph of 61, Pompey was never a truly formidable figure. His personal vanity, his passion for the outward trappings of glory, his political obtuseness and indecisiveness, his fatal urge to please those in titular authority – all combined to make him, even in his moment of glory, a subtly ridiculous figure. The weak and petulant mouth, the studied *anastolē*, the self-complacent smirk of the Copenhagen bust, echoed in other portraits,[43] all hint eloquently at this side of his character, which the literary evidence amply confirms.

From the very first, his sedulous aping of Alexander earned him derision among many of his Roman acquaintances.[44] Crassus treated his title of 'Magnus' as a joke.[45] It is probably to his tame Alexander-style court historian, Theophanes of Mytilene, whom he picked up during his Eastern campaign,[46] that we originally owe such ingenious excuses as Pompey being turned back, while on Alexander's route for the Caspian, by a 'multitude of deadly serpents',[47] and various other nagging comparisons with Alexander, sometimes indeed to the latter's disadvantage – e.g., that Pompey, besides repeating history by taking on a second King Darius, a Mede, had also defeated the Iberians of the Caucasus, which Alexander had never managed – or found the time – to do.[48] In his triumph of 61, which offered more than a hint that its celebrant was promoting himself as the New Dionysus,[49] Pompey either wore, or was said by his enemies to have worn, Alexander's own military cloak.[50] His partisans, presumably with his approval if not at his express dictation, reduced his age on this occasion, for obvious reasons, to thirty-three: in fact he was already forty-five.[51] His conceit was only matched by his failure to appreciate the realities of power, the limitations of his personal *auctoritas*. Months before his triumph, on returning from what had been, even by Roman standards, an immensely successful campaign, he voluntarily dismissed his legions once they were ashore at Brundisium.[52] Caesar, who tartly observed that Sulla didn't know his ABC when he laid down his dictatorship,[53] was unlikely henceforth to show overmuch respect for a man who so demonstrably preferred the baubles of power to its political substance. Most important of all for our present purposes, he surely reflected that Pompey, with his devotion to Alexander and his respect for the constitutional forms of the Republic,[54] was, in the last resort, a follower rather than a leader, and that this, essentially, was what *imitatio* implied in those who practised it.

If Caesar in fact made such a deduction in 61, nothing about Pompey's subsequent career – the inept political vacillations, the constant wavering between ambition and duty – can have given him cause to alter his opinion. The fiasco of Pompey's initial role in the Civil War was only partially redeemed by the *mauvais quart d'heure* which, rallying his old military skills, he contrived to give Caesar at Dyrrhachium.[55] After the final defeat of Pharsalus it was, characteristically enough, in deference to the arguments of Theophanes that he made his disastrous flight to Egypt,[56] where his brutal decapitation and wretched obsequies[57] long provided moralists with a handy *topos* on the mutabilities of fortune.[58] Such was the man whom everyone in Rome, during Caesar's lifetime, would instantly associate with the practice of Alexander-*imitatio*. The comparison, if not wholly odious, could hardly be thought encouraging. During his early career – as the Gades incident clearly suggests – Caesar would have thought twice before consciously emulating Alexander, chiefly because of the immediate competition. As the Macedonian's self-proclaimed military *epigonos*, Pompey, at least up to the year 61, enjoyed overwhelming superiority. After Pharsalus, on the other hand, Caesar was unlikely to adopt a pose so closely identified with his now dead and discredited opponent. At this point, moreover, he may well have felt that as general and statesman he could stand on his own unique record, without the need to emulate or imitate anybody.[59]

WE SHOULD ALSO CONSIDER, in general terms, and quite apart from the special case which Pompey represented, just what kind of prospective advantage could be got by a Roman politician or soldier, in the first century BC, from deliberately associating himself with Alexander of Macedon. How was the Macedonian regarded in Rome at this time? To what extent had the historical Alexander already given way to a creation of myth? Here we must distinguish carefully between two interrelated strands in the overall fabric. There is, first, the educated Graeco-Roman tradition of scholarship, that dealt with Alexander in terms already laid down by Callisthenes, Aristobulus, Cleitarchus, and other early Alexander-historians,[60] and which seems to have been well-established in Rome by the time of the late Republic. When Cato of Utica wanted to denigrate Pompey's victories in the East, he remarked that 'the whole Mithridatic war had been fought against *mulierculae* [mere women]',[61] an insult the full effect of which can only be appreciated when one knows that it was originally made by Alexander of Epirus, contrasting his own hard-fought Italian campaign with that of Alexander the Great in Asia.[62] Which of the two Alexanders faced greater opposition was, in fact, a regular debating point.[63] The tradition gave some scope for moral and philosophical discussion: Polybius, for instance, who had a somewhat ambivalent distrust of kings in general,[64] made Alexander's achievements one topic in a quasi-Thucydidean debate; his own attitude may be judged from the fact that in the surviving portions of the *Histories* he mentions the sack of Thebes no less than five times.[65] As a Greek, nevertheless, he possibly saw in Alexander's achievements some compensation for the subjugation of his own country by Rome. The more casual allusions in Cicero – to Alexander's birth and education, his relations with Callisthenes or Black Cleitus, his destruction of Thebes, his portraits by Apelles and Lysippus, his supposed encounter with Diogenes[67] – make it quite clear that by the mid-first century BC all levels of the historiographic traditon were familiar to educated Romans.[68]

This is as we might expect. It is when we begin to search for the emotional and symbolic impact of Alexander's achievements – that heady phenomenon so familiar to us from all subsequent periods of world history – that the evidence, quite simply, dries up. No subsequent investigations, however detailed or learned, have seriously modified the blunt conclusion reached by Franz Weber in 1909: that up to about 50 BC – that is, until the emergence of Pompey and Caesar as quasi-independent *imperatores* – Rome's attitude to Alexander remained one of bland indifference, which subsequently turned, by and large, to one of distaste.[69] In historical terms the second of these two reactions is much easier to understand than the first. The Republican opposition to Julio-Claudian imperialism, backed by Stoic theory and numbering many writers among its adherents,[70] naturally bracketed Caesar and Alexander together as murderous tyrants. The most striking expression of such a theme is to be found in Book 10 of Lucan's *De Bello Civili*,[71] where Caesar's alleged visit to the tomb of Alexander – here described as *felix praedo*, 'a lucky condottiere', and *proles vaesana Philippi*, 'Philip's mad offspring' – leads into a vigorous rhetorical condemnation of the Macedonian as world-conqueror, insatiable, bloodthirsty, *sidus iniquum / gentibus*, 'a comet of disaster to mankind'. Lucan's habitual exaggerations aside, this is a perfectly tenable view of Alexander's career;[72] more interesting for us in this context is the link with Caesar. If writers as diverse as Lucan, Plutarch, Appian, Velleius Paterculus[73] and, above all, Cicero[74] could see the two conquerors' lives as parallel enough to suggest *comparatio*, how strong an argument is that for Caesar having modelled himself deliberately on his famous predecessor? How far, alternatively, should we discount these comparisons on the grounds of political prejudice, and the misleading hindsight produced by new conditions under the Empire?

Before attempting to answer such questions, we must turn back to a period much nearer Alexander's own lifetime, and establish, if we can, the perspective in which Caesar himself would have viewed the Alexander tradition. Our evidence is sparse, but suggestive. Livy (9.18.6), in an admittedly polemical excursus, doubts whether the Romans of Alexander's day had even heard his name. The claim is exaggerated, yet symptomatic. There can be no doubt that the news of Alexander's conquests spread to Magna Graecia, and thence to Rome, well within his lifetime. It seems more than likely, as Weippert argues,[75] that a Roman embassy[76] did, in fact, join those making the journey to Babylon in 323:[77] the rumours of a major Western expedition then circulating[78] would alone have sufficed to make such a diplomatic mission prudent. But in June Alexander died. We have no contemporary evidence for Rome's attitude to him in the years that immediately followed. Pliny offers an *argumentum ex silentio:* when, towards the end of the fourth century BC, the Romans erected a public statue to the bravest Greek, their choice fell on Alcibiades rather than Alexander. It is just possible, too, that the Livian tradition drew on an older stratum of annalistic contempt. Certainly Livy regarded Papirius Cursor, consul and dictator, hero of the Second Samnite War, as more than a match for the Macedonian.[79] Similarly, a speech attributed by Plutarch to Appius Claudius Caecus, urging the senate to further military action against King Pyrrhus, after the battle of Heraclea in 280, claims that had Alexander come to Italy, he would have ended up either dead or a fugitive, and in any case minus his title of *invictus.*[80] The whole of Livy's *Alexanderexkurs* (9.17-19) may, as Breitenbach argues,[81] have been designed as propaganda to promote Roman military *virtus*, but the form such promotion takes is in itself interesting. It suggests, once again, that the only aspect of Alexander with which Romans concerned themselves was the invincible military adventurer: it also hints at a self-confident (and amply justified) faith in the superior military resources of the Republic.[82]

Florus asserts[83] that the Romans who fought the Macedonian wars (215-167 BC) felt themselves to be matched against Alexander rather than their titular opponent Philip V – in other words, that they had to overcome the legend of Macedonian invincibility. Though this evidence is without value for what Romans of the third century BC actually thought, it is in fact not likely that they were over-impressed, and the outcome must have given them considerable satisfaction. The victories of Cynoscephalae (197) and Pydna (167), won by legionary tactics and legionary discipline, dispelled for ever the myth of the insuperable phalanx, just as a similar Spartan myth had ended two centuries earlier at Leuctra;[84] and in 146 Macedonia became a Roman province. It is early in this period, *c.*200 BC, that we find the first extant reference to Alexander in Roman literature, by Plautus;[85] as we might by now expect, it has an ambivalent edge to it. The slave Tranio, in the *Mostellaria*, remarks: 'They say Alexander the Great and Agathocles were a pair who did really big things. How about me for a third? Just look at the immortal deeds I perform single-handed!' Fraenkel's arguments[86] that these words are Plautus' own, and not a mere translation of Philemon, have found general acceptance.[87] In any case they must represent the kind of allusion to which a Roman audience would respond.

The most remarkable thing about the phrase, however, is its offhandedness. At a time when Rome was engaged in a struggle against Alexander's military legacy, her most popular and prolific playwright referred to him only once[88] – and then in the same breath as the minor-league military despot and condottiere Agathocles of Syracuse.[89] The hard truth of the matter is that a Roman audience knew, and cared, more about Agathocles, who had at least operated in South Italy,[90] than they did about Alexander, whose exploits had taken place far away, in unknown and unimaginable outposts of Asia.[91] We can hardly argue, on the basis of this allusion, that by the end of the third century BC Alexander's name and fame had exactly set the Tiber on fire. Yet Plautus' words have, in one sense, a more than casual interest for us, since they mark the first known occasion on which Alexander is described as 'the Great'.[92] Paradoxically, though some Greeks lost no time in attaching the title 'ho Megas' to Demetrius Poliorcetes and to Antiochus III,[93] it is not until the first century AD that any surviving Greek text so described Alexander.[94] As Spranger remarks, they marvelled at his greatness, but refrained from calling him 'Great'.[95]

The Romans seem to have had no such reticence,[96] and indeed most scholars[97] assert that it was Rome that first bestowed on Alexander the title by which he is best known today. This paradox rests, however, on a highly fragile *argumentum ex silentio*, not least since the title is more often than not associated with military achievement.[98] That distinguished Roman soldiers of the third century could, no less than their Greek or Macedonian counterparts, provide a focus for myth and legend we learn from the remarkable case of Scipio Africanus[99] – though how far Alexander can be said to have dictated the myth is very much open to doubt. Most of our evidence is late and retrospective, but Polybius, writing about 150, clearly was familiar with the myth, and did his best to discredit it.[100] Scipio's mother, *ut fama est*,[101] was visited before his birth by a divine snake, and he was rumoured, accordingly, to be the son of Jupiter, so that when he visited the Capitol, the temple dogs never barked at him. The parallel with the legend of Alexander's birth is obvious,[102] though the motif, it must be said, is world-wide,[103] and in Greece was also attached to Aristomenes and Aratus.[104] Numerous other parallels have been adduced, most of them far-fetched, the best-known – and least convincing – being that between the ebb in the lagoon at Scipio's capture of New Carthage[105] and Alexander's enjoyment of *proskynesis* from the waves while circumventing Mt Climax.[106] We can get no real idea from this material whether Scipio – even with his admitted Greek sympathies[107] – ever consciously attempted to emulate Alexander: the evidence, taken overall, would suggest that he did not.[108] Though Polybius several times refers to him as *ho*

Megas,[109] it is quite uncertain what importance, if any, should be attached to this. [110] Perhaps the most we can say is that a myth grew up around him, to which he was not entirely averse,[111] and in particular that he cultivated some kind of relationship with Jupiter – which suggested a home-grown rather than an imported legend. The rest can safely be ascribed to later Greek or Roman propaganda.

SUCH, IN BRIEF, IS THE EVIDENCE for Alexander-*imitatio* in Rome before the mid-first century BC. It amounts to very little, Though Alexander's career seems to have been studied with some interest by Greek-educated intellectuals, it never engaged the passions of any Republican statesman before Pompey, or fired the creative imaginations of Roman poets at any period whatsoever[112] – except, in Lucan's case, to the furious rhetoric of contempt (see n. 71 and p.199 above.) Two constant elements run through our *testimonia*. First, insofar as Alexander meant anything to a Roman audience, it was in the plain role of military conqueror, with no hint of intellectual or philosophical pretensions, even in areas that might have had advantages for Rome, e.g. the concept of universal empire, if not the brotherhood of man. Second, this attitude almost invariably carried the corollary that Rome could beat Alexander at his own game. Even Cicero's wry comment to Atticus, 'a rather better general than you or me', although sincere enough, could hardly be termed fulsome. It was also made just after Cicero himself had been hailed *Imperator* by his own troops at Issus, in October 51 BC (*Att.* 5.20.3, cf. 2.20.3). *Verb.sap.* Even Polybius, whose admiration for Alexander was considerable (see n. 65), spends some time depreciating the Macedonian phalanx at the expense of the Roman legion (cf. n.84). To the average Roman, Alexander was simply a less familiar version of Agathocles or Pyrrhus, an unpredictable foreign autocrat who indulged in conquest for its own sake (a habit Rome ostensibly deplored), was both king and tyrant (terms of abuse in Roman politics), neglected his administrative responsibilities,[113] had an un-Republican habit of murdering his subordinates, and insisted, embarrassingly, on being worshipped as a god. Though a time was not far distant when the long-suffering SPQR would endure most of these vagaries *faute de mieux*, no Republican politician with an eye to his future career would ever – at least before 49 BC – identify himself too closely with so un-Roman a figure. Even Pompey was careful, in his conscious *imitatio*, never to go beyond the symbols and trappings of purely military glory,[114] and even so it seems clear that much of his enemies' criticism (e.g. that he was aiming at a dictatorship) sprang from a basic distrust of his self-professed resemblance to Alexander. As an instrument for propaganda, in short, the Macedonian was a highly debatable asset.

What, then, was Caesar's attitude to him? *Aemulatio*, as we have seen, in the sense that Alexander had achieved so much so young. But how far, and in what way, might he employ the Macedonian as a model for his own conduct, or to advertise his own virtues? As our investigation has shown, tangible evidence for such conscious exploitation is at best nugatory, and more often than not negative in its conclusions. Let us now see what can be gleaned from those essays in *comparatio* provided by contemporary or near-contemporary witnesses. Once again we are struck – not, I would argue, fortuitously – by a singular dearth of material. No *imperator* of the late Republic has left us an explicit assessment of Alexander, and what we learn about him from Caesar's contemporaries can be – indeed, has been – listed in a footnote less than one moderate-sized page in length.[115] The one exception is Cicero, and Cicero, as we shall see, offers us little but hedging clichés. Strabo, it is true, describing Caesar's benefits to Ilium in the Troad, argues that he acted through *aemulatio* of, or an affinity to, Alexander;[116] he also, however, makes it amply clear that Caesar's main object was to strengthen his own genealogical ties, through the *gens Iulia*, with Aeneas and Venus[117] – a significant act, but not linked, except in the most superficial way, to Alexander-*imitatio*.

For direct comparisons, indeed – odious or otherwise – we are virtually limited to three not over-impressive sources, all too late for comfort: Lucan, Velleius, and Appian. We do not possess a formal comparison by Plutarch for his *Lives* of Alexander and Caesar: whether he ever composed one or not[118] remains, therefore, from our point of view, a strictly academic problem. Cicero's evidence is a special case, which I will examine separately.

Lucan's attitude, already discussed,[119] which simply saw Alexander and Caesar both as extreme instances of the ambitious tyrant, is heavily influenced by post-Augustan anti-imperialist propaganda. Anachronistic or not, however, its single-minded assessment of both men exclusively in terms of military conquest is absolutely characteristic. Both Velleius and Appian[120] unintentionally illustrate one obvious point that modern scholarship tends, for whatever reason, to obscure: i.e. that a comparison of two individuals, A and B, especially in matters of character or *ethos*, does not require that B shall have copied all his habits from A as though he had no mind of his own. After certifying Caesar's descent from Venus, and expatiating on his courage, intelligence and generosity, Velleius concludes: 'In the magnitude of his ambitions, in the rapidity of his military operations, and in his endurance of danger, he closely resembled Alexander the Great.'[121] He adds a caveat: this comparison held good only when Alexander was sober and otherwise in control of his passions, since Caesar ate and slept no more than was necessary to preserve life, never for pleasure.[122] (What, one wonders, did he make of Caesar's reputation for sexual indefatigability?[123]) Now obviously men do not acquire courage and ambition by *imitatio*: these are innate qualities. The one attribute listed here by Velleius, himself a soldier, which Caesar might indeed have derived from Alexander is that famous *celeritas bellandi* on which Appian, among others, comments.[124] I shall return to this later. Appian's prolonged comparison, in fact, like Velleius' brief one, yields little in the way of conscious *imitatio*. Both men, he says, are ambitious, reckless, hard on themselves physically, and dependent to a degree on daring and luck, *tolme kai tyche*. Both on occasion take a cavalier attitude to soothsayers and prophecy (§§ 636-46). Both are intellectually inquisitive (§ 647), good looking, of divine ancestry, generous in victory, and followed with fierce loyalty, despite mutinies, by their troops (§§ 632-4). Both died while planning fresh campaigns (§ 631).

There is very little of substance to be got from such threadbare stuff, and some of Appian's overdrawn parallels – such as that between Alexander at Mt Climax (cf. p.201 above and n. 106) and Caesar's abortive attempt to cross the Adriatic in a storm – hardly inspire confidence. Nor, I assume, would even the most dogmatic exponent of Alexander-*Nachahmung* suggest that Caesar not only set up his Parthian campaign, but also arranged to die before its inception, just to follow obediently in the steps of the Master.[125] In fact, for our purposes the *differences* that Appian notes are more important than the similarities. He reminds us, for example, that Caesar, in sharp contrast to Alexander *aníkētos*, suffered several humiliating defeats in the course of his career[126] – something that *comparatio* could not fail to stress. Equally significant is Appian's observation (§ 635) that, whereas Alexander was a reigning king *ab initio*, Caesar pursued his star *ex idioteias*, beginning as a private citizen,[127] within the very different framework and political conventions – however he might bend them – of the Roman Republic.

THIS WOULD SEEM AN APPROPRIATE POINT at which to introduce the testimony of Cicero, which, as so often with Cicero, is at once prolix and elusive, articulate, yet hard to pin down to a consistent point of view. We are not, for the moment at least, directly concerned with what Cicero thought about Caesar – in particular, whether or not he aimed at deification or kingship in his own lifetime[128] – but simply with his views, if any, on Caesar's relationship and attitude to Alexander.

Cicero refers to Alexander on about thirty occasions, sometimes in neutral terms,[129] sometimes admiringly,[130] sometimes with clear moral disapproval[131] but almost always in the context of a stock rhetorical *exemplum*.[132] Weber (pp. 43-44) argued that his attitude underwent a radical change from 48 BC, clearly because of Caesar's threat to the Republic. This theory has been challenged,[133] on the grounds that the young Cicero seems just as ready to damn Alexander (*De Invent.* 1.93) as the old Cicero is to praise him (*Phil.* 5.48). The objection does not convince me. Literary *topoi* might go on without reference to the realities of human life, but Cicero's correspondence vividly demonstrated the horror he felt at the prospect of a Roman tyranny: this was something which, unlike a *topos*, hit home personally. Two key passages, both concerned with Alexander, well illustrate his unhappy state of mind.[134] After the victory of Munda in March 45 Caesar was busy writing his virulent *Anticato* pamphlet, at least in part to counter the effect of Cicero's *Cato*.[135] Hirtius had also produced a similar *feuilleton* attacking the hero of Utica, which Cicero read in May, and wrote of with contempt.[136] It was precisely now that Atticus, acting on behalf of Caesar's agents Balbus and Oppius, invited Cicero to write Caesar a *symbouleutikós*, a public letter of advice. Cicero tried, though such a task clearly went against the grain. 'I can think of nothing,' he wrote Atticus on 9 May, 'though I have Aristotle's and Theopompus' *Letters to Alexander* beside me. But where is the similarity? What they wrote was calculated both to do credit to the writers and to please Alexander. Can you think of anything analogous? I can't.'[137] One sympathises. Cicero's instinct, I suspect, was to give the same advice that Juvenal's student of rhetoric offered Sulla (1.16-17): 'privatus ut altum dormiret'. At all events, a preliminary draft went to Atticus on 13 May (*Att.* 13.26.2). It contained, as Cicero remarked (*Att.* 12.51.2), 'nothing unbefitting a loyal citizen – loyal, however, as the times permit'. Atticus recommended forwarding the letter to Caesar. Oppius and Balbus wanted something far more positive. The text came back post-haste; Cicero was humiliated (*Att.* 13.2). On 25 May he gave up the project altogether, professedly grateful to his critics 'for wanting so many changes that there is no point writing the thing afresh' (*Att.* 13.27.1), and stating brutally: 'What other material had I for my letter except flattery?'[138]

Atticus must have urged him to reconsider his decision, and this produced the letter (*Att.* 13.2.28) which is most crucial for us. 'In mentem nihil venit,' he writes back: he can think of nothing. What was the advice given in Alexander's case? 'A young man, fired by a passion for true glory and desiring some advice which would tend to his immortal fame, is exhorted to honourable distinction. Plenty to say there!'[139] But 'ego quid possum?' Cicero asks rhetorically: the clear answer is 'Nothing'. His draft, he suggests, was too morally highminded for its audience; it could even have provoked reprisals. 'Are you not aware,' he asks Atticus, 'that even that most famous student of Aristotle's, despite his fine intellect and modest behaviour became proud, cruel and overbearing the moment he assumed the title of king?' [140] What this letter may reveal about Caesar's immediate intentions is a moot point.[141] In the present context what we want Cicero to tell us is at whose instigation Alexander got into the *symbouleutikós* to begin with; and this, characteristically, we never learn. Weinstock[142] states, without argument, that Caesar not only requested this literary exercise himself, but insisted on the parallel with Alexander. Were this in fact true, we would possess evidence, as rare as it was valuable, for Caesar's indeed having employed Alexander as a model in his political propaganda campaign. Unfortunately for us, and despite his (in general) well-deserved reputation for preferring *testimonia* to theorising,[143] Weinstock had not one scrap of evidence on which to base such an assumption. We simply do not know whether the idea originated in Caesar's head or in Cicero's, though by now it should not be hard to guess. Cicero employed what, as a man of letters, he took to be a flattering historical comparison; the politician in Caesar was not amused. But this remains mere speculation. We cannot even tell – since the letter itself does not survive – whether Alexander was set up as a model of heroism or an awful warning: Cicero seems to change his mind on this score between one paragraph and the next. What Caesar himself felt about Alexander remains as baffling as ever.[144] We do not even know whether the *symbouleutikós* reached Caesar in draft; it probably got no further than Balbus and Oppius.

BY A PROCESS OF ELIMINATION we are now reduced to the dim area of merely circumstantial evidence where too many scholars in the past have begun their investigations rather than ending them. Some of the prize exhibits here need not detain us long. These include Caesar's famous cloven-hoofed horse, paraded by the faithful – though not by our ancient sources[145] – as a case of what we might, I suppose, call Bucephalas-*Nachahmung*; the Lysippan statue of Alexander on which Caesar replaced the original head with one portraying himself, a not uncommon practice, and in this case probably done at least as much out of admiration for Lysippus as in any spirit of *aemulatio* towards Alexander;[146] and the ingenious suggestion that Caesar wrote his *commentarii* in coy emulation of the Macedonian *hypomnēmata* and *ephēmerides*, regardless of the fact that Alexander did not compose these himself.[147]

A good deal of extraneous dead wood can be cleared away in this fashion, but at the end we are still left with some major problems. If we take the Gades episode at all seriously, then the first question we must ask ourselves is this: in the light of the evidence we have examined, and of Caesar's own life as we know it, how – if at all – might Alexander-*imitatio* have helped him *at each successive stage of his career*?

The debt-ridden Caesar who gazed at Alexander's statue, and sighed to think how late he had left the achievement of his amibitions, was a very different man from the *dictator perpetuus*, wealthy beyond the dreams even of a Crassus,[148] showered with honours by a subservient Senate packed with his own nominees, whose crowded programme of reform, self-promotion, and the final solution of the Eastern problem was only cut short by his assassination. As this investigation has, I hope, demonstrated, there is no conclusive proof that either of these two Caesars actively exploited the Alexander tradition, and a good deal which suggests that they may have stayed carefully clear of it; but one thing we can claim, with some confidence, is that if they *did* practise Alexander-*Nachahmung*, it was for different purposes and in very different ways.

It is hardly coincidental that by far the greater part of our circumstantial evidence refers to the period at the very end of Caesar's life, when his position was unique, and (except by assassins' daggers) virtually unassailable. I have no doubt, despite the ingenious counter-arguments of my fellow countrymen over the past half-century,[149] that from 45 at the latest Caesar envisaged deification in his own lifetime,[150] and some kind of monarchical status, whether or not this involved the ambivalent title of *rex*.[151] The details of this complex ongoing debate, though fascinating, do not immediately concern us here. What we have to determine, quite simply, is whether either concept, deification or kingship, can, on the evidence, be traced back to Alexander. Again, the evidence is largely negative. Indeed, much of it points in quite another direction, one which it would be far more reasonable for Caesar to take, just as Scipio Africanus may have done (see pp. 201-2 above). Various commentators, from Lily Ross Taylor onwards,[152] have remarked how carefully Caesar stressed his Roman or Etruscan antecedents as regards any claim to royal or divine status: his association with Romulus and Quirinus, his descent from the Alban kings, his Etruscan gold wreath, his scarlet boots, his triumphal toga.[153] Here we see a source of ethnic and patriotic propaganda immeasurably superior to any that could be derived from the achievements of a foreign conqueror. Caesar may have mixed sex and power-politics in his dealings with Cleopatra,[154] but there is no serious evidence that he aimed to set up a Hellenistic-style monarchy based on Alexandria,[155] and the violent opposition stirred up by mere rumours of such intentions on Antony's part[156] made it clear, in retrospect, how wise he had been.

There is one area in which the influence of Alexander might still be claimed, with some show of plausibility, for this final period, and that is the concept of world-conquest, of military supremacy and universal empire (see p. 182 above). Yet even here the evidence remains patchy. Dio[157] reports the erection in the temple of Quirinus of a statue – probably Caesar's likeness, though the text is ambiguous on this point – dedicated to 'the unconquered god'. This, of course, was a title regularly associated with Alexander;[158] within his lifetime the Athenians had probably dedicated a statue to him bearing an identical inscription.[159] A case of *aemulatio*? Perhaps. Even more puzzling is another statue, also described by Dio,[160] which portrayed Caesar standing on a bronze globe, symbolic of victory, and bore an inscription describing him as *hēmitheos* (demi-god) – or whatever the Latin equivalent of that may have been. There are good Roman antecedents for the victory globe; the nearest Greek parallel is not Alexander but Demetrius Poliorcetes; and in any case Caesar had the inscription erased – though whether because it said too much or too little is open to doubt.[161]

Examples of this sort could be multiplied to little purpose.[162] More important is to ask whether the notion of world-conquest and world-empire was one which Caesar, even at his most megalomaniac,[163] and despite the propaganda of his enemies, had any driving urge to embrace, much less justify by Greek precedents. Here the test case is his projected Parthian campaign. Perhaps in romantic reaction against Mommsen, who saw nothing more in the plan than a case of 'frontier rectification',[164] Meyer, in his influential study of Caesar's rise to supreme power,[165] argued that this

Eastern expedition represented 'the renewal and complete fulfilment of Alexander's world-monarchy', a view that depended largely on one over-blown passage in Plutarch (*Caes.* 58.2-5), but nevertheless managed to convince a number of scholars, including Lily Ross Taylor.[166] Yet in fact Mommsen was only stating a *reductio ad absurdum* of the truth. Parthia and Armenia represented a very real danger to Rome's Eastern frontiers that was never satisfactorily resolved till Trajan's day.[167] If Caesar planned to take sixteen legions and 10,000 cavalry on his Parthian campaign,[168] that was not in mere *aemulatio* of Alexander or of anyone else; it was a tribute to a formidable enemy. The defeat of Crassus at Carrhae nine years earlier (53 BC)[169] had given him a warning he could no longer ignore, and a strong secondary motive for a punitive expedition. We can regard the war as unjustified, if we choose;[170] just as we can, with rather better reason, describe Caesar as 'the greatest brigand of them all';[171] the fact remains that the brigand was a canny pragmatist, with well-defined objectives, whose ambition operated in terms of *Realpolitik*. Psychologically he stood poles apart from Alexander. He had never dreamed of marching to the world's end, nor would he have done so now. On the eastern frontier, as in Gaul, the most he aimed at – both Vogt and Gelzer demonstrate this with some cogency[172] – was a completion of the Roman *orbis terrarum*. For such a programme the actual achievements or, worse, the projected *letzte Pläne* of Alexander would, as propaganda, embarrass rather than inspire.

We see, then, that what we may term Alexander's ideology – for many modern students still his chief claim to fame – never caught on, certainly not before the Augustan period, and then only to a very limited extent, with the Roman public. It is therefore highly unlikely to have served as a basis for *imitatio*, and our remarkable lack of evidence on this score should provoke no surprise. Further, what holds good for Caesar's short period of supreme authority must be true *a fortiori* of his earlier career, when he was obliged at least to pay lip-service to the *mos maiorum* and the political ideals of the Republic. The only avenue for a legitimate exploitation of Alexander in political terms – through his military achievements – had already been monopolised by Pompey. We might expect – a point no scholar seems to have raised – that any commander who supposedly modelled himself with such devotion on Alexander would at least take the trouble to familiarise himself with the great Macedonian's generalship, and profit by it himself. But not even this seems to have been the case. We have Plutarch's word for it that Caesar studied Alexander's campaigns,[173] but he must have read them with other problems on his mind. Just how and where he *did* acquire his military skills is one of history's more tantalising puzzles. If he had really, as Russell suggests, spent his ten years in Gaul learning 'the trade of generalship by passing slowly through the stages of apprentice, journeyman, and master', the sheer luck involved in his bare survival, let alone his absolute victory, would have been incalculable: *tyche* can only be credited with just so much.

Another popular theory is that of the Instinctive Genius: Armstrong, for instance, seriously suggests that Caesar 'followed the rules of strategy unconsciously, much as M. Jourdain wrote prose without knowing it'.[174] He certainly did not learn from Alexander. The most striking and fundamental difference between them lay in their use of cavalry. For Alexander this arm formed the key to every major battle, whereas Caesar – good horseman though he was[175] – relied on *auxilia* for his cavalry, and treated it in the main as a convenient means of rapid transport rather than as a flexible combat unit.[176] Domaszewski's attempt[177] to demonstrate Caesar's strategical dependence on techniques employed by Alexander with the phalanx is unconvincing and has won no acceptance. Alexander's masterly control of commissariat and intelligence was something that Caesar could have imitated to his profit;[178] even the speed and dash, the *celeritas*,[179] which they shared – together, surely, with all first-class ancient generals except Fabius Cunctator – was hampered, in Caesar's case, by that notorious legionary addiction to entrenchment which he had inherited, along with so much else, from Marius.[180]

LET ME BRIEFLY SUMMARISE my conclusions. A study of the available evidence suggests that Alexander's historical achievements, and indeed the Alexander legend, never made any appreciable impact on the Romans of the Republic, who found them not only alien and remote, but also in many ways fundamentally antipathetic. Such cases of *imitatio* as can be identified are exceptions rather than the rule, and betray special objectives: Pompey's military self-promotion, Mark Antony's propaganda in favour of a Hellenistic-style kingdom, his own role as the New Dionysus.[181] Caesar's career reveals no preoccupation with Alexander whatsoever beyond an urge to eclipse him in terms of achievement – a case of *aemulatio* rather than *imitatio* – and possibly, at the very end, one or two promotional devices borrowed to help secure a royal deification that was, in itself, an essentially Roman phenomenon. Even here it is doubtful whether conscious *imitatio* was involved, since what we have to do with are astral symbols, radiate crowns, globes, diadems, and all the rest of the portentous flummery with which Ptolemaic and Seleucid rulers were so adept at hedging their kingship.[182] Such things had little connection with the Alexander tradition, and none at all with the historical Alexander.[183] Finally, as a field commander Caesar shows no clear signs of having studied Alexander's campaigns: he might have benefited had he done so. He went his own way, and changed the world in the process; that at least both men had in common. The moral that emerges is familiar and uncomfortable: men of genius – however perverted that genius may be – blaze trails and set trends, while lesser mortals eagerly follow them, waving a banner with the strange device of *imitatio*. Adcock, in short, was right after all. This may be thought an unduly negative conclusion; but as historians we like to believe we are in the business of exploding myths rather than promoting them.

XIII

CARMEN ET ERROR:
THE ENIGMA OF
OVID'S EXILE

THE FACTS OF OVID'S BANISHMENT are well known, its true reason mysterious. The problem, as Sir Ronald Syme observed [1] with commendable meiosis, 'has long engaged the attention of the erudite, the ingenious, the frivolous'. The last-named group, as readers of Thibault[2] will know, forms by far the largest category: no need to waste time on it here.[3] Thibault's three main categories suffice to contain all subsequent serious research.[4] Till the nineteenth century the rule was *cherchez la femme*: then variations of political conspiracy became popular; latterly the *Zeitgeist* has had its turn, with Ovid's general attitude of smart crypto-atheistical urban hedonism provoking a violent reaction from the Augustan moral reformists.[5] No specific explanation so far advanced exactly fits the facts.

Of the three main theories, however, two can be dismissed out of hand:[6] it is the contention of this article that, on our available evidence, *only* a political solution to the problem is acceptable; and, as a corollary, that of the two reasons, the *carmen* and the *error*, alleged for Ovid's *relegatio*, the first was mere diversionary camouflage designed to distract public attention from the real issues at stake.[7] The weakness of the case for the *Ars Amatoria* as the *main* cause of exile, apart from the fact that this contradicts Ovid's own explicit testimony,[8] has always been the irrational delay between publication and punishment: there is no reason why Augustus should have waited so long to strike (his *auctoritas* and *imperium* were quite adequate to eliminate Ovid whenever the urge took him), and then have struck, *on that basis*, so improbably hard.[9]

In default of new evidence the mystery may well, as Thibault thought,[10] prove insoluble: the best we can hope to do is to narrow down the possibilities, lay out the fundamental evidence, and – most important – eliminate all speculation that conflicts with it. Wilkinson[11] is not the only scholar to express justifiable astonishment at the frequency with which modern theorists ignore statements that Ovid 'could not have dared to publish if they were untrue'. Thus, Ovid makes it clear, again and again, that his *error*, however secret, was a *specific offence*, so that though his social and religious attitudes may well have made him unpopular in official circles, they cannot have been the direct occasion of his *relegatio*. That at once disposes of the *Zeitgeist* theory. Further, since he emphasises that his offence was to have kept quiet about something he had *seen*,[12] we can at once also rule out any personal involvement with a highly connected lady as having been responsible for his downfall. Adultery (cf. Thibault 54) is not an ocular offence. *Cherchez la femme*, then, will not do either. This still leaves open the possibility of Ovid's having played some part in furthering the sexual indiscretions of others: but the pander's role alone, unless masking other more serious (i.e., politically coloured) offences, is unlikely to have brought such dire retribution on his head. It is worth remembering that D. Iunius Silanus, accused of adultery with Julia II, was not only given leave to withdraw from Rome in voluntary exile but in AD 20 was allowed back by Tiberius, on the intercession of his brother Marcus.[13]

The direct evidence all stems from Ovid himself. Oddly, though the exile of so famous a poet must have been a *cause célèbre*, the first surviving witness apart from Statius to mention it is Jerome, in AD 381.[14] Accidental loss of all key *testimonia* has been advanced, not altogether convincingly, as an explanation for this curious silence.[15] In any case, Ovid's personal evidence remains crucial. Without new evidence we cannot prove that he is not lying: but he had good reason, if not to tell the whole truth, at least to avoid officially embarrassing falsehoods. Like Thibault (116), I start from the working hypothesis that his statements, consistent enough with one another (except over the *degree* of his guilt), may well be self-serving, but that his worst fault is likely to be the glossing or suppression of personally embarrassing details. Nevertheless, despite Augustus' stern veto on any publication of the facts, Ovid's obsession with posterity drove him to scatter hints, some of them highly suggestive. Circumstantial evidence is provided, as we shall see, by sources dealing with the political drama of the Augustan succession.[16] Later witnesses[17] are derivative, or fantastic, or both, and in any case virtually useless.

Let us remind ourselves of the basic facts of the case. In the autumn of AD 8, probably as the result of information laid by some personal enemy or *delator*,[18] a serious alleged indiscretion (*error, culpa*) on Ovid's part came to the attention of Augustus and a restricted circle of other influential persons, including Ovid's friend and patron Cotta Maximus.[19] At first Cotta was angry with Ovid: he also, interestingly, professed to share the pained reaction of the Princeps:

> Ira quidem primo fuerat tua iusta nec ipso
> lenior offensus qui mihi iure fuit,

> quique dolor pectus tetigisset Caesaris alti
> illum iurabas protinus esse tuum.
> (*EP* 2.3.61-64)

At first you were angry, and with good reason,
    as relentless as he whom my offence
had rightly pricked: the distress that touched great Caesar,
    that, you swore forthwith, was yours as well.

However, when he learned the true facts of the case (ibid.65-66), anger turned to irritated sympathy ('diceris erratis ingemuisse meis'), and he quickly wrote Ovid a letter from Elba, where he was staying,[20] saying he was sure Augustus could be placated (ibid. 67-68). Before the Princeps took action, Ovid travelled north to consult Cotta. Even then, when Cotta asked him if the report was true, he still prevaricated, through a mixture of fear, shame, and emotional distress (ibid. 85-90). An imperial summons now arrived ordering the poet back to Rome for a private hearing[21] before Augustus himself. Ovid seems to have been subjected to a severe tongue-lashing (*Tr.* 2.133-34) by the outraged emperor: there was, to insure secrecy, no formal trial. Ovid was to be banished, in perpetuity, to the remote coastal settlement of Tomis, near the mouth of the Danube estuary in the still unsettled province of Moesia. At least his life had been spared.[22] The banishment was of the type known as *relegatio*, in which the victim retained his property and citizenship but had his place of exile – most often an island – specified.[23] Ovid's *Ars Amatoria* was also banned – an unusual step – from Rome's three public libraries, though, since he had not been condemned by senatorial decree, the book could not be burned.[24] The poet was required to leave Rome by December, a stipulation that made his journey both unpleasant and dangerous.[25] In the case of *relegatio* a pardon was always, in theory, possible, and the edict would become invalid, unless confirmed by his successor, on the death of the emperor who issued it.[26]

    Carmen et error: that the *Ars* was in fact one count of a double indictment, Ovid assures us on numerous occasions.[27] The main objection to the poem seems to have been to its didactic nature, the notion of Ovid as a conscious propagandist for seduction reduced to a fine art, a teacher, in short, of adultery: 'arguor obsceni doctor adulterii'.[28] He makes it quite clear, however, that the second charge against him, habitually referred to as his 'mistake' or 'indiscretion' (*culpa, error*), was the more serious of the two, [29] and he advises the Thracian prince Cotys not to probe its nature but to be satisfied with the first, more public charge –

> Nec quicquam, quod lege uetor committere, feci:
>   est tamen his grauior noxa fatenda mihi.
> Neue roges quae sit, stultam conscripsimus Artem:

innocuas nobis haec uetat esse manus.
Ecquid praeterea peccarim quaerere noli,
    ut lateat sola culpa sub Arte mea.

                    (*EP* 2.9.71-76)

Indeed, I've committed no act that the law forbids me
    yet I still must needs confess a graver offence –
don't ask what it is. (I also composed a foolish poem,
    my *Art*: *that* stops my hands from being clean).
Was there a further offence? Don't ask, I beg you –
    let my fault lie beneath my *Art* alone.

– teasing lines calculated to arouse anyone's curiosity. Though Augustus clearly regarded the *Ars* as a subversive poem (which, of course, by his public standards it was),[30] it seems in the first instance to have been used by him as a cover, designed to distract attention from the far more sensitive area in which Ovid's *error* lay. The significant fact is that Ovid was obliged to treat the second count of his indictment as a top-level secret.[31] This official cloak of secrecy, referred to on various occasions, is one of the more significant clues in our possession.

    Augustus' government, like most modern ones, habitually, and effectively, suppressed general circulation of embarrassing or unpalatable facts, as Dio Cassius, in a fascinating and crucial digression,[32] makes very clear. In Ovid's case 'everybody'– i.e., the usual inner circle of *cognoscenti*, everybody who mattered – knew very well what had taken place,[33] but this does not imply (indeed, all our evidence suggests precisely the opposite) any acquaintance with the true facts on the part of the general public. Whatever Ovid's *error* might have been, it could not, by definition, have had to do with a *well-known* scandal – unless, that is, it somehow involved additional, highly embarrassing evidence that revealed that scandal in a new light, and which the Princeps was therefore determined to suppress. Ovid at one point links his downfall to ruinous connections in high places and warns a friend – probably Brutus – against cultivating the great:

    usibus edocto si quicquam credis amico,
        uiue tibi et longe nomina magna fuge.
    uiue tibi, quantumque potes praelustria uita:
        saeuum praelustri fulmen ab arce uenit.

                    (Tr. 3.4.3-6)

If you've any respect for the lessons experience has taught me
    live for yourself, keep clear of all great names:

live for yourself, avoid (as best you may) too-illustrious
   contacts: from that illustrious citadel
a savage bolt descends.

So the scandal involved 'magna nomina', as indeed we might have guessed
from the strenuous campaign to suppress it. Had it not been for this
unfortunate intimacy, Ovid adds (13–14), he might still be happily at large in
Rome. It is just conceivable that the lost works of Seneca, Aufidius Bassus,
Cremutius Cordus, or, above all, Suetonius contained the whole truth of the
matter.[34] Yet the total silence of the next four centuries – and, more
damagingly, of extant authors such as Tacitus – argues strongly against such
ex post facto knowledge.[35] The balance of probability is that the secret was
indeed well kept, that comparatively few were privy to it, and that for all
practical purposes the truth died with Ovid, as he said it should.[36]

    What other hints does Ovid give us? His *error*, he claims, was unpremed-
itated, without any thought of personal gain, yet at the same time the result of
a complex chain of events.[37] It was not – a fact Ovid several times emphasises,
but which, as we shall see, conflicts with other aspects of his own testimony –
a legally indictable crime: 'quicquid id est, ut non facinus, sic culpa uocanda
est.'[38] 'Yet don't talk of a "crime", say rather, "culpable error".' In particular,
he had committed neither murder, poisoning, nor forgery,[39] nor was he guilty
of treasonable action, or even treasonable talk, against Augustus.[40] That he
felt called upon to make such disclaimers is in itself significant. In fact, he
asserts, he had not *done* anything at all; rather, he had *seen* a crime committed
by others, which apparently, to begin with, he had not recognized for what it
was: 'inscia quod crimen uiderunt lumina, plector/peccatumque oculos est
habuisse meum.[41] ('Unwitting, I witnessed a crime: for that I'm afflicted: my
offence is that I had eyes'.) This *crimen* he elsewhere (*Tr.* 3.6.28) describes as
funestum, an ambiguous epithet (see below, p.222). It was, he insists, a 'more
serious injury' (*gravior noxa*) than any legal crime (*EP* 2.9.71–77). Yet if he
was, as he claims, a mere witness, wherein did his culpability lie? Clearly, in
not reporting the incident once he had recognized it for what it was. As he tells
us, a word at the right moment, in the proper quarter, might have saved him.

     cuique ego narrabam secreti quicquid habebam,
       excepto quod me perdidit, unus eras.
     id quoque si scisses, saluo fruerere sodali,
       consilioque forem sospes, amice, tuo.[42]

To you alone I'd reveal my unpublished problems – always
   barring the one that destroyed me. If you'd known
that too, you'd now be enjoying your comrade's untrammelled
   company: through your advice, friend, I'd be safe.

Why, then, did he keep silent? Again he himself gives us the answer: he was scared and so did nothing,[43] in the vain hope that the scandal would blow over.

From this it sounds as though Ovid's role in the affair was accessory, perhaps peripheral[44] – that of the smart but innocent man-about-town, the fashionable *praeceptor amoris* of the literary salons, taken up by Rome's promiscuous *beau monde*,[45] who stumbled (whether accidentally or not) into a dangerous situation, and then panicked. He repeatedly castigates himself – just as we would expect under the circumstances – for having been naïve and gullible.[46] Yet this mere error of judgment[47] was, nevertheless, an improper act[48] (*peccatum*) of which he felt ashamed and confused: 'uel quia peccaui citra scelus, utque pudore/non caret, inuidia sic mea culpa caret' (*Tr* 5.8.23-24) 'My error fell short of crime, /and though it's not free from/shame, there's no odium to it.' Worse, it not only caused Augustus deep personal pain but was in some sense a direct offence against him.[49] In what sense? It has often been suggested,[50] at least in part on the basis of the suggestive terminology Ovid employs (see n. 49 above), that Ovid's offence came under the heading of *laesa maiestas*. This is persuasive and may well be true, but we have to bear in mind that Ovid never actually says so. He repeatedly describes the Princeps as *laesus*, but the *maiestas* we have to infer for ourselves. Also, *maiestas*, however loosely defined and capriciously applied, was without a doubt a legal crime. Ovid may be contradicting himself, or hair-splitting for his own benefit: it would be unwise to place too much reliance on this thesis. *Maiestas*, however, would well suit an offence for which, had he wished, the Princeps could have imposed the death penalty (*Tr* 1.1.20). Though the *culpa*, Ovid insists elsewhere (*Tr* 1.2.95-98), contained no *facinus*, it remained indefensible.

Though the wave of public dislike for Ovid that his *relegatio* produced can be explained by society's rejection of any official scapegoat, it is interesting that the immediate reaction even of Cotta Maximus (who not only learned the true facts but was Ovid's patron) seems to have been one of anger.[51] This fact gains in significance when we recall that Cotta Maximus and his brother Messallinus were both – certainly from the time his accession was assured – strong partisans of Tiberius.[52] Cotta was hostile to Germanicus and his family: apart from the blanket appeal at *Tr* 2.161-70, Ovid takes care to cultivate the two groups separately.[53] While it is unlikely that Cotta would have extended patronage to Ovid in the first place if he himself were a dedicated Tiberian *ab initio* while the poet openly favoured the Julian succession (more probably, both were to a great extent opportunistic), it does very much look as though in AD 8 Ovid's position was one that could seriously embarrass any ambitious political conformist associated with him.

What *were* his basic relationships to Julians and Claudians,[54] and did they differ in any significant respect? To some degree, like most of his contemporaries, Ovid was a time-server. His fulsome tribute to Gaius Caesar, Augustus' grandson, was written at a time (*c.* 1 BC) when Tiberius was still in eclipse and Gaius looked a likely winner;[55] while from exile he launched his appeals, not only to the Princeps himself but also – with fine impartiality – to Livia, Tiberius, and Germanicus.[56] Yet, before his *relegatio*, encomiastic references to Livia or Tiberius are notable in their absence, and even afterwards they show a marked contrast with the appeals to Germanicus. Ovid's attitude to the imperial Claudians is one of distant self-abasement. In a long, detailed brief to his third wife (*EP* 3.1.114-66) on how to approach Livia, the empress is drawn as a remote and chilly deity, to be addressed only at the propitious moment and then in a grovelling manner. Though this advice is similar to that generally offered to emissaries about to approach great persons,[57] its tone is strikingly constrained and nervous. True, as the wife of an emperor regularly flattered as a god, Livia could scarcely rank much lower than a goddess – but some goddesses are warm and accessible, whereas this one plainly is not. Ovid's approaches to Germanicus, on the other hand, altogether lack the fawning quality apparent in his dealings with Livia and Tiberius: they show not only clear hopes for favourable intercession but also genuine warm admiration and liking. This warmth cannot be entirely explained by Ovid's presumption (*EP* 4.8.67) on the common tie of poetry, even though it was to Germanicus that he rededicated the *Fasti*. He also, be it noted, prayed for Germanicus' succession (*EP* 2.5.75). Germanicus was not only a Julian on the distaff side (through his mother Antonia's descent from Augustus' sister Octavia) but also possessed, to a marked degree, the *clementia* and *humanitas* Tiberius so conspicuously lacked.[58] Had Ovid survived a year or two longer, his hopes – already set back by the failure of his appeals to Tiberius and Livia – would have been dashed yet again. In AD 19, Germanicus died, perhaps by poisoning; and this left Tiberius' position virtually unassailable, since his other forcibly adopted son, Agrippa Postumus, the brother of Julia II, had been executed, with no trial or publicity, within a few days of Augustus' death.[59]

The cumulative impression left by this evidence is, after every allowance has been made for time-serving, flattery, and opportunism, that Ovid's natural sympathies had always lain with the Julian rather than the Claudian faction. This impression is reinforced by Tiberius' refusal to remit or commute the poet's exile on the death of Augustus. Why were he and Livia so obdurate? It can only have been because the events that led to Ovid's *relegatio* in some way affected them personally, and that at once points towards the unsavoury struggle between Julians and Claudians over the succession. Livia and Tiberius, in point of fact, were far more vindictive against the Julians and their adherents than Augustus himself was. It is true that after the events of AD 8 the Princeps habitually referred to Agrippa Postumus and the two Julias as his 'three boils'[60] and, with refined cruelty, made Julia II, in exile on Trimerus, dependent for subsistence on her grandmother Livia.[61] Yet he could never bring himself to execute his own flesh and blood,[62] continually hedged his bets over the succession, and right to the end kept not only the two

Julias but also Agrippa Postumus very much alive, even if in close sequestra-tion.[63] Tiberius and Livia, on the contrary, lost no time in procuring the deaths of both Agrippa and Julia I the moment Augustus succumbed to his fatal illness.[64] Though their connection with Germanicus' death, however widely suspected, remains non-proven (cf. Tac. *Ann.*3.16), they are, at the very least, unlikely to have had much sympathy for his self-proclaimed partisans.

Such is the evidence at our disposal. Ovid always had one eye on posterity and is, I suspect, more likely to have been hinting at the truth (like the child incapable of keeping a secret) than lying,[65] though he also almost certainly played down his own culpability in order to win a reprieve or reduction of sentence.[66] We are looking, to recapitulate,[67] for an indiscretion that took place in high society, was unpremeditated but part of a complex and dangerous situation, was not *per se* indictable yet could have brought Ovid a death sentence (not, perhaps, quite so paradoxical a claim as might at first sight appear to be the case), brought Ovid no profit, and in fact consisted simply of his having witnessed – perhaps without full understanding at the time – an offence committed by others. In particular he stresses the fact that he had taken no treasonable *action* against Augustus, that he was innocent of murder or forgery. Had he reported the incident he might have remained a free man, but he was afraid to do so. He was also, he admits, naïve and gullible. Further, his *error* wounded Augustus deeply and was, indeed, a direct offence against him. Ovid's language suggests that it may have been in some sense subsumable under the general heading of *laesa maiestas*. In any case he felt bitterly ashamed of it. It also occasioned strong and lasting animus in Tiberius and his adherents. He was obligated to keep it secret, though influential circles in Rome seem to have known the truth.

What does this pattern suggest? Ovid's own statements, taken in conjunction with the pattern of historical events during the last decade or so of Augustus' reign, all point toward some more or less unwitting political *bêtise*, linked with the deadly factional struggle between Julians and Claudians for the succession and carefully camouflaged by official public charges suggesting mere moral turpitude. This last, as Syme has often pointed out, was a useful device, particularly valuable in dealing with the two Julias, to distract attention from more serious and politically dangerous offences.[68] Only in political and, probably, quasi-conspiratorial circumstances does the lifelong *relegatio*, by private imperial fiat, of a mere witness – let alone the possibility of his execution for a legally non-indictable offence – even begin to make sense. Such circumstances indeed existed in the years immediately prior to Ovid's exile, and it is to them that we now must turn.

In 2 BC a group of ambitious aristocrats had tried to establish themselves, through Augustus' daughter Julia I, in a position from which they could, after the death (whether natural or induced) of the Princeps, take over effective control of the empire. The plot failed. If there was, as one source

217

indicates, a scheme to murder Augustus, this must have motivated the latter's reluctant shift toward a 'Tiberian solution'.[69] As we might expect, it was Julia's sexual promiscuity, a welcome smokescreen, that received most of the attention when the scandal broke, rather than the political activities of Iullus Antonius and his associates.[70] The refusal of the 'Julian faction' to admit defeat, then or later, was doubtless due to Augustus' own persistent ambivalence over the succession. By AD 4, two of his three grandsons were dead, in circumstances at least suspicious enough to start a rumour that Livia had somehow done away with them for her son's benefit.[71] About the same time, perhaps in response to the very considerable public criticism Julia I's banishment still aroused, Augustus had his daughter transferred from the island of Pandateria to a less rigorous place of exile, Rhegium.[72] Tiberius, whose earlier disgrace had encouraged the attempted pro-Julian coup of 2 BC, was now adopted, *faute de mieux*, by the aging Princeps – though at the same time, characteristically, Augustus made the new heir-apparent himself adopt not only his nephew Germanicus but also Augustus' last surviving grandson, Julia II's brother Agrippa Postumus.[73] That the former was poisoned and the latter executed need surprise no one.

The years that followed, in particular the period between AD 6 and 9 (during which Ovid's *relegatio* took place) saw Augustus' regime pass through an acutely critical phase.[74] There were wars and uprisings in Illyria and Pannonia, a serious recruiting problem, increased taxation of senators and *equites* (with the added risk of disaffection that this brought), famine in Italy, and growing rumours – sometimes hard to confirm – of rebellion and conspiracy.[75] Such circumstances could hardly fail to provoke some attempt by the 'Julian faction' to capitalise on Augustus' weakness and the general state of crisis. The natural figureheads for any succession plot would inevitably be the two Julias and Agrippa Postumus. Tiberius and his supporters, recognising this, devoted considerable time and ingenuity to neutralising all three. The first victim of this renewed Julio-Claudian conflict was Agrippa Postumus: only he, as Barbara Levick justly observes, 'stood between the descendants of Livia and monopoly of power'.[76] His advancement was thwarted: rumours were spread regarding his intractable and brutish character, ungovernable temper, and general irresponsibility.[77] In the autumn of AD 6, Augustus was induced by Livia to sever Agrippa legally from the *gens Iulia*, by the process of emancipation known as *abdicatio*.[78] Agrippa was banished, first to Surrentum, then, by senatorial decree (late AD 7) to the small island of Planasia near Elba. His banishment was made permanent, he was placed under military guard, and his property become forfeit to the state's newly constituted military treasury.[79]

Under normal circumstances only the most heinous of crimes, in particular those definable as *perduellio* or *laesa maiestas*, could have resulted in such treatment. Was Agrippa involved in a conspiracy, or was he merely the victim of Tiberian machinations? Tacitus goes out of his way to assert that he had been involved in no scandal – 'nullius . . . flagitii conpertum.' But the case for involvement is strong. Rogers is not the only scholar to suggest that 'the Tacitean tradition is a misrepresentation of the facts, deriving, presumably, from propaganda of Julia's party'.[80] Violent propaganda against Augustus had certainly been circulating in Agrippa's name, if not actually by him.[81]

Such evidence, though suggestive, remains circumstantial. However, we do possess specific testimony[82] in Dio Cassius and Suetonius pointing to the existence of considerable public unrest at this period and to a number of abortive conspiracies and attempts at revolution (their chronology remains uncertain), which Augustus is said to have detected and suppressed before they could become really dangerous. Writing of the year AD 6, Dio Cassius describes a situation in which high taxation and food shortages had created enough public resentment to make the idea of change of government attractive. He refers to openly treasonable talk and the posting of propaganda broadsheets: elsewhere (Suet. *Div.Aug.*51.1) we read of an anti-Augustan letter circulated in Agrippa's name. The front man for all this activity, P. Plautius Rufus,[83] turns up again in a short list of failed coups mentioned by Suetonius, where he is associated with Julia II's husband, L. Aemilius Paullus, as a co-conspirator. Suetonius goes on to mention other plotters, including the elderly L. Audasius (also under indictment for forgery), Asinius Epicadus, 'a half-breed of Parthian descent', and Telephus, a woman's social slave-secretary. Audasius and Epicadus, he continues, 'had intended to abduct his daughter Julia and his grandson Agrippa from the islands where they were confined, and take them to the armed forces, while Telephus – apparently convinced that fate had destined him for power – would launch an attack on Augustus and the senate.'[84] It would help us if Suetonius had made it clearer to what extent these various activities were coordinated; but the Julian link does strongly suggest that Aemilius Paullus, Plautius Rufus, Audasius, and Epicadus were all involved in the same anti-Tiberian conspiracy, their object being to secure Agrippa Postumus' succession through the support of the legions. A Julian candidate, they will have argued, would prove far more popular than the crabbed and gloomy Tiberius. Julia I's immense popularity[85] – in pleasing contrast to the terror disseminated by Livia – would both have made this plan look feasible and explained the need for her presence as well as that of her son Agrippa, the actual candidate for the throne.

Much about Suetonius' notice excites suspicion, but its central point remains all too plausible. The same is true of that notorious Juvenalian scholium which, amid much tendentious nonsense, gives us the valuable information that Aemilius Paullus was executed[86] for the crime of *laesa maiestas* (clearly as a result of the unsuccessful rising described above) and that his wife, Julia II, was exiled at the same time.[87] The attempted coup must have taken place in the spring or early summer of AD 8.[88] As we might expect, the charge against Julia II, like that used to dispose of her mother, was sexual rather than political: adultery with D. Iunius Silanus. Yet she suffered exile for life: the son she bore on Trimerus was, at Augustus' express command, exposed: her palatial town house was razed to the ground, and the Princeps forbade her ashes to be placed in his Mausoleum. All this is far more redolent of treason than of loose morals. Further, whereas Augustus executed or exiled ('morte aut fuga puniuit') Julia and her accomplices, Silanus, the adulterer, was, as we have seen, merely deprived of the emperor's *amicitia* and returned to Rome without difficulty in AD 20, Tiberius expressing pleasure that he was back from his lengthy travels ('e peregrinatione longinqua').[89] The contrast is instructive. Neither Tiberius nor his mother showed any spark of compassion for Agrippa Postumus, the two Julias, or their political associates – among whom Ovid must surely be included. Yet Silanus, who had simply done what Ovid preached (with unconvincing disclaimers) in the *Ars Amatoria*, got off virtually scot-free.

All this gives us some very clear pointers as to what Ovid's secret *error* may have been, and it certainly helps us to determine what it was *not*. If adultery with Augustus' granddaughter – presumably free of more political and therefore more dangerous connections – earned the offender such a mild slap on the wrist and constituted no obstacle to reconciliation with Tiberius after the latter's accession, it becomes hard to argue that a mere act of voyeurism or procurements – lending a house for assignation, witnessing incest or other illegitimate intercourse, giving advice generally on sexual matters[90] – would incur a sentence of lifelong exile, with no remission after Augustus' death. Even earlier, by the time he came to write Book I of the *Epistulae ex Ponto* (*c.* AD 12), Ovid had virtually abandoned all hope of recall and was instead concentrating on his more frequently expressed alternative petition, for a change of domicile:

> hoc mihi si superi, quorum sumus omnia, credent,
> forsitan exigua dignus habebor ope,
> inque locum Scythico uacuum mutabor ab arcu:
> plus isto, duri, si precer, oris ero.
> (*EP* 1.1.77-80)

If the high gods whose pawn I am believe my statement, maybe
  I'll be held worthy of some slight relief,
be granted a transfer to somewhere beyond Scythian bowshot:
  to pray for more would be mere effrontery.

His hopes were briefly raised, in AD 14, by rumours that Augustus was now more kindly disposed towards him (*EP* 4.6.15-26). But on August 19 of that year the aged Princeps died, and Ovid's last lingering hopes for reprieve died with him, as the poet himself had grimly foreseen.[91] From Tiberius and Livia he could expect no mercy, now or ever.

It seems clear, then, that Ovid was in some sense a partisan of the 'Julian faction'. Later Christian tradition linked his name with Julia I, and though the notion that Julia was the model for Corinna[92] sounds like mere monkish fantasising, it is more than likely that the most fashionable elegiac poet in Rome should have frequented Julia's salon. She was a noted intellectual and wit, besides being the kind of sexual sophisticate who would have appreciated Ovid's *nequitiae* to the full.[93] Her scandalous conduct, whether sexual or political or both, caused her father Augustus deep personal pain,[94] and a similar reaction could well have been expected from him to any further scandal in which she was involved: hence Ovid's repeated allusions to Augustus' *wounds*.[95] When Ovid was interrogated by the Princeps (*Tr.* 2.133.34) after the exposure of Aemilius Paullus' plot, did he perhaps incur lasting displeasure by refusing, or declaring himself unable, to name names? Though the plot had been scotched and its principals – insofar as they were known – had been dealt with 'morte aut fuga,' had the evil been completely rooted out? As late as AD 14, Agrippa's slave Clemens (who bore a striking physical resemblance to his master) not only impersonated the executed Julian claimant but, on reaching Rome, at once received a remarkable amount of support from important quarters.[96] The 'Julian faction' was not only still alive but had wide potential backing.

Though in the exilic poems Ovid goes out of his way to stress that he had *done* nothing treasonable, that he had not himself conspired against Augustus,[97] such disclaimers strongly suggest the guilty witness[98] anxious to minimise his own involvement as an accessory before or after the fact. It is particularly curious that he should go out of his way to deny having been guilty of murder or forgery since, as we have seen, L. Audasius was, precisely, 'falsarum tabularum reus', while an attempt on Augustus' life, just as in 2 BC, formed part of the plot.[99] It may well be that the fatal knowledge Ovid acquired – and, even more fatally, kept to himself – concerned the execution of the coup itself. What we will never know is how active and conscious a role he really played, despite his much-reiterated claim to have been a mere innocent and gullible observer. What was it he witnessed? A privy meeting of conspirators? And if he was betrayed to Augustus, as he must have been, by a *delator*, how did that *delator* know what it was that Ovid knew?

The most economical explanation, of course, is that both men had been privy to the plot, with the *delator* being granted immunity in return for his revelations. Though Ovid almost certainly took no active part in the coup, it is hard to believe him wholly unaware, long before, of what was in the wind, or to argue thathis knowledge came to him by mere casual accident. Others, clearly, were in a position to observe him, and in due course one such witness reported convincingly on the poet's behaviour. After a halfhearted attempt to deny the charge,[100] Ovid thenceforth admitted his guilt.[101] Had the charge been a fabrication, had his knowledge of the plot been gained by some accident impossible to prove, he would undoubtedly have maintained his innocence throughout: he had everything to gain and nothing to lose. The evidence must have been irrefutable, which virtually limits us to a police spy or ex-Julian informer. Guilt by association and silence seems the likeliest verdict.

If Ovid, in whatever circumstances, learned about the plans for this Julian coup against Augustus (and, *a fortiori*, Tiberius), then the hints he scatters throughout the poems of exile make complete and immediate sense. *Magna nomina* (*Tr.* 3.3.4) were indeed involved. The insistence by Augustus on official secrecy becomes more than understandable, especially in the disturbed political climate then prevailing. Ovid's unwillingness to go to the authorities will have sprung not only from fear but also from a disinclination (which he could never thereafter acknowledge) to betray his Julian friends. No thought of personal gain was involved but, rather, natural loyalty: the situation governing the succession struggle was indeed complex, indeed bred great evils (*Tr.* 4.4.38). Though he had, he insists, taken no action himself his silence about what he knew was in itself culpable and could, as he admits, have earned him the death penalty *in camera*. His knowledge was indeed *funestum* (*Tr.* 3.6.28): potentially to Augustus, in the event to Ovid himself. The hostile reaction of highly placed opportunists now safely aboard the Claudian bandwagon, the deadly and unremitting enmity of Livia and Tiberius – what, given the circumstances, could be more predictable?

Though Ovid's constant sniping at the morals and dignity of the *pax Augusta* provided an extra incentive to those selecting his place of exile, his *relegatio* had solid political motivation behind it. On the other hand, his public reputation as the arch-exponent of fashionable erotic heterodoxy provided Augustus with ideal camouflage[102] for more crucial matters. Ironically, he was relying upon Ovid to supply, gratis, convincing support for the cover-charge of sexual misconduct brought against Julia II: like mother, like daughter. This, of course, explains the public banning of the *Ars* almost a decade after its publication, and, similarly, the bracketing of *carmen* with *error* as grounds for Ovid's exile. Since the charge against the *Ars* was nonsensical (though possessed of a certain vague, if irrational, social plausibility in the light of the *lex Iulia* and Augustan moral reforms in general),[103] Ovid, as a good rhetorician, could safely be left to refute it at eye-catching length and in loudly self-exculpatory tones, while exercising discretion over his less easily justifiable brush with dynastic power politics. This explains why he was not only allowed, but encouraged, to correspond freely with friends in Rome (*EP* 3.6.11-12) and to publish his exilic poems. The literary *praeceptor amoris* found himself, in the end, treated as a mere political pawn.

XIV

WIT, SEX AND TOPICALITY: THE PROBLEMS CONFRONTING A TRANSLATOR OF OVID'S LOVE POETRY

NY WOULD-BE TRANSLATOR of Ovid begins with an awkward historical legacy. From Marlowe's day onward there has been a persistent vogue for translating Ovid into the rhymed iambic couplets so popular with Dryden, Pope and other eighteenth-century poets. The habit is far from dead even today: Ovid still seems to be regarded, even if only at subconscious level, as a kind of honorary English Augustan. In 1954 A. E. Watt performed this metamorphosis on the whole of the *Metamorphoses*, a transformation act so monstrous that the Picasso line-drawings illustrating his text seemed tame by comparison. L. P. Wilkinson chose the same medium for the numerous illustrative extracts he cites in *Ovid Recalled*. So good a young scholar as D. A. Little praised these versions fulsomely;[1] yet, immensely ingenious though they are, they do not sound anything like Ovid.

Quite apart from the matter of rhyme and assonance – a device that Ovid uses cleverly and sparingly, not with the predictable regularity of a metronome – there remain the awkward facts that a hexameter is not only dactylic as opposed to iambic, but is one foot longer than the pentameter; on top of that, it has what in English verse would be called a feminine, i.e. disyllabic, ending, whereas the pentameter is cut off abruptly with what used to be known as a half-foot: it is catalectic. Now Ovid was acutely conscious of this distinction. Uneasy about not writing epic, which would have meant using nothing but the hexameter, he made continual little jokes about Elegy's one lame foot when referring to the pentameter.[2] 'Let my verse rise with six stresses,' he says, 'drop to five on the downbeat':[3] the traditional translator, presumably unable to count, with cheerful impartiality gives him five on both, and a chiming rhyme into the bargain. Even in the *Metamorphoses* the use of rhymed couplets to express hexameters sets up associations wholly alien to the original movement of the verse, not least in the matter of overrun: Matthew Arnold's characterisation of the hexameter[4] as possessing, above all, rapidity and directness should be borne in mind here.

What is of prime interest, it seems to me, is to understand why such an odd convention should have persisted for so long. The answer takes us into a brief consideration of what might be termed the 'Homeric Problem' of verse translation. [5] To put it, I hope, succinctly: there are two fundamental and contrasting theories governing the translation of classical poetry, one arguing that the translator should, in the words of F. W. Newman, attempt 'to retain every peculiarity of the original so far as he is able, with the greater care, the more foreign it may happen to be', while the other follows Dryden's precept, which excused anglicisation of the original on the grounds that, as between Dryden and his original, 'my own is of a piece with his, and that *if he were living, and an Englishman*, they are such as he would probably have written' [my emphasis]. In other words, Dryden's principle is a licence to render elegiacs, hexameters, sapphics, alcaics or, if it comes to that, choriambic dimeters in whatever local prosody is popular at the time of writing. Leaf through that perverse anthology of pastiche and pot-pourri, *The Oxford Book of Greek Verse in Translation*, and you will find epigrams in the Housman manner, Greek choruses a long way after Swinburne, and such oddities as Ibycus done up in the idiosyncratic manner of Marvell's 'Ode on the Return of Cromwell from Ireland':

> Them might the subtle muses tell,
> The Heliconian sisters, well:
> > No mortal man may trace
> > Each vessel in its place,

> How Menelaus set his sail
> From Graecian Aulis to prevail
> > In Dardan pasture-land
> > With his bronze-shielded band . . .[6]

Translators, indeed, almost invariably reflect far more of their own age than that of their original; Dryden was simply elevating this unfortunate (and seemingly perennial) human frailty into a positive merit.

The result was that Pope (for instance) could take the end of Book VIII of the *Iliad* (lines 562-5) and produce this:

> A thousand piles the dusky horrors gild,
> And shoot a shady lustre o'er the field.
> Full fifty guards each flaming pile attend
> Whose umbered arms, by fits, thick flashes send;
> Loud neigh the coursers o'er their heaps of corn,
> And ardent warriors wait the rising morn.

We are given six lines for four, a clutch of gratuitous rhyme, and much additional decoration not in the original, including those 'dusky horrors', 'umbered arms', and 'ardent warriors', the last-named having usurped the horses. As Bentley said, with good reason, 'A very pretty poem, Mr Pope, but you must not call it Homer'. Those who so regularly applied the principle to Ovid presumably did so for two main reasons: first, because they knew Ovid was witty and neat, and felt that neatness and wittiness could *only* be produced in English by means of the stopped rhymed couplet; and second, because they were convinced that it was absolutely impossible to reproduce any Latin or Greek metrical pattern adequately in English. The opposing group, on the other hand, would argue with equal passion that the difficulty of the task was no reason for not attempting it, and that what Dryden's followers regarded as the 'equivalent' or 'corresponding' form in English merely set up false associations and took the unwary reader *away* from the original rather than bringing him nearer to it.

The problem of the English hexameter[7] is one that goes back as far as the Elizabethan Age. In 1586 William Webbe, who was associated in his ideas with the better-known Gabriel Harvey, wrote a *Discourse of English Poetrie*, advocating the use of Greek and Latin metres in English. Webbe's own version of Virgil's First Eclogue begins:

Tityrus happilie thou lyste tumbling under a beech tree
All on a fine oate pipe these sweet songs lustillie chaunting:
We, poor soules, go to wracke, and from these coastes be remoued,
And from our pastures sweete: thou Tityr, at ease in a shade plott,
Makst thick grouves to resound with songes of braue Amarillis.

Now the first thing we see about this hexameter is that, inevitably, it is not metrical. As Omond said of Southey's efforts in this field, it 'is simply a triple-time six-cadence line, with falling accents, and without rhyme'.[8] This hints at the reason why almost all English hexameters or elegiacs, however brilliant, and even when sauced up continually with sprung rhythm, inverted stresses, or overrun, have a flat, limp quality that their classical models, however mundane, do not. If I pick an example from Longfellow,[9] that is not only because he did the job better than most, but also because he is here concerned, in verse, with the problem of the elegiac couplet:

Peradventure of old some bard in Ionian islands,
    Walking alone by the sea, hearing the wash of the waves,
Learned the secret from them of the beautiful verse elegiac,
    Breathing into his song motion and sound of the sea.
For as the wave of the sea, upheaving in long undulations,
    Plunges loud on the sands, pauses and turns and retreats,
So the hexameter, rising and singing, with cadence sonorous,
    Falls, and in refluent rhythm back the Pentameter flows.

Most critics, I think, would agree that this is pretty awful stuff; but *why* is it awful? The awkward inversions, the unnaturally stressed syllables or words, are symptoms of something deeper. Tennyson, who was a consummate craftsman and a fair classical scholar, knew the answer by instinct, though he never spelled it out. His lampoon on English elegiacs gets right to the critical heart of the matter:

> These lame hexameters, the strong-winged music of Homer!
> No, but a most burlesque barbarous experiment.
> When was a harsher sound ever heard, ye Muses, in England?
> When did a frog coarser croak upon our Helicon?
> Hexameters no worse than daring Germany gave us,
> Barbarous experiment, barbarous hexameters.

The point he makes so succinctly by demonstration is this. Since all vowels in Latin and Greek have fixed quantities, either naturally or by position, the metrical pattern is independent of – indeed, contrapuntal to – accentual stress and ictus. The two schemes play against each other, producing a strong and springy resonance. In English, on the other hand, we have *only* accentual stress/ictus, and no fixed vowel quantities. Thus the trouble with an English stress equivalent to classical metre is that, having no firm metrical base, it lacks all counterpoint and tension. The usual solution is to create a stress-pattern that coincides at all points with the metrical schema: the line will then sound flat. To realise the truth of this one needs only glance at a line or two of Cotterill's *Odyssey*:[10]

> Now when at last they arrived at the beautiful stream of the river,
> Here the perennial basins they found where water abundant
> Welled up brightly enough for the cleansing of dirtiest raiment.
> So their mules they unloosened from under the yoke of the wagon,
> Letting them wander at will on the bank of the eddying river . . .
>
> (*Od.* 6.85-9)

But, as Tennyson knew, the essence of a classical hexameter or elegiac is that its metrical schema should *not* coincide with the natural stresses of the words forming it: he therefore demonstrated the impossibility of reproducing classical metres in English by carefully creating elegiacs in which, wherever possible, natural stress and metrical schema should be at complete odds with each other. In Latin or Greek this would work excellently; in English it merely sounds awkward and grotesque. In addition, English is largely deficient in inflection, and so cannot achieve that dense flexibility which marks the genre in Latin. As Walter Shewring remarked, 'Early and late attempts in this direction have all in the end come to grief through confusion of quantity with accent, pitch accent with stress accent, and English spelling with English pronunciation'.[11]

The proof, for elegiacs, is contained in such versions of Ovid as Saklatvala's *Art of Love* or Lind's *Tristia*,[12] from which brief extracts should suffice by way of demonstration:

> And now my sport's at an end. From my swans to descend it is timely,
>   Who have borne on their lovely necks this yoke and harness of mine.
> As once the young men, so now let my pupils, the lovely lasses,
>   Write in their trophy and spoils: *"Ovid my master was!"*
>   (*AA* 3.809-12)

> I'm criticised though I am blameless; it's a slender field that I'm plowing;
>   The praise of your deeds would require a plough-land far richer than
>   mine.
> If some little craft is contented to venture upon a small lagoon,
>   It ought not therefore in its rashness trust itself to the broad sea.
>   (*Tr.* 2.327-340)

I seriously doubt whether someone not already familiar with the elegiac metrical pattern would be able to scan these translations – the second one in particular – as they were intended. Note, apart from the flatness, the variable number of extra non-stressed syllables in anacrusis at the beginning of each line, the occasional violation of syllabic count (even on the caesura: 'rash*ness*'), the need to stress, in Tennysonian fashion, improbable words, or, worse, syllables ('lágoon'), the arch inversions ('my master was' – one syllable short there, too): all the result of trying to fight a metrical pattern with the weapons of a stress language.

Worse still, any attempt at variation, unless handled with the skill (and diacritical signs) of a Gerard Manley Hopkins, is liable to baffle a reader used to sensing the natural stress of a line. What kind of pentameter, for instance, is Lind's 'You will find in its entire contents not a single line that is sweet' (*Tr.* 5.1.4) or, even more baffling still, 'Take care that my funeral rites are not ignored, without even a sound' (ibid. 14)? The first requires the discounting of 'you will', 'entire contents' pronounced with a heavy stress on the *first* syllable of each word, the swallowing of 'not', a stress on 'a'; the second calls for the dropping of 'take' and the complete omission of 'are not ig-', though I suppose a slurred 'aren't' would just carry one through. Clearly here we are in a metrical wasteland. On the other hand, there has to be some attempt to produce the *effect* of the original, since otherwise we would still be stuck with the pernicious tradition of 'local equivalence' – rhyming couplets or quatrains, blank verse, or even less appropriate English growths (see below). All translation must be, in some sense, a compromise. How, I asked myself when I first set about translating Ovid, could I save even a semblance of the Latin elegiac couplet, in a way that would keep Ovid, hopefully, crisp and witty, yet sounding like himself rather than a flaccid pastiche of Pope?

There was one very interesting and in some ways successful model before me, that of Guy Lee's *Amores*.[13] This was the work of a sensitive and well-read literary scholar who knew very well Ovid's penchant for making puns and sly allusions (literary, political, or erotic), and, more important, for achieving effects that can only be brought off successfully in a heavily inflected language where the juxtaposition of words is solely for emphasis and not essential to the meaning. Lee's answer, however, almost invariably, is to omit what he can't get across. He also, as he himself admits, very often finds Ovid flat and long-winded (his epithets), and therefore boils down his decorative effects to nothing, remarking[14] that this is the converse of what students of classical verse composition are required to do when turning English poems into Latin, thus offering us two fallacies for the price of one. He reminds us that H. A. J. Munro turned Thomas Carew's lines 'He that loves a rosy cheek/Or a coral lip admires' into the following Latin elegiac couplet:

> cui facies cordi roseos imitata colores
> labrave curalii tincta rubore placent,

which has to be his excuse for translating:

> accipe per longos tibi qui deseruiat annos,
> accipe qui pura norit amare fide (*Am.* 1.3.5–6)

as 'I'll be your slave for life,/your ever faithful lover', or indeed the delectable-sounding:

> illa magas artes Aeaeaque carmina nouit
> inque caput liquidas arte recuruat aquas (*Am.* 1.8.5–6)

as 'She's the local witch – /Can reverse the flow of water', which apart from anything else completely loses the *pattern* of the two lines on which Ovid hangs so much, along with the verbal beauty. I've often thought that if Lee got at Propertius, in his version 'Sunt apud infernos tot milia formosarum', surely one of the most haunting lines in all Latin, would probably emerge as something like 'Hell's full of cuties'. The staccato, variable free verse that Lee defends on the grounds of avoiding monotony (201) makes hay of the whole elegiac concept, even (to take one obvious and gross example) in very often presenting a couplet – and the couplets are spaced out from each other in this version – with its second line both longer and stronger than its first. Lee's *Amores* jettisons a whole mass of fustian, and is sharply alive to jokes and nuances; but in reaction against its predecessors it boils all the formal richness out of the poems. What it offers us is Ovid dehydrated, almost in capsule form.

The solution that most appealed to me was one that had been developed over several decades, primarily by Cecil Day Lewis and Richmond Lattimore, who saw that the way to produce some real stress equivalent to the hexameter was to go for the beat, the ictus, since this was native to English, and let the metre, within limits, take care of itself. They worked out a loose, flexible line (but varied on occasion with one stress less or more) and a variable, predominantly feminine ending, that could take easy overrun, moved swiftly, and to a great degree countered the determination of the English language to climb uphill, where possible in iambic patterns, if given half a chance. Saintsbury had foreseen some of the dangers: 'Good dactylic movements in English', he observed,[15] 'tip themselves up and become anapaestic . . the so-called "Accentual" hexameter . . . is, when it is good verse, not a classical hexameter at all, but a five-anapaest line with anacrusis and hypercatalexis.' That is true, on occasion, of both Lattimore and Day Lewis. But does it matter? This line at least catches the precipitate striding movement of the hexameter, while preserving its basic structure, including the caesura. What is sacrificed is the linguistically unattainable ideal of true metrical equivalence.

The relaxation sometimes tempted Day Lewis especially into slang, at inappropriate moments.[16] But the overall sense of epic speed and flow were captured as never before. Let me quote two parallel passages: Hermes' flight to Ogygia from the *Odyssey*, and Mercury's similar mission to Aeneas in the *Aeneid*:[17]

(i)   He stood on Pieria and launched himself from the bright air
across the sea and sped the wave tops, like a shearwater
who along the deadly deep ways of the barren salt sea
goes hunting fish and sprays quick-beating wings in the salt brine.
In such a likeness Hermes rode over much tossing water.

(ii)   Here first did Mercury pause, hovering on beautifully-balanced
Wings: then stooped, dived bodily down to the sea below,
Like a bird which along the shore and around the promontories
Goes fishing, flying low, wave-hopping over the water.
Even so did Mercury skim between earth and sky
Towards the Libyan coast, cutting his path through the winds.

My own apprenticeship to this line was served by translating Homer for the BBC Third Programme (as it then was) back in the Fifties, and, a decade later, Juvenal for Penguin Classics. In Homer's case it offered speed, variety, formulaic strength, and chances for surging rhetoric, as in the arming of Agamemnon:[18]

Then, last, he grasped
His two tough sharpened spears, each pointed with keen bronze:
And the light gleamed back to heaven from arms and armour,

> And Athena and Hera sent the thunder pealing
> In salute to the king of great and golden Mycenae.

But it was Juvenal who showed me how the almost infinite adaptability of the line could be utilised for pointing up wit and satire – as here in the middle of his anti-Greek diatribe:[19]

> . . . Quick wit, unlimited nerve, a gift
> Of the gab that outsmarts a professional public speaker –
> These are their characteristics. What do you reckon
> That fellow's profession to be? He has brought a whole bundle
> Of personalities with him – schoolmaster, rhetorician,
> Surveyor, artist, masseur, diviner, tightrope-walker,
> Magician or quack, your versatile hungry Greekling
> Is all by turns. Tell him to fly – he's airborne.

The elegiac couplet poses somewhat different problems from those of the epic hexameter. In particular, it is hard to avoid the feeling, in English, of rhythmic monotony, if only because the opportunity for unlimited runovers is going to be severely reduced, since, *inter alia*, so many couplets, in Latin, form self-contained sentences. To make a sharp contrast between hexameter and pentameter is easy enough. Curtail the pentameter by at least a foot, and give it a masculine ending by setting a sharp stress on the final syllable. At the same time *always* give the hexameter a feminine ending. This solution was arrived at independently by G.S. Fraser, in some Ovid translations he did for a radio feature I wrote about twenty-five years ago,[20] and by Gilbert Highet in his book *Poets in a Landscape*.[21]

Let us see how the device works. Here, first, is Fraser: the opening of Penelope's letter to Ulysses:[22]

> Your Penelope writes to you, long-delayed Ulysses –
>   yet send no letter home, come home yourself!
> Tall Troy is down now, loathed of Danaan daughters:
>   was Troy, was Priam worth the cost to me?
> Long since that adulterer's ship sought Lacedaemonia:
>   would the mad waters had then whelmed him down!

Now compare Highet's version of Ovid's complaint to Cypassis, Corinna's lady's-maid:[23]

> Expert in ornamenting hair in a thousand fashions,
>   but pretty enough to set a goddess' curls,
> Cypassis, my sophisticated fellow-sinner,
>   deft at serving *her*, defter for me –
> who could have betrayed the mingling of our bodies?

> how did Corinna sense your love-affair?
> Surely I did not blush? or stumble over a word
>   that gave some evidence of our stolen love?
> Of course I said the man who loved a servant-girl
>   must be a hopeless idiot – of course!
> But the Thessalian hero loved the slave Briseis,
>   captive Cassandra fired Mycenae's king.
> Achilles and Agamemnon fell. I am no stronger:
>   so, *honi soit qui mal y pense*, say I.

It is clear at once that Highet has gone further than Fraser in exploring the flexibilities of the form (so far, in fact, that at line 7 and 9 he seems to lose the feminine ending to his hexameter altogether). Fraser is in serious danger of falling into the rocking-horse mode that remains the prime hazard for elegiacs: that is, unvarying stopped – if not rhyming – couplets, each rhythmically identical to the last. Highet's rhythms are subtler, and he has a sharp eye, like Guy Lee, for Ovidian sophistication, but he is still very much in thrall to the tyranny of the couplet. Over the short haul this may not obtrude on the reader's ear; but when, as in the *Art of Love*, he has to plough through hundreds of lines without a break, the old absence of metrical counterpoint, Latin's saving grace, produces a sense of relentless, repetitive undulation.

Bearing these dangers in mind, I decided to employ overrun wherever possible, and also to exploit the rhythmic contrast between the two lines of the couplet to the uttermost, sometimes reducing the pentameter to as few as three or even on occasion two stresses, and extending the hexameter with an extra stress in override, as it were, while on occasion cutting it back to a five-beat line. These devices are not so apparent in my version of the Cypassis poem as elsewhere, since it is comparatively short. However, you can observe both the overruns and (on the matter of tone) a more – I hope – relaxed, teasing colloquial approach than Highet's: here closer to Lee (who starts off 'Cypassis, incomparable coiffeuse/who should start a salon on Olympus' – nice mood, but too far from the Latin), but linguistically trying to preserve Ovid's patterns:

> O expert in creating a thousand hairstyles, worthy
>   to have none but goddesses for your clientele,
> Cypassis! – and (as I know from our stolen pleasures)
>   no country beginner: just right
> for your mistress, but righter for me – what malicious gossip
>   put the finger on us? How did Corinna know
> about our sleeping together? I didn't blush, did I,
>   or blurt out some telltale phrase?
> I'm sorry I told her no man in his proper senses
>   could go overboard for a maid –
> Achilles fell madly in love with *his* maid Briseis,

> Agamemnon was besotted by the slave-
> priestess Cassandra. I can't pretend to be socially up on
> those two – then why should I despise
> what's endorsed by royalty? Anyway, when Corinna
> shot *you* a dirty look, you blushed right up.

Now the immediate criticism of this format is going to be that it evokes no recognisable patterns in the mind of an English reader; and that, in turn, raises the perennial question, yet again, of what a translation, a verse translation in particular, is *for*. What we may term, for short, the Dryden theory (see above, p.224) seems to assume tacit familiarity with the original, to invite applause for clever and appreciable pastiche. In the English Augustan Age this was, of course, the main motive for translation: anyone interested enough to read a new English version of Ovid or Virgil could almost certainly read them in Latin as well. The object was to produce a skilled assimilation to the literary mode of the moment, however alien that might be from the poet's own intentions. How, as Dryden asked, would he have handled the matter had he been writing in the translator's time and country? This produced, *inter alia*, Gilbert Murray's vastly popular versions of Greek tragedy, with the iambic *epeisodia* done over in rhyming couplets, and the choruses revamped as Swinburne-and-water; or (my favourite oddity) J. W. Mackail's *Odyssey* in the Fitzgerald *Rubaiyat* stanza:[24]

> Now at the hour when brightest shone on high
> The star that comes to herald up the sky
> The Dawning of the Morning, even then
> The ship sea-travelling to the isle drew nigh.
>
> The fields of Ithaca a haven hold
> Called after Phorcys' name, the Sea-God old.
> Two jutting headlands breaking sheer in cliff
> Stretch seaward, and the harbour-mouth enfold . . .

It also produced, more recently, such metaphrastic curiosities, brilliant in their own right, yet arguably not translations in the basic sense of conveying a text to those who lack its language, as Pound's *Homage to Sextus Propertius*, Ted Hughes' version of Seneca's *Oedipus*, or Christopher Logue's marvellous variations on Homer (I am thinking particularly of Achilles' fight with the Scamander) that were originally broadcast on the BBC Third Programme.[25] It would, I suppose, be surprising if an age of *Rezeptionsgeschichte*, determined to enthrone the critic as an integral element of the creative process, did not offer similar privileges to the translator.

This trend militates strongly against another, equally strong, movement in modern translation: the sense of responsibility to one's original, and, in a different sense, to the reader, who today, nine times out of ten, knows nothing whatsoever of the original language, and is far more interested in getting an accurate impression of the poet's own texture and rhythms than in applauding the irrelevant ingenuity of a translator with a gift for clever pastiche. Let me give an example. One critic of my Ovid translation (from the safe anonymity of a reader's report) accused it of 'egregious dullness', and picked on the opening of Book II of the *Ars Amatoria*:[26]

> Cry hurrah, and hurrah again, for a splendid triumph –
>   the quarry I sought has fallen into my toils.
> Each happy lover now rates my verses higher
>   than Homer's or Hesiod's, awards them the palm
> of victory. He's as cheerful as Paris was, sailing away from
>   warlike Sparta, the guest who stole a bride,
> or Pelops, the stranger, the winner of Hippodameia
>   after that chariot-race.
> Why hurry, young man? Your ship's still in mid-passage,
>   and the harbor I seek is far away.
> Through my verses, it's true, you may have *acquired* a mistress,
>   but that's not enough. If my art
> Caught her, my art must keep her. To guard a conquest's
>   as tricky as making it. There was luck in the chase,
> but *this* task will call for skill. If ever I needed support from
>   Venus and Son, and Erato – the Muse
> erotic by name – it's now, for my too-ambitious project
>   to relate some techniques that might restrain
> that fickle young globe-trotter, Love. He's winged and flighty,
>   hard to pin down . . .

Why my critic thought this version dull may be deduced by the rendering he offered, with evident approval, in its place (the fruit of what sounds like a fairly swinging Comp. Lit. seminar):

> O, shout hurray! and then whoopee!
> The long-sought prize is fallen to me!
> Beneath the old men's startled eyes
> I take the Nobel Loving Prize.
> So Paris felt, with Priam's bride,
> escaping o'er the shining tide.
>
> So Pelops on his foreign wheels
> showed Hippo's car some cleanish heels.
> But what's your hurry, callow youth?
> You're far from court, and that's the truth.
> I won your dolly by my art:

Her body's yours, but where's her heart?
You can't rely on Lady Luck
for more than just an easy fuck.

Erato, Muse of loving name,
O Venus, Cupid, play my game!
My plan's ambitious: O what joy,
to pen that wayward, wandering boy!
His frown's a smile, his smile's a frown:
the problem is to pin him down.

As Bentley might have said, 'A very pretty poem, Mr X., but you must not call it Ovid'. Quite apart from incidental matters of accuracy, interpretation and taste (never mind the anachronisms and rhymes: Ovid never used a four-letter word in his whole career) what we have here is a fundamental divergence over method. What my critic wanted, in effect, was Dryden's licence: the old rhyming couplet, shorn of one foot and sauced up with contemporary allusions – a neat, recognisable package to which (as the current catch-phrase goes, dangling its transitive verb with insouciant abandon) modern readers can relate. It is, I think, no accident, as I suggested above, that pastiche translation is gaining ground again in an era of criticism when authors' intentions come a very poor second to critics' interpretative and structural – or deconstructional – fancies. The old joke about translations being like women – if they're faithful they're not beautiful, and *vice versa* – is getting a new lease of life.

I, on the other hand, start from the proposition that all translations are, in effect, crutches, second-best substitutes for those who cannot read the original, rather than material designed to provide pasticheurs and infertile poets with a creative shot in the arm. Though it remains, admittedly, impossible to fully capture one's original text in translation, that does not relieve a translator of the permanent obligation to get as close to that unattainable ideal as he can.[27] I would like, now, to examine some of the specific problems that this intention raises in producing an English version of Ovid's erotic poems.

Of the three elements in my title – wit, sex, topicality – the sex, I found, was by far the easiest to deal with. Despite the traditional air of *nequitia – froufrou* might be a better word for it – that hangs around the *Amores* and the *Art of Love*,[28] Ovid almost never goes in for explicit sexual details. The penultimate line of *Amores* 1.5 is far more characteristic. Having catalogued Corinna's physical charms, and folded her into his siesta-time embrace, Ovid then writes: 'Cetera quis nescit? lassi requieuimus ambo' – 'Fill in the rest for yourselves! tired at last, we lay sleeping'.[29] To borrow his own favourite image, what he offers, particularly in the *Art of Love*, is a guide to sexual siege-warfare and night-exercises.[30] Pursuit forms the essence and major attraction of the game.[31] Ovid spends nearly three books telling men and women how to manoeuvre during the chase, and no more than a few perfunctory lines[32] instructing them how to act when their quarry is safely bedded. This is very mild stuff indeed. Choose sexual positions, he tells the ladies, that conceal your physical defects (e.g. if you have striations from childbirth, have intercourse *a tergo*). Try to achieve simultaneous mutual orgasm – but if you can't come, fake it. No problems for a modern translator here: we are in familiar territory.

Significantly, Ovid tends to be far more violent – sometimes, indeed, downright embarrassing – when describing what he finds *repellent* about women. This is a side of his erotic persona that for some reason has attracted little attention. His evocation of ladies' dressing-tables[33] has a Swiftian quality about it; it reminds me of Jimmy Porter's remarks in *Look Back in Anger*: 'When you see a woman in front of her bedroom mirror, you realise what a refined sort of butcher she is. Did you ever see some dirty old Arab, sticking his fingers into some mess of lamb fat and gristle? Well, she's like that'.[34] 'Quem non offendat toto faex inlita uultu,/Cum fluit in tepidos pondere lapsa sinus?' (*AA* 3.211-12) For Ovid, women in their natural, unmasked state are not merely uncivilised, lacking in *cultus*, but actively disgusting.[35] In the *Remedia*[36] there occurs the following passage:

> Quo tua non possunt offendi pectora facto,
> forsitan hoc alio iudice crimen erit.
> Ille quod obscenas in aperto corpore partes
> uiderat, in cursu qui fuit, haesit amor:
> Ille quod a Veneris rebus surgente puella
> uidit in immundo signa pudenda toro.

Here we have two problems: how to translate *obscenas partes* in a way that conveys the curled lip of disgust without overloading the English, and how to convey the delicious double allusion of *pudenda*, as adjective and noun, implying that the man not only saw stains on a dirty bed, but associated them with his partner's vaginal secretions. I tried 'obscene parts', on the principle of adhering to the Latin whenever possible, but that sounded too heavy. In the end I came up with the following:

> What could not give the least offence to your own feelings
>   in another man's judgment might well
> Be a cause for reproach. One lover was stopped in mid-performance
>   by a glimpse of the girl's slit as she spread
> her legs, another by pudendal stains on the bedsheets
>   when she got up after the act.

'Slit' conveys distaste but is not over-emphatic; 'pudendal' (surprisingly, not a coined neologism, but well-attested, and instantly comprehensible) conveys both senses of Ovid's ambiguity. At least what we achieve here is an approximation.

This kind of *double-entendre* is, in fact, a regular Ovidian device,[37] and its punning allusions can cause the translator severe headaches. Sometimes the sexual teasing can be matched up with an identical English metaphor: the mistress's 'threshold' and 'grotto' (*RA* 786-9) clearly refer to her anatomy as well as to her house, and can so be read in any language, There is also in the same passage (783-6) a mythic allusion skewed to point a *risqué* allusion. Of Agamemnon Ovid writes: 'Nam sibi quod nunquam tactam Briseida iurat/ per sceptrum, sceptrum non putat esse deos.' Commentators[38] have not been slow to point out that in Homer it is Achilles rather than Agamemnon who swears by the sceptre:[39] but they all seem to have missed the point of Ovid's switch. What he clearly had in mind was the kind of situation envisaged in one of the Priapea[40] (whether actually Ovid's own early work or not remains a moot point):

> Hoc sceptrum, quod ab arbore ut recisum est,
> nulla iam poterit virere fronde,
> sceptrum, quod pathicae petunt puellae,
> quod quidam cupiunt tenere reges,
> cui dant oscula nobiles cinaedi,
> intra viscera furis ibit usque
> ad pubem capulumque coleorum.

Here Priapus parodies Homer's speech in reference to his own huge phallus-as-sceptrum: clearly the joke was both well-known and popular. Ovid, then, is making a salty joke, for which the sceptre is essential.

His Latin, as so often, is ambiguous: 'numquam tactam Briseida iurat/per sceptrum' can mean not only that Agamemnon swore by his 'sceptre', i.e. phallus, but also (taking *per* instrumentally) that Briseis had never been 'touched' by it, i.e. was *intacta virgo*. How to suggest this in translation? 'He swore that Briseis was still a virgin, by his sceptre,/But a sceptre (he figured) is no god.' I did wonder whether 'sceptre' might not, in English, be too free of any phallic associations, and thought of substituting 'staff of office', but decided it was preferable to keep the Latin word and image.

A great deal of Ovid's wit is of this sexually allusive sort: 'nocuerunt carmina semper' (*Am.* 3.12.13) can mean both 'my poems have brought nothing but trouble', and 'spells have always been dangerous': the *praeceptor amoris* suddenly takes on the nervous persona of a Sorcerer's Apprentice dabbling in aphrodisiacs. (Ovid repeatedly plays with the word *carmen* in its double sense, promoting poetry as the true magic.[41]) In his address to Bagoas (*Am.*2.2.63-4), Ovid insists that he and his beloved 'non ad miscenda coimus/ toxica': *miscenda* and *coimus* both suggest sexual intercourse as well as an assignation. How to catch this in English? Perhaps 'we don't come together for the decoction /of poisonous doses'? In *Am.* 2.15 Ovid plays with the notion of achieving close proximity to his beloved as a ring, *anulus*, but cannot resist punning on *anulus* as anus too – 'felix, a domina tractaberis, anule, nostra': luckily 'ring' in English carries the same double connotation. Consider *Am.* 3.15.4, 'nec me deliciae dedecuere meae'. The meaning most scholars attach to these words is, roughly, 'My poems may be erotic, but I'm respectable'. That is certainly one possible meaning. But *deliciae* can mean, apart from light verse, both 'darling' and 'sensuality', while the verb *dedecet* can convey the notion of 'unbecomingness' as well as 'dishonour'. So the phrase can also imply 'my girl-friend was quite smart enough for me', 'my elegies lived up to my reputation', or even 'my sensuality never failed me'. What is the poor translator to do? The best I could manage was 'A man whose delights have never let him down'.

There is a whole series of words on which Ovid puns, regularly and ingeniously, to produce sexual double meanings: *membrum, testis, neruus, latus, coire, miscere, surgere, cadere, iacere* and so on. At *AA* 1.412 the 'naufraga membra ratis' suggest erotic no less than maritime failure: a 'dismembered vessel', perhaps? *AA* 1.632 contains a marvellous ambiguity, 'pollicito testes quoslibet adde deos', which can mean either 'Call any gods you like to witness your promises' or 'Promise any sexual performance you like and throw the gods in too': my version is 'Invoke any gods you please/To endorse your performance'. The same joke turns up at *Am* 3.3.19, where the gods whom Ovid's mistress has falsely invoked are described as 'sine pondere testes', i.e. both worthless witnesses and half-cock performers. Try 'puff-ball witnesses'. We find it yet again at *AA* 3.398: 'fructus abest, facies cum bona teste caret' can mean either 'A pretty face, unseen, gets no results', or 'A pretty girl, if never balled, won't get pregnant'. My version: 'Fruitless, the pretty face that goes alone'. The 'adultera clauis' of *AA* 3.643 is not only a duplicate key but a duplicitous cock, just as *ianua* in the following line has vaginal connotations: that one defeated me altogether. Ovid, like Horace, is well aware that *neruus* often means not 'nerve' or 'muscle' but the penis. See *Am.* 2.20.24: 'pondere non neruis corpora nostra carent' – 'Though I'm a lightweight, I'm hard'.

Examples of this sort could be multiplied: how to convey them in English without losing the dry and elegant touch of the original is another matter. The constant danger is of sounding vulgar – something Ovid never is. Yet the pitfalls of sexual allusion are as nothing to the difficulty of reproducing the verbal effects that this technically dazzling poet achieves by neat juxtapositions in a heavily inflected language. 'Spectatum ueniunt, ueniunt spectentur ut ipsae', (*AA* 1.99) pins down, for ever, the behaviour of pretty women in an auditorium. But how catch that perfect chiasmus – all done in six words, too? Ten was the fewest I could manage: 'As spectators they come, come, too, to be inspected/themselves' – strained, and it loses the crispness, but perhaps better than nothing. Oddly, by comparison the famous couplet (*AA* 2.23-4)

Daedalus ut clausit conceptum crimine matris
Semibouemque uirum semiuirumque bouem

proved quite easy to manage by redistributing some of the weight between
hexameter and pentameter:

When Daedalus had built his labyrinth to imprison
the bull-man, man-bull conceived through a queen's guilt . . .

That last example brings me to the problem of topicality, of glossing for an
alien audience references they cannot be expected to know, names (famous in
their own day) which will mean nothing to them. All Ovid says to indicate
the imprisonment in the Labyrinth is *clausit* – 'he shut [him] up'. We need the
word *labyrinth* itself to remind us that what Ovid is talking about is the
Minotaur. I first dealt with this problem in detail when translating Juvenal,
and there in my introduction[42] I referred to the 'unfamiliar names, the
obscure topical or historical allusions that translators are for ever having to
break off in midpassage and explain to the layman. Nothing is calculated to
annoy a reader more . . than a text where every other line requires, and gets,
some detailed marginal gloss before it can be understood.' Here Ovid, like
Juvenal, provides endless problems. He, too, 'is full of recondite references
that he takes for granted his readers will understand: he is writing for
educated Romans who knew their own myths and history' and were familiar
with all prominent figures of the day, not to mention a great number from
their immediate or remote past. Here Ovid too is helped by what I then
termed the 'silent gloss' – that is, the tacit insertion of a word or brief phrase
to point up the reference. Sometimes nominative substitution helps. Ovid is
very fond of periphrastic allusion: when he talks about the 'Maeonian and
Ascraean sages' I will translate these characters, *tout court*, as Homer and
Hesiod. A stylistic trick, hard for modern taste to swallow, is lost; much
clarity is gained. But mythic parallels and *exempla* are so much part and parcel
of Ovid's method that the reader has to be credited with at least a basic
working knowledge of the main myths and legends, and referred to running
notes as a kind of life-raft if he feels in danger of sinking.

The same is true of, say, Roman topography and the associations it carries.
Consider the following passage[43] from the *Art of Love*:

Tu modo Pompeia lentus spatiare sub umbra,
    Cum sol Herculei terga leonis adit:
Aut ubi muneribus nati sua munera mater
    Addidit, externo marmore diues opus.
Nec tibi uitetur quae, priscis sparsa tabellis,
    Porticus auctoris Livia nomen habet:
Quaque parare necem miseris patruelibus ausae
    Belides et stricto stat ferus ense pater.

My translation invokes all the aids outlined above, but I still found myself writing over two pages of commentary on these lines:

> Here's what to do. When the sun's on the back of Hercules'
>   Lion, stroll down some shady colonnade,
> Pompey's, say, or Octavia's (for her dead son Marcellus:
>   Extravagant marble facings: R.I.P.),
> Or Livia's, with its gallery of genuine Old Masters,
>   Or the Danaids' portico (note
> The art-work: Danaus' daughters plotting mischief for their cousins,
>   Father attitudinising with drawn sword).

The Ovidian will at once notice the silent glosses. I have inserted the names of Octavia and Marcellus, and clarified Ovid's obscure reminder that the library in the Portico of Octavia (itself dedicated by Augustus) was built in memory of her son.[44] I have also glossed Belus' daughters (Belides) – or, more precisely, grand-daughters – as the better-known Danaids. But there is still much for which the reader must turn to the notes for enlightenment: e.g. the puzzling reference to 'the back of Hercules' lion', impossible either to omit or to gloss.[45] Such solutions are not, cannot be, perfect; but then all translation, verse translation especially, is an unending series of compromises between conflicting and often incompatible demands. In Ovid's case, if I have succeeded in keeping some proportion of any of these qualities – the balanced formal structure of the elegiac couplet, the elegant sexual innuendo, the crispness of aphorism, the well-read mythical and literary allusiveness, with its simultaneous flattery of, and demands on, the reader's cultural heritage, the sparkle and wit and fun – without, at the same time, losing too many of the landmarks that an intelligent non–classicist requires for his enjoyment of foreign poetry, then I shall feel that my task has been well worth while.[46]

XV

JUVENAL REVISITED

Y ACQUAINTANCE WITH JUVENAL – Hamlet's 'satirical rogue' – dates back, I am somewhat horrified to realise, almost half a century, so that his animadversions on the disadvantages of old age – the baboon-like wrinkles, the dripping noses, the ruined tastebuds, the sluggish sexual performance ('iacet exiguus cum ramice neruus'), and what Shakespeare, embroidering as usual on his original, sums up as 'a plentiful lack of wit, together with most weak hams'[1] – have come, in the course of time, a little too close for comfort. I was introduced to Juvenal very young, at school, by a form-master who was always going on *ad nauseam* about the virtues of good taste: a habit I had not yet learnt to identify as the sure mark of an uncreative middle-class snob and conformist. The ironic joke, of course, was that anyone less in good taste (at any rate of the mimsy genteel sort) than Juvenal it would be very hard to imagine. Two satires in, I realised I had found, in this snarling, envious sniper at corruption, social climbing, and sham pretensions, a most congenial literary companion. When my translation was first published, the anonymous reviewer for the *Times Literary Supplement*, arguing (rightly, I think) that author and translator needed a special rapport, was kind enough to say that I apparently enjoyed such a relationship with Juvenal. He then added, demurely: 'Somehow one cannot quite imagine Mr Green translating the *Little Flowers* of St Francis.'

At the impressionable, not to mention nervous, age of sixteen, then, I found myself precociously elevated into the Classical Sixth (more or less equivalent to an enhanced twelfth grade) of an English public, meaning private, school. Charterhouse in those days had not yet gone coed. It enjoyed a well-deserved reputation for turning out amateur soccer stars, mad Anglican bishops, stockbrokers either dull or crooked, blimpish major generals, classical scholars, and literary misfits such as Robert Graves or Simon Raven, this last category on the *pathei mathos* principle of attaining wisdom through suffering, an Aeschylean conceit in which I have never believed: suffering, far from producing wisdom, merely makes people self-pitying, petty-minded, and querulous. I was certainly querulous enough when our classics master, that genial literary sadist A. L. Irvine (nicknamed 'The Uncle', though never was there a less avuncular man), produced, during the first week of classes, Duff's text of Juvenal's third and tenth satires, accompanied by cyclostyled copies of Samuel Johnson's imitations, 'London' and 'The Vanity of Human Wishes', and set us to translate the Latin at sight, while committing the English to memory by way of what he termed 'a little prep' (a characteristically unacknowledged theft from Kipling). Had the phrase been then in use, I should have been tempted to describe this imposition as 'cruel and unusual punishment'.

Looking back today, though, from the safe vantage-point of age, I can see just how much *mathos* (and indeed more than mere learning: real understanding and appreciation) emerged from my baptism by philological fire. Indeed, the full realisation dawned on me very early on in the decade or so it took me – among innumerable other obligations – to complete my translation of Juvenal for Penguin Classics. As I wrote in 1967, 'this was by far the best introduction to a notoriously difficult poet that one could hope for. Sink or swim, one stumbled through the unfamiliar vocabulary and allusions; and only those who have committed, say, the passage on the fall of Sejanus to memory can really begin to appreciate Juvenal's technical virtuosity, his subtle control of rhythm and sound-effects, his dense, hard verbal brilliance:'[2]

> . . . descendunt statuae restemque sequuntur,
> ipsas deinde rotas bigarum impacta securis
> caedit, et immeritis franguntur crura caballis;
> iam strident ignes, iam follibus atque caminis
> ardet adoratum populo caput et crepat ingens
> Seianus, deinde ex facie toto orbe secunda
> fiunt urceoli pelues sartago matellae.
>
> *Sat.* 10.58–64

> . . . the ropes are hauled, down come the statues,
> axes demolish their chariot-wheels, the unoffending
> legs of their horses are broken. And now the fire
> roars up in the furnace, now flames hiss under the bellows;
> the head of the people's darling glows red-hot, great Sejanus
> crackles and melts. That face only yesterday ranked
> second in all the world. Now it's so much scrap-metal,
> to be turned into jugs and basins, frying-pans, chamber-pots.

I didn't, then, know who Sejanus was (though under threat of lengthy extra impositions I soon found out): what I recognised, immediately and by sympathetic instinct, was a master of language, a passionate dramatiser, a man with a grudge in his heart and fire in his belly, who could move me more – Catullus came later – than any Roman poet I had yet read.

This congeniality of attitude was obviously an important factor (as my *TLS* reviewer recognised) when, after many years, I set about turning Juvenal into English. At the time, however, it merely succeeded in getting me into deeper and deeper trouble with Mr Irvine. I was meant to admire Dr Johnson's frumpish Augustan pastiche: when, in an essay, I complained of the Great Cham's pompous abstractions, pumped-up Christian platitudes (for the most part ineptly optimistic, and thus anti-Juvenalian to the nth degree), as well as the middle-class sanitisation, i.e. censorship, of Juvenal's vigorous and vulgar specific details (often obscene, too, but readers of Duff weren't supposed to know that), I found myself taken to task, neither for the first nor the last time, as immature, callow, prurient, and, above all, that perennial complaint, *sadly lacking in good taste*. Times, happily, change; and recently Professor Niall Rudd – who also had the idea of juxtaposing these four poems of Johnson and Juvenal – brought virtually the same charges against 'The Vanity of Human Wishes' as I did,[3] and. far from incurring opprobrium, published his animadversions to general academic approval. But when I wrote my schoolboy objections, in 1941, the sexual and social revolution lay a long way ahead still, and my *arbiter elegantiarum* was this damnable Scotsman (at least Johnson had the right ideas there, I thought), whose Holy Trinity, often declared, consisted of Classics, Cricket, and Christianity, between which he had somehow contrived to eliminate, at least to his own satisfaction, all incompatibilities. Against this self-generated and self-fulfilling cosmos, which also managed to include Plato's *Phaedrus* and *Symposium* while denying the very existence of physical homosexuality, my adolescent slings and arrows stood very little chance. I could, and did, mock these inveterate city-dwellers for their attacks on the City, but that was a cheap shot and old-hat into the bargain.

On the other hand adolescence, fuelled and inflamed by what Dylan Thomas politely euphemised as 'the force that through the green fuse drives the flower', has always been very quick to spot, and capitalise on, instances of censorship, above all – shades of Dr Bowdler! – censorship involving sex. I and my contemporaries in the Classical Sixth very soon became experts at detecting the tactful omissions in school editions (of Aristophanes in particular) and running them to ground in the excellent school library. This was how I first acquired the basic techniques of scholarly research. Indeed, our endeavours to wrench improper secrets from what Gibbon termed 'the decent obscurity of a learned language' – endeavours not notably helped by Liddell and Scott, who merely translated them into Latin, or Lewis and Short, who, deprived of this refuge, copped out by talking in vague blanket terms of 'lewdness' or '*sens. obsc.*' – won us unmerited admiration from the somewhat other-worldly librarian, a man with a profound speech impediment, who declared himself most impressed by this singleminded pursuit of classical learning among the young. (I sometimes wonder if he was quite as innocent as he let on.) In point of fact, for all the wrong reasons, we *did* learn a good deal: not least about the hazards of translation and the seamier side of human nature.

Oddly – or perhaps not so oddly – our arcane researches brought us to Juvenal, in the first instance, by way of Martial. What Housman demurely termed 'the unpretending school edition of Mr J. D. Duff',[4] from which we worked, told us that satirist and epigrammatist were friends in Rome. Three epigrams, the first two of AD 92/3, the third datable to AD 101-2 , offered snapshots of the friends exchanging presents, of Juvenal sweating uphill in a heavy toga to pay his respects in great men's antechambers.[5] We found sex in these epigrams – more of that in a moment – but something about the indignities of the client-patron relationship, so central to Juvenal's attacks on society, also rubbed off on us. Our enquiries brought us treasure-trove in the shape of Walter Ker's two Loeb volumes of Martial, complete with parallel translations.[6] The librarian kept most Loeb volumes beyond our reach, on the (not unjustified) grounds that they would be used as illegal ponies, or trots; but since Martial, for reasons we soon discovered, was not on the curriculum, and the copies on hand had been presented by a most distin-guished Old Boy, Sir Stephen Gaselee, we managed to obtain access to them. It took us very little time to discover that all the really racy epigrams had been translated, not into English, but into *Italian* – thereby, one might suppose, slurring no less than three ethnic groups simultaneously, and causing us considerable frustration. A quick search revealed the improbable presence among us of Ezra Pound's son, who suffered under the baptismal names of Omar Shakespear, and whose upbringing in Rapallo presumed fluency in Italian. Unfortunately he turned out to be so innocent a child that even knowing Italian he had no more idea what was going on in these epigrams than we did. Dictionary and grammar in hand we managed to figure out some of them for ourselves, and found them rewarding; but our prime target (not least, I fear, as a weapon in our guerrilla warfare against Mr Irvine) was still Juvenal.

Here what struck us first was a simple matter of mathematics. Juvenal, we knew, had published sixteen satires. Duff gave us fourteen only, and inspection of the line-numbering in Satire 6 made it clear (Duff being an honest man, though perhaps not quite so averse to pretence as Housman thought) that the censor's scissors had been busily at work here too. The first major edition we found in the library was that of Professor J.E.B. Mayor (1886). We would have endorsed, had we known it, Housman's verdict on Mayor's commentary, that one turned to it for many things but not for help in trouble, since Mayor omitted Satire 6 altogether, along – naturally – with Satires 2 and 9, the ones that Duff had found over-strong meat for his young English audience. Nothing daunted, we moved on to the next edition on the shelves, that of Ludwig Friedländer (1895). Friedländer, with Teutonic thoroughness un-inhibited by English *pudeur*, had indeed written a voluminous commentary on all sixteen satires. Unfortunately, it was in German. Out came the dictionaries again: we enlisted the help of like-minded friends specialising in modern languages; we slashed away, aided by A.E. Housman's brilliantly bloody-minded edition *editorum in usum*, at the dense maquis of Juvenal's censored Latin, delighted to learn that, until Housman explicated the notorious O passage, our elders and betters had been similarly baffled by it. Our academic zeal knew no bounds. But what we found surprised and – though we would have died rather than admit this – shocked us. Martial's four-letter words and grossly comic sexual or, better, scatological situations we found vastly entertaining. 'Quis ridere potest fatui poppysmata cunni?' he asked:[7] 'Who could laugh at' – well, the last three words are perhaps better left untranslated. *We* could laugh, and did. But what we found in Juvenal was sick, and very often sick-making, disgust: *facit indignatio uersum*. Just as the weight-lifting hoyden of Satire 6 'drinks/ and spews by turns, like some big snake that's tumbled/ into a wine-vat', so Juvenal, with fascinated repulsion, kept coming back, again and again, to those aspects of Roman life – women, hypocrites, sadists, climbers – that made his sensitive gorge rise. It was an interesting and unexpected lesson.[8]

Very little has ever been written about Juvenal's *praefanda*, his rhetorical exploitation of obscenity. Perhaps this is not surprising. Yet – as I found out very young – it constitutes a major weapon in his satirical arsenal. It is also never an end in itself, but always used to attack some ulterior target: pretentiousness, avarice, cruelty. Unlike Martial, he avoids taboo words. He does not need them. In his hand ordinary language magically takes on emetic characteristics. A splendid instance of this – duly signalled to the schoolboy by Duff's truncated line-numbering – occurs in Satire 1. Juvenal is listing social anomalies that specially annoy him. Married eunuchs, topless female hunters, working-class millionaires, informers, and (my case in point) socially pushy gigolos, 'men who earn legacies in bed, who rise to the top/ via that quickest, most popular route – *uetulae uesica beatae*'.[9] I translated this 'the satisfied desires/ of some rich old matron', but my English, alas, missed the scabrous force of the Latin altogether. The alliterative contempt of the first two words is underscored by the use of the vernacular *uetulae*, for which 'old bag' might be the closest equivalent, and even more by the unique employment, in this context, of the term *uesica* – which in fact means 'bladder' – to describe this elderly lady's vagina, the clear implication being that at her age the only part of it still in effective working order is, or should be, the urinary tract. To cap everything else, *beatae* conveys a double meaning: wealthy (i.e. 'blessed' with this world's goods), and blissfully happy (i.e. experiencing orgasm). To pack all this into three words is for Juvenal a remarkable, but by no means an isolated, achievement. Perhaps the most notorious instance is the couplet in Satire 2 describing the results of Domitian's alleged incest with his niece Julia, 'cum tot abortiuis fecundam Iulia uuluam/ solueret et patruo similes effunderet offas', where, as I have pointed out,[10] the sluggish heaves and explosive bursts of the Latin irresistibly suggest uterine contractions followed by the expulsion of the embryo. [11]

My quasi-illicit exploration of the second and ninth satires, together with those parts of the sixth rejected by Duff, stimulated my curiosity in a way now highly unfashionable: it evoked the ghostly profile of a living human being, and made me want to find out more about him. In those innocent days no one had yet come forward to inform us, with peremptory assurance, that authorial intention was irrelevant, that the work was, literally, in the eye of the beholder, that critical reader-response and *Rezeptionsgeschichte* were what mattered, that judging the literary value of a poem or play in any abiding sense was a self-deluding mirage, that a menu or a seed catalogue could be deconstructed in just the same way as the *Iliad*, that the true creative artist was the translator, and that in any case the apparent 'character' of author or narrator must always be viewed as a mere literary mask, a *persona*, an artificial manipulation of traditional formalised *topoi*, i.e. rhetorical clichés. Juvenal, as readers of Professor W.S. Anderson[12] will know, has been no more immune than the next man to this kind of treatment. Though obviously useful to the extent of correcting excessive faith in what has been termed the 'biographical fallacy', this entire movement (I have to make clear from the start) strikes me as not only misconceived but positively dangerous, destruction rather than deconstruction, moral and aesthetic nihilism winding up in a literary cul-de-sac, fuelled by professional academic theorists with fond memories of the Sixties and a conscious or unconscious hatred of all creative art: intellectuals to whom the notions of absolute objective truth or sustainable moral value-judgments are, for a variety of ideological reasons, pure anathema. When I ask myself whether creator or interpreter is more important in the ultimate scheme of things (and never mind the attempt to gussy up the status of interpretation by giving it the pseudo-Hellenistic label of 'hermeneutics'[13]), then I only have to ask myself which of the two could more easily survive without the other. Mistletoe needs oak; cuckoo must find nest: the parasite cannot exist apart from its involuntary host.

This move to cut the author loose from his work, while (as I say) a salutary corrective to biographical literalism – Bundy's work on the formal and encomiastic nature of the Pindaric ode is a splendid example of the theory's virtues as well as its excesses[14] – can also be seen as a profoundly anti-historical symptom, part of the persistent assault on so-called 'bourgeois objectivism' (that honourable and far from pejorative ideal, von Ranke's aim of recapturing the past *wie es eigentlich gewesen*), the deliberate undermining of the concept of actual and retrievable truth, so often embarrassing to prophets, theorists, or ideological system-makers. If literature is no part of the historical process, but a mere intellectual game of which the rules can be refashioned by any player, wherein does its value lie, except as a suspect vehicle for academic careerism? And how can it be related to the beliefs and cultural evolution of the society that generated it, let alone to the individual whose vision drew it into being? Just how far this dissociative principle can go was lately demonstrated by a not over-imaginative English classicist, who proved, to his own satisfaction, if not to that of any historian, by *argumenta ex silentio* and a list of putative geographical and climatic errors, that Ovid was in fact never exiled to Tomis at all, but simply sat in Rome for the last decade of his life playing with the rhetoric of exilic themes. [15]

I thus have two serious strikes against me: I am an historian, which means that I believe in the objective existence of truth, and have no great faith in the binding force of critical theory; and not only do I passionately love literature, but I never forget that it was written for real people, in an actual society, at a specific point in time. My position in academe thus somewhat recalls that of Juvenal's friend Umbricius (another character whose very existence has been doubted: Umbricius, *umbra*, the shadow-man[16]), who asked: 'What can I do in Rome? I never learnt how/ to lie. If a book is bad, I cannot puff it . . ./ astrological clap-trap/ is not in my stars.'[17] All signification is *not* relative, is *not* arbitrary.[18] I do not regard it as the chief function of my profession to play literary games that generate their own rules. The retrojection of such modern theories, with a fine disregard for changing historical circumstance, on to ancient authors is something I have always found irritatingly perverse. 'The royal road to Juvenal,' wrote that old *Scrutiny* wheelhorse H.A. Mason, 'is through profound enjoyment of the poetry of Eliot and Pound.'[19] Unswerving admirer of Eliot though I have always been, I beg to differ. God knows that critics have always enjoyed telling contemporary poets how to write: but to extend their protreptic dominance to antiquity as well – unloading on it all their accumulated modern baggage, from the *persona* theory to (of course) the sovereignty of the critical reader – is an act of anachronistic arrogance that withers compassion at the root. In an excellent recent article, 'Was Juvenal a Structuralist?'[20] with the revealing sub-title 'A look at anachronisms in literary criticism', Kevin McCabe writes: 'Far from remembering that their vaunted critical standards were simply a strategy for recommending the modernist writers to an unsympathetic public, they came to think that these standards were the only appropriate criteria for judging literature of any period.' Amen to that.

The effect on Juvenal, in the last twenty years or so, has been to turn the *Satires* into a series of contrived, semi-dramatic performances, structurally exotic and wholly remote from real life, performed by a literary quick-change artist with a bundle of formal masks behind which to hide, and a bagful of moral bromides and stock rhetorical tropes or literary allusions to suit every occasion. The expression on the mask may change from savage indignation (Satires 1–6) to transitional uncertainty (Satires 7–9) and, finally, Democritean amusement with a touch of recurrent asperity (Satires 10–16),[21] yet the poet himself remains as blankly elusive, almost to the point of invisibility, as the Cheshire Cat's grin. This is not the troubled and complex individual that I began to discover as a schoolboy, with whom I lived, in increasing familiarity, for the best part of a decade as a translator, and whose work forms part of the bedrock on which European moral and social discourse still rests today. It is, however unfashionably, Juvenal himself who primarily concerns me.

Now though a creative writer – the dramatist or novelist in particular – may indeed project a variety of fictionalised mouthpieces for his or her own purposes, a recognisable personality still tends to pervade them all: in a very real sense the writer *is* all his characters. Thus though it is no accident that *persona*-theorists unduly stress the dramatic element in works (such as Juvenal's satires or Ovid's erotic poetry) which, on the face of it, offer a unified voice more or less congruent with that of the author, this does not make nearly as much difference as they suppose. In cases where the writer's life is well-documented – I am thinking especially of Byron and Eliot, who make a nice contrast in this respect – it is clear that public and private face are symbiotically related. To be sure, Byron is not identical with Juan, any more than Eliot is identical with Prufrock; but we only need try to imagine a Prufrock by Byron or a Juan by Eliot to sense the creative limits that authorial personality imposes. Eliot as hedonist, Byron as puritan: these are paradoxical humours that no one, in the face of a clear biographical record, would reasonably attempt to assert. The danger comes when, as in the case of Juvenal, the personal evidence is scanty and, in places, implausible or plain contradictory. Despite occasional nuggets of hard fact, the numerous *Lives* extant give, as a whole, the impression of having been cobbled together, largely from one another or an imperceptive reading of Juvenal's own work, by a group of dim scholiasts desperate for a few crumbs out of which to construct a biography.[22] In such circumstances, of course, a critical theory that completely removes Juvenal's work from the man himself and his historical context can be made to look extremely attractive. The temptation must, nevertheless, be resisted.

What in fact do we know about the satirist's life? Rather less, I must confess, than I thought we did twenty years ago,[23] which was not all that much even then. I still favour AD 55, indicated by one *vita*, as the year of his birth; AD 67, suggested by some on very slender grounds – Juvenal will have referred to the consulship of Fonteius Capito in that year because it was when he was born[24] – seems to me a decade too late. But the evidence of the now-lost inscription [CIL 10.5382] from Aquinum, dependent as it is on tendentious restoration, dissolves on close analysis;[25] and with it vanish the commander of Dalmatian auxiliaries (units in fact not raised till the Marcomannic wars of Marcus Aurelius[26]), the campaigns in Britain, the joint-mayor of Aquinum, the honorary priest of the deified Vespasian. The inscription almost certainly refers to a relative, but one of much later date: all we can deduce from it for our Juvenal is a family tradition of fairly prominent provincial respectability. We no longer need to rationalise Juvenal's obvious civilian-oriented anti-militarism. Aquinum (*Sat.* 3.319 combined with the inscription) was surely his birthplace. But the inscription hardly supports the claim of the best-known *vita* that he was the son or adopted son of a rich freedman, let alone (on the basis of his friendship with Martial) of a *Spanish* freedman. The family, even if not equestrian, sounds solidly bourgeois. This implausible detail may well have been borrowed from the life of Horace, who was indeed *libertino patre natus*, and made much of the fact, by a scholiast who thought all satirists carried an identical chip on their literary shoulder. Again, Juvenal's own class-conscious sneers at *arrivistes* of this sort have not been given sufficient weight. 'Quis tulerit Gracchos de seditione querentes?' he wrote (*Sat.* 2.24). And who would stand for freedmen's sons attacking social climbers?[26] On the other hand, the statement in the same *vita* that 'he was a declaimer until about middle age, more as a hobby than because he was preparing himself for a career as a professional declaimer or barrister'[27] is confirmed by a telltale phrase ('. . .et melius nos/egimus') thrown off in Satire 7 (124-5) during a long tirade on the unprofitability of a career at the bar.[28]

'There still remains,' as I wrote in 1967, 'the enigmatic problem of his exile.'[29] Time has done little to resolve the enigma. Then, I believed, like Highet,[30] that Juvenal was exiled to Egypt by Domitian, between AD 93-96, for an indiscreet attack (*Sat.*7.87-92) on an actor with extensive powers of patronage at court. This reconstruction has since come under heavy attack. It is argued, with some plausibility, that the savagery exhibited by Domitian during his latter years, in response to real or imagined slights, makes it inconceivable that Juvenal would have suffered mere exile rather than execution for his *lèse-majesté:* Helvidius Priscus and Hermogenes of Tarsus had lost their heads for far less serious offences.[31] Similarly, Juvenal would hardly have been so rash, in such a climate, as to wantonly provoke the imperial wrath after so many years of discreet silence. I agree. The trouble is that the ancient *Lives*, which contradict each other so maddeningly on almost every detail of Juvenal's supposed exile, are united in upholding the claim that he did, somewhere, at some time, for some reason, suffer banishment. If we challenge this assertion, as most modern commentators now do,[32] we need to explain how it gained credence in the first place. It is worth noting, in this context, that Juvenal himself never says one word about being exiled. This apparent reticence forms a striking contrast to the loud complaints of Cicero or Seneca during their brief relegations,[33] and *a fortiori* to the single-mindedness of Ovid, who devoted his entire literary output, for the last decade of his life, to this one theme. The argument from silence here at least merits consideration.

The one *vita* that is habitually reprinted, and is often regarded (on flimsy grounds, I feel) as the basis for all the rest, must again form our starting-point here.[34] It claims that in middle age Juvenal composed and uttered ('*dixit*', says the scholiast, which suggests private circulation), a short squib *paucorum uersuum* satirising Paris the *pantomimus* and his jobbing of commissions. There is no clear indication whether this Paris was the one who performed under Nero or his successor at the court of Domitian: both, we may note, were executed by their imperial masters, the first in 67, the second in 83.[35] However, it is generally assumed, with some plausibility, that if this attack was made, it was aimed – before 83 – at Domitian's then-living favourite, and kept very private, in the manner of *samizdat* literature today, enjoying at best a limited underground circulation. The *Life* confirms this: 'For a long time he did not venture to entrust anything even to quite a small audience.'[36] The question is, how long? Presumably at least till after the death of Domitian in 96. He then began giving highly successful readings, 'to packed audiences', *magna frequentia*. At some later point he apparently felt confident enough to insert in Satire 7 those lines (90–92) which, the *Lives* allege, got him exiled. It is true that the satire would read very well without them:

> What nobles cannot bestow, you must truck for to an actor.
> Why bother to haunt the spacious ante-rooms
> of the great? Colonels and Governors, the ballet appoints
> every man jack of them.

The last line of this squib, with reference to mythical characters portrayed in the ballet repertoire, says, literally, 'Pelopea creates Prefects, Philomela tribunes': 'praefectos Pelopea facit, Philomela tribunos'. At that time, *tum*, says the *Life*, 'there was an actor [unnamed, be it noted] who was a court favourite, and many of his fans were being promoted daily'.[37] At *what* time, we may well ask? It is generally agreed that the *princeps* to whom appeal is made, at the beginning of Satire 7, for literary patronage is Hadrian.[38] We are thus confronted with yet another paradox: that even in this new and supposedly more tolerant era, a satirist hoping for imperial preferment from a famous and touchy aesthete would go out of his way to insult one of that aesthete's favourites. Gérard, to get round this difficulty, theorises that Juvenal did not insert his squib into Satire 7 till as late as 136 or 137, when he had become disillusioned with Hadrian's meanness and Hellenising vulgarities: his target, Gérard claims, was the court favourite Titus Aelius Alcibiades, who had procured the Prefecture of Egypt – 'praefectos Pelopea facit' – for C. Avidius Heliodorus.[39] This would at least agree with the *vita*, which states that Juvenal was in his eighties at the time of exile, and was sent to Egypt as a kind of joke, to 'match his trivial and humorous offence' ('ut leui atque ioculari delicto par esset'). Another *Life* preserves the *mot* allegedly uttered by the Emperor on posting Juvenal (ostensibly as commander of a cohort, we are told, though an octogenarian!) to the Great Oasis: 'Well, Philomela's promoted *you*, too.'[40] The *Lives* all agree that Juvenal very soon died in exile 'angore et taedio', 'of vexation and disgust'.

How much, if any, of this odd story should we believe? If Juvenal *did* suffer exile, the scenario I have outlined is the only one that makes consistent historical sense of the evidence. Yet even here doubt creeps in. Why, as I said earlier, should Juvenal go out of his way to alienate Hadrian? And what Princeps in his right mind, even as a black joke, would appoint an elderly sedentary civilian commander of a cohort? Throughout these late biographical notices, composed after Juvenal came back into fashion in the fourth century AD[41] we get the unmistakable impression that (as so often with ancient authors) commentators are quarrying their subject's text to supplement an inadequate or non-existent external record. Hence the wild (and occasionally lunatic) guesses as to which Emperor – Nero? Domitian? Trajan? Hadrian? – exiled Juvenal, or even to where: Scotland figures in our sources as well as Egypt,[42] obviously because of *Sat.* 2.159-161, 'and northern Britain/ with its short clear nights'[43] – not an observation that suggests autopsy – or the knowing references in Satire 4 to British chariot-fighting and Richborough oysters.[44] It can be argued, similarly, [45] that the whole scenario of exile arose from a need to explain Juvenal's alleged presence, at an advanced age, in Egypt, and that his assignation *ad cohortis curam* by the scholiast was prompted by his concern with military matters in Satire 16, which, being unfinished, suggested to the imaginative biographer, making bricks from a bare minimum of straw, that he had died before completing it. Yet the evidence in the *Satires* of Juvenal's personal acquaintance with Egypt depends solely on an ambiguous three-word parenthesis (15.45), 'quantum ipse notaui', thrown off apropos a comparison in self-indulgence between the rural Egyptian peasant and the urban sophisticates of Canopus. The Latin strictly means 'so far as my personal observation goes',[46] i.e. 'to judge by the Egyptians I have met'. This need not have been in Egypt. Rome (as Juvenal himself stresses at xenophobic length and frequency) was jam-packed with foreigners, Egyptians included.[47] The whole picture of exile begins to look more and more like a fourth-century chimera, dreamed up by commentators who had noticed the Julio-Claudian and Flavian predilection for deporting, if not defenestrating, disrespectful scribblers, and wanted to inject a little drama into an otherwise virtually blank career.

Revisiting Juvenal, in short, has convinced me (I repeat) that we know a good deal less about him than I once supposed, and that perhaps we have sometimes been looking in the wrong places. Courtney's claim[48] that our sure knowledge 'consists solely of the evidence of Martial and the few remarks in his own writing' comes pretty close to the truth. From Martial we know that in 92/3 – long before Juvenal had gone public with his invective – the two writers were close friends. Martial praises Juvenal as *facundus*, eloquent, sends him a present of 'Saturnalian nuts' from his smallholding, inveighs against some unknown mischief-maker's attempts to cause trouble between them.[49] All this, be it noted, at the very height of Domitian's reign of terror: had Juvenal in fact incurred the Emperor's displeasure in 93, as has often been argued, the cautious Martial would never have made public admission of their friendship. Later, in 102, under Trajan, Martial from his rural retreat at Bilbilis in Spain draws a vivid picture of Juvenal engaged on the same demeaning client's round that we know so well from Satires 1, 3, and 5, none of which was published (whenever written) till about 110.[50] If Juvenal began life as an independent *rentier*, a provincial of good, perhaps even equestrian, family from Aquinum, who spent his formative years till middle-age as a literary and rhetorical dilettante, it seems clear that by the time he was fifty he had lost his capital. We do not know how, but his hysterical denunciations of gambling[51] suggest one possible answer. In old age, perhaps by inheritance or patronage, his circumstances seem to have improved again.

It is also surely significant that all three of these epigrams contain mild sexual improprieties which we can presume were to the recipient's taste. The malicious acquaintance is accused of employing his tongue for other less mentionable purposes besides the dissemination of slander. The apples in Martial's orchard have been bestowed upon *lasciuis puellis*, randy girls, by ithyphallic Priapus, the garden god, with his *mentula luxuriosa*: and, most interestingly, the delights of country living that Martial enumerates for his city-bound friend include an adolescent *uenator*, 'a huntsman, the sort that you'd want to have off in some secret glade'.[52] By a somewhat circuitous route we have arrived back at Satires 2, 6, and 9, and Juvenal's attitude to sex. Martial's cute young huntsman reminds us of Juvenal's recommendation – set parenthetically in a misogynistic torrent of abuse against women and marriage – that it's much better to sleep with boys, who don't quarrel with you in bed, nag you for presents, or complain because your sexual athleticism lacks a truly Priapic dimension.[53] Martial, it seems clear, knew his friend's tastes. But, it will instantly be objected, what about Juvenal's notorious *attacks* on homosexuality? Close scrutiny of these at once reveals that, insofar as the satirist is castigating sexual perversion *per se* (rather than hypocrisy, avarice, meanness, or breach of class protocol), what excites his anger and contempt – a highly conventional reaction – is the adult invert, the transvestite queen, the middle-aged or elderly *fellator*, above all the habitually sodomised, those whom Aristophanes labelled the *euryproktoi*, with their smooth, enlarged, and depilated rear passages.[54] For Naevolus, the 'two-legged donkey' (*bipedem asellum*), the bisexual male prostitute of Satire 9, Juvenal has nothing but sympathy, as a short-changed fellow-client; it is the donkey's stingy employer, the bitch-queen Virro, who really excites his fury. Here, as in so many other respects, Juvenal shows himself a stickler for respectable ancient mores. Like any Greek *kalos k'agathos,* of the archaic or classical period, he restricted the legitimate object of homosexual affections to the adolescent boy, *eromenos* or *pusio*, prescribed by tradition. Beyond the first beard lay forbidden territory. Not for him the adult gay lifestyle: Juvenal was a straight, buttoned-down, middle-class social pederast.

Yes, but, I can hear the post-Andersonian critic complaining, are not all these attitudes a series of well-known literary conventions, aspects of the traditional satirical *persona*? The answer, of course, is that some of them are and some of them aren't, and the student of Juvenal must learn to distinguish between the two sorts. Juvenal's undoubted bookishness, his immense debt to his literary predecessors,[55] should not blind us to the human profile that his work can be made to yield. Indeed, the very *nature* of that bookishness can provide us with valuable pointers. A most striking example is provided by his various attacks on vice in high places, particularly at the Imperial court. It is these that lack personal knowledge, that smell of the literary lamp. The effeminate Otho prinking before battle comes from Juvenal's contemporaries Suetonius and Tacitus, reinforced with a parodic dash of Virgil.[56] Satire 4, which portrays Domitian's cabinet solemnly deliberating about a giant turbot, seems to have been a parody of Statius' *De Bello Germanico*.[57] Much of Juvenal's scabrous anecdotage about the Claudians is drawn from Tacitus or Seneca;[58] it has been plausibly argued[59] that the lurid personal material untraceable to these sources – above all Messalina awaiting her clients in the brothel, or 'marrying' young Gaius Silius[60] – was drawn from the lost *Memoirs* of Agrippina, thus explaining his otherwise puzzling 'sensational and intimate knowledge of private matters in the palace'.[61] Juvenal's acquaintance with Imperial and court scandal came at second or third hand. For him one vicious emperor was very like another: I doubt very much whether he ever met one in the flesh. His notorious proposal to use *exempla* from among 'the famous dead, whose ashes/rest beside the Latin and the Flaminian ways'[62] was logical enough, since whether his subjects were dead or alive, he took all material of this sort from books anyway.

No: where Juvenal reveals personal experience, with unforgettable passion and vividness, is in the unique montage he offers us of day-to-day life in Rome, viewed through the acerbic eyes of a class-conscious, resentful, well-read, xenophobic, envious, slightly down-at-heels provincial poet, who perhaps had once enjoyed a modest competence, went through a spell of shabby poverty in his fifties, and towards the end of his life seems to have found some kind of financial security once again. The house in Rome – apparently a family legacy –, the little farm out at Tivoli, with its homespun servants, the relaxed tone of meditation that marks many of the later satires: these things are not, surely, mere calculated literary affectations, designed to enhance a new *persona*.[63]

On the other hand they do offer a striking change from the demeaning daily round of the impoverished client that is confirmed for us by Martial and plays so large a part in Juvenal's earlier work. We see this wretched creature snubbed by scornful gigolos, shoved off the ladder of preferment by crooks and con-men, scrambling for scrappy hand-outs from contemptuous patrons, in competition with ex-slaves, public officials and malingerers; too honest to lie, too class-bound to do a job of work, sneering at astrology, with a conscience that refuses to aid and abet adulterers, murderers, or provincial governors on the make; bitching away about slippery Greek arrivistes, Stoic informers, and the *captatores* who do poor clients out of hoped-for legacies;

exposed to unpleasant ridicule on account of his dirty patched toga, his split and cobbled shoes; living in hope of a favourable glance from some scornful patron, indifferent if not actively sadistic; scared in his garret at the prospect of being roasted alive in one of Rome's all-too-frequent fires, or having a jerry-built apartment house collapse about his ears; deafened by Rome's ceaseless clamour, mud-spattered and crowded in the streets, the target for slops and worse from upper windows and physical assault at the hands of young bloods; fobbed off at dinner with cheap and nasty food while his so-called host gorges himself on rich delicacies; snarling away at the mercenary rapacity of women, as cynical as Dr Johnson over the hazards and meannesses of literary patronage, the niggardly rewards won by poets; sniping enviously, in the name of virtue-the-true-nobility, at blue-blooded pedigrees.[64] *Tranquillitas*, we may feel, does not arrive one moment too soon.

It has often been alleged[65] that the picture of Roman society presented by Juvenal differs so radically from that to be found in the correspondence of his exact contemporary, the Younger Pliny, as to cast serious doubt on the accuracy of the satirist's observation. Melodramatic fiction, in short, served up by a Jeremiah-like *persona* who tears into corruption with all the relish of a vulture working its way through ripe carrion. This, of course, is both imperceptive and tendentious. No one would doubt – to take a modern parallel – that George Orwell and Harold Nicolson both recorded their honest impressions of England in the Thirties and Forties, or that they enjoyed a very similar upper-class education: yet they happened to inhabit totally different worlds. So with Juvenal and Pliny: the well-heeled and well-connected administrator-cum-*littérateur* who corresponded with, and undertook diplomatic missions for, the Emperor Trajan, saw a very different side of things from the shabby Grub Street pederast in pursuit of hand-outs and patronage. Where Pliny understood the realities of power, and could deal with the Princeps as a human being, Juvenal was restricted to the near-abstract moral caricatures formulated by nostalgic crypto-Republican fellow-writers. The difference was fundamental.

It is no accident, I feel, that in my reconsideration of Juvenal what has changed most is my assessment of the major landmarks in his life, which, as we have seen, all depend on highly suspect *external* evidence: the dubiously restored Aquinum inscription, *Lives* manufactured to create what fourth-century commentators saw as an appropriate background for an 'opposition poet' who grew up under Nero and the Flavians, above all under Domitian.[66] This fictional character, so officially respectable, with his military commands, his provincial *pietas*, the *cachet* of a virtuous exile – *two* exiles, if we are to believe an ingenious thesis out of Rumania[67] – stands in total contradiction to the peevish threadbare urban scribbler, the anti-militaristic civilian, the nasty misogynist and nagging moral grumbler who emerges from the *Satires* themselves. This prickly figure I first got to know as a schoolboy; the enforced intimacy of translation deepened our familiarity; and visiting with him again in our common old age – these days I too prefer peaceful sunbathing to the races[68] – has simply reinforced my original estimate of all his idiosyncrasies.

Such personal character-hunting is, as I am well aware, a no-no in contemporary literary studies. This does not bother me overmuch. With a satirist in particular we need to know the individual motives, *uotum, timor, ira, uoluptas*, the overall moral and psychological stance determining his angle of attack, his special prejudices and obsessions. Where, as they say, is Juvenal coming from? The random, ad hoc quality noticeable in so much modern scholarship on his work is largely due to a failure to face this fundamental problem; and there are many theses and articles that make much more sense when viewed against the central – and highly modern – paradox of his character.[69] Juvenal was a typical product of his age in that he regarded his society, above all its class-system, as a fixed, immutable datum. This was one of the first facts I ever grasped about him. Twenty years ago I wrote:[70] 'His approach to any social problem is, basically, one of static conservatism. He may have thought that the client-patron relationship was fundamentally degrading [or, as I would now argue, had been debased from its original grounding in *amicitia*[71]], but he never envisaged its abolition . . . His most violent invective . . is reserved for those who, in one way or another, threaten to disrupt the existing pattern of society, to inject some mobility[72] and dynamism into the class-structure.' Hence the attacks on arrivistes and social climbers, all of whom threaten not only the fixed order of things, but Juvenal's own position as a *déclassé*, but still gentlemanly, *rentier*.[73] This is no freedman's son; indeed, the freedman's son is one of his most dangerous competitors.

The paradox, of course, lies in the irreconcilable contrast between his necessarily romanticised view of the past (from which the present always in the *Satires* represents a moral decline) and the detached urban sophistication to which he was heir, and which constantly drove him to debunk the traditional myths and shaggy primitivism that formed part and parcel of the *mos maiorum*, the peasant Republicanism of the old days that he was constantly proclaiming as his ideal.[74] This is a dilemma with which we are uncomfortably familiar today: our emotions, too, demand comforting traditional beliefs, against which our intellect and reason obstinately rebel. The antique code of conduct on which Juvenal bases his moral judgments is summed up in Book III of Cicero's *De Officiis*:[75] those farming virtues of small town thrift and hard work that had scant relevance, in his day, to what Horace termed the 'fumum et opes strepitumque Romae', the smoke and wealth and clamour of the City.[76] A perilous gap had opened up between sentimental moral dream and political reality. Hence the yearning back to a Golden Age, the endless charges of corruption and decline, the jeremiads against Rome's socially destructive loss of simplicity and poverty, the commercialisation of *officium* (public and personal responsibility), the emergence of moneyed upstarts, the abrogation of principle by scions of the old aristocracy.[77] Juvenal, as Courtney says, can neither understand nor tolerate 'the fact that change in Rome's role necessarily changed the nature of the community and the city; Roman writers, convinced that "moribus antiquis res stat Romana uirisque" [that Rome's welfare was rooted in her ancient traditions and manpower], often seem to wish to put the clock back without surrendering the time gained'.[78] Juvenal's complex and dramatic sense of irony[79] failed to perceive the inherent contradiction in which he was involved. But we can understand it today, all too well; and on that understanding – social and moral even more than literary – any real appreciation of the Satires must, ultimately, be based.[80]

XVI

MEDIUM AND MESSAGE RECONSIDERED: THE CHANGING FUNCTIONS OF CLASSICAL TRANSLATION

T
HAT TRANSLATION has always been a crucial element in the transmission of Western culture is, of course, a truism. In the Renaissance Giordano Bruno was reported by Florio to have asserted that 'from translation all Science had its offspring'. Samuel Daniel's preparatory poem to Florio's own version of Montaigne has a memorable phrase about the 'intertraffique of the mind'. Goethe, whose work in this field ranged through Spanish, Italian, English, French, Persian and Slavic as well as classical Latin and Greek, wrote to Carlyle (July 1827): 'Say what one will of the inadequacy of translation, it remains one of the most important and valuable concerns in the whole of world affairs.'[1] (A cynic might remark that whatever he translated, from whatever language, turned somehow into more or less pure Goethe, but no matter.) It remains true, what is more, that to a quite extraordinary extent the world concern Goethe spoke of has been concentrated on a cluster of classical Ur-texts: 'If, as Whitehead pronounced,' writes George Steiner[2], 'Western philosophy is a footnote to Plato, our epic tradition, verse theatre, odes, elegies, and pastoral are mainly a footnote to Homer, Pindar, and the Greek tragedians.' It should, then, illuminate the condition of this classical heritage to examine the role which translation has played in its transmission. Is it, after all, an unmixed blessing?

Perhaps I should state, at the outset, my qualifications – such as they are – for attempting so herculean a task: not for purposes of self-promotion, but rather to warn my audience, beforehand, where my prejudices are likely to lie. For over thirty years now I have practised, among other things, the functions of professional translator and professional ancient historian – an unusual, but I think profitable, combination. As a translator I have tackled poetry – both ancient and modern – fiction, and several areas of scholarship, working variously in Latin, French, Italian, and both ancient and modern Greek. Like most such practitioners, I have not found translation theory – in particular its more recent linguistic, structural, and semiotic manifestations[3]– of much enlightenment or assistance. The theorising seems largely irrelevant; its few practical recommendations are either platitudinous or jejune; the jargon[4] is pretentious, obfuscatory, often misleading, and wholly unnecessary; while the definitions are perhaps most kindly describable as random attributes. One of the more seriously regarded theorists[5] offers the following as the six basic types of literary translation: (i) phonemic, i.e. capture the sound: (ii) semantic equivalence, i.e. get the meaning: (iii) verse into prose: (iv) prosodic, i.e. capture the metre: (v) render the source text – whatever its nature – into rhyming verse: (vi) translate verse into verse, though not necessarily into analogous metre. The six are treated as mutually exclusive. Comment on the arbitrary ingredients of this Irish stew would be superfluous.

It is in my capacity as an historian that such problems concern me most deeply. My introductory chapter (pp 15 ff above) laid stress on the foreshortening of human perspective induced by a rejection of the past, which meant, also, a comparable turning away from the legacy that past has bequeathed to us. I would like, now, to take my argument a little further. History is, ultimately, dependent on words, on what has been termed 'a selective use of the past tense'. Historians, through their successive and partial recreations of past culture, build up, layer by layer, a multifaceted image or icon of the Graeco-Roman complex from which all Western civilisation is, ultimately, derived. Our grasp on that civilisation depends, in the last resort, on successive acts of translation or interpretation. Yet each generation's interpretation differs: every reading is made from a 'distinctive angle of vision'.[6] This was what Croce meant when he claimed that all history is contemporary history. What is more, the functions of historian and translator tend to overlap, especially when dealing with the ancient world. Each time I study a Greek inscription, or puzzle over the narrative conventions of Thucydides, or attempt to elucidate the social niceties underlying Cicero's private correspondence, I find myself (as one distinguished modern historian puts it) 'becoming more and more the translator in the technical sense'.[7] The languages, that is, remain crucial.

The historian, moreover, has a responsibility which the literary critic does not, and which today, indeed, cuts clean across fashionable critical mores: he must (to quote Steiner again) 'determine not only *what* was said . . . but what was *meant* to be said', whereas for the critic 'there is a sense in which successive misreadings or imitative reenactments of a literary text constitute a new yet possibly valid "meaning".'[8] The historian, in short, is committed to a belief in at least the partial retrieval of truth, rather than to a game which sets up its own rules: though, by a nice paradox, his guidelines, more often than not, will be, in the last resort, axiomatic fictions themselves. Like the experimental scientist, the historian is, or should be, acutely aware that he constitutes a mutable factor in his own operations, and remains always a victim, however unwilling, of the principle of observer error. Still, this at least leaves him more resigned to the inevitability of each generation or culture interpreting the world afresh in its own terms and (perhaps more important) for its own benefit. Steiner's examples – 'The Platonism of the Renaissance [he writes] is not that of Shelley, Hölderlin's Oedipus is not the Everyman of Freud or the limping shaman of Lévi-Strauss,' etc.[9] – represent for any serious historian a mere string of platitudes. The past is, can only be, viewed through the refractory, and constantly changing, lens of the present.[10]

At the same time, the evolution of this endless struggle to grasp and communicate our cultural roots, from Graeco-Roman antiquity through the Middle Ages and Renaissance down to our own times, clearly possesses enormous historical and emotional significance for us. Interpretation is at the heart of the matter throughout. How did translators' ideals and motives and principles change in their changing cultural context? Why, at any given point, was one work, or type of work, selected rather than another? How significant were the choices, or – perhaps even more important – the omissions? To what extent was translation in the Renaissance and later influenced by principles established in Graeco-Roman times? What can we learn from the censorship, tacit or open, of sensitive material, or the silent addition of matter not to be found in the original text? I find it interesting (to say the least) that almost no one has tackled this aspect of what non-historians sometimes refer to as the 'diachronic hermeneutic', and that those few who have [11] virtually ignore its socio-historical dimension. Worse, they run its time-factor through a kind of scrambler, so that all places and periods, from Ciceronian Rome through Renaissance Italy and Dryden's London to modern Paris, are liable to jostle together in the same paragraph. This may strike a blow for synchronicity, but it is highly frustrating for those of us who are old-fashioned enough to believe that what one should do in such cases is to begin at the beginning, go on to the end, and then stop.

It is noteworthy that there are certain features in the history of translation which recur, unchanged, from antiquity to the present day. Perhaps the most constant, certainly the most indisputable (though often disputed), is the sense that wholly successful translation is impossible, a contradiction in terms. This melancholy truth has run into a lot of flak lately from advocates of the Exact Translation Hypothesis [ETH], according to which 'anything that can be said in one natural language can be translated exactly into any other language',[12] an axiom also of machine-translation theorists. Such theorists – as opposed to practitioners – are loath to admit that their science (as they maintain) or exact art (as others more correctly argue) exists only as a crutch for human infirmity: that the sole reason they are in business is the curse of Babel, the inability of the vast majority of mankind to understand other people's languages. The Buddhist sage Kumarajiva[13] put it in a nutshell: 'Translation,' he declared, 'is just like chewing food that is to be fed to others. If one cannot chew food oneself, one has to be given food that has been already chewed. Such food however is bound to be poorer in taste and flavour than the original.' Dante, Samuel Johnson, Mme Dacier, Von Humboldt and many others, in all periods, have made the same point.[14] When an English critic told Anatole France 'that translation was an impossible thing', he replied: 'Precisely, my friend: the recognition of that truth is a necessary preliminary to success in the art.'[15]

Some linguists and philosophers, indeed, would carry the argument even further and claim that not merely translation, but *all* communication is impossible.[16] While in theory this may be true, life, practically speaking, has to go on. Translation, like politics, remains the art of the possible, however flawed or incomplete, and to dismiss its validity 'because it is not always possible and never perfect is absurd'.[17] Indeed, one of translation's more striking historical features has always been its robust indifference to theory as such. Even Louis Kelly is forced to admit that 'had translation depended for its survival on theory, it would have died out long before Cicero'. [18] It has indeed been doubted whether the theorists (who anyway seem more interested in savaging each other's papers) even really believe in their own theories,[19] or whether translation exists in the abstract at all, rather than as an accumulated body of praxis.[20]

Such doubts strike me as both realistic and sensible. What they imply is not so much a supposed Anglo-Saxon aversion to theory *per se* – something translation theorists have not been slow to allege[21] – as, rather, an understanding that the business of translation, with all its inadequacies and ad hoc makeshift compromises, is simply not amenable to the kind of consistent rational systematisation that any overall theory presupposes. Attempts to circumvent this obstacle by arguing that translation theory merely aims 'to reach an understanding of the processes undertaken in the act of translation, and not, as is so commonly misunderstood, to provide a set of norms for effecting the perfect translation'[22] – i.e., that it should be descriptive rather than prescriptive – are somewhat disingenuous: even a taxonomy, in the last resort, offers a normative structure. And what are the chances, anyway, of an accumulation of metaphrastic practices achieving taxonomic status? There is, indeed, a fundamental frustration familiar, and peculiar, to all working translators, engendered by the intellectual recognition of inherent and irremediable inadequacy. It has even been suggested[23] that this gives rise to 'a particular sadness . . . a special *miseria* of translation, a melancholy after Babel'.*Post paraphrasin triste omne animal.*

Be that as it may, such a recognition highlights the limitations of translation theory, and explains the historical rarity of new or basic theoretical pronouncements on the subject.[24] While technical working hints abound, for over two and a half millennia there has been virtually no change in the narrow range of options agreed on as available for the translator, or in the equally circumscribed conflict over just what translation – literary translation in particular – could, or should, attempt to achieve. Such consistency at least deserves our serious consideration. It also suggests, with some force, that translation theorists in particular may have been asking the wrong questions. When we have examined all the linguists' diagrams – platitudes done up to resemble electric circuits – when we have ploughed through the obiter dicta on signifiers and signified, coding and decoding, Karl Buhler's symbols, symptoms, and signals,[25] deep structures, contextualisation, *langue* and *parole*, *Sprachvermittlung*, polyvalence, and the rest of the jargon, what still emerges is a simple, constant oscillation between the two opposed poles of close fidelity (linguistic, stylistic, semantic, or any of these in combination), and autonomous, creative embellishment, with strategic equivalence lurking somewhere in the middle as a pragmatic compromise.[26] Letter and spirit, sense vs. literalism, Lefevere's 'reader-oriented' or 'text-oriented' versions[27] – the same basic binary opposition declares itself throughout.

The one brute fact of which every practising translator is acutely conscious, but theorists occasionally tend to forget, is that whatever text is produced will not, in any sense, be the original.[28] No translator, however ingenious, can reproduce the sound-patterns of an alien tongue: attempts at so-called 'phonemic translation', of which the Zukofsky Catullus remains the most notorious example, are mere grotesque curiosities. 'Et qui sis, fama loquetur anus', Catullus wrote: 'And that old woman Rumour will tell what you are.' What does the phonemic version give us? 'Wait queer, Sis Fame'll liquidate your anus.'[29] We are forcibly reminded of the alien barriers between languages, the grim *raison d'être* of translations as such, the wishful thinking embodied in the myth of Babel – one universal prelapsarian language to replace the 5000-odd at present spoken, a return to the Golden Age *Ursprache* of Eden.[30] Other aspects of the case are not much better. Prosodic equivalence between a language governed by metrics and one dependent on stress-rhythms is chancy at best; in a confrontation between irreconcilable conventions (e.g. to rhyme or not to rhyme) it is the foreign original which more often than not loses out. Familiarity may sometimes breed contempt, but it is also seductively comforting. Worse, every autonomous language generates its own socio-cultural matrix, often in the form of stubbornly recalcitrant idioms which resist all attempts at close verbal transference, and force even the 'text-oriented' translator, however conscientious, into the cultural-equivalence game, dressing up his foreign source in a recognisable domestic guise. Confronted with *l'esprit de l'escalier*, he cannot, if he wants to stay in business, talk about 'the spirit of the staircase'. The vivid idioms of contemporary Greek offer even worse challenges to the literal minded. What is to be done about a language which indicates the rejection of a suitor by announcing that he is eating macaroni pie, pulls the snake out of the hole rather than chestnuts out of the fire, and declares 'It's raining over there' (*péra vréchei*), not by way of warning us to carry an umbrella, but to show that the speaker just couldn't care less?

All this, of course, assumes objectivity and honesty in the translator, a rarer condition than might be supposed. Thus there is, as I have suggested, a certain element of unreality about the questions regularly asked. Should the translator's object be to convey the alien quality of his original, however much violence that may do to the language into which he is translating, and the culture it represents? Or should he rather follow the example of Denham and Dryden,[31] and make Homer or Virgil speak as he imagines they might have done had they been born in the translator's own nation and age? Despite much debate, an historian, surveying the evidence down the ages, might well argue that the translator has not, on the face of it, got much choice in the matter; that *whichever* position he assumes, the result will be much the same: a reflection, not of the alien culture he is transposing, but of his own age and social context. The translator, in fact, is far more preconditioned than he knows. I shall return to this point later [see p.268]. Before we flatter ourselves, as during the past twenty or thirty years we have tended to, that nowadays we respect our originals more than our predecessors did, we might reflect on the literary accident (it is nothing more) that after Eliot, Pound, H.D. and the Imagists, unrhymed free verse, of a kind that looked vaguely like an Aeschylean chorus or the triadic strophes of Pindar, was assimilated into the English poetic repertoire, so that translators soon found an obvious, *and accepted*, new option available to them.[32] Their apparent fidelity (for which they took the credit) was still governed by contemporary fashion.

This brings us back, by a somewhat circuitous route, to the preservation of our classical heritage. It is a cliché today that, while fewer and fewer people are proficient in Latin and Greek, the availability of ancient literature in translation is at its peak: has, indeed, become an essential element in the teaching of countless university courses. To some extent, of course, the illusory nature of this process – even, perhaps especially, in the case of good literary translations – is recognised, if not stressed. We all know that any student, say, who thinks that he or she is getting *echt* Pindar from the Lattimore version, and then compares that with Bowra, and both with Nisetich (let alone with the Greek text) is in for a rude shock. Philosophers have always been uneasily aware that to teach Plato or the Presocratics in translation was asking for trouble: cognate words have shifted their meaning, semantic implications are fiercely disputed, current social, moral, even political or religious assumptions are liable to infect even the most judicious version. Francis Cornford emphasised this wittily when he remarked, apropos *Republic* 549B, that 'one who opened Jowett's version at random and lighted on the statement that the best guardian for a man's "virtue" is "philosophy tempered with music", might run away with the idea that, in order to avoid irregular relations with women, he had better play the violin in the intervals of studying metaphysics'. He adds: 'There may be some truth in this; but only after reading widely in other parts of the book would he discover that it was not quite what Plato meant.'[33]

In any case, to lay such stress as is at present fashionable on the purely linguistic and literary problems of translation (which, as we have seen, are both limited and unchanging) tends to distract attention from larger, more affective issues. Historically speaking, the temptations, both conscious and unconscious, facing any serious translator are legion. Cornford, for instance, was too polite to ask just how much Jowett's militant Christianity had affected his interpretation of Plato, even the vocabulary he used: the answer is, a very great deal.[34] The same is true, *a fortiori*, of Victorian approaches to Aeschylean Zeus-oriented plays such as the *Agamemnon* or *Prometheus*, in which the Father of Gods and Men tended to feature as a kind of lightly Hellenised monotheistic Jahweh, beneficent or vengeful according to circumstance. The *Prometheus*, of course, has also been peculiarly vulnerable to Marxist distortions. Translations can be, and often are, censored or slanted for political no less than religious reasons: the various versions of, say, *Das Kapital* or *Mein Kampf* are highly revealing in this respect.

Sometimes the act of translation in itself, as with Tyndale's Bible, is a perilous gesture, a literal matter of life or death: one thinks, today, of the *samizdat* literature circulating clandestinely in Russia. In 1546 Etienne Dolet was burnt at the stake for attributing to Plato, in his version of the *Axiochus* and the *Hipparchus*, a disbelief in the immortality of the soul.[35] As Highet observed,[36] 'this must be one of the most drastic punishments for mistranslation ever recorded'. Today the risks remain. In 1945 the Japanese government responded to the Allies' ultimatum after Potsdam with a statement containing the word *mokusatsu*, meaning that response to the proposal would be *delayed* pending discussion. But the translation received in Washington suggested that the proposal would be *ignored*; and this, seen in the context of earlier Japanese intransigence, may well have helped to seal the fate of Hiroshima and Nagasaki.[37] Similarly, during the US-Iranian hostage negotiations of 1980-81 (conducted variously in English, Farsi, French and Arabic), a Persian noun that could mean anything from 'guarantee' to 'understanding' was taken one way in London, the other in Tehran.[38] More often, fortunately, such *malentendus* do no more than generate unkind cross-cultural laughter. One remembers the American interpreter for President Carter in Warsaw who made him say 'When I abandoned [rather than 'left'] the US', and talk of the Poles' 'lusts' instead of their 'longings';[39] not to mention the version of the slogan 'Come alive with Pepsi' prepared for the Chinese, which meant, literally 'Pepsi brings your ancestors back from the grave'.[40]

The classical corpus has not been exposed, quite, to hazards of this sort (hostile critics of Pound's *Homage to Sextus Propertius* might differ), but its very real vicissitudes in translation have certainly been as much social, political and religious as literary or linguistic. Communication has always been a weapon, and very often the prime aim with the message is to scramble it. The Babel myth is instructive in this respect. 'Go to, let us go down, and there confound their language, that they may not understand one another's speech.'[41] The early history of the Near East suggests, at best, a limited use of translation, and for a narrow range of functions (which are, however, revealing and symptomatic). Religious texts (including the Sumerian epic of Gilgamesh, if epic is the right name for it) were translated into Hurrian and, later, Hittite. The same is true of the law-code of Hammurabi. The Tell-el-Amarna letters of the late Bronze Age testify to the need then, as always, for competent diplomatic interpreter-translators between governments: the curious use of Akkadian, in cuneiform, as an international language had its drawbacks.[42] The Library of Assurbanipal in seventh-century Nineveh contained a variety of medical and magical texts in translation. But the most striking example of translation from this area and period is the great inscription which in 518 BC Darius I of Persia set up at Behistun, and copies of which were distributed throughout the empire. This was Darius' self-promoting, and possibly tendentious, autobiographical testament, prepared in Persian, Elamite, Akkadian, and 'in Aryan, which was not done before'.[43] In 522 Darius had been the King's spear-bearer in Egypt.[44] A year later, after much fierce fighting against an alleged pretender who may have been a genuine claimant to the throne, he was established as King himself. Scholars still debate whether Darius was a liar and usurper or the true restorer of the Achaemenid line.[45] But in either case, what we have here is a classic instance of translation as political propaganda.

What is more, the overall pattern that emerges from these various instances offers a clear foretaste of things to come. The prime concerns are religious, legalistic, diplomatic, practical, prescriptive. The message is all-important, the medium scarcely considered. The problems normally associated with translation thus scarcely arise. We are so used to thinking of it as a primarily *literary* phenomenon that we often forget how modern a development this is, how small a role aesthetics played in translation until the eighteenth century. What we assume to be literary appreciation more often than not turns out, on closer inspection, to be a quest for practical advice or moral protreptics. The Greeks, convinced that their own culture and language were the only ones worth having, and that the definition of a barbarian was a person who *did not speak Greek*, but rather chose to go *ba-ba-ba* in some inferior lingo of his own, followed their reasoning (as always) to its logical conclusion, and translated almost nothing from any other tongue.[46] This is particularly striking in the case of Ptolemaic Egypt, which had a rich literature of its own, totally ignored by the culture-conscious Greek intellectuals of Alexandria. Such translations into Greek as we find are made by Egyptian interpreters, and consist for the most part of flattering decrees issued by the native priesthood in honour of their current Macedonian overlord.[47] Once again, literary translation is conspicuous by its absence. The obvious apparent exception is Ptolemy II's commissioning of the Septuagint; but this too lacked aesthetic inspiration, being a Greek version of Scripture made for Alexandria's Jewish community, which had by now largely forgotten its Hebrew and Aramaic.[48]

The true literary breakthrough (though still encumbered to a striking degree with practical, moral, and political considerations) only came with the absorption of the Greek world by Rome, when in return, as Horace wrote,[49] 'captive Greece captivated her savage victor, and brought the arts into rustic Latium'. The process was haphazard, epidemic, and the fruit of violence and rapine. Livius Andronicus (c.284-204 BC) marks its beginning. He was a half-Greek, half-Italian schoolmaster, the product of bilingual Magna Graecia. Brought to Rome as a slave after the capture of Tarentum in 272, he continued to teach, and about 250 produced the first Latin *Odyssey* for his pupils.[50] This was in the old Roman accentual line known as the Saturnian, roughly the equivalent to the nursery-rhyme 'The Queen was in her parlour † eating bread and honey'. The Greek hexameter had not yet been transplanted to Rome. Over two centuries later Horace records that Livius' *Odyssey* was still a school text. Extant fragments reveal that Livius sometimes expanded, sometimes mistranslated his original, and also started the practice of converting Greek into Roman deities, so that Poseidon becomes Neptune, Kronos Saturn, Zeus Jupiter. Again, the pointers are significant. The transposition of metre and myth into local terms started a fashion of cultural equivalence that has had enormous influence; while the notion of translation as an exercise for schoolchildren or students is central to the rhetorical principles handed down by Cicero, Horace and Quintilian to the Middle Ages and the Renaissance.[53] Perhaps the most important aspect of the latter practice is that it concentrates exclusively on the interests of the translator, and ignores even a hypothetical audience. This, too, was a development with lasting consequences.

Rome's acclimatisation to Greek culture was rapid. Each victory in South Italy, Sicily or Greece – Syracuse (212), Capua (211), Cynoscephalae (197), Pydna (168), the Achaean League (146) – brought in a fresh flood of looted pictures, statues, and manuscripts, a new wave of educated Greek slaves to teach the children of Rome's upper classes. The first private library in Rome, based on spoils taken from King Perseus of Macedon, was founded by Aemilius Paullus in 167.[54] Nearly a century later, Sulla ransacked Athens for MSS of Aristotle and Theophrastus.[55] By Cicero's day the educational process had gone so far that any well-bred person was expected to be fluent in Greek as a matter of course: the well-to-do acquired the equivalent of a university education in Athens. Thus the key to Roman translation and translation theory of the Augustan age is bilingualism: 'The translated text was read *through* the source text',[56] in sharp contrast to the position of monoglot readers restricted to the translation itself. This fact – since the pronouncements of Cicero, Horace and Quintilian in particular were highly influential on later practitioners, such as St Jerome – very often, as we shall see, came to dominate the thinking of translators in periods when it was highly inappropriate: that is, when the prime need was for vernacular translations aimed at those with no Latin or Greek whatsoever.

To our way of thinking the prescriptive advice associated with Cicero and his immediate successors is elementary enough. While preparing a version of the Greek orator Aeschines, Cicero emphasised that his aim was to catch the essential substance and style, not translating Greek terms literally, even though approximating to them in type, 'and following the words only insofar as they do not offend against Roman idiom'[57] – a revealing caveat. Elsewhere in the same essay [58] he puts the anti-literalist case with even greater concision: 'I have not felt obliged to render word for word; but I have kept intact the style and force of the language.' Horace in his *Art of Poetry*[59] echoes this advice: 'As a faithful interpreter you will not be at pains to translate word for word.' At the same time he exhorts his readers, would-be writers above all, to keep Greek models in mind twenty-four hours of the day.[60] For a Roman man of letters or rhetorician Greek literature was there to be copied, imitated, translated, paraphrased, and perhaps, with luck, improved on. Translation, it was held, enriched the native tongue. Thus the embellishment factor was always strong, and translation of this sort tended to be viewed primarily as a *literary exercise*,[61] for the bilingual translator's own benefit. Examples include Catullus' slick versions of Sappho and Callimachus, mimetic *jeux d'esprit* facilitated by the close structural and metrical congruence between Latin and Greek, [62] and, in a less direct sense, Horace's imitations and metrical adaptations of the Aeolic poets and Archilochus.[63]

Yet such specifically literary translations formed no more than a limited sub-group of those known from the Roman world. Popular entertainment created its own demands. Greek New Comedy was raided, without compunction, for plots (much as Shakespeare in turn was to ransack North's Plutarch), and freely revamped for the amusement of coarse Roman audiences,[64] in a process aptly known, from its habit of purloining passages belonging to different plays and running them together, as *contaminatio*. Then as now, too, pornography was much in demand. About 100 BC L. Cornelius Sisenna translated the erotic *Milesian Tales* of Aristeides: Roman officers on active service used to carry copies in their baggage,[65] as their modern counterparts carry the products of the Olympia Press. There was a steady flow, as always, of technical treatises. The Carthaginian Mago's handbook on agriculture was put into Latin by order of the Senate. Pompey's freedman, the scholar Pompeius Lenaeus, translated a number of medical documents acquired along with the treasure of Mithridates.[67] Cicero may have spent time wrestling with what Lucretius termed the 'poverty of his native tongue' ('patrii sermonis egestas') in order to force Plato into a Latin that lacked adequate philosophical vocabulary;[68] but by far his best-known translation, of which later versions were also produced by Germanicus, Statius' father, and Avienus, was that versified astronomical handbook, somewhere between a star-chart and Old Moore's Almanac, the *Phaenomena* of Aratus.[69] Since this was heavily laced with Stoic cosmologising, it had a double attraction: practical know-how reinforced with moral uplift. The same formula was precisely what most attracted the translators of the Renaissance.

Lastly in this odd catalogue we may note a characteristic specimen of political translation – from Latin into Greek this time, following the flow of power rather than culture – which has to be reckoned even more tendentious than the Behistun inscription of Darius I. I refer, of course, to the Greek edition of Augustus' *Res Gestae*, that notorious and manipulative apologia for a career of world-conquest and the bureaucratic organisation that followed. The Latin version was written for Roman consumption, and is unashamedly ethnocentric and chauvinistic in tone, embodying Virgil's famous recommendation to go easy on the defeated and subservient, but to blitz the stiffnecked ('parcere subiectis et debellare superbos').[70] The Greek text, however, the so-called Monumentum Ancyranum, carefully revamps this mood of imperial self-satisfaction into a crusade of liberation from oppression; it also plays down Antony, whom the East had supported, at the expense of Brutus and Cassius, 'conspirators' who had not only murdered Caesar, but inflicted much suffering on the Balkans through their protracted military campaigns and requisitions. The entire message, in fact, has been subtly reworked, with sly verbal touches and more than Orwellian relish, to eliminate Roman domestic propaganda and butter up the provincials.[71] *Traduttori, traditori*, says the old Italian proverb: here, for once, the real translator-traitors can be observed at their work of disinformation.

We see, then, that Rome bequeathed to the translators of the Middle Ages a tradition based on pragmatism, propaganda, school usage, and, as far as literary theory went, a preference for embellishment and freedom over mere literalism – a preference which the Renaissance was to exploit in no uncertain fashion. The record also strikingly confirms Fitzmaurice-Kelly's judgment, that 'at all times, and in all countries, translations have usually been produced for utilitarian purposes, and not from artistic motives.'[72] The free or creative translation has been in and out of fashion ever since. However, the triumph of Christianity introduced a whole new series of motives and assumptions for the translator, and these for the most part ran flat counter to the classical tradition. The one area where they overlapped was that of propaganda, or proselytisation, as Christians preferred to call it. The persuasive techniques of the Early Fathers often, in fact, bear an uncomfortably close resemblance to those we have observed on the Monumentum Ancyranum. More important, the emphasis was shifted back from translator to audience. In the beginning was the Word, the Logos, and amid the confusion of tongues after Babel the main object was to have that message conveyed, accurately, to a widespread audience in the vernacular.

There were, however, two significant counter-trends that militated against this process. First, at least from the time of St Jerome, the creator of the Vulgate (AD 384), it was widely held that in Scripture, as opposed to secular writings, 'even the order of the words is a sacred mystery'.[73] This belief promoted literalism to a point where it not infrequently made near-nonsense of Holy Writ, and began to exercise a malign influence on non-religious translation as well.[74] Second, although the Greek East continued to disseminate religious and classical texts in a wide variety of vernacular versions, while the great Moorish translation centre of Toledo produced Arabic texts of Greek works, especially by Aristotle, that would otherwise have been lost to posterity,[75] nevertheless ecclesiastical and feudal authorities in the Catholic West came to frown on all attempts to make the Scriptures, in particular, available to the populace at large. The Logos was to be reserved for authority to define and expound. The first of these trends at least had the virtue of sharpening the translator's always shaky sense of responsibility to his text, and put some sort of a brake on the excesses of autonomous fancy. The second, as is well known, at least from Tyndale's time, precipitated an acute political, no less than religious, struggle during the English and German Renaissance, when the essentially middle-class and Protestant demand for vernacular Bibles became a burning issue in every sense of the word.[76]

The belief that Catholicism 'had exerted its influence upon the nation by fostering ignorance'[77] acted as a spur to translators in the Elizabethan age. Modern opinions to the contrary notwithstanding, [78] literary and aesthetic considerations, once again, played almost no part in this movement. Prior to 1477 – unless we count Boethius' *Consolation of Philosophy*, which attracted translators as diverse as King Alfred, Chaucer, and Queen Elizabeth herself, primarily as a manual on how to conduct oneself in adversity[79] – no classical work had been translated into English directly from Latin, let alone from Greek. A survey of those works actually translated between 1477 and 1620,[80] from Caxton to Chapman, is in many ways startling, and puts something of a tarnish on the so-called 'Golden Age' of translation. Counter-tensions are everywhere. Bible-inspired literalism fights the flowery excesses of Euphuism, and generally loses. The Horatian advice to translate sense for sense rather than word for word is carried to its logical extreme, and sometimes beyond. The Protestant enthusiasm for spreading the moral word runs up against a still-powerful Catholic resistance to the whole idea of vernacular translation as such.[81] Interest in literature for literature's sake is conspicuous by its absence. The overwhelming preference, predictable by now, is for moral homilies, practical handbooks, and what the fastidious Roger Ascham referred to as 'bold bawdrye'. 'It is not too much to say', Lathrop wrote in 1933, 'that almost no classic Greek works at all were translated, and that none entered the stream of English literature.' [82] Till the mid-sixteenth century there is 'no history, no lyric, no satire, no oratory, no drama',[83] *at all* and the situation does not noticeably improve during the next fifty years. Cicero is represented solely as a moralist: the vast bulk of his oratory and correspondence remains untouched. Aristophanes and Plato (the latter except for one spurious dialogue) are ignored: so are Catullus, Propertius, and even Juvenal, whereas Artemidorus' manual on dream-interpretation gets no less than four separate translations during the century. Most extraordinary of all, no one touches Greek tragedy. Aeschylus, in fact, has to wait until 1777, though all Seneca's melodramas were available by 1581, as students of Jacobean theatre will be uncomfortably well aware.

The rise of a new kind of reading public, the Tudor Protestant middle class, was clearly analogous to that at Rome during the late Republic. In both cases literary self-consciousness arrives late on the scene, with the so-called Augustan period: no accident that the Roman label was reapplied in the eighteenth century. Even then the aesthetic factor remains uncertain, being fatally susceptible to the fluctuations of translation's indissoluble link to the politics, religion, culture, and, above all, the social niceties, the decorum of its age. John Studley, in the preface to his translation of Seneca's *Medea* (1556), announced that he had changed the first chorus 'because in it I saw nothing but a heap of profane stories and profane idols'.[84] This kind of devaluation of source to the benefit of the host-culture's ethos is perennial. If Dryden's Virgil was to speak as an Englishman, he had to take on English moral decorum along with the *persona*.

This was liable to produce some amusing cultural cross-eddies. The down-to-earth Thomas Hobbes, in his translation of the *Odyssey*, exactly caught Penelope's furious reproach [*Od.* 19.91–92] to the treacherous maid Melantho: 'Bold bitch, said she, I know what deeds you've done.' Such Anglo-Saxon frankness was too much for Pope, who translated the same line as 'Loquacious insolent, she cries, forbear!' The euphemism won hearty approval from Lord Woodhouselee in his *Essay on the Principles of Translation* (1790),[85] on the grounds that such epithets 'would sound extremely offensive' in a lady 'whom the poet painted as a model of female dignity and propriety', and that Pope therefore 'has in fact been *more faithful* [my emphasis] to the sense of the original, by accommodating the expressions of the speaker to that character which a modern reader must conceive to belong to her'. Penelope, in short, has been Augustanised, and on principle. Homer's proprieties are not good enough; the susceptible eighteenth-century reader must be spoon-fed with his own.

We see, once again, that it is not a simple matter of conscious choice whether the translator will stress fidelity to his original or the accommodation of his audience. Strive he never so hard to sink himself in the tone, form, rhythms, structure and substance of his original, everything is against him. He cannot escape the medium through which he expresses himself. Whatever he produces will still reveal, with deadly accuracy, the unmistakable idiom of his own age. Richard Stanyhurst in the sixteenth century and Cecil Day Lewis in the twentieth both professed to be working to evoke the true Virgil. Yet in each case the chains of period remained unbroken. 'Quod she, shall hee scape thus? Shall a stranger giue me the slampam?/ With such departure my regal segnorye frumping?' is as unmistakably Elizabethan as 'Where are you off to, Aeneas? Don't welsh on your marriage contract!' is post-war modernist. About all the two extracts have in common, apart from an attempt to represent the hexameter, is their weakness for quickly obsolete slang.[86]

Catullus' sea-nymphs, too, move with the times. A Victorian scholar made them 'unveil limbs flushing naked about them/ stark to the nursing breasts from foam and billow arising'; the contemporary poet, rejecting such roses and raptures of virtue, offers us instead 'naked sea-nymphs sticking out of the water showing their tits'.[87] The real curse of Babel is parochialism.

Examples could be multiplied from every period since the Renaissance. Cowley's Pindar is extravagantly metaphysical, Pope's Homer breathes the very essence of eighteenth-century Augustanism, Shelley's Homeric *Hymns* are buzzing with Beauty, Liberty, and dreams of the New Jerusalem,[88] Gilbert Murray's Euripidean choruses, as Eliot unkindly but accurately pointed out,[89] pastiche the 'fluid haze of Swinburne', the Chicago Greek Tragedy series coasts along on a poetic tide created by Eliot, Pound, and Dylan Thomas; Ted Hughes' Oedipus is *Crow* in drag, Tony Harrison's *Phaedra Britannica* is a curdling mix of *The Elder Statesman* and *Look Back in Anger*. Today rhetoric, euphuism and metaphrase seem to be on the way in again, cheered on in convoluted phraseology by modish semioticians. The pendulum continues to oscillate. Stanyhurst had the right attitude to this sort of thing: 'Good God what a frye of such *wooden rythmours* dooth swarme in stacioners shops, who neauer enstructed in any grammar schoole, not atayning too thee paringes of thee Latin or Greeke tongue, yeet lyke blynd bayards rush on forward, fostring theyre vayne conceits wyth such over-weening silly follyes, as they reck not too bee condemned of thee learned for ignorant, so they bee commended of thee ignorant for learned.'[90]

Translation since the Renaissance, then, exhibits not only a tidal ebb and flow between fidelity and freedom, but also, closely linked with this, a corresponding social swing between the needs of audience and translator. In the Elizabethan period the emergent Protestant middle class, which had like its most brilliant representative, little Latin and less Greek, showed an almost insatiable urge for edification in the vernacular. By the eighteenth century this urge had largely been satisfied, scholarship had re-established itself, new canons of decorum were being laid down and translators were once more writing for themselves and for one another, with both them and their readers evaluating text through original. The early nineteenth century brought back a wider audience, fired with dreams of idealised Greek democracy through which they hazily viewed an assortment of more or less violent revolutions. The end of the Victorian era saw the scholars and *littérateurs* dominant once more. For some decades now we have enjoyed a phase of eager if uninstructed public interest parallel to that visible in Tudor England; but as I have suggested, there are already signs that we are moving back towards a new Alexandrianism. I see no evidence that this process of systole and diastole is conscious or deliberate, much less controllable. In this as in everything else, translation remains hopelessly at the mercy of its environment.

A quarter of a century ago I believed that something could be done – indeed, was being done – to resolve this dilemma.[91] Now I am by no means so confident. Renewed study of five centuries' translation of the classics, and an uncomfortable awareness that today – with courses in world literature flourishing as never before – the vast majority of American readers (to look no further) has access to Greek and Roman literature only in English, and for the most part in contemporary English at that, has left me perhaps unreasonably depressed. In the preface to his sympathetic version of Virgil's *Georgics* (1940) Day Lewis argued that 'every classical poem worth translating should be translated afresh every fifty years', and by now we are in a position to see why. Half loaves, I agree, are better than no bread: but do we really have so ineradicable a need to be cosseted by our own changing theories and assumptions?

I would like to conclude with some wise, if bleak, words of Henry Thoreau's on this subject, and in citing them I hope I shall not be suspected of merely attempting to drum up business for my own academic profession. In the third chapter of *Walden* Thoreau wrote:[92] 'Those who have not learned to read the ancient classics in the language in which they were written must have a very imperfect knowledge of the history of the human race; for it is remarkable that no transcription of them has ever been made into any modern tongue, unless our civilisation itself may be regarded as such a transcript.' No more damning or total dismissal of all translations has ever been made. Roger Ascham, too, knew the proper worth of translations: at the very end of his life, in *The Scholemaster* (1568/70) he lamented that 'even the best translation is for mere necessitie but an evill imped wing to flie withall, or a hevie stompe leg of wood to go withall'. In my own capacity as a humble crutch-maker I can only concur. But as a lifelong student of Greek and Latin I beseech all those who can, by hook or crook, make the effort, to beat the curse of Babel by mastering the languages in which two of the greatest, and most influential, literatures the world has ever known are written, and by doing so break free from the tyranny imposed by their own culture. 'For even' – to quote Ascham again – 'as a hauke flieth not hie with one wing: even so a man reacheth not to excellency with one tong.'[93] This is a hard investment; but once made, it will reward the investor a thousandfold, until his dying day.

NOTES AND
REFERENCES

CHAPTER I

1 Arist. fr. 15 Plezia = Demetrius *De Elocut*. 144: ὡς ὁ 'Αριστοτέλης, 'ὅσῳ γάρ,' φησί, 'μονώτης εἰμί, φιλομυθότερος γέγονα' – the endemic danger, surely, facing all researchers. Lord Hailsham's remark in his Presidential address to the Classical Association ('It is apparently a requirement in a developed human society that it should have classics, and the point is that you cannot select what classics you will have') is more to the point than might appear at first sight. See *Proc. Class. Assoc.* 58 (1961) 11.

2 Karl F. Morrison, *The Mimetic Tradition of Reform in the West* (1982) ix-xiv, 391 ff.

3 See Peter Kidson, 'The Figural Arts', in *The Legacy of Greece: a new appraisal*, ed. M.I. Finley (1981) 427-8.

4 W.A. Oldfather, 'The future of the English vocabulary', *Class. Outlook* 19 (1942) 33-34.

5 Alfred North Whitehead, *Process and Reality* (1929) 63: 'The safest general characterization of the European philosophical tradition is that it consists of a series of footnotes to Plato.' Whitehead, never loath *épater les bourgeois*, was more than a little prone to startling and conceptually suspect aphorisms: further on in the same work (142 ff.) he brackets the *Timaeus* with Newton's *Scholium* as 'the two great cosmological documents governing Western thought'. *Caveat emptor.*

6 In Germany, as in France, there have been occasional official attempts to stem the influx of foreign terminologies: what I always remember about Hitler is his determination to have the telephone referred to as a *Fernsprecher*. As for Teutonic mythology, the brilliant Wagnerian lampoons of Anna Russell do more to set this in its true perspective than any polemic could, and offer a salutary counterblast to the whole Bayreuth mystique.

7 'In a list of 426 difficult but useful words compiled by the Freshman English staff at the University of Arizona for special vocabulary study . . . 404 are derived from the classical languages': Donald M. Ayers, *English words from Latin and Greek elements* (1965) 12. Cf. also J.F. MacDonald, 'The influence of Latin on English prose style', *Phoenix* 5 (1951) 33.

8 See the penetrating remarks of Alan E. Samuel, *From Athens to Alexandria: Hellenism and Social Goals in Ptolemaic Egypt* (1983) 25 ff., esp. 32: 'The fundamental economic theory . . . is that which aims at stability in the economy.'

9 Cf. Asa Briggs, *A Social History of England* (1983) 106.

10 See in particular Martin Ostwald, *Nomos and the Beginnings of the Athenian Democracy* (1969), esp. 137 ff., and K. Adshead, *Politics of the Archaic Peloponnese* (1986) 88.

11 Aristoph., *Clouds* 42 ff., *Acharn.* 457, 478 and elsewhere.

12 See, e.g., Arist., *Pol.* 8.6.1-7.11 = 1340b 20-1342b 35. Cf. W. Donlan, 'Social vocabulary and its relation to political propaganda in fifth-century Athens', *Quad. Urb. Cult. Class.* 27 (1978) 95–111.

13 Ibid. 1342a, 19–21: '. . . ὁ θεατὴς διττός, ὁ μὲν ἐλεύθερος καὶ πεπαιδευμένος, ὁ δὲ φορτικὸς ἐκ βαναύσων καὶ θητῶν καὶ ἄλλων τοιούτων συγκείμενος . . .'

14 The attitude of that brilliant scientific pioneer Archimedes in the 3rd cent. BC is typical in this regard: cf. Plut. *Marcell.* 14, a key passage too often dismissed as mere prejudicial hyperbole.

15 Lewis Mumford, *Stanford Conference on the Humanities: The Humanities look ahead* (1943) 135.

16 Like all such anecdotes, this one is retailed in several variant versions. That quoted above is told by Bishop Strong, who had it on the authority of Canon Liddon: see J.B. Skemp, 'The permanent value of Greek studies', *Durham Univ. Journ.* 13 (1952) 37, drawing on the 1st (1941) edition of the *Oxford Dictionary of Quotations.* The 3rd edition, however, (1979) reports the sermon in question as having been preached on Christmas Day rather than at Easter, and offers a considerably toned-down text: 'Nor can I do better, in conclusion, than impress upon you the study of Greek literature, which not only elevates above the vulgar herd, but leads not infrequently to positions of considerable emolument.' The source for this is the Rev. W. Tuckwell, *Reminiscences of Oxford* (2nd ed. 1907) 124.

17 Richard Hofstadter, *Anti-Intellectualism in American Life* (1962) 238; cf. 82–83, 116 ff. For a vigorous restatement of, and attack on, this rejection of the past see N. Foerster, *The Humanities and the Common Man* (1946) 13–14: 'The great books of the past are demonstrably full of error [it is argued], and in any case do not much concern us who are not Greeks or Elizabethans but modern Americans. If we need belles-lettres let them be not Homer and Dante and the other classics but contemporary literature, which grows out of and reflects our environment, deals in a "meaningful" way with our problems. Human nature changes, and ours is ours. So strong is this attitude that it is

tactically unwise, in many universities, to use in academic circles such words as "the past", "tradition", "heritage", "classical", "medieval", save in a tone of studied contempt.'

18 George Santayana, *Life of Reason* (1905–6), vol.I, ch. xii ('Flux and constancy in human nature'), who also observes that 'progress, far from consisting in change, depends on retentiveness'. The statement in the text is frequently misquoted as 'Those who do not understand history are doomed to repeat it'.

19 See Macdonald (n.7 above) 39. Modern Greece has complicated this issue by equating the mandarin tradition (*katharévousa*) with reactionary conservatism and the Hellenising ideal, while the vernacular (*dhemotikí*) has come to represent radical populism and post-Byzantine Orthodox ethnicity, so that successive governments have prescribed each in turn, particularly for use in schools, according to their political persuasions. It is worth noting, too, that the Euphuistic excesses of Renaissance prose, based on Cicero and Seneca, came under attack as early as 1664, from a special committee of the scientifically oriented Royal Society. The members of this committee (including Dryden and John Evelyn) went on record as 'preferring the language of Artizans, Countrymen and Merchants before that of Wits and Scholars'. Cf. W. Beare, 'Scholars and scientists', *Proc. Class. Assoc.* 59 (1962) 15–16.

20 M. Kline, *Mathematics and the Search for Knowledge* (1985) 152 ff.

21 See, e.g., R.R. Bolgar, *The Classical Heritage and its Beneficiaries* (1954) 389 ff.; R.L. Calhoun in *The Meaning of the Humanities*, ed. T.M. Greene (1938) 121; R.M. Ogilvie, *Latin and Greek: A History of the Influence of the Classics on English Life from 1600 to 1918* (1964) 182 ff.; R. Pound, 'The humanities in an absolutist world,' *The Humanities after the War*, ed. N. Foerster (1944) 10 ff.; H.C. Baldry, *The Classics in the Modern World* (1949) 7; W.H. Alexander, 'The Classics and Survival Values', *The Humanities for our time,* W.R. Agard and others (1949) 127; Georg Mann, 'The Decline of the Humanities, or, Where's the Bloody Horse?', *Arion* 1.2 (1962) 101.

22 Cf. Alexander (n.21 above) 128–9.

23 Frank M. Turner, *The Greek Heritage in Victorian Britain* (1981) 171 ff.

24 Ogilvie (n.21 above) 172 ff.

25 See the cogent arguments of G.S. Kirk in *The Nature of Greek Myths* (1974) 73-75, and in *Myth: Its Meaning and Function in Ancient and other Cultures* (1970) 275 ff.

26 Claude Lévi-Strauss, *Structural Anthropology* trs. C. Jacobson & B.G. Schoepf (1963, 1967) 209 ff.

27 Ted Hughes, *Crow* (1971) 63-65.

28 Hom. *Il*.23.679 ff., with schol. *ad loc.*; *Od.* 11.271 ff.; Hes. *WD* 161-3; Ps-Hom. *Theb.* ap. Athen. 11.465e.

29 Also made into an excellent state-of-the-art survey of the problem today: Michael Wood, *In Search of the Trojan War* (1985). This work, which evinces throughout a (carefully controlled) will to believe, makes an interesting contrast with the published papers of the first Greenbank Colloquium in Liverpool (1981), issued as *The Trojan War: Its Historicity and Context*, ed. L. Foxhall & J.K. Davies (1984), where academic scepticism places the onus of proof squarely on the shoulders of the credulous. The contrast emerges even more clearly in some of the reviews: N.R.E. Fisher, dealing with the Liverpool colloquium in *Greece & Rome* 33 (1986) 90-91, not only praises its general scepticism (which is fair enough) but also the fact that it 'does not follow any TV series, has no illustrations, evokes no images of small cities, windy plains, or tight jeans' – a purely gratuitous piece of academic spite (and, one suspects, envy).

30 See now *Myth, Scandal and History: The Heinrich Schliemann Controversy and a first edition of the Mycenaean Diary*, ed. W.M. Calder III and D.A. Traill (1986), esp. 17 ff., 110 ff.

31 See W.B. Stanford & J.V. Luce, *The Quest for Ulysses* (1974) 216, with figs. 182-3.

32 Simone Weil: *The Iliad, or, The Poem of Force*, trs. Mary McCarthy (1956), esp. 31 ff.

33 W.H. Auden, *Collected Poems*, ed. E. Mendelson (1976) 454.

34 T.S. Eliot, 'Tradition and the Individual Talent', *The Sacred Wood* (3rd ed. 1932) 52.

35 Louis MacNeice, *Collected Poems*, ed. E.R. Dodds (1966) 530.

36 Kit Wright, 'Fortunes of War', reprinted (from *The Bear Looked over the Mountain*) in *The Penguin Book of Light Verse*, ed. Gavin Ewart (1980) 587-9.

37 Yannis Ritsos, *The Fourth Dimension* [Τέταρτη Διάσταση], (12th ed. Athens, 1982). Cf. also M. Colakis, 'Classical Mythology in Yannis Ritsos's Dramatic Monologues', *Class. & Mod. Lit.* 4 (1983/4) 117-130.

38 See R.G. Tanner, 'The Dramas of T.S. Eliot and their Greek models', *Greece & Rome* 17 (1970) 124-7.

39 M. O. Lee, 'Orpheus and Euridice: some modern versions', *Class. Journ.*56 (1961) 307-313.

40 See in particular R. Trousson, *Le Thème de Prométhée dans la Littérature Européenne*, 2 vols. (1964), esp. ix, 451 ff.

41 See, e.g., 'The Humanities Today', *Essays in Antiquity* (1960) 1-25, and the title essay in *The Shadow of the Parthenon* (1972) 11-46.

42 Foerster (n.17 above) 10-13.

43 Baldry (n.21 above) 5.

44 Bolgar (n.21 above) 389.

45 Xen. *Mem.* 3.7.6, cf. 1.2.9; Sen. *Ep. Mor.* xc, *passim*; above, pp.17ff., with nn. 11-14.

46 For a *reductio ad absurdum* of the mechanising and *pastichiste* skills implicit in Greek and Latin verse composition see the fascinating account by D.W. Blandford, 'The Eureka', *Greece & Rome* 10 (1963) 71-78, of a machine invented during the mid-Victorian age by one John Clark, capable of turning out no less than 26,000,000 different Latin hexameters (admittedly of very poor quality). The significant point, however, is that not only did someone think such a device worth developing, but also got it exhibited at the Egyptian Hall in Piccadilly, where it attracted large audiences. Times have indeed changed.

47 R.L. Calhoun (n.21 above) 121.

48 The actual Greek phrase is λάθε βιώσας: Epicurus fr. 551 Usener = fr. 86 Bailey. A similar withdrawal on the part of modern humanists has been analysed by Mann (n.21 above) 101-4.

49 For a representative sample of such defensive writing see, e.g., D.B. King, 'Why read Latin literature?', *Class. Bull.* 29 (1953) 55-57; E.A. Quain, 'The ancients speak to the modern world', *Class. World* 42 (1948/49) 153-6; N.I. Herescu, 'Homo, humus, humanitas: préface à un humanisme contemporain', *Bull. Assoc. G. Budé* 5 (1948) 64-76; J. Malye, 'De l'humanisme', ibid. 53-57. For the retreat into high-flown abstract waffle try D.M. Pippidi, 'Le sens actuel de l'humanisme', *Lettres d'humanité* 6 (1946) 5-22; and for a particularly gross exercise in mindless nationalism (*ethnikismós*), T. Aghnides, 'What ancient Greece means to the modern Greek', *Bull. John Rylands Libr.* 27 (1942/43) 260-270. The attack on layabouts is cited from N.J. De Witt's article 'The community, culture and the classics', *Class. Weekly* 39 (1945/46) 18-20. De Witt's specialty, ironically enough, was Epicureanism.

50 Gilbert Chinan, *The Meaning of the Humanities* (n.21 above) 155.

51 See in particular McLuhan's *Understanding Media: the extensions of man* (2nd ed. 1964), with the penetrating criticisms of Rebecca West, *McLuhan and the future of literature* (1969), and Sidney Finkelstein, *Sense and Nonsense of McLuhan* (1968), esp. ii, 15 ff., 'McLuhanese history vs, real history'. It is encouraging to note that already the multiple copies of such works as *The Gutenberg Galaxy* (1962) are mouldering unread on the shelves of university libraries.

52 Ogilvie (n.21 above) 182-3.

53 W.W. Tarn, rev. G.T. Griffith, *Hellenistic Civilisation* (3rd ed. 1952) 347.

54 J.F. Mountford, 'Investment in the Classics', *Proc. Class. Assoc.* 60 (1963) 9-23, esp. 18-20. It is interesting to note how many post-war Presidential addresses to the Classical Association kept harping on variations of the same theme: see, e.g., Viscount Samuel, 'The classical age and our own', ibid. 50 (1953) 7-17; Lord Soulbury, 'Classics and politics', ibid. 46 (1949) 8-22; Lord Hailsham, ' "Vos exemplaria Graeca . . . " ' ibid. 58 (1961) 9-15 (the prevalence of titled Presidents, mostly conservative, is itself symptomatic); and cf. such comparable statements as those of Beare (n.19 above) 9-19; C.M. Bowra, *A classical education* (1945); D. von Bothmer, 'The classical contribution to Western civilisation', *Bull. Met. Mus. Art* 7 (1948/49)

205-218; K. von Fritz, 'The position of classical studies in our time', *Lampas* 6 (1973) 290-303.

55 MacNeice (n.35 above) 125-6.

56 Often cited: see e.g., Baldry (n.21 above) 21, and G. Highet, *The Classical Tradition* (1949) 494, who took it from Bowra (n.54 above). Possibly apocryphal, but most often attributed to a headmaster of Shrewsbury School.

57 Auden (n.33 above) 263. For a salutary stress on the importance of permanent truths, by a scientist, see Sir Cyril Hinshelwood, 'Classics among the intellectual disciplines', *Proc. Class. Assoc.* 56 (1959) 9-22, esp. 14.

58 E.R. Dodds, 'Classical teaching in an altered climate', *Proc. Class. Assoc.* 61 (1964) 11-23, esp. 15.

59 For the classic attack on Plato and his influence, see K.R. Popper, *The Open Society and its Enemies* (4th ed. 1962), vol. I, *The Spell of Plato*, esp. 86 ff. Attempted refutations of Popper (for a representative selection see *Plato, Popper and Politics*, ed. R. Bambrough, 1967) have failed to nullify his main conclusions.

60 Popper (n.59 above), vol. II, *Hegel and Marx, passim.*

61 T.S. Eliot, *Selected Essays* (3rd ed. 1951) 514-6; Dodds (n.58 above) 13-14.

62 Harold Nicolson, 'Marginal Comment', *Spectator* 6269 (20 Aug. 1948) 236. His obiter dictum did not stop him from expatiating, in the same article, on the totalitarian content of Plato's *Republic* and *Laws*; but then political realism was never one of Nicolson's strong suits.

CHAPTER III

1 John Donne, *Devotions upon emergent occasions* (1623), Meditation xvii.

2 Plato, *Phaed.* 109A-B: ἡμᾶς οἰκεῖν . . . ἐν σμικρῷ τινι μορίῳ, ὥσπερ περὶ τέλμα μύρμηκας ἢ βατράχους περὶ τὴν θάλατταν οἰκοῦντας . . .

3 Hdt. 8.144, in a speech by Athenian representatives addressed to the Spartan mission in Athens at a time (479) when Alexander of Macedon was also there, as an emissary from

Mardonius, attempting (8.140) to detach Athens from the Hellenic alliance and bring her powerful fleet over to the Persian side; they inveighed against such a move, *inter alia*, τὸ Ἑλληνικὸν ἐὸν ὅμαιμόν τε καὶ ὁμόγλωσσον καὶ θεῶν ἰδρύματά τε κοινὰ καὶ θυσίαι ἤθεά τε ὁμότροπα.

4 C. M. Woodhouse, *The Story of Modern Greece* (1968). 131-2.

5 Thuc. 3.70-84 *passim*.

6 Strabo 1.3.19, C.60: οἱ δὲ καὶ τὴν Λέσβον τῆς Ἴδης ἀπερρωγέναι πεπιστεύκασι.

7 Bürchner, 'Lesbos', *PWK* xii (1925) (hereafter 'Bürchner') col. 2111; Naval Intelligence Division (Great Britain), *Geographical Handbook*, series 18, *Greece* (1944) vol. iii ('Regional Geography') 448-9, 493-4.

8 G. M. Choutzaios, Τὸ Ἀπολιθωμένο Δάσος τῆς Λέσβου (1979) 183 (English summary); cf. 50 ff. for a full description (in modern Greek) of the process of petrification, and 71 ff. for a list of the tree-species petrified.

9 Vitruv. 1.6.1.

10 Fr. 47 L-P: Ἔρος δ᾽ ἐτίναξέ μοι φρένας, ὡς ἄνεμος κατ᾽ ὄρος δρύσιν ἐμπέτων.

11 κατώρης, fr. 183 L-P.

12 Theophr. *Hist.Plant.*3.9.5., *Caus. Plant.* 2.6.4.; cf. Plin *HN* 16.46; J. D. Kondis, Λέσβος καὶ ἡ Μικρασιατική της Περιοχή (1978) (hereafter 'Kondis, *Lesbos*') 27, para.96.

13 Plin.*HN* 5.139: Pyrrha hausta est mari (this suggests the effects of a *tsunami*), Arisbe terrarum motu subuersa. Cf. Kondis, *Lesbos* 345, paras. 805 ff. Many early travellers, including Clavijo, Didot, and Hauttecoeur, refer to seismic activity on Lesbos.

14 F. Fouqué, 'Rapport sur les tremblements de terre de Céphalonie et de Métélin en 1867', *Arch. Miss. Scient.* 4 (1868) 445-458.

15 M. A. Walker, *Old Tracks and New Landmarks* (1897) 190.

16 C. T. Newton, *Travels and Discoveries in the Levant* (1865), vol.i, 86-87, gives an excellent account of Karinai, remarking in conclusion what a blessed thing it was that this place was far beyond the reach of cockneys, and that its silence was never profaned by the sound of champagne-corks and the din of knives and forks rattling against the sides of the pigeon-pies of European picnics.' Today it has been discovered, and its little taverna exploited, by Greek tourists from Thessaloniki. I think Newton might well have preferred his cockneys.

17 *IG* xii (2) no.4; cf. Hiller von Gärtringen, *Inscriptiones Graecae Insularum Maris Aegaei praeter Delum: Supplementum* (1939) (hereafter 'Von Gärtringen') 2.

18 J.D. Kondis, Τὸ Ρωμαικὸ ὑδραγωγεῖο τῆς Μυτιλήνης', *Lesviaka* 6 (1973) 77-81.

19 Though substantially less than what was visible to early travellers such as Choiseul-Gouffier, or even, later, to Alexander Conze: see his *Reise auf der Insel Lesbos* (1865) (hereafter 'Conze') 55 ff., and the comments of P. Lindau, *An der Westküste Klein-Asiens* (2nd ed. 1900) 58-59, who observes that Conze 'hat im Jahre 1858 noch dreizehn mehr oder minder gut erhaltene Pfeiler gesehen; jetzt stehen derer nur noch zwölf. . . Conze sah von den obern Ziegelbogen noch vier; jetzt stehen nur noch drei . . .' Today the number of uprights remains the same, but there are only *two* intact upper arches.

20 M. Boutan, 'Rapport sur la topographie et l'histoire de l'île de Lesbos', *Arch. Miss. Scient, et Litt.* 5 (1856) (hereafter 'Boutan') 288. Boutan's topographical (as opposed to his historical) work is extremely valuable (cf. below, n.74). In 1855 he saw an incomplete arch about 3-400 yds outside the city, in a small gorge, 'mais elle menace ruine, et la chute d'une seule pierre fera bientôt tout écrouler.'

21 J. D. Kondis, Λεσβιακὸ Πολύπτυχο ἀπὸ τὴν ἱστορία, τὴν τέχνη καὶ τὴ λογοτεχνία (1973) (hereafter 'Kondis, *Dossier*') 119; R. Koldewey, *Die antiken Baureste der Insel Lesbos* (1890) (hereafter 'Koldewey') 65-68.

22 L. De Launay, *Chez les Grecs de Turquie: autour de la Mer Egée* (1897) 56-57.

23 Longus, 1: διείληπται γὰρ εὐρίποις ἐπεισρεούσης τῆς θαλάττης καὶ κεκόσμηται γεφύραις ξεστοῦ καὶ λευκοῦ λίθου; DS 13.79.6; Paus. 8.30.2. The presence of these bridges, in perhaps the second century AD, and Strabo's earlier failure to mention the canal in his description of the two harbours (13.2.2, C.617), suggest that it had lost its earlier strategical importance, and was now being used only for small craft. Its subsequent abandonment would then be logical enough.

24   M. M. Patrick, *Sappho and the Island of Lesbos* (1912) 66.

25   Cf. Boutan 337 for the 'Anatolian connection': he argues that the island's fate 'est fatalement attaché à celui de l'Asie Mineure, que le maître de Smyrne et de l'Ionie doit aussi régner sur Lesbos. C'est là une nécessité politique, contre laquelle les Lesbiens se sont inutilement débattus à toutes les époques de leur histoire. Leur île est une sorte d'avant-poste que les maîtres de l'Asie Mineure ne peuvent à aucun prix laisser à une race étrangère.' This is true as far as it goes, but ignores the equally strong counter-claim of the Greek world to Lesbos as an integral part of the 'Aegean circle'.

26   W. Lamb, *Excavations at Thermi in Lesbos* (1936) (hereafter 'Lamb, *Thermi*'), and 'Antissa', *Ann.Brit.Sch.Ath.* 31 (1930/31) 166–178; 32 (1931/32) 41–46.

27   Strabo 12.2.2, C.617, τῶν Πυρραίων Εὔριπον; cf. Arist. *Hist.Anim.* 544a 21 and elsewhere; *Part.Anim.* 680b 1; *Gen.Anim.* 763b 1.

28   A useful summary (with map, pl. 34) in H.-G. Buchholz, *Methymna: Archäologische Beiträge zur Topographie und Geschichte von Nordlesbos* (1975) (hereafter 'Buchholz, *Methymna*') 121 ff. Cf. J.M. Cook *CAH* II,ii, 776 ff.

29   See, e.g., Cook (n.28) 777: 'With such mythical fabrications we shall not be concerned in this chapter.'

30   Lamb, *Thermi* 208.

31   *CAH* I,ii, 377; Lamb, *Thermi* 374.

32   *CAH* I,ii, 371-2, 384.

33   *CAH* I,ii, 682, dating the reoccupation in the Troy V period and comparing it with the establishment of Poliochni VI on Lemnos. Lamb, *Thermi* 72,212 leaves the date more open-ended in the Middle Bronze period.

34   Lamb, *Thermi* 72, 212-3.

35   DS 5.81.1-8, cf. 3.55.7.

36   DS 5.81.3-4; Dion.Hal. AR 1.18.1; schol. Hom.*Il.* 24.544.

37   DS 5.82.1-2: λοιμικὴ κατάστασις . . . διὰ τὴν τοῦ ἀέρος φθοράν; cf. C. G. Doumas, *Thera* (1983) chs. vi-vii, 134-150, for an up-to-date discussion of the evidence, current theories, and the date of the eruption.

38   Eusebius, *Canon* (ed. Schoene vol. ii) 26-27 (= Ann. Abraham 497).

39   The tradition of Macareus expanding his power to Chios, Samos, Cos and Rhodes appears to be based on a misunderstanding of the term Μακάρων νήσους used to describe them and Lesbos. Diodorus (5.82.2-3) makes this clear when he gives two alternative explanations of the title: (a) that it was due to τῆς εὐπορίας τῶν ἀγαθῶν, which is surely correct, and (b) that through the efforts of Macareus his sons got the mastery of the other islands, which must be based on an associative misinterpretation of the word Μακάρων.

40   Blegen, *CAH* II,ii, 163 and elsewhere, set the end of the Trojan War *c*.1250, with the destruction of Troy VIIa. This agrees with the date given by Ps.-Hdt. *Vit.Hom.* 38 (incidentally the only source to set up a sequence of absolute rather than relative dates, calculated in years not generations, and keyed to a known and chronologically certain departure-point, Xerxes' invasion of 480) and also by Herodotus himself (2.145), who reckoned over 800 years from this day (? *c*.440 at time of writing) to the Trojan war. Blegen (ibid.) demonstrates that during Troy VIIb1 the Trojans reoccupied the site: grey Minyan, red-washed, and tan ware continued more or less as before. This agrees with the evidence of Strabo, 13.1.40, C.608. VIIb1 lasted until *c*.1200 (during which time there is evidence for the Trojans occupying themselves as pirates, Strabo 3.2.13, C.150, which suggests a possible connection with the Sea Peoples); there was then 'an abrupt change of culture' (Blegen 164), with new crude pottery (*Buckelkeramik*) traced across the Hellespont to Thrace and (?) Hungary. This again is precisely supported by Xanthos of Lydia, cited by Strabo (14.5.29, C.680; cf. 10.3.22, C.473; 13.1.8, C.586; 13.1.21, C.590), who talks of an invasion by Thracians and Phrygians at this time. The more traditional alternative date for the fall of Troy, *c*.1200-1180, fits this second take-over very well, and I am assuming the sequence in my calculations.

41   Hom. *Il.* 24.543-5.

42 See F. Lochner-Hüttenbach, *Die Pelasger* (1960), who sifts all the evidence as well as can be done. I would not go so far as A. B. Lloyd, *Herodotus Book II Commentary 1-98* (1976) 232, who writes the Pelasgians off as 'largely a figment of the Greek imagination'.

43 Cf. DS 5.81.1. For Macareus as king and lawgiver see 5.82.4.

44 DS 5.81.6-7; Steph.Byz. s.v. Methymna, Issa, Antissa, Arisba; cf. S.L.Plehn, *Lesbiacorum Liber* (1826) (hereafter 'Plehn') 25-26.

45 DS 5.81.6: Λέσβος ὁ Λαπίθου τοῦ Αἰόλου τοῦ Ἱππότου. . .Cf. Steph. Byz. s.v. Aimonia.

46 DS 5.81.7; 3.55.7, where it is stated that Mytilene was founded by the Amazon Myrina, who conquered the island and named the city after her sister, who had been joint commander. For Mytilene's eclipse of Thermi cf. Cook, *CAH*³ II,ii, 778.

47 C. J. Cadoux, *Ancient Smyrna* (1938) 32, 57.

48 *HH Apoll.* 1.37, 'Macar's Aeolian seat', noted by Cook, *CAH*³ II,ii, 778, though his assertion that the expansion of Mytilene was the work of 'Aeolians' seems open to doubt.

49 DS 5.84 *passim;* Apollod, 3.15.7-8, and for the new archaeological evidence the summary of the paper by Iris Love, *AIA Abstracts* 8 (1983) 18. Cf. G. L. Huxley, *The Early Ionians* (1966) (hereafter 'Huxley') 15-16.

50 Strabo 13.2.3, C.617: θαυμαστόν τι χρῆμα.

51 Apollod. *Epit.* 3.32-33 *passim;* Aristobulus FGrH 139 F6; cf. Hom. *Il.* 2.688 ff., 9.60,291 ff., 20.90 ff., 188 ff. Cf. W. Leaf, *Troy: A study in Homeric geography* (1912) 397-399; Huxley (n.49) 19.

52 E. L. Shields, 'Lesbos in the Trojan War', *CJ* 13 (1917/18) 672 (hereafter 'Shields').

53 Hom. *Il.* 9.128-130, 270 ff.; *Od.* 5.349, 9.322, cf. 4.342. Note Briseis as 'the girl from Brisa', Shields 673-4.

54 Parthenios xxi *passim,* xxvi 3.

55 Hom. *Il.* 9.129

56 Buchholz 126-7: 'Auf die Siedlung in Palaia-Methymna wie auch den archaischen Ort in Dabia-West passt des einen Vergleich mit Theben und Troja herausfordende Epitheton aber nicht. Erst seit dem fünften Jahrhundert waren mit der Einbeziehung des späteren Burgbergs der Gattelusi . . . Voraussetzungen gegeben, die sowohl ein ὑψίπυλος wie überhaupt die Kunde von der Uneinnehmbarkeit der Stadt rechtfertigten.'

57 Lamb, *Thermi* 72, 213.

58 Paus. 8.5.1-2; Hdt. 9.26.2.

59 Huxley (n.49) 19-20 with further reff.; *CAH*³ II,ii, 368-370. A convenient summary of the 'Troy VI theory' is in M. Wood, *In Search of the Trojan War* (1985) 225-231. This up-to-date report on archaeological and scholarly progress in the Troy debate has been unfairly denigrated by specialists. For the views of the latter see *The Trojan War: its historicity and context,* ed. L. Foxhall and J.K. Davies (1984), esp. 63 ff. Cf. above, n.29 to Ch.I.

60 *CAH*³ II,ii, 352-3, 659.

61 Ps.-Hdt. *Vit.Hom.* 38 (cf n.40 above); J. Bérard, 'La migration éolienne', *Rev. Arch.* (1959) (i) (hereafter 'Bérard') 17.

62 Strabo 13.1.3, C.582; full *testimonia* in Bérard, 22 ff.

63 Strabo ibid.; Thuc. 1.12.3; Tzetzes on Lycophr. *Alex.* 1374. The pseudo-Herodotean date wins confirmation from other sources. Orestes, born at the beginning of the Trojan War (1270/60) was generally agreed to have died *aet.* 70 (schol. Eur. *Orest.* 1645 = FGrH 12 F25, Hom. *Il.* 1.142, *Od.* 3.305), i.e. c. 1200/1190. He planned a colonising expedition, but did not live to carry it out (Bérard 3-4). During his reign (Paus. 1.41.2) and again after his death (Ps.-Apoll. 2.8.2) the Heracleidae invaded the Peloponnese. On this second occasion Orestes' son Penthilos was driven out into Thrace (Strabo 13.1.3, C.582, dating the event 60 years after the Trojan War, i.e. 1200/1190, immediately after Orestes' death). According to Velleius Paterculus (1.1.4) he had reigned for three years, well within the margin of error. Strabo (ibid.) gives the generational sequence Penthilos-Arch-elaos-Gras, with Gras finally completing the migration. Allowing 30 years per generation from 1200/1190 would place Gras's expedition 1140-30, or allowing 33 ¹/³ years (three generations to the century), c. 1123. Gras is also put 100 years (= 3 generations) after Orestes by Tzetzes (*loc. cit.*). Thucydides, who clearly used the late date for the capture of Troy, places the final return of the Heracleidae and Dorians to the Peloponnese 80 years later (1.12.3), i.e. *c.* 1120, shortly before the occupation of Melos.

64 Strabo 13.3.3., C.621, who says of the Pelasgian ἔθνος that it ηὔξήθη τε ἐπὶ πολὺ καὶ ἀθρόαν ἔλαβε τὴν ἔκλειψιν, καὶ μάλιστα κατὰ τὴν τῶν Αἰολέων καὶ τῶν Ἰώνων περαίωσιν εἰς τὴν Ἀσίαν.

65 Strabo 9.2.5., C.402, cf. 9.2.3, C.401.

66 C. D. Buck, *The Greek Dialects* (1955) 135; A. Meillet, *Aperçu d'une histoire de la langue grecque* (1948) 62, 75; J. B. Hainsworth, *CAH²* III,i, 854 ff.

67 E.g. Herbst, 'Mytilene', *PWK* 16 (1933) col. 1413: 'Ins helle Licht der Geschichte tritt M. erst im 6.Jhdt. v.Chr.', and, more recently, Buchholz, *Methymna* 138: 'Bis hinab zum Beginn des siebenten Jahrhunderts v.Chr. ist echte methymnaïsche Geschichte so gut wie nicht rekonstruierbar . . .'; also Kondis, *Lesbos* 59, para.238, who argues that 'μέσα στὸ δεύτερο μισὸ τοῦ 7ου αἰ. π.χ. ρίχνεται τὸ πρῶτο ἱκανοποιητικὸ φῶς στὴν ἱστορία τῆς Λέσβου'.

68 W. Lamb, 'Antissa', *Ann.Brit.Sch.Ath.* 32 (1931/32) 41-46 with pls. 17-19; cf. A.M. Snodgrass, *The Dark Age of Greece* (1971) 408-9, and N. Coldstream, *Geometric Greece* (1977) 262-3.

69 For the Μυτιληναίων Αἰγιαλός see Scylax 97; Theophr. fr.167 = Athen. 2.62b; Strabo 13.1.49, C.606, 51, C.607; Livy 35.31.13; Hiller von Gärtringen no. 142; for the Ἀκταῖαι Πόλεις Thuc. 3.50.3, 4.52.3; Strabo 13.1.62-63, C.612. Cf. Kondis, *Lesbos* 77, para. 341.

70 Strabo 13.1.3., C.582, 13.1.61, C.612.

71 Sigeion: Strabo 13.1.38, C.599; Arisbe, Hdt. 1.51.1, cf. Buchholz, *Methymna* 139.

72 Arist. *Pol.* 5.8.13, 1311b 26-31.

73 Alcaeus fr. 129 L-P: τόδε Λέσβιοι . . . εὔδειλον τέμενος μέγα ξῦνον κάτεσσαν . . .

74 First discovered by Boutan in 1855 (cf. Boutan 311 ff.), and excavated by Koldewey (Koldewey 47 ff. with pls. 16-26) in 1855-6. For

the identification of the site see L. Robert, *REA* 62 (1960) 308-315, and for a good recent evaluation of the architecture, H. Plommer, 'The temple of Messa on Lesbos', in *Coins, Culture and History of the Ancient World,* ed. L. Casson (1981) 177-186.

75 Alcaeus fr. 130B L-P 13-19, cf. schol. A on Hom. *Il.* 9.129.

76 V. Scully, 'The capitals of Klopedi', *Architect. Rev.* 135 (1964) 129-134 = *The Earth, The Temple and the Gods* (2nd. ed. 1979) app.2, 222-5. Cf. Huxley (n.49) 91.

77 R. L. Scranton, *Greek Walls* (1941) 27: the whole chapter ('Lesbian Masonry', 25-44) is of great interest.

78 Arist. *Nic.Eth.* 1137b 30.

79 Kondis, *Dossier* 81 with fig. 45.

80 Strabo 13.1.39, C.599. Periander arbitrated in favour of Athens, but Mytilene clearly regained the city at some point, since later we find Peisistratus recovering it once more for Athens.

81 Thuc. 3.1-6, 8-16, 18-19, 27-30, 35-50 *passim.*

82 Cf. T. J. Quinn, *Athens and Samos, Lesbos and Chios 478-404 B.C.* (1981) 30 ff.

83 Thuc. 8.22.2.

84 Xen. *Hell.* 4.8.28.

85 IG ii² 42 = Ditt. *Syll.³* 149. Cf. H. Pistorius, *Beiträge zur Geschichte von Lesbos im vierten Jahrhundert v.Chr.* (1913) 38.

86 A. J. Heisserer, *Alexander the Great and the Greeks: The Epigraphic Evidence* (1980) 77-78, 83-85, 92-95, 118 ff., 136-7.

87 For a concise account of these events see Huxley (n.49) 86 ff.

88 DS 37.27.1.

89 Livy *per.* lxxxix; Suet. *Div.Jul.* 2.

90 Plut. *Pomp,* 42: εἰς Μιτυλήνην ἀφικόμενος τήν τε πόλιν ἠλευθέρωσε διὰ Θεοφάνη, καὶ τὸν ἀγῶνα τὸν πάτριον ἐθεάσατο τῶν ποιητῶν, ὑπόθεσιν μίαν ἔχοντα τὰς ἐκείνου πράξεις. ἡσθεὶς δὲ τῷ θεάτρῳ περιεγράψατο τὸ εἶδος αὐτοῦ καὶ τὸν τύπον, ὡς ὅμοιον ἀπεργασόμενος τὸ ἐν Ῥώμῃ, μεῖζον δὲ καὶ σεμνότερον. Cf. Strabo 13.2.3,

C.617-8. The theatre in Rome was opened in 55 BC, and could accommodate 40,000 spectators: S. B. Platner, rev. T. Ashby, *A Topographical Dictionary of Ancient Rome* (1929) 516, cf. 428-9, 555; E. Nash, *A Pictorial Dictionary of Ancient Rome* (1968) vol. ii, 423-8.

91 For Alcaeus's στασιωτικὰ ποιήματα see Strabo 13.2.3, C.617; Sappho's exile (probably to Syracuse): Marm. Par. ep. 36 (p. 12 Jacoby) = Campbell *test.* 5 (*Greek Lyric 1: Sappho Alcaeus,* 1982) 9.

92 Huxley 85 with further reff.

93 Fr. 106 L-P: πέρροχος ὡς ὅτ' ἄοιδος ὁ Λέσβιος ἀλλοδάποισιν.

94 See S. Charitonidis, L. Kahil, R. Ginouvès, *Les mosaïques de la maison du Ménandre à Mytilène* (1970) 97 ff. with pls. 1-8.

95 *P.Oxy.* 1800 fr. 1 = Campbell *test.* 1; Athen. 13.596c-d; Ovid *Her.* 15.63-70, 117-120; cf. Sappho fr. 202 Campbell and further *testimonia* there.

96 *IG* xii(2) 514 = Boutan 314, Conze fig. 16 no. 2.

97 *Acts* 16.10-17; 17.1-2, 15; 18.1, 18-23; 19.1; 20.6, 13-16. Cf. V. Aivaliotis, "Ὁ 'Απόστολος Παῦλος στῆ Μυτιλήνη', *Poimen* 36 (1968) 82-84.

98 Acts 19.25-40.

99 C. Buondelmonti, *Liber Insularum Archipelagi* (1406: ed. E. Legrand, 1897) 77, 234.

100 Buondelmonti, ibid.; O. Dapper, *Description exacte des isles de l'archipel . . .* (trs. from the Flemish, 1703) 235, who asserts that the island has since been free of snakes (a fiction), and in particular Gavriel, Archbishop of Methymna, Περιγραφὴ τῆς Λέσβου (ed. I. M. Phoundoulis, 1960) 31, describing Mesa, where μένουσι κτὶσματα παλαιότατα διεφθαρμένα. Λέγεται, κατὰ παράδοσιν, ὅτι ἦν ποτε δράκων φοβερὸς ἐκεῖ μὴ ἐῶν τινα παρελθεῖν τοῦ τόπου, ἐν δὲ τῷ τὸν ἅγιον Παῦλον ἐνδημῆσαι εἰς Λέσβον καὶ τῶν ἐκεῖσε πιστῶν δεηθέντων, διὰ προσευχῆς ἐθανάτωσεν αὐτόν.

101 Cic. *De Leg. Agrar.* 2.16.40: urbs et natura ac situ et . . . pulchritudine imprimis nobilis.

102 Theopompus ap. Athen. 12.532b (Timotheus of Athens).

103 Arist. *Gen. Anim.* 3.11.763b; *Hist. Anim.* 9.37.621b; cf. H.D.P. Lee, 'Place-names and the date of Aristotle's biological works', *CQ* 42 (1948) 61-67.

104 Longus 4.2.2-6; cf. 3.33.4; *proem.* 1.1; 1.1.2; 1.4.3; 1.23.2; 2.12.2; 2.13.2; 4.10.3.

105 Cf. P. Green, 'Longus, Antiphon, and the topography of Lesbos', *JHS* 102 (1982) 210-214.

106 A. M. Scarcella, 'La donna nel romanzo di Longo Sofista', *Giorn. Ital di Filol.* xxiv (1972) 63-84.

107 Longus (ed. G. Dalmeyda) i 4.1-3, i 7.2, iv 39.2. It would be natural to seek such a cave, if one existed, near the source of the island's one perennial river, the Voúvaris (see below), but this area (like much of Lesbos) is now (August 1980) off-limits on grounds of military security. It is an odd coincidence (but, I would judge, no more than that, unless a garbled memory of *Daphnis and Chloe* itself) that a shepherd should have told me a highly circumstantial story of how once, out in the hills and blind drunk, he stumbled on just such a cave, *full of statues* – but after sobering up could never remember his way back there!

108 Longus i 1, cf. Paus, viii 30.2, Strabo xiii 2.2, Diod. xiii 79.5-6, and R. Herbst, 'Mytilene', *RE* xvi (1933) 1417-19.

109 Longus ii 1.1-4, iv 10.3, iv 2.2, iii 33.4, ii 13.12. It is not necessary to argue, with P. Grimal, 'Le jardin de Lamon à Lesbos', *Rev. Arch.* xlix (1957) 211-14, that Lamo's orchard derives from an Oriental literary tradition: every fruit that Longus mentions can be found growing on the island today. See Dori Diálektos, Ὁ Νόμος Λέσβου⁴ (1980) 9-65, and the Naval Intelligence Division's *Geographical Handbook for Greece* (1945) iii, *Regional Geography* 510-13.

110 Proem i 1: καλὸν μὲν καὶ τὸ ἄλσος, πολύδενδρον, ἀνθηρόν, κατάρρυτον, μία πηγὴ πάντα ἔτρεφε καὶ τὰ ἄνθη καὶ τὰ δένδρα . . .

111 See the Budé edn² (1960) ed. G. Dalmeyda, xiv-xv.

112 Fr. 338 L-P: ὕει μὲν ὁ Ζεῦς, ἐκ δ' ὀράνω μέγας / χείμων, πεπάγαισιν δ' ὑδάτων ῥόαι.

113 Alcaeus frr. 397, 367, 347(a), 345.

114 Sappho frr. 136, 105(a), 117A, 156 (Campbell), 96 (ἀελίω δύντος ἀ βροδοδάκτυλος σελάννα πάντα περρέχασ' ἄστρα), 168C, 2 (Campbell: I use his translation).

115 P.C. Candargy, *La végétation de l'île de Lesbos (Mytilene) (1899) xxxvi, 1-39.*

CHAPTER V

1 Cf. Frank Schulze, 'On Blockbusters', *Art in America* 67.2 (1979) 101; Carter Ratcliff, 'Tut, Exxon and Anita Loos', ibid. 94.

2 See Grace Glueck, 'Where Tut money is going', *New York Times*, 23 March, 1979.

3 Ratcliff (n. 1 above) 96.

4 Cf. the percipient analysis by C.H.V. Sutherland, *Gold: Its Beauty, Power and Allure* (3rd rev. ed. 1969), esp. 20ff.

5 For a popular treatment of Rameses II see now William MacQuitty, *Rameses the Great, Master of the World* (1978). As T.G.H. James points out in his foreword, this pharaoh was no slouch at self-promotion, and did a PR job on his own much-puffed achievements that is producing results to this day.

6 See the admirable, and aptly titled, monograph by Brian M. Fagan, *The Rape of the Nile: Tomb Robbers, Tourists, and Archaeologists in Egypt* (1975), for a vivid account of this process down the ages. Mr Fagan's well-documented sketch of Belzoni is particularly revealing.

7 Thomas Hoving, *Tutankhamun: the untold story* (1978). Cf. the contrasting reviews by T.G.H. James, *New York Times Book Review*, 12 Nov. 1978, 48, 52 ('the revelations, even if all true, are not as scandalous as they are made out to be'), and Karl E. Meyer, *New Republic*, 6 Jan. 1979, 36-38, together with Meyer's own exposé of the antiquities racket in *The Plundered Past* (1973). It is fascinating, in the light of this new material, to reread that gripping report, *The Discovery of the Tomb of Tutankhamun*, by Carter himself and A.C. Mace (repr. 1977, with a good new introduction by Jon Manchip White): rather like having a second shot at Agatha Christie's *The Murder of Roger Ackroyd* after being alerted to the narrator's significant omissions.

8 The 'X-raying of the pyramids': Ahmed Fakhry, *The Pyramids* (2nd ed., 1969) 259 ff.

The Akhenaten temple project at Karnak has been recently described by Donald B. Redford in 'The razed temple of Akhnaten', *Scientific American*, Dec. 1978, 136-147. A thorough survey of recent work in the predynastic field is provided by Michael A. Hoffman's *Egypt before the Pharaohs: The Prehistoric Foundations of Egyptian Civilisation* (1979).

9 See W.B. Emery, *Archaic Egypt* (1961), esp. chs v and ix, with the relevant illustrations; W. Westendorf, *Painting, Sculpture and Architecture of Ancient Egypt* (1968), 23ff.

10 See Miriam Lichtheim, *Ancient Egyptian Literature, vol.1: The Old and Middle Kingdoms* (1973) 15-80. Adolf Erman's *The Ancient Egyptians: a sourcebook of their writings* (reissued 1978), first translated into English in 1927 and unrevised since, is now (though excellent in its day) in many respects obsolete, and should be used with caution. This plethora of material is not restricted to Egypt: it also comes from Mesopotamia, Assyria, the Hittite empire and the eastern Mediterranean – including, now, the vast new finds at Ebla. See James B. Pritchard, *Ancient Near Eastern Texts* [ANET] (3rd ed. 1969), and the two-volume paperback abridgement of this work, *The Ancient Near East: an anthology of texts and pictures* (1958, 1975).

11 Lichtheim, *op.cit.* vol.2, *The New Kingdom* (1976), offers the best edited and most attractive translations. Cf. also W.K. Simpson (ed.), *The Literature of Ancient Egypt* (1972), a useful but less complete (and less adequately annotated) anthology. The didactic literature (mostly in the form of 'instructions' to sons or successors) has encouraged William MacQuitty to produce, in *The Wisdom of the Ancient Egyptians* (1978), an anthology of snippets that reads rather like a cross between Samuel Smiles's *Self-Help* and *Thoughts of Chairman Mao*. There's obviously a market for this sort of thing, since the volume forms part of a series.

12 See Hermann Kees, *Ancient Egypt: a cultural topography* (1961: repr. 1977), esp. 47ff. This exhaustive text (originally written as articles for Pauly-Wissowa's *Reallexikon*) can be supplemented with the numerous photographs in a topographically planned survey such as *Egypt Observed* (1979), by Henri Gougand and Colette Gouvion.

13 Lichtheim, *op.cit.*(n.10 above) vol.1, 194ff.

14 See Alan B. Lloyd, *Herodotus Book II*, vol.1, *Introduction* (1975), 49ff., and Plato, *Laws* 656D–657B, 799A–B.

15 See E.A. Wallis Budge, *The Egyptian Book of the Dead* (1895, repr. 1967): and on Egyptian religion in general the same author's *Egyptian Religion: Egyptian Ideas of the Future Life* and *Egyptian Magic* (both 1899, repr. 1979): also Henri Frankfort, *Ancient Egyptian Religion* (1948, repr. 1961), and Alan W. Shorter, *The Egyptian Gods: a handbook* (1937, repr. 1978).

16 Barbara Mertz, *Temples, Tombs and Hieroglyphs* (rev. ed. 1978) 67. This sensible, entertaining book, modestly described by its author as 'a popular history of ancient Egypt', is the work of a scholar trained at the Oriental Institute in Chicago. Together with its companion volume, *Red Land, Black Land: Daily Life in Ancient Egypt* (rev. ed. 1978), it offers one of the most stimulating, and solidly grounded, general introductions to Egyptian culture available on the American market today. See also J.E. Manchip White, *Ancient Egypt: its culture and history* (rev. ed. 1970), less brightly chatty than Dr Mertz, but equally authoritative (White learnt his Egyptology at Cambridge from S.R.K. Glanville). Drier than either, but a monument of learning, is the late Sir Alan Gardiner's *Egypt of the Pharaohs* (1961). Among the more popular syntheses, Warner Hutchinson's *Ancient Egypt* (1978) is succinct and, on the whole, reliable.

17 See the dissection of Velikovsky's theories by Carl Sagan in *Broca's Brain* (1979) ch. vii, 'Venus and Dr Velikovsky', 81–127: and on Von Däniken the equally powerful arguments of John Scarborough, 'The gods in the image of Man: Von Däniken's new myths', *Bulletin of the Science Fiction Writers of America*, vol. 10 no. 3 (winter 1974–75), Academic Affairs Section, 20–25. Such attacks, it should be noted, affect neither beliefs nor sales, as (to take a more weighty example) Pieter Geyl, Hugh Trevor-Roper, and other serious historians found when they tried to explode the credibility of Arnold Toynbee's *A Study of History*.

18 E.A. Wallis Budge, *The Egyptian Book of the Dead* (n.15 above); *An Egyptian Hieroglyphic Dictionary* (2 vols., 1920, repr. 1978). The transliteration of hieroglyphs is complicated by the fact that, as in Hebrew or Arabic, there was no indication of the vowels: and that (a much more serious problem) we have no idea, except through the late and Hellenised medium of Coptic, what those vowels may have been – a lack that has not stopped Egyptologists, Budge included, from supplying them. This is understandable: to transliterate (for example) the word for a scribe's equipment as *mnhd* may show scholarly caution, but makes for difficulties in pronunciation. See Gardiner (n.16 above) ch.ii, esp. 22ff.

19 Piazzi Smyth's *Our Inheritance in the Great Pyramid* (4th ed. 1880) has been reissued as *The Great Pyramid: its secrets and mysteries revealed* (1978). Recent contributions to this odd literature include Peter Tompkins, *Secrets of the Great Pyramid* (1971), Peter Lemesurier's *The Great Pyramid Decoded* (1977, repr. 1979), and John Anthony West's *Serpent in the Sky: the High Wisdom of Ancient Egypt* (1979), from which I quote above, and which operates in a somewhat wider field. On top of everything else the author is rabidly anti-evolutionary (one section of his bibliography is disarmingly labelled 'Progress, Darwinian Evolution, and other Fantasies'), and cashes in on the obvious difficulties and conflicting theories of interpretation which bedevil Egyptian as all other ancient texts, by suggesting that such lofty guardians of ancient wisdom could not have demeaned themselves to utter the gobbledegook put in their mouths by modern professors, a circular argument that possesses its own offbeat charm.

20 See, e.g., G. Pat Flanagan, *Pyramid Power* (1973), a remarkable blend of elementary physics and pure hocus-pocus; and Norman Stark, *The First Practical Pyramid Book* (1977). Cf. Hoving, *op.cit.* (n.7 above), p.14. It is not hard to see how this kind of thing gains credence in some quarters, and there is always the long arm of coincidence to help things along. As it happens, I can report a nice instance of this myself. About five minutes after I finished the first draft of this section I began shivering violently, ran a high (103°F) fever, and retired to bed with 'flu. On recovery, I returned to the piece, and promptly, like Philoctetes, developed an inflamed and swollen foot. Driving to the clinic, I found myself jammed in line behind a car with the licence number TUT 777. By pyramidologists' logic, who could doubt that I was being hexed by angry transcendental forces?

21 *Ancient Egypt* (n.15 above), 89.

22 Just how complex and symbolic these texts could be, yet at the same time how totally deficient in any kind of conceptual or rational thought, is well demonstrated by the complete sequence of inscriptions preserved on the four shrines of Tutankhamun, a mind-numbing collection of prayers, myths, and interminably repetitive incantations, now edited and translated by Alexandre Piankoff as *The Shrines of Tut-Ankh-Amon* (1955, repr. 1977).

23 The parallels between modern American and ancient Egyptian embalming – 'the painting of the dead man's face, the burial of jewellery and trinkets in the coffin, the ornate and expensive coffin itself' (Mertz, *Red Land, Black Land* 282ff.) – have often been noted, and should be at once apparent to readers of Evelyn Waugh's *The Loved One* or Jessica Mitford's *The American Way of Death*. Mertz also draws attention to the two cultures' parallel addiction to a variety of oblique euphemisms for the fact of death. Fortunately, the Egyptian habit of pickling the viscera of the deceased in four canopic jars does not seem to have caught on with American morticians.

24 See in particular *The Egypt Story: its art, its monuments, its people, its history* (1979), with a plethora of fine photographs by Fred J. Maroon, and an intelligent, impressionistic text by the novelist P.H. Newby, himself a former resident of Cairo and Alexandria. Cf. also the illustrations to *Egypt Observed* (n.12 above).

CHAPTER VI

1 *Hom. Hymn to [Pyth.] Apollo,* 281 ff.

2 Georges Roux, *Delphes: son oracle et ses dieux* (1976) [hereafter 'Roux'], 39–40.

3 Lucian, *Bis. Accus.* 1.

4 Roux 70.

5 Roux 5, 157–8.

6 H.W. Parke, *Greek Oracles* (1967) [hereafter 'Parke'], 32 ff.; Robertson (n.40 below), 361–2; Roux 34.

7 Parke 108.

8 Roux 212–3: 'Une fois de plus, Delphes fut seulement le réflecteur de l'hellénisme. Sa crise fut celle de la Grèce: prospère lorsqu'elle était puissante, le sanctuaire périclita lorsque, épuisée, elle s'endormit.'

9 Parke 46–49.

10 E.R. Dodds, *The Greeks and the Irrational* (1951) [hereafter 'Dodds'], 75.

11 R.B. Onians, *The Origins of European Thought* (2nd ed. 1954), *passim*.

12 Parke 79.

13 Diod. Sic. 16.58.8; cf. Roux 100–116 with plan; Parke 77–8.

14 Parke 98–99.

15 Hdt. 1.50–51 *passim*.

16 Hdt. 1.87.

17 As argued by Roux, 211–212; cf. Parke 97.

18 Parke 259 ff.

19 See, e.g., Aristoph. *Birds* 958–990.

20 Thuc. 8.1.1; cf. Plut. *Nic.* 13.

21 Roux 211–212.

22 In Greek, σώζειν τὰ φαινόμενα; see Simplicius' *Commentary* on the *De Caelo* of Aristotle, ed. I.L. Heiberg, *Comment. in Aristot. Graeca* (1894) vii, 422, cf. 488, 492–3.

23 Cf. Roux 164: 'Supposer qu'il [le prophète] se substituait au dieu comme inspirateur serait imputer à Delphes l'organisation d'une supercherie permanente . . . Et qui croira que les Pères de l'Eglise auraient dédaigné d'exploiter une aussi facile accusation si elle avait eu la moindre apparence de vérité?'

24 Dodds 74.

25 Xen. *Anab.* 3.1.5.

26 Dodds, 74–75, puts the case more strongly than I would: 'The prestige of the Oracle must have been pretty deeply rooted to survive its scandalous behaviour during the Persian Wars. Apollo on that occasion showed neither prescience nor patriotism, yet his people did not turn away from him in disgust; on the contrary, his clumsy attempts to cover his tracks and eat his words appear to have been accepted without question.'

27 Parke 131 ff.

28 Fontenrose 42; cf. 34 for a very similar statement.

29 Parke 259 ff.

30 H.J. Rose, *Modern Methods in Classical Mythology* (1930), 20.

31 M. Dobson, *Helios* 10 (1983) 187 ff.

32 N. Robertson, *Phoenix* 36 (1982) 359.

33 Parke 79.

34 Diod. Sic. 16.26.2-4.

35 Eur. 35. 973 Nauck: μάντις δ' ἄριστος ὅστις εἰκάζει καλῶς. Cf. Plut. *Mor.* 432C.

36 Herakleitos fr. 244 Kirk-Raven-Schofield = Plut. *Mor.* 404E.

37 Parke 79.

38 Plut. *Mor.* 759A-B: ἡ Πυθία τοῦ τρίποδος ἐκβᾶσα καὶ τοῦ πνεύματος ἐν γαλήνῃ καὶ ἡσυχίᾳ διατελεῖ.

39 Plut. *Mor.* 397C: μόνας τὰς φαντασίας παρίστησι καὶ φῶς ἐν τῇ ψυχῇ ποιεῖ πρὸς τὸ μέλλον.

40 See, e.g., the notices by F. Brenk, *Gnomon* 52 (1980) 700-706; J. Mikalson, *Class. World* 74 (1980) 179-80; P. Walcot, *Greece and Rome* 27 (1980) 104 (a brief note only); N. Robertson, *Phoenix* 36 (1982) 358-363; M. Dobson, *Helios* 10 (1983) 187-194; J. Bremmer, *Mnemosyne* 36 (1984) 441-2. I have not seen S. Platthy's review in the *Journ. of Magic Hist.* 1 (1979) 119-123.

CHAPTER VII

1 See A.W.H. Adkins, 'Clouds, Mysteries, Socrates and Plato', *Antichthon* 4 (1970) 13-24, where it is argued convincingly that Socrates employed initiation-language in philosophical discussion and further that Aristophanes deliberately held this practice up to ridicule in the *Clouds*. It is interesting, though probably coincidental, that in the *Theaetetus* Socrates goes on (156A) to identify the ἀρχή of his thinkers' secret opinions as the notion ὡς τὸ πᾶν κίνησις ἦν (cf. p.116 and n.17). W.K.C. Guthrie, *A*

History of Greek Philosophy, vol.iii (1969) 374, suggests that Aristophanes may have described Socrates and his companions as a *thiasos* 'for comic effect and adding such picturesque details as the ban on revealing its "mysteries" to any but the initiated disciples', but he does not cite either of these Platonic passages.

2 εἰσὶν δὲ οὗτοι οἱ οὐδὲν ἄλλο οἰόμενοι εἶναι ἢ οὗ ἂν δύνωται ἀπρὶξ τοῖν χεροῖν λαβέσθαι, πράξεις δὲ καὶ πᾶν τὸ ἀόρατον οὐκ ἀποδεχόμενοι ὡς ἐν οὐσίας μέρει.

3 Gilbert Murray, *Greek Studies* (1947) 66 ff.; cf. E.R. Dodds, *The Greeks and the Irrational* (1951) 179-80.

4 K.J. Dover, *Arethusa* 6 (1973) 70; cf. *JHS* 86 (1966) 47. The Platonic epigram: Schmid-Stählin, *Gesch. Griech. Lit.* I4 (1946) 451 n.3: the story about Dionysius, *Vit. Aristoph.* 9, p.xlv Bergk.

5 See, e.g., G.E.R. Lloyd, *Polarity and Analogy* (1966) 421 ff.; S. Sambursky, *The Physical World of the Greeks* (1956) ch.i, 'The Scientific Approach', 1-25; Bruno Snell, *The Discovery of the Mind* (1953) ch. x, 'The Origin of Scientific Thought', 227-245; B.E. Perry, 'The early Greek capacity for viewing things separately', *TAPA* 68 (1937) 403-27.

6 G.S. Kirk, *Homer and the Epic* (1965) 132. For a good account of parataxis see P. Chantraine, *Grammaire Homérique*, vol. ii (1953) 351 ff.

7 Dodds (n.3 above) 116-20, 180-85.

8 The classic treatment is that by F.A. von Hayek, *The Counter-Revolution of Science: Studies in the Abuse of Reason* (1955).

9 *Clouds* 76-77, 116-18, 238-41, 244-45, 433-34, 484-85, 738-39, 1154-62.

10 *Clouds* 202 ff., 259, 338-39, 648, 1231, 1283-84.

11 Anaximander: [Hippocr.] *Nat.Puer.* 17 (= Littré vol. vii, 498). Anaximenes: J.M. Robinson, *An Introduction to early Greek Philosophy* (1968) 44-45. Empedocles: Diels-Kranz [hereafter 'DK'] 31 B35, A49, A30, A51; Arist. *De Caelo* 2.1.284a 25. Anaxagoras: DK 59 B13, B15, B16. The Atomists: DK 68 B167, A3, A69; Theophr. *De Vertig.* 1 (p.136 Wimmer); Lucr. 5.419-431; cf. Guthrie (n.1) vol. ii, 174, 300 ff.,

400, 410, 423. Rotation of the heavenly bodies: DK 59 A12 (Anaxagoras). Spontaneous generation: DK 59 B13, B4 (Anaxagoras). Rise of civilisation: DK 59 B4 (Anaxagoras). Dizziness: Theophr. ibid. Stones in the bladder: [Hippocr.] Morb.4.55 (= Littré vol. vii, 600, reading ὑπὸ δίνης with Heidel, cf. Robinson, op.cit. 325).

12 Cf. Dover's commentary on this passage, *Aristophanes: Clouds* (1968) 150.

13 Dover, ibid. xxxv.1

14 Dover, ibid, xlii-iii.

15 On this line see Dover, ibid. 91.

16 Theognis 729-30 West; R.B. Onians, *The Origins of European Thought* (2nd ed. 1954) 86-87.

17 ἡ κινήσεως τάξις, Plat. *Laws* 665A; cf. Arist. Probl. 882b 2: πᾶς ῥυθμὸς ὡρισμένη μετρεῖται κινήσει.

18 Alcibiades is said to have erased the record of a charge by rubbing it off it with a dampened finger (Athen. 9.407B-C); cf. J. Hatzfeld, *Alcibiade* (2nd ed., 1951) 132. Hatzfeld argues that the anecdote, involving the comic poet Hegemon of Thasos (against whom the charge had been brought) 'ne mérite peut-être pas beaucoup de créance'. I see no particular reason to regard it with more scepticism than any one of a dozen similar stories.

19 For 'calling down the moon' as a magical ritual see W. Roscher, *Ueber Selene und Verwandtes* (1890) 87, 89, 177 ff., 344 ff. Menander associated Thessalian witches with this process: Pliny *HN* 30.7, cf. A.S.F. Gow, *Theocritus* (1950) 2, 34. See also Plat. *Gorg.* 513A 5-6, with Dodds' note (p.350); also Daremberg-Saglio s.v. 'Magia', III.2 p.1516 with fig. 4785. It has been suggested to me that Socrates' apparent approval of Strepsiades' solutions at 749 ff. and 764 ff. militates against the argument which sees Socrates, *qua* exponent of the New Intellectualism, in conflict with the pragmatic and archaic thought-patterns of Strepsiades. But Socrates' two interjections (εὖ γε 757; σοφῶς γε 773) are both heavily ironic; and only a line or two later (781 ff.) his patience with this rustic non-conceptualising pupil abruptly runs out.

20. Anaximander frs. 101-2 Kirk-Raven; Hdt. 4.36.2, 5.49; cf. A.E.M. Johnston, 'The

earliest preserved Greek map: a new Ionian coin type', *JHS* 87 (1967) 86-94 with pl. ix, cf. pls. x-xi. See also O.A.W. Dilke, *Greek and Roman Maps* (1985) 22-31, 146-47.

21 See 212-13, παρατέταται – παρετάθη, which we may roughly approximate in English by the two usages of the phrase 'laid out'. For other Strepsiadic puns and portmanteau neologisms see, e.g., *Clouds* 24, 33, 74, 166, 243, 730, 857, 1108-09.

22 Dover, op.cit.(above, n.12) xxxv.

23 Whether or not Aristophanes intended his audience to believe Strepsiades' assertion (1481-85) that it was Hermes who told him to set the *phrontisterion* on fire is a moot point. What the spectators might well recall, however, was that famous incident, within living memory, when 'the Crotoniates revolted against the political power of the Pythagoreans, trapped the leaders of the sect in a house where they met . . . and incinerated both house and leaders' (E.C. Kopff, 'Nubes 1493 ff.: Was Socrates Murdered?', *GRByS* 18, 1977, 116). For the purposes of this analysis I am working from the revised text as we have it, and I do not speculate on the degree to which Aristophanes originally favoured the sophistic arguments of the Unjust Argument. It is, however, suggestive that Dover (xciii-xciv) thinks the first version may have 'ended with the triumph of Pheidippides over his wretched father' and thus have 'presented without irony or disguise the bleak reality which in *Knights* is overlaid by the conventional comic ending'.

24 See, e.g., 247-48, 263-74, 291-92, 296-97, 398-402, 423-24, 818-19, 825 ff., 1235, 1241-42, 1468-71, 1476-77; and cf. Adkins, op. cit.(n.1) 24.

25 See n.8 above.

26 See Guthrie, op. cit. (n.1 above) vol. ii, 369-77, for a convenient summary of Diogenes' views.

27 Dodds, op. cit. (n.3 above) ch. vi, 'Rationalism and Reaction in the Classical Age', 179 ff.

CHAPTER IX

1 Just how far things have moved in a very short time may be deduced from C.J. Fordyce's edition of Catullus, published in 1961, which omitted no less than 31 poems because they 'did not lend themselves to comment in English'. Earlier evidence is abundant, ranging from the habitual suppression of the second and ninth satires of Juvenal from all exegetic commentaries to such *curiosa* as Pickard-Cambridge's habit of airbrushing out the erections from ancient representations of satyr-drama (to which he devoted a good proportion of his scholarly career), or W.W. Tarn's determined efforts to clean up Alexander's sex-life (for which see his *Alexander the Great*, 1948, vol. 2, Appendix 18, 319-326), or the habit – now at last abandoned – of translating Martial's more obscene epigrams not into English but into *Italian* (see p. 243).

2 E.g. Sir Kenneth Dover, *Greek Homosexuality* (1978), and Sarah B. Pomeroy, *Goddesses, Whores, Wives and Slaves* (1975).

3 The value of this, of course, varies, as students of Claude Lévi-Strauss are well aware; perhaps the Freudian approach has done more than any other to obfuscate the historical issue by overlaying ancient fantasies with modern ones. See, e.g., Philip E. Slater, *The Glory of Hera* (1968), and, for a fundamentally sane eritique of these various approaches, G.S. Kirk, *Myth: its meaning and functions* (1970).

4 Homer's Ionian patrons: G.L. Huxley, *The Early Ionians* (1966) 43; expurgations: G. Murray, *The Rise of the Greek Epic* (4th ed. 1934) ch. v, 120ff.; Achilles and Patroclus, Dover, *op. cit.* 53, 197-8, and cf. note 8 below.

5 The double standard clearly applies to Odysseus. When he finds that twelve of the serving women in his palace have been putting out for the wooers he has just slaughtered, he tells Telemachus and Eumaeus, first, to have these girls remove the bodies and clean up the mess, and then to put them all to the sword (Telemachus, however, feeling that they do not deserve a 'clean death', partly because they put out, and partly because they insulted his mother (? by putting out), hangs them all instead): Od. 22.417-472, esp. 440-5, 461ff.

6 Helen is also, of course, a survivor: as MacNeice wrote, 'the whore and the buffoon will come off best' (a good classicist, he might have had Helen and Menelaus in mind), and Helen's reappearance in the *Odyssey* (4.120ff.) after the war, every inch the respectable married society matron, is one of the great comic scenes in world literature.

7 Aeschylus, for one, was far more explicit: frs. 228-9 of his play *The Myrmidons* clearly refer to intercrural intercourse. Cf. p. 137.

8 Dover, ibid., citing Aeschines 1.142 (the speech *Against Timarchus*). See also the admirable article by W.M. Clarke, 'Achilles and Patroclus in love', *Hermes* 106 (1978) 381-396, esp. n. 38, where Clarke observes that in the *Iliad* 'we see the reticence of the author, and presumably his audience, to label a love that, in any case, requires no name to be understood'.

9 I would not include in this category such phenomena as the temporary Athenian law, passed at a time during the Peloponnesian War when husbands were in short supply, permitting de facto bigamy (i.e. legitimising offspring by concubines), or Plato's frigid notion that warriors who distinguished themselves on the battlefield should be given special sexual privileges when on furlough: see Diog. Laert. 2.26, cf. D.M. MacDowell, *The Law in Classical Athens*, 1978, 90; Plato, *Rep.* 460b, 468b-c. Such measures are utilitarian rather than aimed at the pleasure principle; indeed, Plato's contempt for the sexual act is notorious, and his exposition of sexual eugenics in the *Republic* must rank – along with Lucretius' tirade, *De Rerum Natura* 4.1030-1287, cf. p. 150 – among the most antaphrodisiac passages in all literature.

10 For an excellent analysis of the continuing tradition, which takes full advantage of the anthropological and sociological fieldwork carried out by such researchers as Campbell, Friedl, Peristiany and Sanders, see Peter Walcot, *Greek Peasants, ancient and modern: A comparison of social and moral values* (1970), esp. chs ii-iii.

11 One of Hesiod's fears is excessive sexual demands by a wife: *WD* 704-5, and cf. 585-8, where he claims that in high summer women are most insatiable, but men dried out and at their lowest ebb, a generalisation which should amuse habitués of Hellenic cruises. For the prevalence of such fears see H.R. Hays, *The Dangerous Sex: The Myth of Feminine Evil* (1964), esp. 239ff.

12 Phocylides, fr. 2 Diehl, expresses similar sentiments, again praising the bee-wife. See also the admirable edition of Semonides' poem by Prof. Hugh Lloyd-Jones, *Females of the Species* (1975): his introduction contains some illuminating general remarks (25ff.) on women in Greek literature.

13 By a kind of selective breeding process such chauvinistic attitudes also produced a few really powerful and sexually dominating matriarchs: the real-life analogues of mythical characters such as Clytemnestra or Medea would be Cimon's sister Elpinice and, in the 4th cent. BC, Philip II's terrible wife Olympias.

14 We should beware, as Dover very properly reminds us, of assuming without question, in default of confirmatory evidence, that poems purporting to describe details of the writer's own life are, in fact, autobiographical: see 'The poetry of Archilochus', *Fondation Hardt Entretiens* vol. X, *Archiloque* (1964), 183-212, esp. 206ff. But in Archilochus' case I suspect a kind of sexual exhibitionism that took especial pleasure in self-revelation, and was calculated to shock.

15 'Kick the empty-headed rabble!', he snorts (*Theog.* 847): note also his significant complaint, common in an era when capital first began to erode traditional privileges, that 'money is what holds most power for all men' (*Theog.* 718). The bulk of his erotic addresses to Kyrnos are gathered at the end of the *Theognidea* (lines 1231ff.), perhaps a late act of sequestration by medieval Christian scribes who were disconcerted at finding homosexuality – in fact very characteristically – allied to moral protreptics: see Martin L. West, *Studies in Greek Elegy and Iambus* (1974) 43ff., and cf. the Suda s.v. Theognis (1).

16 Now conveniently catalogued by Dover, *op. cit.* 206ff.; he also reproduces a good many of them. Cf. John Boardman, *Athenian Black Figure Vases* (1974) 210: 'Male homosexual activity is so commonly shown that it acquires iconographic conventions of its own . . . The scenes appear regularly from about 560 on.'

17 A seeming exception would be the famous temple prostitutes of Corinth, or Eryx in Sicily or Comana in Asia Minor: see Strabo 8.6.20, C.378, 6.2.6, C.272, 12.3.36, C.559; Athenaeus 13.573 *passim*; Diod. Sic. 4.83. But in the first place it is nowhere expressly stated that these prostitutes actually had intercourse *in the temple* of Ma or Aphrodite; and in any case there are few taboos of this sort that do not have a formalised ritual exception.

18 Cf. T.B.L. Webster, *The Tragedies of Euripides* (1967) 64ff.

19 Plato, *Symp.* 207b, 208e-209d *passim*, cf. *Phaedr.* 250e: well discussed by Dover, *op. cit.* 163, 167; cf. also his excellent monograph *Greek Popular Morality in the time of Plato and Aristotle* (1974) 206-7. Hereafter 'Dover *GPM*'.

20 On this fascinating topic see G. Devereux, 'Greek pseudo-homosexuality and the "Greek Miracle" ', *Symbolae Osloenses* 13 (1967) 69-92, cf. Dover *op. cit.* 81ff.

21 Most accounts of Alcibiades are still absurdly over-eulogistic: for a salutary corrective see E.F. Bloedow, *Alcibiades Reexamined* (1973); and for Alcibiades' philosophic-erotic relations with Socrates, M. Gagarin, 'Socrates' *Hybris* and Alcibiades' Failure', *Phoenix* 31 (1977) 22-37. The standard biography is that by Jean Hatzfeld, *Alcibiade* (2nd ed. 1951). See also my article 'Alcibiades: a Lion in the State', *Internat. Hist. Mag.* 17 (1974) 8-23.

22 The paradoxes of the Athenian attitude to homosexuality become a little more manageable if one constantly bears in mind that *only* the courting of adolescent boys (in particular those whose beards had not yet begun to grow: a significant point, since this emphasises their girlishness) by older – but normally not middle-aged or elderly – men was regarded as socially acceptable; whereas *all* homosexual activity *between adults*, above all *passive promiscuity* by adult effeminates (and indeed even over-eagerness on the part of an adolescent *eromenos*) provoked social disapproval or derision. Any male citizen who prostituted his favours was debarred from many civic rights, including that of addressing the Assembly. Cf. Dover ch. ii, 19ff., analysing Aeschines' speech *Against Timarchos*.

23 See pp. 112 ff.

24 By a nice paradox, the two things about Plato that have always ensured his popularity, with post-Christian moralists and aesthetes alike, are, first, his hauntingly brilliant characterisations and crystalline prose style (which, like Proust's, can often reconcile the reader to illogical or antipathetical propositions); and second, his simultaneous obsession with Eros and disapproval of physical sex. What hair-splitting Augustinian could resist a preacher who both argued that *paiderastia* was the best route to philosophical appreciation of beauty, and damned homosexual intercourse as 'contrary to nature' (*Laws* 636a-c, 836d-e)?

25 Dover *GPM* 211.

26 See, e.g., Antiphon 1.14-20; Aristoph. *Eccles.* 225-8. *Thesm.* 478ff.; Andocides 4.14, 4.33; Lysias 1.6-26, 14.29; and cf. Jeffrey Henderson, *The Maculate Muse: Obscene Language in Attic Comedy* (1975) 183ff. On incest see R. and E. Blum, *Health and Healing in Rural Greece* (1965) 49.

27 Herodotus 1.8-10, 61; 2.89; 5.92 n.3; 9.112.

28 Cf. Pomeroy, *op. cit.* (n.2 above) 98-114.

29 Sappho might seem to present an early exception, and in ways I think she does; the island of Lesbos – small enough for isolation, large enough to sustain an independent world – was a natural enclave (see pp.46-7 above). Yet even Sappho often regards love as a plague to the senses: the student of mine who said that her famous list of symptoms (fr.31 Lobel-Page, vv.7-16) – sweat, pallor, voice-failure, and so on – sounded more appropriate for cholera than for passion (in the modern sense, understood) had a point. Evidence for passion as madness or an affliction: Dover *GPM* 77, 125, 137, 208.

30 On Aphrodite Urania and Aphrodite Pandemos see Plato, *Symp.* 180e-181c, cf. Xen., *Symp.* 8.9, Paus. 1.22.3.

31 See Dover *GPM* 205-207.

32 See John Ferguson, *The Heritage of Hellenism* (1973) 27ff., and Lewis Mumford, *The Culture of Cities* (1938, repr. 1970), esp.. chs i-ii.

33 See A. Audollent, *Defixionum Tabellae* (1904); S. Eitrem, 'La Magie comme motif littéraire chez les Grecs et les Romains', *Symbolae Osloenses* 21 (1941) 39-83; K. Preisendanz, *Papyri Graecae magicae* (1928-31); E. Tavenner, *Studies in Magic from Latin Literature* (1916); G. Luck, *Hexen und Zauberei in der Römischen Dichtung* (1962); A.M. Tupet, *La Magie dans la poésie latine* (1976), esp. pt ii, 107ff.

CHAPTER X

1 E.N. Borza, 'The Macedonian royal tombs at Vergina: some cautionary notes', *Arch. News* 10.4 (1981) 81-82 with nn. 59-60; J.P. Adams, 'The *larnakes* from Tomb II at Vergina', *Arch. News* 12.1-2 (1983) 3-4 with nn. 16-34.

2 Deborah Trustman, 'Museums and Hype: the Alexander show', *Atlantic Monthly* (Dec. 1980) 73.

3 Judith Weinraub, *The Washington Star*, 13 Nov. 1980, C-1, C-4; cf. J. Carter Brown in *The Search for Alexander: an Exhibition* (1980) 6.

4 C.M. Woodhouse, *The Story of Modern Greece* (1968) 184 ff.

5 R. Clogg, *A Short History of Modern Greece* (1979) 163-4.

6 E. Badian, 'Greeks and Macedonians', in *Macedonia and Greece in Late Classical and Early Hellenistic Times*, ed. B. Barr Sharrar and E.N. Borza [Studies in the Hist. of Art, vol. 10] (1982) 33-51. This key discussion of the problem predictably stirred up quite breathtaking displays of emotional *ethnikismós* in those Greeks attending the seminar (cf. p.154 above). One reputable archaeologist asserted, in my presence, that of course Badian only took this 'anti-Greek' line because he was a Jew – and then seemed honestly puzzled by the frosty reaction that followed.

7 Demetrius *De Eloc.* §283; Plut. *Vit. Phoc.* 22; cf. my *Alexander of Macedon* (1974) 477.

8 *The Search for Alexander: an Exhibition* (1980) 20.

9 M. Andronikos, *The Royal Graves at Vergina* (1978) 5-6, n.2.

10 Trustman (n.2 above) 73.

11 Israel Shenker, 'Treasures of the Age of Alexander and Philip of Macedon go on World Tour', *Smithsonian* (Nov. 1980) 132.

12 Trustman (n.2 above) 78.

13 Thrasymachus fr. F2 Diels-Kranz, cited by Badian (n.6 above) 35.

14 Shenker (n.11 above) 138.

15 N.G.L. Hammond, *A History of Macedonia*, Vol.I (1972) 431-5, esp. 433; Vol.II (with G.T. Griffith, 1979) 29.

16   Badian (n.6 above) 38.

17   'On the Malice of Herodotus', usually cited in Latin as *De Malignitate Herodoti, Mor.* 854E-874C: see esp. 855B-857F, 874C.

18   Shenker (n.11 above) 132, 134.

19   Published in *Archaia Makedonia* I (1970) 65, and subsequently repeated in his *History of Macedonia*, Vol.I, 56-58 (cf. maps at 124 and 140), repeated in Vol. II, 13, and in his article ' "Philip's tomb" in historical context', *GRByS* 19 (1978) 331-350. Cf. my article 'The royal tombs of Vergina: a historical analysis', in *Philip II, Alexander the Great and the Macedonian Heritage*, ed. W.L. Adams and E.N. Borza (1982) 129-151 [hereafter 'Green, "Royal Tombs" '], esp. 136-7.

20   See in particular 'Vergina: the royal graves in the Great Tumulus', *Athen. Arch. Annals* 10 (1977) 1-72 [in fact not published till 1979]; 'Regal Treasures from a Macedonian tomb', *Nat. Geogr.* 154 (July 1978) 54-77; 'The royal tomb of Philip II' [note title], *Archaeology* 31 (Sept.-Oct. 1978) 33-41; a short monograph, *The Royal Graves at Vergina* (Athens 1978, cf. n.9 above: a reprint of item 1 above); 'The royal tombs at Aigai (Vergina)', in *Philip of Macedon*, ed. M.B. Hatzopoulos and L.D. Loukopoulos (Athens 1980) 188-194; 'The royal tombs at Vergina: a brief account of the excavations', a contribution to the exhibition catalogue (n.8 above) 26-38; and *Vergina: the Royal Tombs and Other Antiquities* (Athens 1984: published in several languages, including Greek, English, French and German).

21   His nearest approach to a detailed rebuttal of criticism has been in his article 'The royal tomb at Vergina and the problem of the dead', *Athens Annals of Arch.* 13 (1980) 168-178, which still leaves a number of loose ends untied.

22   Most notably from Professor Hammond, *GRByS* 19 (1978) 331-350; and cf. his later article, 'The end of Philip', in *Philip of Macedon* (n.20 above) 166-175. See also R. Lane Fox, *The Search for Alexander* (1980) 77-95, and S.M. Burstein, 'The tomb of Philip II', *Echos du Monde Classique/Classical Views* 26 (1982) 143-163.

23   Quint. Curt. 10.7.2-10; Arrian, *Succ.* 1.1A and B; Justin 13.2.8-3.1; Diod. Sic. 18.2.2-4.

24   Diyllos, *FGrH* 73 Fl; Diod. Sic. 19.52.5

25   Evidence assembled in Green, 'Royal Tombs' (n.19 above) 129-133, 146-7.

26   Diod. Sic. 19.52.4, 105.1-2; Paus. 9.7.2; Justin 15.2.3-5.

27   Green, 'Royal Tombs' 130-1, 147.

28   Ibid. 148. For Cleopatra-Eurydice's dispatch by Olympias see Justin 9.7.12, cf. 12.6.14 and Paus. 8.7.7.

29   Green, 'Royal Tombs' 149.

30   E.N. Borza, 'Those Vergina tombs again', *Arch. News* II (1982) 9.

31   Susan I. Rotroff, 'Spool saltcellars in the Athenian Agora', *Hesperia* 53 (1984) 343-354, cf. *AJA* 84 (1980) 228-9 and 86 (1982) 283.

32   P.W. Lehmann, 'The so-called tomb of Philip II: a different interpretation', *AJA* 84 (1980) 527-31; 'The so-called tomb of Philip II: an addendum', *AJA* 86 (1982) 437-442, cf. *Athens Annals of Arch.* 14 (1981 [1982]) 134-144; A.M.P. Giallombardo and B. Tripodi, 'Le tombe regali de Vergina: quale Filippo?', *Annali della R. Scuola Normale Superiore di Pisa*, Sezione di Lettere, ser.III, 10.3 (1980) 889-1001, cf. *Magna Grecia* 16 (1981) 14-17; W.L. Adams, 'The royal Macedonian tomb at Vergina,' *Anc. World* 3.3 (1980) 67-72.

33   See T.D. Boyd, 'The arch and the vault in Greek architecture', *AJA* 82 (1978) 83-100, esp. 89 n.24; other evidence assembled in Green, 'Royal Tombs' 134 n.10. Cf. E.A. Fredricksmeyer, 'Again the so-called tomb of Philip II', *AJA* 85 (1981) 330-4.

34   Green, 'Royal Tombs' 134-5; Borza (n.1 above) 77-78.

35   Adams (n.32 above) 69-70.

36   See Borza (n.34 above) 78-81; Green, 'Royal Tombs' 149-150 with n.58.

37   Evidence in Green, 'Royal Tombs' 135; cf. Demosth. 18.67, Justin 9.3.2.

38   Lehmann, *AJA* 84 (1980) 528 n.9; Adams (n.32 above) 70 and n.37.

39   Ed. H. Diels and W. Schubart (Teubner) 12.36-13.12. On the leg wounds see in particular 12.64-66: 'Pleuratas the Illyrian charged him during an Illyrian campaign and wounded him with his lance in the right shin . . . ' and 13.3-7, 'he received a third wound during his attack on the Triballi when during a charge one of the enemy thrust a sarissa [*sic*] through his right thigh, laming him'. The reading *klein* (collarbone) for *knēmēn* (shin) depends on the assumption that Demosthenes' report (18.67) is exhaustive, and that therefore the broken collarbone to which he refers must be a wound mentioned by Didymus, especially since Didymus does not refer to a broken collarbone himself. I see no reason for Philip not having suffered both wounds.

40 Andronikos (n.9 above) 46: ' . . . measurement showed that the left greave is 3.50 cm. shorter. The greaves are also shaped differently: the left greave has a more pronounced bulge over the knee muscle.'

41 Personal information, Dr George Kitzmiller.

42 Andronikos (n.9 above) 48; also his article in *Philip of Macedon* (n.20 above) 204-5, and Hammond, *GRByS* 19 (1978) 332-3.

43 Andronikos (n.21 above) 169-70.

44 Green, 'Royal Tombs' 151.

CHAPTER XII

1 'Victor and Invictus', *HThR* 50 (1957) 236; in his subsequent book, *Divus Julius* (1971), Weinstock backed off from the kind of overt comparison he had made in his article, and his references to Alexander remain peripheral: see, e.g., 21, 86ff., 333 f.

2 Eduard Meyer, *Caesars Monarchie und das Principat des Pompeius: innere Geschichte Roms von 66 bis 44 v. Chr.* (1922, repr. 1963) 465-473, esp. 472: 'Die Monarchie Caesars is ihrer Idee nach die Wiederaufnahme und volle Durchführung der Weltmonarchie Alexanders,' etc.

3 N.J. De Witt, 'Caesar and the Alexander legend', *CW* 36 (1942-43) 51-52, cf. *TAPhA* 73 (1942) 342-5, and J. Gagé, *REA* 42 (1940) 425-438.

4 Often with explicit acceptance of the views propagated by W.W. Tarn (e.g. in *PBA* (1933) 123-166, and *Alexander the Great* (1948 II 399 ff.): see De Witt 52.

5 L.R. Taylor, *The divinity of the Roman Emperor*

(1931), esp. 74-77; strongly influenced by Meyer (see 75 n.42).

6 D. Michel, *Alexander als Vorbild für Pompeius, Caesar und Marcus Antonius* (1967), esp. 67-107, 134.

7 Ibid. 67: 'Die moderne Forschung hat die Frage nach der Alexander-Nachahmung Caesars *beinahe ausnahmslos* bejaht' (italics mine).

8 *CAH* IX (1932) 718-740, esp. 739. Cf. also the sober judgment expressed by M. Gelzer in his *Caesar: Politician and statesman*, trs. P. Needham (1969) 322 n.7 (-323).

9 D. Kienast, 'Augustus und Alexander', *Gymnasium* 76 (1969) 430-455. See in particular 440: 'Trotz der in der Literatur immer wieder geäusserten Auffassung eines besonders engen Verhältnisses gerade Caesars zu Alexander lässt sich nicht erweisen, dass sich der Dictator den Makedonenkönig zu seinem Vorbild erwählt hätte.'

10 O. Weippert, *Alexander-Imitatio und römische Politik in republikanisher Zeit* (1972), esp. 105-192.

11 J.S. Richardson, *JRS* 64 (1974) 238.

12 See my *Alexander of Macedon* (1974) 40-41, 532 n. 29, 541 n. 58.

13 See n.11 above.

14 Cf. Cic. *De Orat.* 1.60.257; 3.29.117, where the double function of *comparatio* – to assess likeness, and judge probability – is stressed; *De Offic.* 1.43.152; Livy 22.8.2; Tac. *Dial.* 23.2.

15 See e.g., Appian, *BC* 2.149-154,619ff.; Strabo 13.1.27, C 594-5; Vell. Pat. 2.41; Livy 9.16.9-19.17; and cf. p.196 above.

16 Cf. Cic. *Rhet. Her.* 1.3, *De Orat.* 3.53.204, *Phil.* 14.6.17, *De Offic.* 3.1.1; Sen. *Ep.* 65.3 ('omnis ars naturae imitatio est').

17 *Aemulatio* can, of course, include *imitatio* as one of its methods (cf. Cic. *Tusc. Disp.* 4.18.7), but need not do so: cf. Livy 28.21.4; Vell. Pat. 1.17.5 ('aluntur aemulatione ingenia'). It can also often be competitive, even hostile: Cic. *Tusc. Disp.* 4.26.56; Livy 26.38.10, 44.25.2; Pliny, *HN* 13.70.

18 As Michel and Weippert both to some extent do; cf. also J.B. Nadell, *Alexander and the Romans* (1959) chs. iii-iv.

19 This embarrassing omission was noted long ago by Franz Weber, *Alexander der Grosse im Urteil der Griechen und Römer bis in die konstantinische Zeit* (1909) 45. Lucan, it is true, claims (10.19-20) that Caesar visited Alexander's tomb in Egypt, a claim plausible enough *per se*; but no other account of the Egyptian campaign refers to such an episode, and Lucan may have invented it on the analogy of subsequent better-attested visits by Augustus (Suet. *Div. Aug.* 18.1, Dio Cass. 51.16.5) and Caligula (Suet. *Cal.* 52, Dio Cass. 59.17.3). Cf. Appian, *BC* 2.89.376, and the discussions by Nadell 82, Weippert 118 with n.1, and especially H. Christensen, 'Alexander der Grosse bei den römischen Dichtern', *Neue Jahrb. f. klass. Altert.* 23 (1909) 122 with n.2. Even if true, such a visit would surely have been due to pure historical curiosity (both Augustus and Caligula seem to have had the tourist's – and the vandal's – instinct in such matters) rather than to any hypothetical urge for symbolic *aemulatio*. On Lucan's attitude to Caesar see pp.199 and 203 below, with nn.71 and 119.

20 Suet. *Div. Jul.* 7.1; Dio Cass. 37.52.2; Plut. *Caes.* 11.3. The last-named source is sometimes cited as dating the incident to Caesar's subsequent proconsulship: see, e.g., H. Strasburger, *Caesars Eintritt in die Geschichte* (1938) 95-96, accepted by Gelzer (n.8 above) p.32 and n.2. In fact it does nothing of the sort. ὁμοίως δὲ πάλιν ἐν Ἰβηρίᾳ, Plutarch begins, which leaves the date wide open; and in any case the whole point is lost if Caesar is portrayed as being considerably *older* than Alexander at the time of the latter's death. The sensible remarks of H.E. Butler and M. Cary in their edition of Suetonius' *Divus Julius* (hereafter 'Butler-Cary'), p.51, still have considerable cogency. Cf. T. Rice Holmes, *The Roman Republic and the founder of the Empire* I (1923) 224-5 with n.5; 440-1; W. Steidle, *Sueton und die antike Biographie* (1951) 18 with n.5; P. Treves, 'Cesare e Alessandro', *Cesare nel bimillenario dell morte* (1956) 69. On the date (69) see L.R. Taylor, 'Caesar's early career', *CPh* 36 (1941) 123-4; cf. Gelzer 31.

21 Gagé (n.3 above) 428-432. As he makes quite clear, the entire episode is highly speculative; but if a statue of Alexander *was* ever set up in this temple – the existence of which is itself well-attested – then Pydna (167) provides a reasonable *terminus post quem,* and Fabius

Aemilianus' sacrifice to Hercules of Gades (Appian, *Iber.* 65) a fitting occasion.

22 The story in this form is told by Suetonius (*Div. Jul.* 7.1) and Dio (37.52.2), the latter incorrectly assigned to Caesar's praetorship by Butler-Cary 51.

23 Plut. *Caes.* 11.3 (cf. n.20 above).

24 *HThR* 50 (1957) 232.

25 Weippert (n.10 above) 108: 'Ueber ihre Historizität lässt sich schwer urteilen – an sich wird man sagen dürfen, dass sie sehr nach eigener Konstruktion *ex eventu* aussieht.'

26 Suet. *Div. Jul.* 7.2; Dio Cass. 1.c.

27 TAPhA 73 (1942) 343.

28 *Julius Caesar and Rome* (1967) 35.

29 Strasburger (n.20 above) 94-96; cf. Weippert 109ff.

30 Suet. *Div. Jul.* 1.2-3; Plut. *Caes.* 1.1, 5.1-7; Gelzer (n.8 above) 21.

31 Hdt. 6.107.1; Artemidorus, *Oneirocr.* 1.79 (pp. 91-92 Pack).

32 Confirmation, however slight, is supplied by Strabo's account (13.1.27, C 594) of his treatment of the Ilians: πολὺ πλέον [than Sulla] αὐτῶν προυνόησε, ζηλώσας ἅμα καὶ Ἀλέξανδρον. For further discussion of this passage see p.203 and nn.116-17.

33 *Phil.* 5.17.48: 'tertio et tricesimo anno mortem obiit, quae est aetas nostris legibus decem annis minor quam consularis.' Cf. *Brut.* 81.282; Sall. *Hist.* 3.88 M.

34 See, e.g., F.S. Johansen, 'Antichi ritratti di Caio Giulio Cesaro nella scultura', *Analecta* Romana 4 (1967) 7-68; J.M.C. Toynbee, 'Portraits of Julius Caesar', *G&R* 4 (1957) 2-9, further developed in her *Roman Imperial portraits* (1978) 30-39.

35 As Pompey did: see Plut. *Pomp.* 2.1-2, and R. Winkes, 'Physiognomonia: Probleme der Charakterinterpretation römischer Porträts', *Aufstieg und Niedergang der Römischen Welt,* I 4 (1973) 903-4. Cf. Michel (n.6 above) 37, 55-56, and (on the handicap of Caesar's baldness) 103; also Weippert 119.

36 From Venus and Ancus Marcius: Suet. *Div. Jul.* 6.1, cf. Weinstock, *Divus Julius* 17-18; Weippert 120-1, 163-5; Michel 69-71; and in particular Elizabeth Rawson, 'Caesar's heritage', *JRS* 65 (1975) 152ff.; also T.P. Wiseman, 'Legendary genealogies in late Republican Rome', *G&R* 21 (1974) 153-174.

37 See p.207, with nn. 150-3.

38 See my *Alexander of Macedon* (n.12 above) 164-5, 269-70, 273-5, with reff. there cited.

39 Arrian 7.9-10; QC 10.2.15-30; cf. Plut. *Alex.* 71.3. Appian, *BC* 2.151.635, makes the same point.

40 Peter P. Spranger, 'Der Grosse: Untersuchungen des historischen Beinamens in der Antike', *Saeculum* 9 (1958) 38ff., with reff. there cited. Cf. also Kienast (n.9 above) 437ff., Nadell (n.18 above) 30ff., Gelzer, *Pompeius* (1949) 59-60; Weinstock, *Divus Julius* 37-39, Michel 37ff., Weippert 56ff., 103-4. The key reference is in Sallust, *Hist.* 3.88 M: 'Sed Pompeius a prima adulescentia sermone fautorum similem fore se credens Alexandro regi, facta consultaque eius quidem aemulus erat.'

41 Plut. *Pomp.* 13.3-5, cf. Nadell 37.

42 For Pompey's achievements in Asia see Gelzer, *Pompeius* ch. vi, 87ff., and J. van Ooteghem, S.J., *Pompée le Grand, Bâtisseur d'Empire* (1954) 204-253. The date of his first triumph: E. Badian, *Hermes* 83 (1955) 107-118, cf. *Hermes* 39 (1961) 254-6.

43 For a convenient conspectus see Michel, pls. xiv-xx, and Toynbee, *Roman Imperial portraits* 24-28.

44 Plut. *Pomp.* 2.2: ὥστε καὶ χλευάζοντας αὐτὸν ἐνίους ἤδη καλεῖν ᾿Αλέξανδρον.

45 Plut. *Caes.* 7.1, cf. Spranger (n.40 above) 39 with n.112.

46 Cic. *Pro Arch.* 10; Val. Max. 8.14.3; Plut. *Pomp.* 37.3 (with an allusion to his penchant for making malicious propaganda on his master's behalf). Another historian who wrote up Pompey's campaign was Posidonius: Strabo 1.1.6, C 492.

47 Plut. *Pomp.* 36.1: cf. 38.2-3 for his reputed ἔρως καὶ ζῆλος to extend his conquests to the shores of Ocean.

48 Appian, *Mithr.* 103. 480ff.; 116. 568ff.; Vell. Pat. 2.40.1; Diod. Sic. 40.4; Plut. *Pomp.* 34.

49 G. Wirth, *Alexandre le Grand: image et réalité* (Entretiens sur l'Antiquité classique, vol. 22, Geneva 1976) 187-8. Cf. Weippert 93, and, in general, Pliny, *HN* 7.95-99.

50 Appian, *Mithr.* 117, 577.

51 Plut. *Pomp.* 46.1; cf. A.R. Anderson, 'Heracles and his successors', *HSCPh* 39 (1928) 37-39.

52 Vell. Pat. 2.40.3; Plut. *Pomp.* 43.2; Appian, *Mithr.* 116. 566. The modern literature is immense: convenient accounts in van Ooteghem (n.42 above) 254ff., Gelzer (n.40 above) ch. vii, 121ff., and M. Cary in *CAH* IX 507ff.

53 Suet. *Div. Jul.* 77.1. The authenticity of this remark, attributed to Caesar by Titus Ampius, is often doubted by modern scholars; but as an off-the-cuff utterance, sedulously reported, it strikes me as all too plausible.

54 See, e.g., Weippert 102-4, Wirth 187.

55 An excellent brief account of this episode is given by Gelzer, *Caesar* 233-7.

56 Plut. *Pomp.* 76.5-6.

57 van Ooteghem 633-7.

58 H.R. Breitenbach, 'Der Alexanderexkurs bei Livius', *MH* 26 (1969) 147-8; see in particular Livy 9.17.6, Plut. *Pomp.* 46.1, and Seneca, *Consol. ad Marc.* 20.4. Cf. L. Alfonsi, 'Pompeio in Manilio', *Latomus* 6 (1947) 345-351.

59 Weippert 106, with characteristic forthrightness, is one of the very few scholars to appreciate this point. 'Wie weit', he asks, not altogether rhetorically, 'hat ein solcher Mann ein Vorbild überhaupt nötig – sollte man nicht annehmen dürfen, dass er völlig auf eigenen Füssen stehen kann?'

60 See, e.g., Lionel Pearson, *The lost histories of Alexander the Great* (1960), for a useful general survey.

61 Cic. *Pro Mur.* 31.

62 QC 8.1.37.

63 See, e.g., Livy 9.17.16-17, 9.19.10-11; QC *loc.cit.*; Gell. 17.21.33; cf. Weippert 90, 236-7.

64 Rawson (n.36 above) 151-2.

65 *Hist.* 9.28.8, 34.1-3; cf. R.M. Errington, *Alexandre le Grand* (n.49 above) 175-7.

66 Weber (n.19 above) 41.

67 See *De Div.* 1.23.47, *De Nat. Deor.* 2.27.69, *De Offic.* 2.15.53, *De Orat.* 3.35.141, *Ad Attic.* 12.40.2, 13.28.3 (birth and education); *De Orat.* 2.14.58, *Pro Rab. Post.* 9.23, *Tusc. Disp.* 3.10.21 (Callisthenes); *Tusc. Disp.* 4.37.79 (Black Cleitus); *De Invent.* 1.22.30 (Thebes); *Verr.* 4.60.135, *Acad.* 2.26.85, *Ad Fam.* 5.12.17 (Apelles and Lysippus); *Tusc. Disp.* 5.32.92 (Diogenes). Cf. Weippert 125-7.

68 The appearance of Quintus Curtius Rufus's *Historiae Alexandri,* and the copious references in a work such as Pliny's *Natural History* (see the *Indices* by L. Ian in his Teubner edition, vol. VI (1875) 27), indicate a still wider and more detailed dissemination of material by the end of the Julio-Claudian period.

69 Weber 45: 'Auf römischer Seite steht man anfänglich gleichgültig dem Makedonenkönig gegenüber. Erst um 50 v. Chr., gleichzeitig mit der politischen Wiedergeburt Alexanders auf griechischer Seite, beginnt man, ihm grössere Aufmerksamkeit zu widmen. Im Gegensatz zu der griechischen Beurteilung Alexanders ist die römische eine ungünstige und knüpft in ihrer Tendenz an die makedonische Opposition an, wie sie zu Lebzeiten Alexanders bestand.'

70 G. Boissier, *L'Opposition sous les Césars,* 3rd ed. (1892) 272ff. Cf. my *Essays in Antiquity* (1960) 163ff.

71 10.18-48: cf. Christensen (n.19 above) 121-130, with further reff., and P. Ceauşescu, 'La double image d'Alexandre le Grand à Rome', *Stud Clas* 16 (1974) 2ff., for a detailed survey of the tradition hostile to Alexander during the imperial period.

72 Cf. my *Alexander of Macedon* (n.12 above) 487-8.

73 Cf. n.15 above.

74 Cf. pp.204 ff., with nn.128-144.

75 *Op. cit.* 1ff., esp. 4-5.

76 Arrian 7.15.5-6; Pliny, *HN* 3.57 (citing Cleitarchus).

77 Cf. Green (n.72 above) 469-70 with n.79.

78 Breitenbach (n.58 above) 152-4.

79 The statue to Alcibiades: Pliny, *HN* 34.26 (I am grateful to the late Professor E.T. Salmon for drawing my attention to this passage). Papirius Cursor: Livy 9.16.11-19, cf. Amm. Marc. 30.8.5, with the comments of Nadell (n.18 above) 4.

80 Reported by Plut. *Pyrrh.* 19.1-3 (the claim 19.1); for other sources referring to this speech see the commentary by A.B. Nederlof (1940) 117-8, and cf. Weippert 10ff. Professor Badian reminds me that Appius' speech, or something that at least passed for it, survived to the age of Cicero (see *Brut.* 61). It seems very likely that Plutarch based his own speech, 'indirectly but solidly', as Badian argues, 'on that famous document of Roman *gravitas'*.

81 *Op. cit.* 156.

82 Weippert 16-17.

83 *Epit.* 1.23.2: 'quamvis tum Philippus regno praesideret, Romani tamen dimicare sibi cum rege Alexandro videbantur.'

84 Polybius (*Hist.* 18.28-32, with Walbank's commentary *ad loc.*), after describing the battle of Cynoscephalae, inserts a lengthy excursus on the relative merits of the Macedonian phalanx and the Roman legion, coming down decisively (despite his appreciation of Alexander's military skills: see n.85 above and Weber 41-42) in favour of the latter. Its special virtue, he argues, was its adaptability to any kind of terrain.

85 *Most.* 775-7: 'Alexandrum Magnum atque Agathoclem aiunt maxumas/duo res gessisse: quid mihi fiet tertio,/qui solus facio facinora immortalia?'

86 *Plautinisches im Plautus* (1922) 16-17.

87 E.g. by Spranger (n.40 above) 33; cf. Weippert 18ff.

88 *Mil. Glor.* 777, 'isque Alexandri praestare praedicat formam suam', almost certainly refers to Paris of Troy: see Weippert 17 n.2.

89 H. Berve, *Die Herrschaft des Agathokles* (1952) 4ff., has a full conspectus of the sources; cf. also his shorter account in *Die Tyrannis bei den Griechen* (1967) 441ff., and H. Bengtson, 'Die Westgriechen im Zeitalter des Agathokles und des Pyrrhos', *Griech. Gesch.*[4] (1969) 391-9, with useful general documentation.

90 Bengtson 394.

91 Weippert 21, who adds that Agathocles 'musste ihnen [i.e. the Romans] neben Pyrrhos als der eigentliche Vertreter des hellenistischen Herrschertums erscheinen, energisch, ruhelos', etc. etc.

92 Spranger (n.40 above) 26-28, 36-37; Weippert 19-21, with further literature; F. Pfister, 'Alexander der Grosse: Die Geschichte seines Ruhms in Lichte seiner Beinamen', *Historia* (1964) 37-39.

93 Demetrius' title is attested in an inscription of (?) 302 BC: see N. Kyparissis and W. Peek, *MDAI(A)* 66 (1941) 221ff.; A. Wilhelm, *JŒAI* 35 (1943) 157ff., cf. Spranger 26 with n.26. For Antiochus, a century later, see Appian *Syr.* 1, 1 and Spranger 29-32. His career, as Professor Badian reminds me, certainly suggests Alexander-*imitatio*: was 'ὁ Μέγας' part of this?

94 [Longinus] Περὶ ''Υψους 4.2, cf. Weippert 19.

95 Spranger 32: 'Die Mitwelt hat zwar die Grösse Alexanders staunend anerkannt: "den Grossen" hat sie ihn deswegen nicht genannt.'

96 See, e.g., Cic. *Pro Rab. Post.* 23, *Pro Arch.* 24; Sueius, *Carm.* fr. 4; Nepos, *Eum.* 8.2, 13.1.2.

97 See, e.g., Spranger 33, Weippert 20 (with n.2 for further reff.).

98 This is certainly true of Antiochus III: Appian, after describing his victorious progress (*Syr.*1,1) says καὶ μέγας 'Αντίοχος ἀπὸ τοῦδε κληθείς, etc. It also almost certainly applies in the case of Demetrius Poliorcetes, though Wilhelm (n.93 above) 161 n.25, argues from Plut. *Dem.*2.2 that the title referred to his large build and striking physical appearance.

99 H.H. Scullard, *Scipio Africanus in the Second Punic War* (1930) [hereafter 'SA¹'] 13-31, 71ff., 282-3; id., *Scipio Africanus, soldier and politician* (1970) [hereafter 'SA²'] 18-25, 237; F.W. Walbank, 'The Scipionic legend', *PCPhS* 193 (= n.s. 13) (1967) 54-69; Weippert 37ff., Anderson (n.51 above) 31-37; Nadell (n.18 above) 17ff.

100 *Hist.* 10.2 *passim,* cf. Walbank (n.99 above) 59.

101 Suet. *De Vir. Illustr.* 49; Dio Cass. fr. 57.39; Gell. 6.1; Livy 26.19.3 ff., etc.

102 Cf. Plut. *Alex.* 2.6, with Hamilton's commentary *ad loc.*; also Cic. *De Div.* 2.135 (which rationalises the incident by implication) and Justin 11.11.3-6.

103 See Stith Thompson, *Motif-index of folk-literature* (rev. ed. 1955) I 462, no. B 604.1.

104 Paus. 4.14.7, 2.10.3.

105 Walbank (n.99 above) 64-68, with a full discussion of the sources. Other parallels in Scullard, *SA¹* 282, *SA²* 237, Weippert 38ff.

106 Plut. *Alex.* 17.3-5; Arrian 1.26.1-2; Callisthenes *ap.* schol. T. Eustath. ad Hom. *Il.* 14.29 (= FGrH 124 F 31). Strabo, like Polybius a realist, reports an alternative version (14.3.9, C 666-7) in which Alexander's men were forced to march navel-deep in sea water all day.

107 Scullard, *SA¹* 284 with n.3.

108 Cf. n.21 above; also Scullard, *SA¹* 282, *SA²* 237; Nadell 25-26; Weippert 48-49.

109 *Hist.* 18.35.9, 31.26.1, 27.1, etc.

110 Weippert regards the phrase as a simple translation of 'Scipio Maior'; but see Walbank's *Commentary* on 18.5.39, and H.S. Versnel, *Gymnasium* 81 (1974) 317 (in a review of Weippert).

111 Cf. Livy 26.19.8.

112 This is clearly brought out by Christensen (n.19 above): see esp. 107-8, 130ff.; and cf. Weber (n.19 above) 42ff.

113 Cf. Plut. *Mor.* 207 D 8: the surprise evinced by Augustus, 'that Alexander did not regard it as a greater task to set in order the empire which he had won than to win it', is characteristically Roman.

114 van Ooteghem (n.42 above) 222, 283. Gelzer's notion (*Pompeius* 59 and n.115) that Pompey may have been thought of (or have even considered himself) as a *reincarnation* of Alexander is a pleasant Pythagorean conceit, but not to be taken seriously.

115 Weippert 123-4 with n.1. He observes of this material: 'Was sie über Alexander zu sagen haben, ist erstaunlich wenig und nichtssagend.'

The only word I would query here is *erstaunlich*. By far the most useful item is Sallust, *Hist.* 3.88 (cited n.40 above). Otherwise we are reduced to a fragmentary encomium (*Rhet. Her.* 4.31), and casual references in Gellius (13.4.1-2), Sueius's *Moretum* (fr. 1 = Macrob. *Sat.* 3.18.12), and Nepos' *Life* of Eumenes (1.6, 2.1-4, 3.1, 4.4, 6.1-3, 7 *passim*, 8.2, 13.1-3; cf. *De Reg.* 2.1, 3.1). According to the Suda, s.v. Βάρρων, 'Varro' wrote an Ἐπιτομὴ τῶν κατ' Ἀλέξανδρου τὸν Μακεδόνα, though whether this was the work of the great M. Terentius Varro is impossible to determine.

116 13.1.27, C 594-5. The key phrase is ζηλώσας ἅμα καὶ 'Αλέξανδρον. Caesar is also described as φιλαλέξανδρος.

117 Cf. Suet. *Div. Jul.* 6.1, and for modern interpretations of the Strabo passage, Weippert 117.

118 H. Erbse, 'Die Bedeutung der Synkrisis in den Parallelbiographien Plutarchs', *Hermes* 84 (1956) 403-4, argues that Plutarch never attempted the comparison because it would have presented peculiar difficulties, a view with which I tend to sympathise. See also Alan Wardman, *Plutarch's Lives* (1974) 236-7.

119 Cf. pp.195 and 199 and nn.19, 71 above.

120 Vell. Pat. 2.41.1; Appian, *BC* 2.149.619-154.649.

121 Trs. F.W. Shipley: 'magnitudine cogitationum, celeritate bellandi, patientia periculorum Magno illi Alexandro . . . simillimus'.

122 Cf. Suet. *Div. Jul.* 53.

123 Ibid. 49-52 *passim*.

124 *BC* 2.149.621: ἄμφω . . . τὰ δόξαντα ἐπελθεῖν ταχυτάτω. Cf. Suet. *Div. Jul.* 57. Cicero frequently refers to Caesar's speed of movement in his correspondence: *Att.* 8.9.4, 'τέρας horribili celeritate', cf. ibid. 7.22.1, 10.9.1.

125 Weippert, 115-6, justly observes that 'wenn Appian diese beiden. Stellen in das Prokrustes-Bett seiner Synkrisis gezwungen hat, brauchen wir deshalb darin noch nicht zu folgen'. Nadell, 58, in fact stresses the parallel between Caesar's death and Alexander's, as remarked by Appian, a nice instance of *imitatio* and *comparatio* confused.

126 E.g. the rout of Q. Titurius Sabinus and L. Aurunculeius Cotta by Ambiorix, *BG* 5.24.37, and Pompey's break-out at Dyrrhachium (*BC* 3.58.5-65.3). The effectiveness of Afranius and Petreius in Spain Appian exaggerates for his own purposes: see Gelzer 214-7. It is, however, true that at one point in Africa the Caesarians, as Appian says, λαμπρῶς ἔφευγον. Cf. his *BC* 2.95.397-400; also *Bell. Afr.* 3.18, Dio Cass. 43.2.3-4, Plut. *Caes.* 52.6-9.

127 Cf. p.196 and n.39 above.

128 Cf. p.207 above and nn.150-1 below.

129 Cf. p.199 f. and n.67 above.

130 E.g. *Phil.* 5.48.

131 E.g. *De Rep* 3.24, *De Offic.* 1.90, *Tusc. Disp.* 3.21, *De Invent.* 1.93.

132 Cf. Weippert 125ff., 142-3.

133 By R. Schütz, *Ciceros historisches Kenntnisse* (1913) 44 and n.32, cited by Weippert 140.

134 Cf. Weippert 135ff., and Badian's brief but penetrating remarks in 'The Eunuch Bagoas', *CQ* n.s. 8 (1958) 155-6; also Weinstock (*art. cit.*, n. 1 above) 233-6.

135 Suet. *Div. Jul.* 56.5, Cic. *Orat.* 35.

136 *Att.* 12.40.1, 41.4, 44.1, 45.2, 48.

137 Trs. Shackleton Bailey (V 138). For Theopompus' letter cf. Athen. 6.230 e and 13.595 a = Jacoby *FGrH* 15 F 251 (II 390). For the (spurious) letter of Aristotle see V. Rose, *Arist. fr.* 408, 414-5, cf. Wilamowitz, *Aristot. u. Athen* I 339 n.39, and Weippert 136 n.2.

138 'Atque etiam vereor,' he added, 'ne putet me hoc quasi Catonis μείλιγμα esse voluisse': a very reasonable fear.

139 Trs. Shackleton Bailey (V 169).

140 13.28.3 (translation mine): 'quid? tu non uides ipsum illum Aristoteli discipulum, summo ingenio, summa modestia, postea quam rex appellatus sit, superbum, crudelem, immoderatum fuisse?'

141 Though taken with *Phil.* 2.110 it is, clearly, of the greatest importance and significance: cf. Rawson (n.36 above) 149.

142 Weinstock, *art. cit.* (n.1 above) 233.

143 See J.A. North's review of *Divus Julius* in *JRS* 65 (1975) 171 and 176 (esp. §5).

144 It would be hard to guess this from even the more sensible modern scholarship on the subject: see e.g., Weippert 135ff. Cicero's failure to mention in his correspondence any hint of Alexander-*imitatio* on Caesar's part could possibly be treated as an *argumentum ex silentio* for its never having taken place.

145 Suet. *Div. Jul.* 61 makes no mention of Alexander in this context; Pliny, *HN* 8.154-5 juxtaposes Caesar's horse with Bucephalas in a general catalogue of famous horses, but without suggesting that the two were in any more specific way connected. Cf. Weippert 112-3, Nadell 48-49, and Anderson (n.99 above) 40-41.

146 Statius, *Silv.* 1.1.84-87. Michel (n.6 above) 102 argues that 'die Person Alexanders für Caesar (und seine Umwelt) den Vorrang gegenüber dem Künstler Lysipp haben musste', a highly debatable assertion. Cf. Weippert 113-5, Anderson 1.c., Nadell 49ff., Weinstock 233 with n.136. The practice of rededicating statues (by changing either their heads or their inscriptions) goes back at least to Cicero's day (*Att.* 5.1.26), and was also known in Greece (Paus. 1.2.4, 1.18.3). It was condemned at length by Dio Chrysostom (31.47, 87-9, 90ff., 154-5); according to Pliny (*HN* 35.4) the habit of putting new heads on old statues had become a byword long before his time. Mark Antony appropriated for himself the two colossal statues of Attalus and Eumenes that formerly adorned the 'Monument of Agrippa' by the Propylaea (Plut. *Ant.* 60, cf. *IG* II² 4122). Granius Marcellus incurred a charge of *laesa maiestas* by putting Tiberius' head on a statue of Augustus (Tac. *Ann.* 1.74, cf. Suet. *Tib.* 58); Caligula had his own head attached to a Greek statue of Olympian Zeus (Suet. *Cal.* 22.2). Cf. Pliny, *HN* 35.93, for Claudius replacing Alexander's head with that of Augustus. The entire subject is examined in detail by Horst Blank, *Wiederverwendung alter Statuen als Ehrendenkmäler bei Griechen und Römern* (1969): see esp. 11ff., and (for the climate of opinion which made such actions a commonplace) 113-4. I am grateful to Professor M. Gwyn Morgan for drawing my attention to this fascinating monograph.

147 N.J. De Witt, 'The non-political nature of Caesar's *Commentaries*', *TAPhA* 73 (1942) 342-5.

148 See now Arther Ferrill, 'Caesar's private fortune: wealth and politics in the late Roman Republic', *Indiana Soc. Stud. Quart.* 30 (1977) 101-111.

149 Most notably F.E. Adcock, 'Caesar's position in the State', *CAH* IX (1932) 718-740, and J.P.V.D. Balsdon, in his long review of Gerhard Dobesch's *Caesars Apotheose zu Lebzeiten und sein Ringen um den Königstitel* (1966), *Gnomon* 39 (1967) 150-6. For the division of opinion along broad ethnic lines see now Weippert 189 n.4. As early as 1961, reviewing the 6th revised German edition of Gelzer's *Caesar* in *Gnomon* 33 (1961) 600, Badian sounded a salutary note of caution against excessive scepticism: 'Perhaps we have now gone too far: attempts to deny Caesar's monarchic and divine status just before his death seem to me mistaken.'

150 See now Rawson (n.5 above) 148ff., and Victor Ehrenberg, 'Caesar's final aims', *HSCPh* 68 (1964) 149: both stress the finality of the key passage in Cicero, *Phil.* 2.110.

151 A useful survey of recent scholarship is to be found in Helga Gesche, *Caesar* (*Erträge der Forschung* LI, 1976) 152ff. See in particular Weippert 155ff., Weinstock, *Divus Julius* 70ff.: the most valuable contribution is that of Rawson (n.36 above).

152 *Divinity* (n.5 above) 38-77, cf. Weippert 163ff., Rawson 148ff.

153 *Testimonia* assembled by Rawson, 148. Cf. also A. Alföldi, 'Der neue Romulus', *MH* 8 (1951) 190-215.

154 Weippert 175ff., cf. H. Volkmann, *Cleopatra*, trs. T.J. Cadoux (1958) 65-89.

155 Suet. *Div. Jul.* 79.3 makes it clear that this was a wild rumour only; disproved (Nic. Damasc. §20) by the contents of Caesar's will.

156 John M. Carter, *The Battle of Actium* (1969) 174-199; Volkmann 152ff.; and in particular the evidence assembled by Ceauşescu (n.71 above), 157-8.

157 43.45.3; cf. Michel 84-85.

158 E.g. Plut. *Alex.* 14.4; other instances

collected by Tarn, *Alexander the Great* (1948) II 338ff.

159 Hypereides I (*In Demosth.*) col. 32: ἐβούλετ[ο . . .] στῆσαι εἰκό[να Ἀλεξάν]δρου βασιλ[έως τοῦ ἀνι]κήτου θε[οῦ . . .] Whether the proposal was in fact carried out must remain uncertain; the important thing is that it could be put forward in those terms. Cf. Tarn, *op. cit.* 342-3, with further references.

160 43.14.5, 43.21.2, cf. Michel 85ff., Weippert 160ff., Balsdon (n.149 above) 151.

161 Weinstock, *art. cit.* (n.1 above) 232-3, Taylor (n.5 above) 65; Dobesch (n.149 above) 42.

162 See, e.g., Michel 86ff.

163 It is not necessary to subscribe to the theory so ably argued by J.H. Collins, 'Caesar and the corruption of power', *Historia* 4 (1955) 445-465, that Caesar towards the end of his life was probably in some sense either senile or mentally unbalanced, to perceive a fundamental change of personality during his last years.

164 *Röm. Gesch.*[14] III 467 (cited by Collins 458): ' . . . nicht ungemessene Pläne der Welt-überwindung, sondern bloss wohlerwogene Grenzregulierungen ins Werk zu setzen.'

165 *Caesars Monarchie* (n.2 above) 465ff., esp. 472-5.

166 *Op. cit.* 75. See also H. Strasburger, *Caesar im Urteil seiner Zeitgenossen* (repr. 1968) 60; Collins (note 163 above) 458.

167 N.C. Debevoise, *A political history of Parthia* (1938) 70ff., 213ff., K.H. Ziegler, *Die Beziehungen zwischen Rom und dem Partherreich* (1964) 32ff., 100ff.; and M.A. Levi, 'La guerra contro i Parti', *Cesare nel bimillenario della morte* (1956) 117-128, esp. 124ff.

168 Appian, *BC* 2.110.460.

169 Debevoise (n.167 above) 84ff. Cf. Nadell 55 n.14; Weippert 172ff.

170 Cf. Ziegler (n.167 above) 33.

171 E. Badian, *Roman imperialism in the late Republic,* 2nd ed. (1968) 89-91, a crisply pungent summing-up.

172 *Caesar* 322 n.7 (323), cf. J. Vogt, *Vom Reichsgedanken der Römer* (1942) 65, 178ff. Weippert, 188ff., leans towards the view that he had no clearly formulated plans at all.

173 Plut. *Caes.* 11.3.

174 W.H. Russell, 'Caesar the general', *CW* 50 (1956) 19; D. Armstrong 'The "Blitzkrieg" in Caesar's campaigns', *CJ* 37 (1941) 138-143. G. Veith, 'Caesar als "Vater der Strategie" ' repr. *Caesar,* ed. D. Rasmussen (*Wege der Forschung* XLIII, 1967) 372-8, is a stylised, dogmatic, and ill-documented eulogy which adds little of value.

175 Suet. *Div. Jul.* 57.

176 M. Rambaud, 'La cavalerie de César', *Hommages M. Renard* (1969) II 650ff., esp. 663.

177 'Die Phalangen Alexanders und Caesars Legionen', *SHAW* 1926, 1ff., esp. 79-86.

178 J.F.C. Fuller, *Julius Caesar* (1965) 316ff.

179 For examples of *celeritas* cf. n.124 above; also *BG* 1.13, 72, 7.56, and cf. Armstrong (n.124 above), *passim.*

180 Fuller (n.178 above) 86ff.

181 Michel 109-132; Weippert 193ff.

182 Michel 81ff.

183 E.A. Fredricksmeyer, *CW* 62 (1969) 225.

CHAPTER XIII

1 *History in Ovid* (1978) [hereafter '*HO*'] 216.

2 John C. Thibault, *The Mystery of Ovid's Exile* (1964) [hereafter 'Thibault'] 125-9 and *passim.*

3 We no longer need to wonder, e.g., whether the *praeceptor amoris* gatecrashed a neo-Pythagorean seance, saw Livia nude in her bath, surprised Augustus in the act of pederasty, or caught Julia II committing incest: Thibault *ut supr.* In this category we should also place the various editions of L. Herrmann's dotty ritualistic theory: see *RBPhil* 17 (1938) 695-725; 43 (1965) 40-52; 48 (1970) 38-44. The most recent version, *AC* 44 (1975) 126-40, has Ovid spying on Livia's mature naked charms while improperly observing the rites of the Bona Dea, not for lascivious or political motives but in spirit of disinterested anthropological research (he was doing fieldwork for Book XII of the *Fasti*).

4 He conveniently tabulates and summarises them in chapters 4 (38ff.), 8 (75ff.), and 9 (89ff.). See also F. Della Corte, *I Tristia* (1973) II, 63-69.

5 For characteristic recent developments in these categories see, e.g., Raoul Verdière, 'Un Amour secret d'Ovide,' *AC* 40 (1971) 623-48; F. Corsaro, 'Sulla relegatio di Ovidio,' *Orpheus* 15 (1968) 123-67 (*cherchez la femme*); B.T. Buchert, 'The Reasons for Ovid's Banishment,' *Akroterion* 19 (1974) 44-49 (*Zeitgeist*); Barbara Levick, 'The Fall of Julia the Younger,' *Latomus* 35 (1976) 301-339 [hereafter 'Levick'], further developed in *Tiberius the Politician* (1976) 57ff. [hereafter 'Levick']; Eckhard Meise, *Untersuchungen zur Geschichte der Julischen-Claudischen Dynastie* (1969) 223-35 ('Anhang I: Die Verbannung Ovids') [hereafter 'Meise'] (political conspiracy).

6 Meise 224 reaches an almost identical conclusion, though his categories differ somewhat from mine and Thibault's. However, since he dismisses all of them but one, and since this one coincides with my own choice, the variations remain immaterial. Only the assumption, he argues, that Ovid 'beteiligte sich an einer Verschwörung gegen Augustus oder fügte sich nicht dessen politischen Plänen und Absichten' can lead to a satisfactory solution of the problem, 'denn gegen alle andern lassen sich von vornherein allzu gewichtige Einwände erheben'. Cf. R.C. Zimmermann, 'Die Ursachen von Ovids Verbannung,' *RhM* 81 (1932) 263-74.

7 Syme *HO* 215-29, while linking Ovid's *relegatio* to the disgrace of Julia II and Aemilius Paullus, also revives the old (and, to my mind, fallacious) claim that Augustus acted against the poet *primarily* because of the *Ars Amatoria*: he further suggests, 220, that Ovid may have witnessed 'the staging of a mock funeral for the aged ruler, with suitable recitations in prose or verse', an uncharacteristically footling, not to say pumpkinified, suggestion.

8 *EP* 3.371-72 and elsewhere.

9 Syme does not help his own case by arguing for a (wholly gratuitous) first edition of *AA* Bks 1-2, published, he alleges (13-19, 222) as early as 8 BC. But then he is capable (13) of claiming it to

be 'generally conceded' (which it is not, and with good reason) that *AA* 3.343-4 proves that the second edition of the *Amores* 'came out during the interval, brief indeed, between *AA* 1-2 and *AA* 3'. All that that textually shaky distich in fact shows – *if* we accept the reading *deue tribus libris* – is that the three-book *Amores*[2] was in circulation before Ovid wrote *AA* 3: how long before is a moot point. I hope to return to this problem elsewhere.

10 Thibault 1-2, 121.

11 In his review of Thibault, *Gnomon* 37 (1965) 734. he lists the main points with crisp concision: 'through *stultitia* and *simplicitas* he witnessed, neither illegally nor unexpectedly, a *culpa* prejudicial to the Julian house and painful to the Emperor, and through *timor* failed to act then as he should have done.'

12 *Tr.* 3.5.49-50; cf. *Tr.* 2.103-104, 3.6.27-28.

13 Tac. *Ann.* 3.24.

14 Statius *Silv.* 1.2.254-55; Hieron. *Chron.* Olymp. 184, 199. The Jerome reference is often attributed, though on no compelling grounds, to Suetonius, and is printed by Reifferscheid as fr. 30 of the *De poetis*. For a full conspectus of the non-Ovidian *testimonia* see Della Corte (n.4 above), II, 18-20.

15 E.g., Thibault 22-23.

16 Well analysed, with certain caveats, by Meise 5ff., 229ff., and by Levick *passim*. Cf. Syme *HO* 199ff.; F. Norwood, 'The Riddle of Ovid's *Relegatio*,' *CP* 58 (1963) 150-63 [hereafter 'Norwood']; T. Wiedemann, 'The Political Background to Ovid's Tristia II,' *CQ* 25 (1975) 264-71, and R.S. Rogers, 'The Emperor's Displeasure and Ovid,' *TAPhA* 97 (1966) 373-78.

17 Conveniently assembled by Thibault 20ff.

18 Though his third wife had imperial connexions (*Tr.* 1.6.25, 4.10.73), Ovid was vulnerable to such attacks: witness the manner in which 'Ibis' (whose identity remains quite uncertain) drew the emperor's attention to Ovid's more risqué erotic verse (*Tr.* 2.77-80), slandered the poet behind his back (*Tr.* 3.11.20, *Ibis* 14), and attempted to rob him of his patrimony (*Tr.* 1.6.9-14) through sharp litigation.

Despite Thibault's reservations (16-17), it seems likely that 'Ibis', or someone like him, denounced Ovid to Augustus and hoped, by inducing a charge of *maiestas minuta,* to get the informer's cut from his victim's property. On Ovid's third wife see Syme, *HO* 145-48; cf. A.L. Wheeler, 'Topics from the Life of Ovid,' *AJP* 46 (1925) 25-8. Ovid was *en route* to Tomis by December (*Tr.* 1.11.3), and it seems likely that this unseasonable departure was one immediate condition of his *relegatio,* which we can therefore date in October or, more probably, November.

19 *EP* 2.3.6ff. Cf. Thibault 118; Norwood 161-62.

20 What was Cotta doing on Elba in November? Not, clearly, vacationing. His presence may conceivably have been linked to the iron-mines, which led the Greeks (Strabo 2.5.19, C.123; 5.2.6, C.223-24) to call Elba *Aithalia,* the 'smoky island'; cf. Plin. *NH* 3.81. Yet with his high rank he can scarcely have been a *procurator metallorum,* since this office was normally held by *equites* or freedmen: see J.F. Healy, *Mining and Metallurgy in the Greek and Roman World* (1978) 130-31, with further literature there cited. It is interesting, though probably fortuitous, that Elba forms the nearest point of access to the small island of Planasia (Pianosa), to which, a year previously, Agrippa Postumus had been exiled (Tac. *Ann.* 1.3.5; Dio Cass. 55.32; Suet. *Div. Aug.* 65; cf. p.218 and nn.75-77 below). Pianosa also provided the setting for Joseph Heller's *Catch-22,* an irony that should appeal to Ovidians.

21 Rogers (n.16 above) 373-78.

22 *Tr.* 2.147, 4.45: S.G. Owen, *P. Ovidi Nasonis Tristium Liber Secundus* (1924) [hereafter 'Owen *TrII*] 40-47.

23 *Tr.* 2.135-38, 4.4.46, 5.2.55-58; Mommsen, *Röm. Strafrecht* (1899) 965ff.; Owen *TrII* 43-44; Thibault 8-11 (discussing the legal options for private action on Augustus' part). Rogers (n.16 above) suggests that Augustus was expressing *renuntiatio amicitiae* and gave force to his ruling by means of magisterial *coercitio.* For the options of *relegatio in locum* see Della Corte (n.4 above) II, 96-102.

24 *Tr.* 3.1.59-82, 3.14.5-8; cf. Syme *HO* 229. As Ovid himself reminded his readers (*EP*

1.1.23-24), however else enemies of Caesar (e.g., Brutus, Mark Antony) might be deprived of public honour, at least their writings were left untouched in the libraries. From *Tr.* 3.1.65-74 it looks as though Ovid's other later works were similarly evicted (or denied access), at least from the public shelves.

25 *Tr.* 1.3.5-6, 1.4 *passim,* 1.11.3, 1.11.13ff. Ovid seems also to have been robbed or otherwise swindled by the servants who accompanied him: *Tr.* 1.11.27ff., 4.10.101; *EP* 2.7.61-62. He made the journey to Tomis last as long as he could; his repeated claim (*EP* 3.4.59-60, 4.11.15-16) that an exchange of correspondence between Rome and Tomis could take up to a year is clearly based on his own leisurely progress and is calculated to emphasise the remoteness of the Black Sea. Elswhere (*EP* 4.5.5-8) he shows himself considerably more realistic about the speed of the mail service. It is worth noting that he himself travelled slowly enough for news from Rome to catch up with him at various points (*Tr.* 1.6.15, 1.9.39-40).

26 *Tr.* 2.135, 5.2.8; cf. Owen *TrII* 46; Thibault 11, 138-39.

27 Owen *TrII* 10-11, and Thibault 30-31 provide a convenient conspectus of references. Note in particular *Tr.* 2.207, 'perdiderunt cum me duo crimina, carmen et error'; cf. *Tr.* 4.1.26, where Ovid asserts that his Muse 'mecum iuncti criminis acta rea est', a phrase capable of more than one meaning – see Thibault 32 with nn.80-85 for a conspectus of the main variants – but almost certainly here no more than a restatement of 'duo crimina' which are not to be treated separately. Cf. Schanz-Hosius, *Röm. Lit. Gesch.* (1935) 2, 209, §8 ('Die Ursachen der Verbannung'), and Syme *HO* 222, who writes that 'the carmen and the error are in a tight nexus' (though I do not agree with the reasons he gives for this): *contra* Wilkinson, in his review of Thibault (n.11 above) 735, who argues that 'iuncti criminis' means that 'the Muse was his accomplice in the case of the *Ars* (a conceit)' and adds, without argument, 'those who suppose that [these lines] somehow link the *Ars* with the *error* are mistaken'.

28 *Tr.* 2.212. For similar expressions cf. *Tr.* 2.348; *EP* 2.10.15-16, 3.3.47-48, 3.3.58.

29 *EP* 3.3.71-76.

30 *Tr.* 2.7-10, 345-46; cf. *EP* 4.13.41-42. Ovid suggests at one point that Augustus had never read the poem but had only (like too many modern magistrates) heard carefully culled passages read by ill-wishers (*Tr.*2.77-80), a practice, as he rightly points out, liable to inhibit fair judgment.

31 *Tr.* 1.5.51-52, 2.207-212, 3.6.32, 4.10.100; *EP* 2.2.59, 2.9.73-74, 3.1.147.

32 Dio Cass. 53.19.1-5: the whole passage repays careful study, not least Dio's remarks on the development of secret diplomacy, without recourse to senate or people.

33 *Tr.* 1.1.23, 4.10.99; *EP* 1.7.39: cf. Thibault 118.

34 See Thibault 20-23 for the most recent presentation of this *argumentum ex silentio*. Suetonius' *De poetis*, he says, 'almost certainly included a biographical sketch of Ovid', and '*no reader of Suetonius will doubt* that he would have told his readers all that he knew about a subject so provocative as the exile of the poet' [italics mine]. Of such straw can scholarly bricks be made; and even if we concede both points, just how much Suetonius *did* know about Ovid's exile remains a matter of complete uncertainty.

35 Even Thibault (23) is constrained to admit that 'only the most precarious inferences can be drawn from the silence of the extant writers for there is no context in which failure to mention Ovid's exile would necessarily be significant'.

36 *Tr.* 1.5.51; cf. Norwood 161-62.

37 *Tr.* 3.6.33-44, 4.4.37-38, 4.4.43-44.

38 *EP* 1.6.25: the next line offers the significant caveat, 'omnis an in magnos culpa deos scelus est?' See also *Tr.* 1.2.97-98, 1.3.37-38, 3.1.51-52, 3.11.33-34, and *EP* 2.9.7, etc.; cf. Owen *TrII* 10-11.

39 *EP* 2.9.67-70.

40 *Tr.* 1.5.41-42, 2.51-52, 3.5.45-46; cf. 2.446, 3.5.47-48.

41 *Tr.* 3.5.49-50; cf. 2.103-104, 3.6.27-28.

42 *Tr.* 3.6.11-14; cf. *EP* 2.6.9-12.

43 *Tr.* 4.4.39: *EP* 2.2.17.

44 We should, nevertheless, always be on our guard against Ovid's (virtually inevitable) attempts to minimise or gloss over his own involvement in the affair: cf. Thibault 142 n.62.

45 See now F. Barone, 'Carmen et Error,' *Ovidianum: Acta Conventus Omnium Gentium Ovidianis Studiis Fovendis* (1976) 148. A suggestive modern parallel is the case of the late Stephen Ward, British osteopath, portrait-artist, and discreet procurer, who was taken up (for their own benefit) by members of the Cliveden set and other smart circles in London, but was quickly dropped again – indeed, made a classic scapegoat – at the time of the Profumo–Keeler scandal (1963). For a revealing and well-documented account of this unsavoury episode see Ludovic Kennedy, *The Trial of Stephen Ward* (1964).

46 *Tr.* 1.2.100, 1.5.42, 3.6.35; *EP* 1.6.20, 1.7.44, 2.2.17.

47 *Tr.* 4.10.89-90; *EP* 1.7.39, 2.6.7, 3.3.73, etc.

48 *Tr.* 5.2.60, 5.11.17; *EP* 1.1.66, 1.6.21, 2.2.105, 2.3.33, 2.6.5, etc.

49 The pain is characterised as an unhealable wound (*uulnus*): *Tr.* 2.209-210; *EP* 2.2.57-58. Direct offence: *Tr.* 1.10.42, 2.134, 3.8.39-40, 5.7.8, 5.10.52; *EP* 2.2.21. Its nature is repeatedly hinted at in near-explicit phrases: 'ni fuerit laesi mollior ira dei' (*Tr.* 1.5.84); 'nec ueniam laeso numine casus habet' (*Tr.* 2.108); 'si modo laesi/ ematuruerit Caesaris ira' (*Tr.* 2.123-124); 'numinis ut laesi fiat mansuetior ira' (*Tr.* 3.6.23); 'laesi principis ira' (*Tr.* 4.10.98); 'perstiterit laesi si gravis ira dei' (*EP* 1.4.44; cf. 2.3.68). If the *maiestas* of mere sovereign mortals could be *laesa* (and provoke condign punishment), surely the same, *a fortiori*, was true of a god?

50 See the detailed discussion by Owen (*TrII* 40-43), arguing that Ovid was tried and condemned by the Princeps on this charge *intra cubiculum*. The procedure will have been by *cognitio extra ordinem*. The punishment given was not without precedent in a case of *maiestas*: note the *leue exilium* imposed by Augustus on Cassius Patavinus (Suet. *Div. Aug.* 51); cf. H. Fraenkel, *Ovid: A Poet between Two Worlds* (1945) 111, and Thibault 8-10. Owen repeats his assumption in his commentary on *Tr.* 3.6.23, *Ovid Tristia Book III* (1889) 50, where he states:

'It would appear that technically Ovid's crime was "laesa maiestas", treason.'

51 *Tr.* 1.1.23-24, 2.87; *EP* 2.3.61ff. It has been suggested to me that Ovid had to emphasise this 'anger' of Cotta's to avoid getting his patron into trouble; that does not necessarily (or even probably) mean that the anger was in fact feigned or nonexistent.

52 Owen *TrII* xxxiii-iv. Cf. now the exhaustive prosopographical analysis by Syme: *HO* ch. 7, 'The sons of Messalla,' 114-34, esp. 129-31.

53 Syme *HO* 130, with reff.

54 In an influential article, 'Julians and Claudians,' *Greece and Rome* 22 (1975) 29-38, Barbara Levick has argued, mainly on the grounds of repeated cross-adoptions, that these traditional labels for what even she admits to have been 'family cliques' are misleading and 'must go'. Her own tentative suggestion for a replacement is 'Scribonians' and 'Livians'. Despite her disclaimer, there is a certain amount of pedantry at work here. At least since the time of F.B. Marsh's *The Reign of Tiberius* (1931) it has been well understood that, as used in this context, 'Julians' means Scribonia, Julias I and II, Agrippa Postumus, and their adherents (including, marginally, Germanicus), while 'Claudians' refers to the group supporting Tiberius through Livia. Granted such limitations, the labels are a useful shorthand, and I see no reason to abandon them.

55 *AA* 1.177ff., with the commentary by A.S. Hollis (1977) 65-82. Ovid undoubtedly exaggerates the role Gaius played in the East; in this, however, he took his cue from the Princeps himself, who wished his grandson εὔνοιαν . . . τὴν Πομπηίου, τόλμαν δὲ τὴν Ἀλεξάνδρου, τύχην δὲ τὴν ἑαυτοῦ (Plut. *Mor.* 207F 10; cf. 319D). The general mood can be assessed from *AP* 9.297 (= Hollis app. 3, 153), a shorter but even more hyperbolic *propemptikon* for Gaius by Antipater of Thessalonike. Yet even here Ovid could not keep *nequitia* from creeping in. When he describes Gaius' projected triumph (219ff.), the procession merely serves as a handy talking-point with which to impress a girl.

56 See, e.g., *EP* 3.1.114-66 (Livia), 3.4.87-96, 4.9.105ff. (Tiberius); *EP* 2.1 *passim*, 2.5.41-64,

4.8.23-88 (Germanicus). When the news of Augustus' deification reached Ovid, he also set up a shrine to the new god (having long so described him) and promoted the Augustan cult with sedulous and well-publicised enthusiasm: *EP* 4.9.105ff.

57 Cf., for instance, the briefing given by Horace to Asina, *Epist.* 1.13; though here the tone is far more flippant and light-hearted. Horace, after all, unlike Ovid, had developed a personal relationship with the Princeps.

58 On Germanicus see the evidence in n.55 above. The rededication of the *Fasti: Fast.* 1.3-6 ed. Bömer, with introd. vol. 1, 17ff.; cf. *Tr.* 2.551. Germanicus' character and position vis-à-vis the imperial succession: Suet. *Gaius* 3.3; Tac. *Ann.* 2.73; Dio Cass. 55.13.

59 Forcible adoption of Agrippa Postumus: see Suet. *Tib.* 15.2, where Tiberius is said only to have been adopted by Augustus 'coactus prius ipse Germanicum . . . adoptare'. While it is true that, as Levick points out (*Greece and Rome* 22 [1975] 30), Tiberius was legally required to do this 'because he could not legally do so afterwards, as he was no longer *paterfamilias*', it is hard to imagine him doing so willingly under any circumstances; and the conditions that applied to Germanicus applied with equal force to Agrippa Postumus. The death of Germanicus: Tac. *Ann.* 2.69-73; Dio Cass. 57.18; Suet. *Gaius* 1-7 *passim*. The execution of Agrippa Postumus: Tac. *Ann.* 1.6, 2.39; Suet. *Tib.* 22; Dio Cass. 57.3.5f.; and cf. R.S. Rogers, 'The Conspiracy of Agrippina,' *TAPhA* 62 (1931) 148-49.

60 Suet. *Div. Aug.* 65.4. He was also in the habit of quoting Homer (*Il.* 3.40) to the effect that he should never have married and should have died without issue. When he said this it was (so, rightly, Levick 339) Scribonia and her offspring rather than Livia whom he had in mind.

61 Tac. *Ann.* 4.71. As Norwood (162 n. 8) points out, with commendable understatement, 'by such support her future inactivity in politics was assured'.

62 Cf. Tac. *Ann.* 1.6.

63 Most scholars reject the story of Agrippa Postumus receiving a secret visit from, and reconciliation with, Augustus on Planasia in

AD 14 (Tac. *Ann.* 1.5; cf. Dio Cass. 56.30.1). Levick[2] (64-67) is critical but at least accepts the likelihood that the journey was made. It would, indeed, have been an act entirely consistent with the emperor's previous conduct – and might well have sparked the rumour (*EP* 4.6.15-16) that his attitude towards Ovid, as an adherent of the Julian group, was softening. However, Augustus did not write Agrippa back into his will, which remained that of 3 April 13 (Suet. *Div. Aug.* 101.1).

64 Tac. *Ann.* 1.5-6, 1.53, 2.39-40; Suet. *Tib.* 22.50; Dio Cass. 57.3.5, 18.1a [Zonaras].

65 Thibault 115-16: 'As a methodological norm, we note that no hypothesis should be predicated on . . . the assumption that Ovid is deceiving the reader by misstating his view of the facts . . . We cannot prove that Ovid is not lying, but if he is, the problem becomes by definition insoluble . . . unless new and independent evidence should be discovered.' Cf. 142 n. 62. Perhaps 'insoluble' is over-pessimistic.

66 Meise (228) sees this very clearly: 'Er will wieder nach Rom zurück, er will, dass Augustus seine Aufbannung aufhebt. Da ist es doch ganz natürlich, dass die Bemerkungen über sein Vergehen diesem Zweck dienen, dass er seine Verantwörtlichkeit verringert oder ganz ablehnt und dass er deshalb von einem Irrtum (*error*) spricht.'

67 Cf. Meise 225-72 for a convenient conspectus of the main *testimonia*.

68 Syme, *Tacitus* (1958) vol. 1, 403-404; *The Roman Revolution* (1939) 468; *HO* 194-95, 219-21. Cf. Meise 46-47: 'Schon bei der Bestrafung der ältern Iulia hatte der Prinzeps den wahren Hintergrund, die Verschwörung, nicht als offizielle Begründung der harten Strafen angeben lassen, sondern hatte sein unerbittliches Vorgehen ausdrücklich mit dem sittenlosen Treiben seiner Tochter und ihrer Anhänger motiviert.' It is hard to understand the confident ascription of 'keinen politischen Charakter' to the affair in Schanz-Hosius (n.27 above) 209.

69 Meise 5-27; Syme *HO* 193-98. For the scheme to murder Augustus see Pliny *HN* 7.149: 'adulterium filiae et consilia parricidae palam facta'; and cf. Dio Cass. 55.10.15; Sen. *De Brev. Vit.* 4.6.

70 Sen. *De Ben.* 6.32.1; Vell. Pat. 2.100.3-4; Dio Cass. 55.10.12-15; Suet. *Div. Aug.* 65.1: 'Iulias filiam et neptem omnibus probris contaminatas relegauit'; cf. Plin *HN* 31.9.

71 Tac. *Ann.* 1.3; Dio Cass. 55.10-11.

72 Suet. *Div. Aug.* 65.3; Dio Cass. 55.13.1 [Xiphilinus]; Tac. *Ann.* 1.53.1; Sen. *De Ben.* 6.32.2.

73 Syme, *Roman Revolution* (n.67 above) 431; Levick[1] 312-15. Dio (55.13.1a [Zonaras]-2) suggests that Augustus acted as he did in this matter πῇ μὲν ὑπὸ τῶν πραγμάτων ἀναγκασθείς, πῇ δ' ὑπὸ τῆς 'Ιουλίας ἀναπεισθείς, explaining that Julia ἤδη . . . ἐκ τῆς ὑπερορίας [i.e., seclusion on Pandateria] κατήχθη, and clearly implying a personal interview. This is by no means impossible and can best be dated to the time of Julia's transfer from Pandateria to the mainland. Such a hypothesis would also most conveniently explain the problem of her so-called 'second exile' (schol. Juv. 6.158), on which much time and ingenuity have been spent to little purpose: see, e.g., Meise 38ff. Unfortunately, Dio does not go on to specify just which arrangements Augustus allegedly made through force of circumstances and which at Julia's urging. However, it is not hard to guess that the adoption of Tiberius and his endowment with ten years' tribunician power (though not, perhaps, his dispatch to the German and Pannonian wars) fell into the former category, while the advancement of Agrippa Postumus and Germanicus represented Julia's contribution. This evidence has seldom been seriously considered in the past; it may indeed be a fabrication, but I do not think we can ignore it altogether. Tacitus remarks (*Ann.* 1.3) that Augustus forced the adoption of Germanicus 'quo pluribus munimentis insisteret'.

74 Wiedemann (n.16 above) 265ff.; Syme *HO* 205-206. For a concise, if rhetorical, survey of Augustus' misfortunes during the period see Pliny *HN* 7.149. The most revealing general narrative (containing all the facts mentioned here) is that of Dio Cassius, 55.22-34. This is immediately preceded by a long set-piece discussion between Augustus and Livia [!] on the relative merits of harshness and clemency in ruling an empire – a pale echo of Thucydides' Mytilene debate, more immediately influenced by Seneca's *De clementia*, but not without interest as an illumination of Dio's own thinking: see F. Millar, *A Study of Cassius Dio* (1964) 78-79. The attempt by Della Corte (n.4 above) II, 102-110, to extract from this frigid rhetorical exercise evidence for Augustan policy in dealing with offenders such as Ovid is ingenious but historiographically perverse.

75 Dio Cass. 55.14.1; Suet. *Div. Aug.* 19.1; and cf. Wiedemann (n.16 above) 267-68, and Levick 56-57.

76 Levick¹ 313.

77 Dio Cass. 55.22.4; Vell. Pat. 2.112.7 talks of 'mira prauitate animi atque ingenii' and hints at a putative change in Agrippa's habits, a revelation of the inborn brutish nature he had hitherto concealed (that standby of ancient character-analysis), since he now 'qualis esset apparere coeperat'. Dio (55.32.1) describes him as δουλοπρεπής and given to fits of anger. For Tacitus (*Ann.* 1.3) he was 'rudem sane bonarum artium et robore corporis stolide ferocem'. Suetonius (*Div. Aug.* 65.1) mentions his 'ingenium sordidum ac ferox'. All of this adds up to no more than bluntness, bad temper, and physical strength.

78 Tacitus (*Ann.* 1.3) remarks that Livia 'senem Augustum devinxerat adeo' that he sanctioned Agrippa's removal to Planasia against his own better judgment; there is no reason to suppose that she had not been working against Agrippa on Tiberius' behalf ever since the adoption in AD 4. For Augustus' *abdicatio* of Agrippa see Suet. *Div. Aug.* 65.1 (cf. Vell. Pat. 2.112.7) and the entry for AD 6 in the *Fasti Ostienses* (*Inscr. Ital.* 13.1, p.183), *Agrippa Caesar [abdicatus est]*: reasons for accepting the supplement, Levick² 57. Discussion of *abdicatio*, emancipation, and inheritance: John Crook, *CR* 4 (1954), in a review of W. Schmitthenner's *Oktavian und das Testament Cäsars*, cited by Levick² 57; Levick, 'Abdication and Agrippa Postumus,' *Hist.* 21 (1972) 674-97; S. Jameson, 'Augustus and Agrippa Postumus,' *Hist.* 24 (1975) 287-314.

79 Suet. *Div.Aug.* 65.4; Dio Cass. 55.32.2; Tac. *Ann.* 1.3.6, and cf. 1.6.1. The reasons given are that he was 'nihilo tractabiliorem, immo in dies amentiorem' (Suet.), and, similarly, καὶ οὐ γὰρ ἐσωφρονίζετο (Dio). I no more believe that he had schizophrenia, or any

other mental disease, than does Levick (Levick² 58 with n.43). As she reminds us, 'treating political opponents as if they were insane is a technique still in use'. For the dates of these events see Levick¹ 328-33; cf. *Hist.* 21 (1972) 694-96, and Jameson (n.77 above) 302.

80 Rogers (n.16 above) 148.

81 Suet. *Div. Aug.* 51.1 refers to one Junius Novatus, who 'Agrippae iuuenis nomine asperrimam de se [i.e. Augustus] epistulam in uulgus edidisset'.

82 Dio Cass. 55.27.1-3; Suet. *Div. Aug.* 19.1-2.

83 It looks as though Plautius Rufus survived the events of AD 6 (perhaps, as Dio says, because he was thought not to be responsible for the agitation, and suspicion was directed elsewhere), and, once more working as a discreet agent in the *coulisses*, played a part in the Julian coup of AD 8. Indeed, if the 'Rufus' of Sen. *De Ben.* 3.27.1 is he, which seems likely (see Levick 334 n.124 for an ingenious piece of prosopographical detective work), then he even survived some highly indiscreet remarks, made while drunk, about Augustus' trip north to Ariminum at the time of the coup's suppression.

84 It has often been pointed out (see Meise 29f. for a discussion of the scholarship) that by now Julia was no longer on Pandateria, but at Rhegium: I take this to be a simple associative slip on Suetonius' part (since Agrippa *was* on an island, and Julia had been) rather than a confusion of Julia I with Julia II. The latter, at this stage in the plot, had not yet been officially compromised, much less banished. For the antecedents of Asinius Epicadus, freedman son of a war-captive won by Asinius Pollio, see Levick 337-38. However, I do not think that much can be deduced about this shady character from the political career of his *patronus*, C. Asinius Gallus, despite the latter's mild anti-Tiberianism before the succession, or his subsequent support for Sejanus and final imprisonment and death by starvation (Dio Cass. 58.3.1ff.; Tac. *Ann.* 6.23.1; cf. *PIR²* 1229).

85 See, e.g., Suet. *Div. Aug.* 65.3; Dio Cass. 55.13.1.

86 Syme (*HO* 210-11) theorises, with some ingenuity, that L. Aemilius Paullus was the

Frater Arvalis who died in AD 13/14 (*ILS* 5026), and therefore merely suffered exile in AD 8; since an Arval Brother could only lose his position by death (Plin. *HN* 18.6), banishment, he claims, was no impediment to continuation in office. (Could an Arval, though, perhaps lose his priesthood if he gave up his Roman citizenship in exile?) But whether Aemilius Paullus was executed or exiled makes no essential difference to my main argument.

87 Schol. Juv. 6.158, glossing the phrase 'dedit hunc Agrippa sorori': for our present purpose the key statement is the following, apropos Julia II: 'nupta [sc. Iulia] Aemilio Paulo, cum is maiestatis crimine perisset, ab auo relegata est.'

88 Certainly later than Agrippa's removal to Planasia in the autumn of AD 7. Confirmatory evidence for the date is provided by the fact that the future emperor Claudius, when 'admodum adulescens' (he attained the age of seventeen only on August 1 of AD 8) was forced to give up his fiancée, the daughter of Julia II and Aemilius Paullus, 'quod parentes eius Augustum offenderant' (Suet. *Div. Claud.* 26.1). It is worth emphasising that, since Silanus was convicted of *adultery* (Tac. *Ann.* 3.24), Aemilius Paullus was still alive in AD 8, and the conspiracy in which he took part, and which cost him his life, must be dated to that year: so, rightly, Syme *HO* 207ff., against Levick[1] 334ff., Levick[2] 60ff.

89 Tac. *Ann.* 3.24 *passim*. The comment on Augustus' actions is revealing: 'nam culpam inter viros ac feminas uulgatam gravi nomine laesarum religionum ac uiolatae maiestatis appellando clementiam maiorum suasque ipse leges egrediebatur.' For the exposure of Julia's son, see Suet. *Div. Aug.* 65.4. As Meise (45) stresses: 'offensichtlich wollte der Prinzeps verhindern, dass ein weiterer möglicher Kandidat für den Prinzipat aufwuchs, der später seine Nachfolgeregelung würde stören können.' This would have been as true of a child by Aemilius Paullus as of one by Silanus: Meise (44) scarcely exaggerates when he says that Paullus 'konnte sich . . . auf Grund seiner adligen Herkunft . . . durchaus den Iuliern oder Claudiern ebenbürtig fühlen'. Levick's theory (Levick[1] 336, Levick[2] 61 with n.52) that Paullus died earlier, that Julia in fact married Silanus, and that witnessing this

marriage constituted Ovid's *error*, I find unconvincing on every count.

90 For a survey of such theories see Thibault 55–68 with nn.147–98.

91 *Tr.* 4.9.11–14; *EP* 4.6.16.

92 Sidon. Apollin. 23.157ff.:
. . . et te carmina per libidinosa
notum, Naso tener, Tomosque missum,
quondam Caesareae nimis puellae
ficto nomine subditum Corinnae . . .

93 Macrobius (*Sat.* 2.5) preserves a string of anecdotes about Julia that illustrate both sides of her character.

94 Suet. *Div. Aug.* 65.2–3; Dio Cass. 55.10.12, 55.10.14; cf. Meise 7–9.

95 *Tr.* 2.209; *EP* 2.2.57–58.

96 Tac. *Ann.* 2.40: 'iamque Ostiam inuectum multitudo ingens, iam in Urbe clandestini coetus celebrabant . . . multi e domo principis equitesque ac senatores sustentasse opibus, iuuisse consilio dicerentur.'

97 E.g., *Tr.* 2.51–52, 3.5.45–46; *EP* 1.1.26, 2.9.9ff.; and cf. Owen *TrII* 18–19.

98 See, e.g., *Tr.* 2.103–104, 3.5.49–50.

99 *EP* 2.9.67–70; Suet. *Div. Aug.* 19.1.

100 *EP* 2.3.85–90.

101 E.g., *Tr.* 1.2.95–96, 2.29; *EP* 1.1.59–63, 3.6.9–10.

102 Cf. Meise 44ff.

103 See W.S. Stroh, 'Ovids Liebeskunst und die Ehegesetze des Augustus,' *Gymn.* 86 (1979) 323–51, esp. 324 with nn.3–6; cf. H. Last in *CAH* vol. 10, 443–52; Della Corte (n.4 above) II, 41–43, 49–52.

CHAPTER XIV

1 In *Ovids Ars Amatoria und Remedia Amoris: Untersuchungen zum Aufbau* (1970), ed. E. Zinn, 109.

2 *Am.* 1.1.3–4, 2.17.21–2, 3.1.9–10, 65–6: *RA* 373–4.

3 *Am.* 1.1.27.

4 In his essay *On Translating Homer* (1861): cf. T. H. Savory, *The Art of Translation* (2nd ed. 1968) 44–5; Paul Selver, *The Art of Translating Poetry* (1966) ch. ix, 69ff.

5 Selver, ibid., Savory chs. iv-vi, 49-89; cf. L. Forster, *Aspects of Translation* (1958) 22-4, P. Green, 'Some versions of Aeschylus' in *Essays in Antiquity* (1960) 185ff., and several of the essays in *The Craft and Context of Translation* (1961), ed. W. Arrowsmith and R. Shattuck, in particular those by D. S. Carne-Ross, Kenneth Rexroth, and S. P. Bovie (3-21, 22-37, and 38-56 respectively).

6 The perpetrator of this curiosity was none other than the late Sir Maurice Bowra: see the *Oxford Book of Greek Verse in Translation* (1938) no. 166, 217. Clearly, a discipline which – at least as formerly taught in England – did not hesitate to make students turn Pope into Latin elegiacs or Shakespearian speeches into Greek tragic iambics could not be expected to frown on a converse process.

7 See George Saintsbury, *A History of English Prosody* (1906) vol. i 318-21, vol. ii, ch.v 167-95, and esp. vol. iii, ch. 3, 'The later English hexameter', 394-436; and T. S. Omond, *English Metrists in the Eighteenth and Nineteenth Centuries* (1907) 108-113, 124-5, 134-6, 157-61, 219-20, and Appendix A, 243-55; cf. Selver *op. cit.* 65-87.

8 *Op. cit.* 109.

9 Cited by Selver, *op. cit.* 67.

10 H. B. Cotterill, *Homer's Odyssey* (1911) 85. This is by no means the only attempt to render Homer in English accentual or pseudo-quantitative hexameters: see, e.g., (my list is far from complete) Francis Caulfield's *Odyssey* (1923) and the versions of the *Iliad*, or parts of it, by H. S. Wright (Bks I-IV, 1885), F. H. J. Ritso (Bks I-III, 1861), E. W. Simcox (1865), F. W. Newman (2nd ed. 1871: the first edition had sparked off the famous controversy between Newman and Matthew Arnold, cf. Selver, *op. cit.* 69ff.), A. F. Murison (1933), and George Ernle's *The Wrath of Achilleus* (1922). Ernle's is the most thoroughgoing attempt, not excluding Bridges', to produce rational quantitative metrics in English, and his analytical preface (5-17) is still worth reading, not least for his description of Meredith's experiments with quantity in *Love in the Valley*. But in the end he is still forced, by his own logic, to produce such grotesque pieces of scansion (in what obstinately remains a stress-language) as 'Bălefŭllỹ|brŏught

sŭffĕrĭngs', or 'ănd thĕ găl|lănt Achĭllĕus': and an unwary reader, not knowing what the translator was up to, might well, following his own accentual instincts, take 'Now ever as the battle grew deadlier and the Achaeans' as highly resolved blank verse.

11 In the 'Epilogue on Translation' to his prose version of the *Odyssey* (1980) 308, cf. 303.

12 Beram Saklatvala, *Ovid on Love* (1966); L. R. Lind, *Ovid: Tristia* (1975).

13 *Ovid's Amores*: English translation by Guy Lee (1968).

14 *Op. cit.* 199-200.

15 *Op. cit.* vol. iii 417, 414.

16 Cf. p.268, for his version of *Aen.* 10.649.

17 Homer, *Od.* 5.50-4; Virg. *Aen.* 4.252-7. The English versions are by Lattimore and Day Lewis respectively.

18 Homer, *Il.* 11.41-5.

19 Juv. *Sat.* 3.78-85.

20 Reprinted, with considerable revisions, in my *Essays in Antiquity* (1960) 109-135, under the title 'Venus Clerke Ovyde'.

21 Gilbert Highet, *Poets in a Landscape* (1957): see 12-14 for a brief and characteristically lucid statement on his position as a translator. The specimen quoted here can be found on p.183. For other good examples of Highet's proficiency in this mode see, e.g., pp. 21-2, 30, 32, 86, 87, 92-6, 107-10 (a particularly felicitous version of Propertius 4.11), 170-3, 178-9, 182.

22 Ovid *Her.* 1.1-6.

23 Ovid, *Am.* 2.8.1-14.

24 J. W. Mackail, *The Odyssey* (2nd ed. 1932) 268 (*Od.* 13.93ff.). In his preface Mackail wrote that he had chosen the metre before ever reading Fitzgerald, and says of his translation: 'Its aim throughout must be to suggest . . . the combination of leisureness [*sic*] and rapidity, of swift motion with the stateliness in which, as Aristotle observes, the Homeric hexameter is unequalled'. The idea of inappropriate associations seems not to have occurred to him. For a similar oddity see W.G.T. Barter, *Homer and English Metre* (1862) 'with a literal rendering in the Spenserian stanza of the first book of the

Odyssey', and P.S. Worsley's version, also in Spenserian stanzas (like Sir Richard Fanshawe's *Aeneid* Bk IV of 1648), a work which must have caught the public fancy, since the second edition was published in Edinburgh in 1895.

25 Cf. J.P. Sullivan, *Ezra Pound and Sextus Propertius: a study in creative translation* (1965), especially ch. ii, 'The *Homage* as creative translation', 17ff.; D.S. Carne-Ross (n.5 above) 19-21. Logue's version of Achilles' fight with the Scamander may conveniently be consulted in the Penguin anthology *Mid-Century: English Poetry 1940-60* (1965) 220-7 ('From Book XXI of Homer's *Iliad*'). Cf. also *Arion* 7 (1968) 267-.74, 8 (1969) 465-76, and Logue's *Patrocleia* (1963), a version of Bk XVI.

26 *AA* 2.1-20.

27 Cf. my *Essays in Antiquity* (n.20 above) 202-6.

28 For Ovid's somewhat self-conscious references to his own *nequitia* see *Am.* 2.1.2, cf. 3.11.37, *Tr.* 2.280.

29 *Am.* 1.5.25. My anonymous critic suggested that 'Fill in the rest for yourselves' was intended as sexual *double-entendre*, a thought which, perhaps regrettably, had till then not occurred to me. It might be preferable, and would certainly keep closer to the Latin, to translate: 'Who doesn't know the rest?'

30 See, e.g., *Am.* 1.6.29-34, 1.9.19-20 (and *passim*), 2.12.5-14, 2.18.8-12, *AA* 1.35-6, 131-2, 363-4, 2.233-54.

31 *Am.* 2.19 *passim*, cf. 2.9.9-10, *AA* 3.577-610, and elsewhere.

32 *AA* 3.769-808.

33 *AA* 3.209-35.

34 John Osborne, *Look Back in Anger* (1957) 24.

35 Cf. *AA* 1.277-82, 360, 459 ff., 755-72; 2.372-86; 3.101-32, and E.W. Leach, 'Georgic Imagery in the *Ars Amatoria*', *TAPhA* 95 (1964) 142-54.

36 *RA* 427-32.

37 I am grateful to Professor George Doig for letting me see his unpublished research on this fascinating topic.

38 E.g. G. Nemethy, *P. Ovidii Nasonis Remedia Amoris* (1921) 68; F.W. Lenz, *Heilmittel gegen die Liebe* (1960) 93; A.A.R. Henderson, *P. Ovidi Nasonis Remedia Amoris* (1979) 135.

39 For Achilles' oath see *Il.* 1.233-44; Agamemnon swears by Zeus, Earth, the Sun and the Furies (*Il.* 19.260ff.).

40 *Carm. Priap.* xxv, ed. F. Buecheler (5th ed. 1922) 154. For the question of priority between Ovid and the *Priapea* see R.F. Thomason, *The Priapea and Ovid* (1931), who on linguistic grounds argues for Ovidian authorship: this of course would reinforce the point of the later allusion. The case he makes is strong – see the review by R.S. Radford, *AJPh* 53 (1932) 390-2 – but of necessity not conclusive.

41 *Am.* 2.1.21-8, 3.6 *passim*, 3.9.27-30; *AA* 2.91-106; *RA* 251-2.

42 *Juvenal: The Sixteen Satires* (2nd ed. 1974) 60-1.

43 *AA* 1.67-74.

44 Cf. E. Nash, *Pictorial Dictionary of Ancient Rome* (2nd ed. 1968) vol. ii 254ff.; S.B. Platner and T.Ashby, *A Topographical Dictionary of Ancient Rome* (1929) 427 with further reff.; M.J. Boyd, *Publications of the British School at Rome* 21 (1953) 152ff.; M. Gwyn Morgan, *Hermes* 99 (1971) 480ff.

45 Paul Brandt, *P. Ovidi Nasonis de Arte Amatoria Libri Tres* (1902), 10 suggests, in common with most commentators, that the reference is zodiacal, and means when the sun is in Leo, i.e. during July, the association with Hercules being through his killing of the Nemean Lion (Apollod. 2.5.1, cf. Hes. *Th* 326ff., Theocr. 25.162ff., etc.). But what is required by the context, as advice, would seem to be a *time of day* rather than a month of the year. When the sun *terga leonis adit* suggests noon, or soon after; siesta-time. 'Hercules' lion' will then have been part of a well-known statue-group (as familiar, probably, to Ovid's readers as Landseer's lions in Trafalgar Square would be to a modern Londoner). This may have stood outside the temple of Hercules Custos near the Circus Flaminius: Platner-Ashby (n.44 above) 252 – or perhaps in Pompey's colonnade, the centre of which was laid out as a garden, and contained various works of art (Prop. 2.32.11-12; Plin. *HN* 35.59, 114, 126, 132).

46 This paper was first presented at a seminar in the Classics Department of the University of Ottawa: I am grateful to those students and faculty whose searching comments and criticisms did so much to improve my original draft. A slightly modified version appeared in *The Translator's Art*, ed. W. Radice and B. Reynolds (1987), 92-111. For surviving imperfections I of course assume full responsibility. All translations from Ovid, unless otherwise attributed, are from my Penguin Classics volume, *Ovid: The Erotic Poems* (1982).

CHAPTER XV

1 *Sat.* 10.188-216; Shakespeare, *Hamlet* II.i.201 ff.

2 In Juvenal: *The Sixteen Satires* (1967), 2nd ed. rev. 1974 [hereafter 'Green, *Juvenal*'], p.7.

3 Niall Rudd, *Johnson's Juvenal: 'London' and 'The Vanity of Human Wishes'* (1981), p.xiii.

4 A.E. Housman, *D. Iunii Iuvenalis Saturae* (2nd ed. 1931), p.xxix. He also praised its 'candour', though in the sexual matters that so fascinated Housman this quality is conspicuous by its absence.

5 Mart. 7.24, 91; 12.18; cf. J.D. Duff, *Fourteen Satires of Juvenal* (1898, 2nd ed. 1970), pp. xxi ff., and E. Courtney, *A Commentary on the Satires of Juvenal* (1980) [hereafter 'Courtney'], pp. 2 ff.

6 Walter C.A. Ker, *Martial: Epigrams* (2 vols., 1919).

7 Mart. 7.18.11. For Housman's trenchant animadversions on the O passage, see his *Juvenal* (above, n.4) xxix-xxx, xlviii-ix.

8 *Sat.* 6.431-2: ' . . . sic tamquam alta in dolia longus/ deciderit serpens, bibit et uomit . . . '

9 *Sat.* 1.37 ff.

10 *Sat.* 2.32-33.

11 Green, *Juvenal* 51-52.

12 Anderson's articles on satire have now been conveniently collected in book form: W.S. Anderson, *Essays on Roman Satire* (1982); his six major studies on Juvenal will be found between pp. 197-486. Cf. also H. Frueland Jensen,

'Crime, vice and retribution in Juvenal's satires', *Class. et Med.* 33 (1981/82) 155-168.

13 Cf. Paul Johnson, *Enemies of Society* (1977) p.112.

14 Elroy L. Bundy, *Studia Pindarica I and II* (1962), reprinted as one volume 1986.

15 A.D. Fitton Brown, 'The unreality of Ovid's Tomitan exile', *Liv. Class. Month.* 10.2 (1985) 19-22.

16 A.L. Motto and J.R. Clark, 'Per iter tenebrosum: the mythos of Juvenal 3', *TAPhA* 96 (1965) 275-6.

17 *Sat.* 3.41 ff.: 'quid Romae faciam? mentiri nescio: librum/ si malus est, nequeo laudare . . . motus/ astrorum ignoro.'

18 Cf. B.C. Verstraete, 'New approaches in the literary-critical study of Roman poetry', *EMC/CV* 31.6 (1987) 350.

19 H.A. Mason, 'Is Juvenal a Classic?', in *Critical Essays in Roman Literature: Satire*, ed. J.P. Sullivan (1963) p. 95.

20 In *Greece and Rome* 33.1 (1986) 78-84: the quotation is from p.83.

21 See in particular Alvin Kernan, *The Cankered Muse* (1959) *passim*, and W.S. Anderson, 'The program of Juvenal's later books', *CPh* 57 (1962) 145-160 = *Essays on Roman Satire* [above n.12] pp.277-292.

22 Evidence for the life of Juvenal is assembled by Gilbert Highet, *Juvenal the Satirist* (1954) [hereafter 'Highet'], pp. 1-41, but his conclusions go a good deal beyond what the evidence warrants: better-balanced accounts in Michael Coffey, *Roman Satire* (1976) pp. 119 ff. (cf. his briefer notice in the revised edition of Duff [n.5 above] pp. iv-ix), and Courtney pp. 1-11.

23 Green, *Juvenal* pp. 10-20.

24 *Sat.* 13.16-17; cf. R. Syme, *Tacitus* (1958) vol. ii, pp. 774-5, and Coffey, *Roman Satire* p.lix with n.3.

25 See S. Monti, *Rend. Accad. Arch. Lett. e Bell. Art. di Napoli* 40 (1965) 79-110, conveniently summarised by Courtney, pp. 3-5.

26 Courtney pp. 8-9. On Juvenal's rigid disapproval of those with ideas above their station, see T.P. Malnati, 'Juvenal and Martial on social mobility', *CJ* 83 (1988) 133-141.

27 ' . . . ad mediam fere aetatem declamauit animi magis causa quam quod se scholae aut foro praepararet' (ed. W.V. Clausen, 1959, p.179): the translation is Courtney's.

28 Pointed out by E. Flintoff, 'New light on the early life of Juvenal', *Wien. Stud.* 87 (1984) 156-9.

29 Green, *Juvenal* p.18.

30 Highet, pp. 40-41.

31 Suet. *Dom.* 10; Tac. *Agric.* 45; Plin. *Epp.* 8.14.7; cf. Coffey, *Roman Satire* p.121 with n.18.

32 See, e.g., Courtney pp.5-9; Coffey, *Roman Satire* p.122; P. de Labriolle and F. Villeneuve, *Juvénal: Satires* (1921) pp.xvii-xx ('une pure légende').

33 On Cicero's brief but much agonised-over exile in 58-57 see his *De Dom.* §§97-98 and the further evidence collected by D.R. Shackleton Bailey, *Cicero* (1971) ch. ix, 'The bitter bread of banishment', pp.64-72. On Seneca's complaints about his relegation to Corsica, AD 41-49, see, e.g., his *Ad Polyb. de Consol.* 2,1, 13,2-4, 18.9. In general cf. Ernst Doblhofer's remarkable monograph *Exil und Emigration: zum Erlebnis der Heimatferne in der römischen Literatur* [Impulse der Forschung Band 51] (1987) esp. pp.49ff., 73ff., 163-6.

34 I use Clausen's text (cf. n.27 above).

35 Dio Cass. 63.18; Suet. *Ner.* 54; Dio Cass. 67.3; Suet. *Dom.* 3.10; schol. Juv. *Sat.* 1.1: ' . . . in exilium missus quia dixit uersum illum . . . '

36 ' . . . diu ne modico quidem auditorio quicquam committere ausus est.'

37 'erat tum in deliciis aulae histrio multique fautorum eius cottidie prouehebantur.'

38 See, e.g., Courtney p.1.

39 J. Gérard, *Juvenal et la réalité contemporaine* (1976) pp. 104-115, 339-352.

40 *Vita* E in Jahn's ed. of 1851: cf. Labriolle and Villeneuve (n.32 above) pp. xviii-xx.

41 See, e.g., Coffey, *Roman Satire* pp. 122, 145.

42 Cf. Gérard (above, n.39) pp 104 ff.; E. Cizek, 'Juvénal et certains problèmes de son

temps: les deux exils du poète et leur consé-quences', *Hermes* 105 (1977) 80-101, esp. 81-6.

43 'Orcadas ac minima contentos nocte Britannos'.

44 *Sat.* 2.126-7, 140-2.

45 The best and most concise presentation of this thesis is that of Labriolle and Villeneuve, pp. xvii-xx; cf. Courtney pp.8-10.

46 The translation is Courtney's: on the inter-pretation see his note *ad loc.*, p.599.

47 E.g. Crispinus, the 'Delta-bred house-slave, silt washed down by the Nile' (*Sat.* 1.26-29, cf. 4.1ff.), or Tiberius Julius Alexander (*Sat.* 1.129-131).

48 Courtney p.9.

49 Mart. *Epigr.* 7.24.1-2, 7.91.1-2. Cf. Hilaire Belloc's reproof of the 'remote and ineffectual don/ who dared attack my Chesterton'.

50 Ibid. 12.18.1-6.

51 *Sat.* 1.88-93, 8.9-12, 14.4-5 (did Juvenal inherit the habit?).

52 Mart. *Epigr.* 7.24.7-8; 7.91.3-4; 12.18.22-23, 'uenator sequitur, sed ille quem tu/ secreta cupias habere silua.'

53 *Sat.* 6.34-37.

54 *Sat.* 2 *passim*: 3.95-97; 6.01-16; 8.14-16, 114-5; 9.35-38, 95.

55 Cf. G.B. Townend, 'The literary substrata to Juvenal's Satires', *JHS* 63 (1973) 148-160.

56 *Sat.* 2.99-107: cf. Virg. *Aen.* 3.286, 12.94; Suet. *Otho* 2.2, 12 *passim*.

57 See Courtney pp. 195-6.

58 For a convenient assemblage of references see Jerry Clack, 'To those who fell on Agrippina's pen', *Class. World* 69 (1975) 46 n.2.

59 Clack, ibid. pp. 45-53.

60 *Sat.* 6.115-132, 10.329-345. There were some tit-bits that Juvenal missed, e.g. (if we can believe the Elder Pliny) Messalina's capacity for repeated orgasms: twenty-five in a 24-hour period, achieved in competition with a famous prostitute, whom *nocte ac die superauit quinto atque uicensimo concubitu* (*HN* 10.172).

61 Clack, p.51. For other instances of such unconfirmed details see, e.g., *Sat.* 6.155-8 (Berenice's incest with her brother Agrippa II), and 8.146-182 (the low-life habits of Plautius Lateranus).

62 *Sat.* 1.170-1.

63 See Sat. 11.65ff., 151ff., 171, 190; 12.87-89; and Courtney p.9, who stresses, rightly I think, the emphasis on *tranquillitas* in Sat. 10.

64 Sat. 1.37-38, 73ff., 95ff., 117ff.; 3.41ff., 58ff., 126ff., 147ff., 184ff., 193ff., 232ff., 268ff., 278ff; 5 *passim*; 6 *passim*; 7.36ff.; 8 *passim*.

65 See, e.g., Courtney 32ff. for an uncharacteristically heavy-handed treatment of this problem.

66 Two carefully sceptical articles by Sir Ronald Syme, 'The *patria* of Juvenal', *CPh* 74 (1979) 1-15, and 'Juvenal, Pliny, Tacitus', *AJPh* 100 (1979) 250-278, clear away much of the dubious evidence that has accumulated concerning the poet's background and friends.

67 See E. Cizek [above, n.42] esp. pp. 83 ff.

68 Sat. 11.193-204.

69 A survey of recent Ph.D. dissertations well illustrates this. Vincent Pascucci, 'Juvenal's use of the past to satirise the present' [Brown University, 1979; *Diss. Abs.* 40 (1980) 5851A], demonstrates J.'s idealisation of the past, his use of the *mos maiorum* (ancestral custom) as a moral yardstick; Michael Lowery's 'A study of mythology in the *Satires* of Juvenal' [Indiana University, 1979: *Diss. Abs.* 40 (1980) 4014A-15A] catches the paradox of J.'s ambivalent attitude to myth and epic, ridicule vying with moral enskyment; S.A. Iverson, 'The military theme in Juvenal's satires' [Vanderbilt University, 1975; *Diss. Abs.* 37 (1976) 279A-80A], similarly tries to reconcile J.'s clear anti-militarism with his use of Republican military tradition as a salutary counterweight to the softening luxury engendered by overlong peace. What seems missing in every case is an adequate understanding of J.'s social and moral position *vis-à-vis* present and past.

70 Green, *Juvenal* 23 ff.

71 See R.A. LaFleur, '*Amicus* and *amicitia* in Juvenal', *CB* 51 (1975) 54-58, and '*Amicitia* and the unity of Juvenal's First Book', *Ill.Class. Stud.* 4 (1979) 158-177.

72 See Malnati (n.26 above) 133-4.

73 Courtney, I am pleased to note, in his *Commentary* (1980) arrived (pp. 22ff.) at precisely the same conclusion as I did in 1967, though in an otherwise well-documented section he makes no mention of my findings.

74 Green, *Juvenal* 38ff.

75 Cf. Courtney 23ff.

76 Hor. *Odes* 3.29.12.

77 Examples conveniently assembled by Courtney, 26ff.

78 Courtney 25.

79 Excellently analysed by Alba Claudia Romano, *Irony in Juvenal* [Altertumswissenschaftliche Texte unde Studien, Band 7], Hildesheim 1979.

80 This essay was originally delivered as the inaugural Romano Lecture (20 April 1988) under the auspices of the State University of New York at Binghamton. I am most grateful to Mr Romano himself and his wife for bringing me back to Juvenal after some years away from him, and for entertaining me so charmingly during my visit to Binghamton. My thanks are also due to Professor Gerald E. Kadish and to my old friend Professor Thomas W. Africa, both of whom also contributed substantially to the pleasure of the occasion for me.

CHAPTER XVI

1 Examples cited from George Steiner, *After Babel* (1975) [hereafter 'Steiner'] 248, cf. 257.

2 Steiner 456.

3 The bibliography is enormous and still growing: the following titles offer a representative sampling. I have not included any studies on machine translation. See: S. Bassnett-McGuire, *Translation Studies* (1980); M.S. Batts (ed.), *Translation and Interpretation; the multicultural context: a symposium* (1975); E. Cary, R. Jumpelt (ed.), *Quality in Translation* (1963); J.C. Catford, *A Linguistic Theory of Translation* (1965); R. De Beaugrande, *Factors in a Theory of Poetic Translating* (1978); Jacques Derrida, 'Des Tours de Babel', most conveniently available (prefaced by a somewhat sclerotic English translation) in

J.F. Graham (ed.) *Difference in Translation* (1986) 209-248; R. Firth, 'Linguistic Analysis and Translation', in *For Roman Jakobson*, ed. M. Halle (1956) 133-9; W. Frawley, 'Prolegomenon to a Theory of Translation', in *Translation: Literary, linguistic, and philosophical perspectives*, ed. W. Frawley (1984) 159-175; J.S. Holmes, *The Name and Nature of Translation Studies* (1975), and, with J. Lambert, R. van den Broeck, *Literature in Translation: new perspectives in literary studies* (1978); R. Jakobson, 'On linguistic aspects of translation', *Selected Writings*, vol. ii (1971) 260-6; A. Lefevere, *Translating Poetry: seven strategies and a blueprint* (1975), and numerous other articles and monographs; G. Mounin, *Les Belles Infidèles* (1955) and *Les Problèmes théoriques de la traduction* (1963); P. Newmark, E.A. Nida, *Approaches to Translation* (1981); E.A. Nida, *Language Structure and Translation* (1975); M.G. Rose (ed.), *Translation Spectrum: essays in theory and practice* (1981).

4 Quite apart from the idiotic acronyms SL and TL ('source' and 'target' languages, respectively), the field is strewn with such barbarous pomposities as 'diachronic hermeneutic' (= history of translation, Steiner 27), 'cladogenetic', 'anagenetic', 'polytypic', 'polymorphic' (Lefevere in Holmes-Lambert-Van den Broeck, n.3 above, 25), 'segmentation', an English equivalent for the equally tedious French *découpage*, confusingly fuzzy terms such as Buhler's 'symbol', 'signal' and 'symptom' (P. Newmark, 'An approach to translation', *Babel* 19, 1973, 3 ff.), and much over-enthusiastic borrowing from the clotted vocabularies of that grey area where philosophy, linguistics, and several social sciences have met and coagulated.

5 Lefevere (n.3 above) 4-5.

6 Steiner 29. His whole discussion of this point (29-31) is both penetrating and suggestive.

7 J.H. Hexter, 'The loom of language and the fabrication of imperatives: the case of *Il Principe* and *Utopia*', *Amer. Hist. Rev.* 69 (1964) 946.

8 Steiner 135; cf. F. Crews, *Skeptical Engagements* (1986) 118ff.

9 Steiner 29.

10 Cf. L.G. Kelly, *The True Interpreter: A History of Translation Theory and Practice in the West* (1979) [herafter 'Kelly'] 227: 'The essential variable is what the translator sees in the original, and what he wishes to pass on. Each age and culture translates anew; by their contemporaries translators are judged according to criteria peculiar to times, place and genre.'

11 The prime examples are Kelly (n.10 above) and Steiner (n.1 above).

12 E.L. Keenan, 'Some logical problems in translation', in *Meaning and Translation*, ed. F. Guenther and M. Guenther-Reutter (1978) 157, rightly contests this hypothesis.

13 Cited by Keenan, ibid.

14 Cf. Dante, *Convivio* 1.7 ('E però sappia ciascuno che nulla cosa per legame musaico armonizzata sì può de la sua loquela in altra transmutare, senza rompere tutta sua dolcezza e armonia . . .' etc.); Samuel Johnson, in Boswell's *Life* (1776), cited by T.F. Higham, *The Oxford Book of Greek Verse in Translation* (1938) xxxvii ('Poetry, indeed, cannot be translated: and therefore it is the poets that preserve languages'); Mme Dacier, *Introduction à l'Iliade* (1766) 6, 33, 39; K.W. von Humboldt, letter to A.W. von Schlegel, 23 June 1796: 'Alles Uebersetzen scheint mir schlechterdings ein Versuch zur Auflösung einer unmöglichen Aufgabe.' For Renaissance criticism along similar lines see Y. Lindeman, 'Translation in the Renaissance: a context and a map', *Canad.Rev. Comp. Lit.* 3.2 (1981) 204. General discussion in Kelly 214 ff.

15 Lewis May, 'Concerning Translation', *Edinburgh Rev.* (Jan. 1927) 117.

16 See, e.g., Mounin, *Problèmes* (n.3 above) 170: 'La traduction devient impossible parce que la langage lui-même n'assure pas la communication des hommes entre eux-même la communication unilingue.'

17 Steiner 251.

18 Kelly 219, 4; cf. A. Lefevere, 'Literature, comparative and translated', *Babel* 29 (1983) 70, who says of 'recent academic writing' that it 'has not proved to be of overmuch use to practising translators, and . . . has also not succeeded in bringing translation closer to the center of comparative literature or literary theory'.

19 Mounin, *Les Belles Infidèles* (n.3 above) 7: 'Dans ce domaine de l'intraductibilité, tout se passe comme si vivaient côte à côte une théorie toujours alléguée, mais à laquelle les théoriciens ne croient pas vraiment eux-mêmes, et une pratique à peu près sans influence contre cette théorie.' Cf. Steiner 162 on the habits of academic philosophers.

20 Steiner 272.

21 See, e.g., Bassnett-McGuire (n.3 above) 3: 'The powerful Anglo-Saxon anti-theoretical tradition has proved especially unfortunate with regard to Translation Studies . . . ' etc.

22 Bassnett-McGuire 37. She tries to hedge her bets by arguing that such a theory, even if not formative, should still offer a 'guideline'. Her argument appears to derive (like a good deal in translation theory these days) from a pioneering article by John McFarlane, 'Modes of Translation', *Durham Univ. Journ.* 45 (1953) 77-93, esp. 92-93, which is more modest in its aims and to that degree more persuasive. Cf. my *Essays in Antiquity* (1960) 204.

23 Steiner 269.

24 Steiner ibid.: 'The range of theoretic ideas, as distinct from the wealth of pragmatic notation, remains very small.' Cf. 239 ff.

25 Cited and analysed by Kelly, ch. iii, 68 ff. Some typical diagrams can be studied in R. de Beaugrande (n.3 above) 2-3, 32-33.

26 Steiner 235 draws attention to the 'radical tension between impulses to facsimile and impulses to appropriate recreation'.

27 Cf. Marilyn Gaddis Rose, 'Translation types and conventions', in M.G. Rose (n.3 above) 31-40.

28 Cf. Mounin (n.19 above) 7: 'Tout les arguments contre la traduction se résument en un seul: elle n'est pas l'original.'

29 Catullus 78.10; Celia and Louis Zukofsky, *Catullus* (1969) 78. Lefevere (n.3 above) 26 concedes the near-impossibility of phonemic translation.

30 Steiner 49 ff. It is significant that Steiner himself, a trilingual intellectual of formidably wide reading and literary acuity, should be so sold on the pseudo-rational notion of one monadic world-language, even to the point of giving sympathetic consideration (58-59) to all the dreary mystical rubbish in the Kabbala on

the music of the spheres and the hermetic key to 'die reine Sprache', etc. Two minutes' thought would confirm (a simple argument to which Steiner fervently objects) that the existence of innumerable local languages, gradually shrinking in number as communications improve, is precisely what we might expect, and indeed what the ample evidence attests. Steiner himself notes (50-51) that there were once at least *twice as many* languages as survive today: an obvious indication of attrition through improved communications. Even so, no less than a thousand are still spoken on the island of New Guinea alone. What I suspect here is a visceral intellectual distaste for the non-generalised, unsystematic, largely paratactic multiplication of unrelated entities, an urge to wield Occam's Razor on this polyglot protobabble and reduce it to a rational linguistic unity.

31 See, e.g., Denham's remarks in the preface to his *Destruction of Troy* (1656), ap. T.R. Steiner, *English Translation Theory, 1650-1800* (1975) 65: ' . . . therefore if *Virgil* must needs speak English, it were fit he should speak not only as a man of this nation, but as a man of this age'; and Dryden's similar statement in the *Dedication* to his *Aeneid* (1697), ibid. 72: 'I have endeavoured to make Virgil speak such English as he would himself have spoken, if he had been born in England, and in this present age.' See also p.224 above and cf. my *Essays in Antiquity* (n.22 above) 189-190. It is interesting to reflect that both Dryden and Pope may well have devoted themselves to translating Virgil and Homer for precisely the same reason that Boris Pasternak spent so much time on Shakespeare.

32 Cf. Lefevere (n.3 above) 114 ff. As he says (115), 'the comparison of translations and original works in the target language could provide the study of the sociology of literature with an easily malleable but reliable and precise tool to ascertain to what extent and with what speed literary innovations reach the general reader.' The answer seems to be, pretty fast. It is not all that long since F.L. Lucas was asserting that 'the rhymeless metres of Greek are too remote from English for successful imitation'.

33 F.M. Cornford, *The Republic of Plato* (1941) v-vi; cf. D.J. Furley, 'Translation from Greek Philosophy', in *Aspects of Translation* (1958) 52 ff.

34 Steiner 344-5.

35 J.E. Sandys, *A History of Classical Scholarship* (1908) vol. ii, 180.

36 G. Highet, *The Classical Tradition* (1949) 118.

37 T.H. Savory, *The Art of Translation* (2nd ed. 1968) 183-4.

38 Ruth A. Roland, *Translating World Affairs* (1982) 3.

39 Roland, ibid. 25.

40 Marcia Nita Doron, 'The Economics and Politics of Translation', in Rose (n.3 above) 164-5.

41 *Genesis* 11.7.

42 See, e.g., Maurice Lambert, 'La traduction il y a 4000 ans', *Babel* 10.1 (1964) 17-20; F.J. Witty, 'Translation Literature: early (Pagan and Christian)', *New Cath. Enc.* 14 (1967) 245 ff.; D. Diringer, *The Alphabet* (2nd rev. ed. 1953) 53.

43 A.T. Olmstead, *History of the Persian Empire* (1948) 107 ff.; R.N. Frye, *The Heritage of Persia* (1963) 84 ff.

44 Hdt. 3.139, cf. Xen. *Cyrop.* 4.2.46.

45 Judicious summary in Frye 86-87. He concludes: 'Although the Behistun inscription bristles with difficulties and there are many points for discussion, the burden of proof for the falsity of the historical account must rest on those who seek to disprove it. They may be right but they have not proved their contention.'

46 Eric Jacobsen, *Translation a Traditional Craft* (1958) 43. I do not know what the 'certain works from the Oriental languages' may be that he alleges (ibid. n.35) the Greeks did translate, unless he is possibly referring to something like Hanno's *Periplus* or other Carthaginian treatises on navigation and agriculture. Cf. B.H. Warmington, *Carthage* (1960) 62-64.

47 For convenient up-to-date translations of these priestly decrees see M.M. Austin, *The Hellenistic World from Alexander to the Roman Conquest* (1981) 366-8 (no. 222, the Canopus Decree of March 238 BC), and 374-8 (no. 227, the 'Rosetta Stone', decree of March 196 BC); on the latter see also now S.M. Burstein, *Translated Documents of Greece and Rome 3: The Hellenistic Age from the Battle of Ipsus to the Death of Kleopatra VII* (1985) 131-4 (no. 103).

48 On the translation of the Septuagint see P.E. Kahle, *The Cairo Geniza* (1947) 132-179.

49 Hor. *Epist.* 2.1.156-7: 'Graecia capta ferum uictorem cepit et artis / intulit agresti Latio . . .'

50 See E.H. Warmington, *Remains of Old Latin*, vol.ii (1936) viii ff.; J.W. Duff, *A Literary History of Rome from the Origins to the Close of the Golden Age* (3rd ed. 1953) 88 ff.

51 Hor. *Epist.* 2.1.69-72.

52 Warmington (n.50 above) 24-42, esp. frs. 1, 2, 15, 16, 18, 27, 30; cf. Duff (n.50 above) 91-92.

53 An excellent analysis in Jacobsen (n.46 above) 39ff.; cf. Bassnett-McGuire (n.3 above) 43-45, 51-52; Kelly 44-45, 81, 163, 180.

54 Plut. *Aem. Paull.* 28; Isidor. *Orig.* 6.5.1.

55 Plut. *Sull.* 26; Strabo 13.1.54.

56 Bassnett-McGuire 45.

57 Cic. *De Opt. Gen. Orat.* 7.23: 'uerba persequens eatenus, ut ea non abhorreant a more nostro . . .'

58 Ibid. 5.14: 'In quibus non uerbum pro uerbo necesse habui reddere, sed genus omne uerborum uimque seruaui.' Cf. *De Offic.* 1.6, 2.60; *De Fin.* 1.4.6, 3.15; *De Leg.* 2.17.

59 Hor. *AP* 133-4: 'nec uerbo uerbum curabis reddere fidus / interpres', most often wrongly translated, as, e.g., in the Loeb version of H.R. Fairclough, 'do not seek to render word for word *as a slavish translator*'. Denigration of 'slavish' fidelity in the translator is a characteristic approach by modern advocates of creative autonomy: see, e.g., Kelly 68 ff., 75, and esp. 207.

60 Ibid. 268-9: 'uos exemplaria Graeca / nocturna uersate manu, uersate diurna'.

61 See, e.g., Cic. *De Orat.* 1.34, §155; Hor. *AP* 51-53; Quint. *Inst.Orat.* 1.9.1-3, 2.14.1-2, 10.5.2-4; Plin. *Epist.* 7.9.2.

62 Cat. 61 ('Ille mi par esse deo uidetur' = Sappho's 'φαίνεταί μοι κῆνος ἴσος θέοισιν', etc.); and 66, the 'Lock of Berenice' ('Idem me ille Conon caelesti in lumine uidit' = 'κήμὲ Κόνων ἔβλεψεν ἐν ἠέρι τὸν βερενίκης' of Callimachus).

63 E.g. Hor. *Odes* 1.9, 1.18, 1.37, where known allusions enable us to pick up the parallel: probably many more to which the key is lost, e.g. 1.10, 1.11, 2.4.

64 Plautus and Terence provide numerous examples. A really startling instance of textual massacre for the supposed benefit of the groundlings is provided by the Latin version of a passage from Menander, the work of Caecilius Statius (d. 168 BC): see Gordon Williams, *Tradition and Originality in Roman poetry* (1968) 363-5, cf. Kelly 79-80; F. Blatt, 'Remarques sur l'histoire des traductions latines', *Class. et Med.*1 (1938) 217-242.

65 Ovid, *Trist.* 2.443-4; Plut. *Crass.* 32.

66 Duff (n.50 above) 193.

67 Plin. *HN* 25.5-7.

68 See J. Humbert, 'A propos de Cicéron traducteur du grec', *Mél. de Phil., de Litt., et d'Hist. Anc. offerts à A. Ernout* (1940) 197-200, who makes the best case he can for 'la langue philosophique des Latins' *not* having been a mere 'calque assez servile du grec', and in the process demonstrates just how freely Cicero operated with the resources at his command. Cf. Kelly 163. A more realistic assessment of Cicero's problems is that by R. Poncelet, *Cicéron traducteur de Platon: l'expression de la pensée complexe en latin classique* (1957), esp. 363 ff. Poncelet's conclusion, paradoxical enough, is that Latin's survival, far from being a triumph of classicism over the *'egestas* ancestrale', was due, precisely, to its handicaps (374): ' . . . le latin a dû persister dans son être *parce qu'il était incapable* de copier le modèle grec. Il n'y a là ni instinct, ni volonté, ni système, ni choix. L'idée fuit la formule latine: il fallait donc suggérer l'idée et laisser au lecteur le soin de penser l'inexprimé . . . ' etc.

69 Cic. *De Nat. Deor.* 2.41. §104, *Ad Att.* 2.1.11, *De Orat.* 1.69.

70 Virg. *Aen.* 6.853.

71 The discussion by D.B. King, 'The Greek Translation of Augustus' *Res Gestae', Trans. Wiscons. Acad.* 41 (1952) 219-228, is fundamental. Cf. also Kelly 99. The one surviving copy is

inscribed on the wall of what is now a mosque in Ankara (hence the name 'Monumentum Ancyranum').

72 J. Fitzmaurice-Kelly, 'Translation', *Enc. Brit.* (1911) vol. xxvii, 183.

73 Hieronymus [St Jerome], *Epist.* 57 *Ad Pammachium* 57.5.2, where Jerome echoes the Horatian prescription 'non uerbum e uerbo sed sensum exprimere de sensu', except 'scripturis sanctis, ubi et uerborum ordo mysterium est'.

74 See Blatt (n.64 above) 220ff. He observes that 'le littéralisme est étroitement lié à la nouvelle religion: ce qui est fatal, c'est que le nouveau principe admis pour les textes sacrés s'empare peu à peu des autres genres littéraires'. At the same time he stresses, correctly, that some Christian translators were very free indeed.

75 On the Toledo School see D.M. Dunlop, 'The work of translation at Toledo', *Babel* 6.2 (1960) 55-59.

76 See, e.g., F.F. Bruce, *History of the Bible in English* (3rd ed. 1978) chs. i-iv; F.R. Amos, *Early Theories of Translation* (1920) ch. ii, 49 ff.; and for Tudor translation as a conscious instrument in the hands of Protestant reformers, C.H. Conley, *The First English Translators of the Classics* (1927) 72 ff.

77 Conley 73.

78 For a characteristically overblown eulogy see, e.g., Charles Whibley's panegyric in the *Cambridge History of English Literature*, vol. iv (1932) 1-25, which begins: 'The translators of Elizabeth's age pursued their craft in the spirit of bold adventure which animated Drake and Hawkins . . . ' etc.

79 See Highet (n.36 above) 41-46, 570-1.

80 See the comprehensive list in H.B. Lathrop, *Translations from the Classics into English from Caxton to Chapman 1477-1620* (1933) 311-318: cf. also the analysis of the period 1550-72 in Conley (n.76 above) 129-154.

81 J.W.H. Atkins, *Camb. Hist. of Eng. Lit.* vol. iii (1932) 444-5; L.B. Wright, 'Translations for the Elizabethan Middle Class', *The Library*, 4th. ser. 13.3 (1932) 312-331 (a particularly acute study); F.M. Salter and H.L.R. Edwards, *The Bibliotheca Historica of Diodorus Siculus trans-*

lated by John Skelton, vol. ii (E.E.T.S. 1957) xxii–iii.

82 Lathrop (n.80 above) 307; Roger Ascham, *The Scholemaster* (1570) ed. J.E.B. Mayor (1863) 81.

83 Lathrop 27.

84 Cited by Amos (n.76 above) 111.

85 Alexander Fraser Tytler, Lord Woodhouselee, *Essay on the Principles of Translation* (1790: Everyman ed., n.d.) 146–7; cf. Kelly 209–210.

86 Virg. *Aen.* 4.590–1: '. . . ibit / hic,' ait, 'et nostris inluserit aduena regnis?', and 10.649: 'Quo fugis, Aenea? thalamos ne desere pactos!' Cf. Day Lewis' introduction to his *Aeneid* (1952); Richard Stanyhurst, *Translation of the first Four Books of the Aeneis of P. Virgilius Maro with other Poetical Devices thereto annexed* (1582), ed. E. Arber (1895) 116; R.G. Austin, *Some English Translations of Virgil* (1956) 9, 19.

87 Catullus 64.17–18: '. . . nudato corpore Nymphas / nutricum tenus extantis e gurgite caeno.' The first translation is that of Ellis, the second by C.H. Sisson: both are cited by Lefevere (n.3 above) 115 ff.

88 See Timothy Webb, *The Violet in the Crucible: Shelley and Translation* (1976) ch. ii, 51 ff.

89 T.S. Eliot, 'Euripides and Professor Murray,' *Selected Essays* (3rd ed., 1951) 57–64.

90 Stanyhurst (n.86 above), Dedication to Lord Dunsany, p.10.

91 See my essay 'Some versions of Aeschylus', *Essays in Antiquity* (n.22 above), 185–215, esp. 199–200, 211 ff.

92 H.D. Thoreau, *Walden* (1854) ch. iii: see *The Variorum Walden,* ed. W. Harding (1962), 99, and the ingenuous editorial confirmation (287) that indeed his meaning is 'that no translation has ever succeeded in fully carrying over the spirit of the original into a new language'. It is interesting that the three authors he singles out are Homer, Virgil, and Aeschylus.

93 Roger Ascham, *The Scholemaster* (n.82 above), 151.

INDEX

321